UNSETTLED

Unsettled

*Refugee Camps and the Making
of Multicultural Britain*

JORDANNA BAILKIN

OXFORD
UNIVERSITY PRESS

OXFORD

UNIVERSITY PRESS

Great Clarendon Street, Oxford, OX2 6DP,
United Kingdom

Oxford University Press is a department of the University of Oxford.
It furthers the University's objective of excellence in research, scholarship,
and education by publishing worldwide. Oxford is a registered trade mark of
Oxford University Press in the UK and in certain other countries

© Jordanna Bailkin 2018

The moral rights of the author have been asserted

First Edition published in 2018

Impression: 1

Published in the United States of America by Oxford University Press
198 Madison Avenue, New York, NY 10016, United States of America

British Library Cataloguing in Publication Data
Data available

Library of Congress Control Number: 2017962348
ISBN 978–0–19–881421–4

Printed and bound by
CPI Group (UK) Ltd, Croydon, CR0 4YY

Acknowledgments

These are strange days to be writing about camps and refugees. In the early days of this project, I believed—perhaps reasonably enough—that camps were created *by* citizens, *for* refugees. The story turned out to be far more complicated than that. I hope I have done justice to the incredibly diverse populations who moved through Britain's refugee camps. Their lives remind us that refugees and citizens have not always seen themselves as sharply divided, whether they live in camps or not.

Another assumption: when I began this book, I thought that I was speaking and writing from one liberal democracy to another. I am no longer sure that this is the case. Yet the truth remains that very few states of any kind today can evade the moral dilemmas of encampment—even if they try to do so by stopping refugees at their borders and thus speeding the creation of camps elsewhere. I am glad to thank the many people who helped me think through what lessons might be learned from the camps of the past—and whether, indeed, they are truly "past" at all.

At a time when funding for scholarly research seems especially precarious, I am very grateful to have been supported by a fellowship from the National Endowment for the Humanities, as well as a Society of Scholars Fellowship from the Walter Chapin Simpson Center for the Humanities at the University of Washington. The Giovanni and Amne Costigan Endowed Professorship and the Jere L. Bacharach Endowed Professorship in International Studies provided vital support for research. Two chairs of the Department of History—Lynn Thomas and Anand Yang— ensured that I would have the time I needed to finish the book, which I much appreciated. I also want to thank the staff at the Department of History at the University of Washington, especially Jeri Park, for making it a pleasure to come to Smith Hall.

Many archivists came to my aid in this project: most notably, Steven Dryden at the British Library Sound Archive, Paul Dudman at the University of East London, David Langbart at the National Archives and Records Administration, and Matthew McMurray at the Royal Voluntary Service Archive and Heritage Collection. Suman Buchar and Jayesh Amin from the "Exiles Project" generously shared their interview contacts, as well as the maps they used for two important exhibitions. I thank Rob Perks for permission to quote from the Central British Fund Kindertransport Interviews and the Vietnamese Oral History Project, both at the British Library. I much appreciated the generosity of my interviewees, and thank Lee Allane, Thanh Cherry, Colin Hodgetts, Chandrika Joshi, Betty Kellar, Vinh Ly, Julia Meiklejohn, Sue Millman, Barbara Nadja, Atul Patel, Henry Pavlovich, Peter Rimmer, and Vinod Tailor for their vivid recollections and their willingness to revisit often complicated times in their lives. Zosia Biegus, Henry Pavlovich, and John Perivolaris also kindly gave me permission to publish photographs from their personal collections.

I have been lucky to share my work with many astute audiences who sharpened my thinking. I thank the organizers and participants at the North American Conference on British Studies, the International Seminar on Decolonization at the National History Center, the Ransom Center at University of Texas at Austin, the Center for British Studies at Berkeley, the Institute of European Studies at Berkeley, the History Colloquium at the University of Washington, the Center for British Studies at Northwestern University, the European History Colloquium at the University of California at Los Angeles, the British Studies Center at Rutgers University, Yale University, the University of Southern California, the Post-Imperial Britain Workshop at Klitgaarden, and Simon Fraser University.

For kindly offering suggestions from their own work (and, in some cases, allowing me to preview it), I thank: Sana Aiyar, Pam Ballinger, Emily Baughan, Roberto Beneduce, Anna Bocking-Welch, Antoinette Burton, Rita Chin, Nicholas Crowson, Nadja Durbach, David Feldman, Ilana Feldman, Aidan Forth, Thavolia Glymph, Jo Guldi, Kennetta Hammond Perry, Becca Herman, Lara Kriegel, Marjorie Levine-Clark, Erik Linstrum, Jana Lipman, Saima Nasar, Susheila Nasta, Radhika Natarajan, Lucy Noakes, Guy Ortolano, Maya Parmar, Tammy Proctor, Erika Rappaport, Caitlin Rathe, Tehila Sasson, Tom Scott-Smith, Caroline Shaw, Penny Sinanoglou, Peter Stansky, Simona Taliani, Becky Taylor, Stuart Ward, Bogusia Wojciechowska, and Glennys Young.

Conversations with the ever-generous Seth Koven, Philippa Levine, and Lou Roberts always left me brimming with ideas. Lou talked through many aspects of moving this book to publication, while also being an excellent lunch companion at the Imperial War Museum. Feedback from Stephen Brooke and Milla Schofield came at just the right time and invigorated me at a moment of fatigue. I am hugely grateful to Deborah Cohen, Sarah Stein, James Vernon, and Andrew Zimmerman for reading (in some cases, more than once) the whole manuscript, and offering invaluable suggestions, critiques, and encouragement.

It has been a delight to work with Oxford University Press; Stephanie Ireland's energy, efficiency, and enthusiasm were noteworthy, as was meticulous work from Cathryn Steele. One of the reviewers for the press revealed himself to be Geoff Eley, whose own work has long inspired me; I thank him and the other readers for their helpful comments. Eric Johnson patiently offered technical assistance with several scans and last-minute snafus. Christina Manetti provided thoughtful translations from the Polish newspaper *Dziennik Polski*, and Bill Nelson dealt with many complex specifications to produce the map; I thank them for their careful work.

While I was writing this book, it was a pleasure to be surrounded by the burgeoning creative projects and growing families of my friends: I thank (and am always in awe of) Rebekah Gross, Abbie Raikes, Viviane Silvera, Sarah Stein, Lynn Thomas, Kate Washington, and Molly Watson. Kate also provided editorial zing during an extraordinarily difficult time for her. My parents and extended family have been a tremendous source of support and fun, whether in Mexico City or Muskoka.

Christopher, Tobias, and Finn are the very best adventurers, but also my absolute favorite people with whom to stay home. Chris deserves the most heartfelt thanks for many reasons (including his insightful comments on "just one more draft"), but especially his generosity many years ago in giving me the sole unclaimed space in our home for my office, ensuring that I would always have a room of my own. I love it, and him.

This book is dedicated to the memory of Stephanie M.H. Camp—so much loved and so much missed—who made everyone feel at home.

Contents

List of Illustrations   xi
Map of Refugee Camps in Britain   xii

   Introduction   1

   Interlude: Before the Camps   16

1. Making Camp   24

2. Feeding and Hungering   71

3. In Need   86

4. Happy Families?   111

5. Mixing Up   134

6. Hard Core   157

   Epilogue: Camps after Encampment   191

Endnotes   215
Bibliography   263
Index   281

List of Illustrations

1.1   Queen Mary of Teck inspecting Nissen huts at Hesdin, July 7, 1917   26

1.2   Members of the Women's Army Auxiliary Corps amidst the ruins of some Nissen huts   27

1.3   The kitchen in a completed temporary house converted from an army Nissen hut   28

1.4   Tennis at an internment camp for German residents at Knockaloe, Isle of Man   36

1.5   "Activities and Inactivities"   37

1.6   Early days of the Basque camp, Eastleigh   42

1.7   Chalets for Jewish children at Dovercourt   44

1.8   Jewish refugees in their room at Kitchener Camp   46

1.9   Airmen of No. 300 Polish Bomber Squadron at RAF Faldingworth   47

1.10   Children at Foxley Camp   53

1.11   Gohel Parshotta at RAF Stradishall   60

1.12   Drawing showing how to use the lavatory at Doniford   61

1.13   Tavistock Scouts visiting Plaisterdown   61

1.14   Ugandan Asian family at Tonfanau   63

1.15   Portrait of man and child at Sopley   67

1.16   Portrait of Thanh Chuong Ly at Sopley   68

1.17   Vietnamese children at Sopley   68

1.18   The barrier at Thorney Island   69

2.1   Typical meal at Kitchener Camp   75

3.1   First communion at Foxley Camp   93

3.2   Corpus Christi procession at Northwick Park   94

3.3   Jazz band at Foxley Camp   95

3.4   Musicians at Northwick Park   96

3.5   Anna Crooks at the Anglo-Egyptian Aid Society   101

4.1   Telegram from Ugandan Asian wives at Maresfield Camp   122

4.2   Vietnamese boy at Sopley   125

4.3   Volunteers tidying up Raleigh Hall   131

4.4   Rock 'n' Roll session at Stradishall   132

5.1   Edith Tudor-Hart, "Basque and English School Boys, North Stoneham Camp"   136

5.2   Group of visitors at Kitchener Camp   137

5.3   Float from Kitchener Camp   138

6.1   Gate at main entrance to Kitchener Camp   182

7.1   Kindertransport statue   206

7.2   Zosia Biegus returns to Northwick Park   207

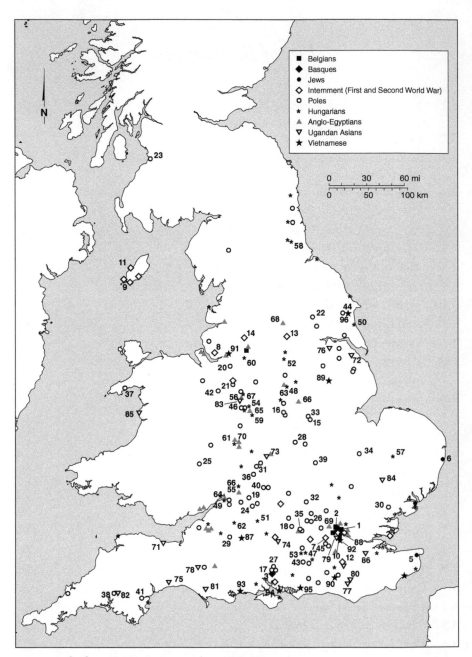

Key sites of refugee camps in twentieth-century Britain.

This map does not represent every place where refugees were housed in Britain, but rather gives a sense of the scope and scale of encampment and indicates the main sites discussed in the text.

Belgians:
1 Alexandra Palace
2 Earl's Court

Basques:
3 North Stoneham

Jews:
4 Dovercourt
5 Kitchener Camp
6 Pakefield

Internment (First and Second World War):
7 Bertram Mills
8 Huyton
9 Isle of Man camps – Port Erin and Port St. Mary, Onchan, Hutchinson
10 Kempton Park
11 Knockaloe
12 Lingfield
13 Lofthouse Park
14 Warth Mills

Poles:
15 Ashby Folville
16 Burton on the Wolds
17 Chandlers Ford
18 Checkendon
19 Daglingworth
20 Delamere Park
21 Doddington
22 East Moor
23 Fairfield
24 Fairford
25 Foxley
26 Great Bower Wood
27 Hiltingbury
28 Husbands Bosworth
29 Keevil
30 Kelvedon
31 Long Marston
32 Marsworth
33 Melton Mowbray
34 Mepal
35 Nettlebed South Hostel
36 Northwick Park
37 Penrhos
38 Plaisterdown
39 Podington
40 Springhill Lodges
41 Stover (later Ilford Park)
42 Tilstock Anglo-Polish Housing Units
43 Tweedsmuir
44 Walton
45 Weston Green
46 Wheaton Aston

Hungarians:
47 Aldershot
48 Alfreton Miners Hostel
49 Bridgend Hostel
50 Catfoss RAF base
51 Chiseldon
52 Crimicar Lane Sanitorium
53 Crookham
54 Drake Hall
55 Eastwood Hostel
56 Frobisher Hall
57 Grange Farm
58 Haverton Hill
59 Hednesford
60 Styal Homes
61 Summerfield Hostel
62 Thorney Pits

Anglo-Egyptians:
63 Alfreton
64 Bridgend Hostel
65 Drake Hall Hostel
66 Eastwood Hostel
67 Frobisher Hostel
68 Greenbanks Hostel
69 Sheepcote Hostel
70 Summerfield Hostel

Ugandan Asians:
71 Doniford
72 Faldingworth
73 Gaydon
74 Greenham Common
75 Heathfield
76 Hemswell
77 Hobbs Barracks
78 Houndstone
79 Kensington Barracks
80 Maresfield
81 Piddlehinton
82 Plaisterdown
83 Raleigh Hall
84 Stradishall
85 Tonfanau
86 West Malling

Vietnamese:
87 Devizes
88 Kensington Barracks
89 Morten Hall
90 Nelson Hall
91 Padgate
92 Raleigh Hall
93 Sopley RAF Centre
94 Sunshine House
95 Thorney Island RAF
96 Watton

Introduction

Today, no one thinks of Britain as a land of camps. Instead, camps seem to happen "elsewhere," from Greece to Palestine to the global South. Yet, over the course of the twentieth century, dozens of British refugee camps housed hundreds of thousands of Belgians, Jews, Basques, Poles, Hungarians, Anglo-Egyptians, Ugandan Asians, and Vietnamese. This book is a testament to these forgotten sites, and the lives lived within them.

The camps were spread out all over Britain, from the heart of London to the most remote corners of North Wales. Refugees lived with thousands of civil servants and a fractious mix of volunteers: ex-army officers, middle-class matrons, and young radicals. They slept in holiday chalets and concrete bunkers, in military bases, prisons, and stately homes. Some camps were tightly controlled, with barbed-wire perimeters and armed guards. At other camps, residents came and left freely. Some camps were virtually ignored by locals; others completely transformed the nature of nearby towns. People could be encamped for just a few days, or for decades.

"Refugee camps" in Britain were never only for refugees. Many camps were peopled with British squatters, as refugees shared space—willingly or not—with Britons who had been ousted from their homes by bombs and poverty. The camps were also repurposed for different groups and generations of refugees, jumbling together those who fled the crises of war and empire. The Hungarians and Anglo-Egyptians competed for spaces when they disembarked in 1956; Ugandan Asians arrived in 1972 to find Poles still encamped from three decades earlier.

In a narrative that extends over eight decades, from the Great War to the 1980s, we can see just how close refugees and citizens used to be, and how far apart they became. The sense of shared experience between Britons and refugees—strongest during and immediately after the Second World War—largely disappeared by the later decades of the twentieth century. Yet this was not a linear trajectory. It was full of fits and starts, shaped by the uneven paths of wealth and poverty. The contemporary notion that the camp marks the absolute division of citizens and non-citizens was not a foregone conclusion. At different moments, camps could signal either the unity of citizens and refugees or their segregation.

As the world's refugee crisis is once again bringing to Europe the challenges of mass encampment, *Unsettled* offers warnings from a liberal democracy's recent past. Rather than thinking of camps as something that happened "elsewhere," this book serves as a reminder that the spaces in which refugees have lived are all around us. It is an effort to recapture the truth that we are standing on their ground.

WHEN WAS A REFUGEE NOT A REFUGEE?

First, a problem: this is a book about refugee camps. But, strikingly, many of the individuals in this book denied that they were refugees. At the same time, the state denied that the places where these people lived were camps. The labels of "refugee" and "camp" were widely used, but not universally accepted. Both the name and the resistance to it are crucial parts of this story.

The word "refugee" entered the English language in the wake of Louis XIV's persecution of Protestants in Catholic France and the English offer of refuge to the Huguenots. During the nineteenth century, refugees in Britain included victims of foreign revolutions, slaves, and persecuted minorities. For many Britons, the refugee was the ideal liberal subject: heroic, morally righteous, and independent.[1] At times, refuge was an alternative to military or diplomatic intervention abroad, an admission that there were limits to Britain's power to end oppression on the world stage.[2] Britain's offer of refuge to foreigners was part of its own national and imperial morality tale.[3]

After the Great War, the refugee was a jarring, anachronistic figure—a reminder that the conflict was not really over.[4] The first official census of refugee populations was conducted in 1922, and refugee aid was further professionalized in the 1920s and 1930s. The newly interventionist states that emerged from the war treated civilians who were "out of place" with anxiety, even as camps for the stateless quickly became normalized.[5] In this improvisational climate, refugees were viewed with a mixture of compassion and concern.

The study of refugees was increasingly systematized after the Second World War.[6] In 1951, the UN Convention Relating to the Status of Refugees defined refugees as individuals who, owing to a "well-founded fear of persecution" for reasons of political opinion, race, religion, nationality, or membership in a particular social group, are outside their country of nationality and are unable or, as a result of such fear, unwilling to return to it. This definition, which reflected the Convention's roots in the early Cold War, characterized refugees as the product of oppressive, totalitarian regimes that preyed on their own citizenry.[7]

International conventions, however, did not fully encompass the distinctiveness of Britain's relationship to the displaced, the expelled, the unsettled.[8] I chart the histories of camps for Belgians fleeing the Germans during the Great War, Basque children threatened by the Spanish Civil War, Jews fleeing Nazi-occupied Europe, Poles who fought for Britain during the Second World War and refused to return to Soviet-occupied Poland, and Hungarians escaping the Soviet invasion in 1956. These camps also served Anglo-Egyptians (British subjects ousted from Egypt during the Suez Crisis), Asians who were expelled from Uganda under Idi Amin's Africanization policy in 1972, and Vietnamese taking flight from the civil war from 1979 to 1981.

"Refuge" is an inadequate concept to describe the complex histories of these groups. Many "refugees" in Britain were actually British subjects, who might (or might not) think of themselves as having come "home." The Ugandan Asians and the Anglo-Egyptians were British subjects; the Poles were offered British citizenship shortly after their arrival. Each group held different relationships to the imperial and wartime pasts, and the laws of citizenship did not always capture the range of their historical connections with Britain. In Britain, it was possible to be both a "refugee" and a "citizen" at once.

Perhaps for this reason, many of the people in this book rejected the word "refugee."[9] They sought other terminologies to make sense of their experiences. For example, some British politicians called the Poles "émigrés," rather than refugees, because they were not in the act of fleeing their homeland. Rather, they were soldiers who had come to Britain in wartime. Others objected that the term "émigré" evoked the memory of French aristocrats who had abandoned the king during the Revolution, and might stigmatize these Polish soldiers as deserters.[10] Anglo-Egyptians, too, denied that they were refugees—which would have implied that they were fleeing their "true" home in Egypt for a foreign land. Instead, they preferred the term "evacuees," which suggested that they were returning to their rightful home in Britain. Britons who were displaced by the Blitz during the Second World War were also known as "evacuees," so this vocabulary of evacuation forged connections between two highly mobile populations.

Many Ugandan Asians agreed with the Anglo-Egyptians: Britain could not call its own citizens refugees. One journalist recounted how he was scolded by a camp leader for describing the Ugandan Asians as "refugees." The administrator emphasized, "It's one thing they have made very clear to me. They say they are English now."[11] Indeed, some Ugandan Asians refused to stay in a camp because they believed it would mark them as refugees, despite their British passports.[12] Manzoor Moghal, who went straight from Heathrow Airport to Leicester, recalled, "I was not willing to go to any refugee camps because I thought that was demeaning, humiliating. We were British citizens with full rights and for us to be treated as refugees was somewhat unfair."[13] For Moghal, life in camp was the ultimate sign of being a refugee.

For others, being a refugee was not just a specific legal status, but also a state of mind. Mahmood Mamdani, now a prominent political scientist at Columbia University, who wrote a memoir of his own experience of the Ugandan Asian expulsion, refused to describe Ugandan Asians as refugees:

> A refugee is not just a person who has been displaced and has lost all or most of their possessions. A refugee is in fact more akin to a child: helpless, devoid of initiative, somebody on whom any kind of charity can be practiced; in short, a totally malleable creature.[14]

At the Kensington Barracks Camp, Mamdani wrote, "I realized that I was truly becoming a 'refugee,' my existence increasingly remote from the world outside, the camp more my real world."[15] According to Mamdani, the true heroism of the Ugandan Asians lay precisely in their refusal to act as helpless, passive victims even in the infantilizing environment of the camps. One could be displaced without adopting the refugee's hopeless mindset.

Yet the state's designation of the people in this book as "refugees" was—while disputed—not without meaning. People in flight deciphered the landscape of possibilities available to them, making decisions about whether to claim the refugee label.[16] Being named as a refugee offered sources of economic aid, but also introduced new forms of vulnerability, constraint, and loss.[17] Furthermore, becoming a "refugee" was a process rather than a single event.[18] Even for those who were willing to be identified as "refugees," this designation had a time limit. One could fall out of—as well as into—refugee status over time, and benefits could be suspended or retracted. People could easily be reclassified as paupers, squatters, or ordinary migrants. No one was supposed to be a refugee forever.

Could Britons be "refugees"? Some certainly thought so. In April of 1946, the BBC broadcast a popular song called, "I'd Like to Be a Refugee from Britain." In an alarming new era of queuing, rationing, and higher taxes, the song predicted a mass exodus of white Britons. It was brought up in Parliament later that year as a sign of just how destabilized some Britons felt. The refrain was: "I want to be a refugee from Britain / The place where I'm no longer free; / If they can carry on without Winston Churchill / They will blooming well have to carry on without me." Such broadcasts reminded listeners that Britons could be unhoused by war and poverty, or so disaffected with their own government that they felt compelled to flee. The language of being a refugee offered a way for Britons to make sense of their own experiences of displacement, homelessness, and alienation.

Who, then, were the unsettled? Refugees were unsettled, but so were Britons. The British state had a long history of using repression and sympathy to constrain the movements of a diverse range of people.[19] As early as the Middle Ages, the British state saw those who lacked a permanent home—the rootless and the roofless—as a threat to social stability. The Tudors passed numerous laws to criminalize the mobility of the poor. By the nineteenth century, any poor person in Britain moving outside their parish could be charged with vagrancy. Aid depended on being settled; mobility detracted from the aid one might receive.[20] Local authorities were not always required to provide relief to "strangers" (Britons who migrated from parish to parish).[21] In colonial settings, European vagrants were prosecuted because they threatened the notion of white superiority.[22] The state's solutions to vagrancy— from flogging laws to workhouses—never eradicated the uncontrolled mobility of the casual poor. The laws were still used in the twentieth century to keep the poor within predictable geographical pathways.

After the Second World War, there were devastating new ways for all Britons (not just the wandering poor) to be displaced. During the war, 3.7 million houses had been destroyed or damaged, or two out of every seven houses in Britain.[23] Another 1.48 million homes were closed or destroyed in slum clearances, displacing more than 3.6 million people.[24] Subsequently, the state sought to manage mobility through a wide array of population redistribution projects, from industrial development schemes to public-sector housing programs to New Towns. Some of these projects aimed to increase the population's social and physical mobility, while others sought to curtail it.

In this context, the "unsettled" took on new meaning. During the postwar decades, the state began to describe as "unsettled" those Britons who—through a distinctive combination of circumstance and personality—found themselves on the move.

The term "unsettled" became a way to make sense of—and bring together—the variety of people whose mobility was perceived as dangerous. The role of the state, in short, was to settle them: not only by providing opportunities for jobs and housing, but also by helping them transform their ways of thinking and being. A settled way of life was increasingly essential to participate fully in modern society. The "unsettled" (of any nationality) were a problem population that transcended the rights of citizenship. Their existence posed ongoing anxieties for the state, which sought to regulate the mobility of citizens as well as refugees.

The ideal of freedom as an imagined space or physical destination—rather than a political or social condition—was prevalent in liberal democracies.[25] Liberal democracies such as Britain often defined freedom as dependent on the physical experience of free movement. But ideal citizens also valued stability, contrasting with lesser subjects who were "excessively" mobile and must be restricted through pass laws and other discriminatory means.[26] The relationship between freedom, physical mobility, and democracy was more complicated than it seemed. Was movement an essential component of freedom? Should it ever be constrained?

This book is not a comprehensive history of the unsettled. Rather, it takes the refugee camp as a place that reveals the unsettled nature of both refugees and citizens, and how the state sought to transform them. The demands of aid tended to merge populations in need rather than isolating them. Within the camp, refugees and citizens might share spaces, meals, and other elements of camp life. They moved in and out of moments of closeness and distance, structured by timelines of war and poverty. In Britain, many people who were categorized as "refugees" were actually British subjects. At the same time, many Britons were so profoundly displaced that they saw themselves—and were unofficially treated—as refugees. Camps—the site of the unsettled—allow us to hold these stories of displacement in tandem.

THE CAMP THAT IS NOT A CAMP

What made a place to house refugees a "refugee camp"? Notably, the refugee camp (unlike the refugee) has no definition in international law. The 1951 UN Convention did not refer to camps at all, perhaps because, historically, most refugees have not been housed in camps. More recent conventions describe them as places where displaced persons are sheltered. In a legal sense, then, the refugee camp is simply a place where refugees live. Today, what we call refugee camps may range from Palestinian camps that function as full-blown cities, to temporary, "illegal" shelters in Calais.[27]

Perhaps the first "refugee camps" (though contemporaries often called them "concentration camps") originated in the South African War (1899–1902).[28] British forces in South Africa presided over more than 100 camps, containing a quarter of a million Boer and African civilians. These camps provided poor relief, of a sort, for the destitute Boers whose land was destroyed by Britain's scorched earth policy.[29] But they also entangled aid and detention—the refugee and the prisoner—in ways that shaped the camps of the future.[30] Residents were treated both as harmless refugees and as dangerous rebels.[31] Estimates suggest that about 20,000 black South Africans and as many as 28,000 Boer civilians died in the camps.[32]

The scale and scope of encampment were fundamentally changed in the twentieth century. The development of the global capitalist economy, two world wars, and the triumph of popular and national sovereignty—all led to the recognition that refugees were likely to be a permanent feature of modern life.[33] Modern politics (and, in particular, modern warfare) demanded spaces to keep people in a suspended state between the flight from their original homes and their full admission to a new country.[34]

The geography of encampment diversified after the Great War. Armenian refugees from Turkey flocked to rudimentary camps run by American Protestant missionaries, and the interwar period witnessed the proliferation of camps in the Balkans, Asia Minor, and the Near East. The exodus of refugees from the Spanish Civil War brought refugee camps into Western Europe. These camps, which were surrounded by barbed wire and (in France) under strict military control, rapidly blurred the line between refugee aid and political quarantine.[35] However, although doctors and nurses were introduced to refugee camps in the 1920s, these camps were just temporary shelters. They were not the highly regulated spaces that they would later become.

During the Second World War, as Liisa Malkki has described, the refugee camp became a standardized, generalizable technology of power in the management of mass displacement. Camps conjured up entire classes of people—doctors, therapists, administrators, and photographers—who were trained to offer aid, but also to judge the capacities and characters of refugees.[36] Through the processes of segregating nationalities, quarantining, public discipline, schooling, and rehabilitation, the modern refugee emerged in the camp as a knowable, nameable figure. Camps were a crucial site in the crafting of what Peter Gatrell has called refugeedom—the matrix of administrative practices, legal norms, social relations, and refugee experiences, as well as their cultural representation.[37] In this way, refugee camps helped to create the refugee.

As a 1948 United Nations report stated, camps for refugees spread "like a cancerous growth" across Europe after the Second World War. These camps jumbled together collaborators and resistance fighters, hardened criminals and teenage innocents, shell-shocked wanderers and dissidents in a "storm-tossed mass of humanity."[38] Eleanor Roosevelt, touring the DP camps in 1946, wrote that "I felt all the time...a kind of spiritual uprooting, a kind of being lost." Aid workers saw the camp as the place where refugees regressed to an infantile state, as they absorbed the traumas of war. In *The Wild Place*, Kathryn Hulme (the UNRRA Director of the Polish DP Camp at Wildflecken, Germany) described the camp as being closed off from the outside world "as effectively as if you inhabited a small planet adrift from earth like a raft in space, you knew only the queer inverted life of the DP camps, which had to be learned step by step because never before had anything quite like it been even imagined."[39]

Scarred by her own experience of internment at Gurs, the German-Jewish philosopher Hannah Arendt described DP camps as "holes of oblivion" for modern pariahs.[40] Ranking Nazi camps as Hell and Soviet labor camps as Purgatory, Arendt categorized refugee camps as Hades—"camps for persons who have become superfluous and bothersome."[41] But for Arendt, refugee camps were fundamentally akin to Nazi and Soviet camps because their inhabitants were "treated as if they no longer existed, as if what happened to them were no longer of interest to anybody, as if they were already dead and some evil spirit gone mad were amusing himself by stopping them for a while between life and death."[42] What mattered most was not the physical reality of barbed wire and violence, but the "skillfully manufactured unreality of those whom it fences in," easing the pathways between Hades, Purgatory, and Hell itself.

Camp officials in Britain saw themselves as undertaking a very different project than their Continental counterparts. But they could not control how refugees saw the camps. Refugees in Britain entered camps with specific political histories, and some—the Poles and the Vietnamese, in particular—had already faced camps elsewhere. In the 1940s, Polish refugees likened British camps to Bergen-Belsen in northern Germany, from which many had recently been released. Czeslaw Maryszczak, a Polish veteran, catalogued the camps he had traversed in his lifetime: labor camps in Siberia, a tent camp in Persia, a timber-constructed camp in India, a mud-hut camp in Uganda, and, finally, a corrugated sheet-metal camp in England.[43] For him, Britain was just another stop in what had already been a long period of encampment around the world.

Different individuals might experience a single camp as a site of unwelcome intrusions, violent discipline, or valuable education. For Mahmood Mamdani, it was Kensington Barracks in London, and not Idi Amin's Uganda, which constituted his first experience in a "totalitarian" society. He described Kensington as a "nightmare in totally controlled living." But, for others, refugee camps offered new outlets for cosmopolitan pleasures. The Welsh middle classes, for example, often dined out at the Ugandan Asian camp in Tonfanau, enjoying what they saw as exotic cuisine. Such contradictory perspectives were echoed in competing views of refugees (they were heroic, they were parasitic) and the camps that housed them (they were luxurious, they were barbaric).

The question of what defined a "camp" was widely debated in Britain. Multiple structures—from army huts to stately country homes—came under this description. Although the housing for Belgians was cheerfully referred to as "camps" at the beginning of the Great War, this term was rejected as "unfortunate" by 1919, when conditions in POW and internment camps were more widely publicized.[44] Still, camps in Britain were both ubiquitous and diverse.[45] In 1939, the British government proposed to spend £1 million building fifty new camps across the country.[46] These camps would serve multiple functions of modern life, promoting discipline and community. They might house refugees evacuated from the danger zones of war, but they could also be holiday sites, or places to train the unemployed. Camps could be used for war or peace—for refugees or citizens. Such projects expressed a vision of universal encampment. Anyone might be encamped, though not everyone would be encamped in the same way. In the 1950s, Zosia Hartman, a displaced Pole, recalled that the Polish camps were renamed "hostels" after civilian depart-ments took over from the War Office.[47] The rebranding of the "camp" as a "hostel" did not indicate a different physical experience, but a change in authority.[48] Many hostels were simply camps that had changed hands. The Poles, however, continued to call these spaces *Obóz*: that is, "the camp."[49]

Race played a role in this longer debate about vocabulary. As the Ugandan Asians arrived, the Home Office struggled with what to call the places where they stayed. The benign term "reception centre" did not seem fully accurate.[50] Stradishall, a Royal Air Force base used to house Ugandan Asians, was described as a "debriefing centre," much like the facilities for returned POWs in the Second World War. The Welcome Committee for British Asians stated, "we reject the idea of camps for British citizens arriving here, 75% of whom are likely to have friends and relatives already here."[51] Camps might be appropriate for "true" refugees, but not for British citizens who were simply temporarily displaced. The establishment of refugee camps for "UK citizens who happened to have brown skins could politically be dynamite."[52] One volunteer at the Thorney Island base, which housed refugees from Vietnam, said her supervisor "did not like" for her to refer to Thorney Island as a camp at all.[53]

One of the most popular euphemisms—for refugees and citizens alike—was the "resettlement center." But what did it mean to be resettled? Everyone admitted that resettlement was an unscientific process, whether for citizens or refugees. Some defined it as a straightforward issue of housing and jobs. But others argued that it encompassed far more than that. Children needed school, and the family needed to adjust to a new way of life.[54] Different groups received vastly unequal resources to transform themselves into a settled way of living. Notably, shelters for homeless Britons were by the 1980s known as "resettlement units." This intermeshed vocabulary of resettlement was no coincidence. Rather, it reflected that the state's ongoing project of regulating mobility constantly demanded new sites and spaces. These sites (and the people within them) were in constant conversation.

As we will see, being "resettled" was deeply unsettling—not only for refugees, but also for those who worked at or lived near the camps. For many, resettlement generated new kinds of loss and disruption. More broadly, this history unsettles contemporary political narratives that depend on a stark division of citizens, migrants, and refugees. It reveals how one state struggled with the contradictions of placing people (including many of its own subjects and citizens) in camps. Refugees were just one of the unsettled populations with which the state coped.

Ultimately, the language of the camp was irresistible. Despite official reluctance, the term "camp" quickly became part of the colloquial idiom, both in government documents and in the press, to describe the spaces where refugees were housed.[55] I have chosen to retain the term "camp" as a way to resist the euphemistic vocabulary of "transit," "reception," and so on.[56] Such innocuous terms obscure the relationship that these sites bear to detention, and the extent to which their residents were unfree. Some of the spaces in this book were more easily recognizable as "camps" than others. But their distinctive combination of aid and confinement makes the vocabulary of the camp the most apt choice.[57]

The philosopher Giorgio Agamben has argued that any space in which the normal order is *de facto* suspended—and when the occurrence of atrocities depends not on the rule of law, but on the civility and ethics of the police—is a camp, regardless of its topography.[58] Agamben's characterization of the refugee camp as a place of the state of exception, where the body of the refugee is reduced to bare life, clearly does not capture the complexity of the British experience—though it comes closer at times than one might have expected. Thus, Britain offers a useful case study for rethinking some of the classic theoretical literature on encampment.

Memoirs of refugee camps have many recurrent tropes of suffering and alienation: bitter cold, inedible food, the strangeness of hearing English voices over loudspeakers.[59] Robert Kee, the British journalist, argued in his 1961 work *Refugee World* that certain sensory, material, and psychic experiences were central to the lives of refugees in camps: overcrowding, a lack of privacy and hygiene, the suspension of the expectation of improvement or change. For Kee, "to be a refugee means to smell certain smells, to share a water-tap with dozens of other people, to sleep in overcrowded rooms, to hear noises day and night through thin walls, to be doing all this for years."[60]

My book diversifies these familiar plots—not because they are false, but because their narratives of privation overlook other kinds of experiences, and make them invisible.[61] In this diversity is hidden a bigger story about the complicated alliances and rifts that were forged in British camps—and ultimately extended beyond them. Bülent Diken and Carsten Bagge Laustsen have argued what defines a space as a camp is "a site of enclosure, abandonment, and ethical conformity, but it necessarily contains lines of escape, openings," which can turn the camp into something else.[62] They conclude, "the camp is not just a matter of walls and fences but also of doors and windows."[63] Instead of trafficking solely in images of misery, I open up more varied experiences that reveal camps—with all their complex cultures and demographics—as spaces of possibility as well as confinement.

SO FAR, SO CLOSE: THE IMPOSSIBILITY OF ENDINGS IN REFUGEE HISTORY

This book explores Britain's distinctive cultures of encampment. The unique physical environments of Britain's camps gave rise to specific kinds of interactions and exchanges, structuring how refugees and Britons thought of themselves and each other. The daily encounters—some fleeting, others more permanent— between refugees and Britons are not always captured by traditional archives, but can be given solidity by the specific places and landscapes in which they occurred.[64]

The most emblematic place for refugees in Britain was the military base.[65] Refugee camps were often housed in abandoned (or not so abandoned) army and air force bases, illustrating how easily missions of aid morphed into martial operations. This militarization of refugee care unsettled any perceived dichotomies between civilian and soldier refugee and citizen.[66] Refugees who were housed on bases were often subject to military surveillance and detention. Thus, camps prompted an often nostalgic mobilization of wartime resources, complicating our sense of the built environment of war and a "break" between war and peace. In the refugee camp, the warfare state and the welfare state converged.[67] Warfare provided the infrastructure of welfare.

Refugee camps laid bare the legacies of war, but also of empire. Refugee aid had always depended on the possibility that troublesome refugees could be moved to imperial outposts. When opportunities for imperial relocations disappeared, British sympathy for refugees plummeted.[68] Later on, imperial decline played a central role in population displacement, generating its own refugees.[69] Refugee camps prompted larger debates about Britain's obligations to other countries. At the time of the Vietnamese refugee crisis, Hong Kong was the most valuable remaining British possession.[70] The admission of refugees from Vietnam—coming through the British colony of Hong Kong—was one of these episodes: not an "epilogue" to decolonization, but part of it. In this sense, none of the camps discussed here were "after" empire at all. The transformations of independence galvanized a new range and depth of entanglements, rather than bringing them to an end.

This is a story of distance and closeness, intimacy and difference. The cultivation of sympathy for unseen and unknown people is a historical and contemporary mystery. To accept that we owe as much to distant strangers as to people we are close to is to reject a core part of what most people believe.[71] Yet refugee care involved precisely such a belief—while also bringing "distant strangers" physically close. This book is part of the history of empathy, a meditation on how people came to care about one another and the historically specific effects of that care.[72] As Leslie Jamison reminds us, empathy is not just remembering to say, "that must be really hard"; it is figuring out how to bring difficulty into the light so it can be seen at all.[73] The history of refugee camps reveals that the suffering of refugees was understood differently—and brought into the light so that it could be seen—at various moments in time.[74]

The work of aid has been criticized for distancing people from one another, creating inequalities between the giver and the receiver. The refugee camp complicates this notion. Licitly or not, many Britons lived in refugee camps—not only giving aid, but also receiving it. Demobilized British soldiers and bombed-out civilians squatted in Polish camps, blurring the boundaries between refugees and citizens. To put it another way, Britons were trying to get into the camps, while refugees were trying to get out.

As Britons moved through states of plenty and deprivation, they shared spaces and dilemmas with refugees in unforeseen ways. Their congregation was not always peaceful, and intimacy did not preclude inequality. Most notably, Britons could leave camps whenever they wanted. At times, citizens and refugees were in deeply unequal relationships, where the power was all to the citizen. At other moments, the camp was simply a staging ground for an encounter between unsettled peoples—some of whom were citizens, and some who were not. The primary axis of difference in this story is not between refugees and citizens, but between the settled and the unsettled.

What appears at first to be a story of British generosity toward desperate foreigners becomes more complicated. The state's sympathy or suspicion toward *all* forms of mobility rose and fell with the displacements of war and empire. The fact that the camps were constantly repurposed and upcycled allows us to explore broader questions about continuities and discontinuities in twentieth-century history.[75] In theory, camps were a spatial manifestation of the gap in rights and experience between citizens and refugees—a sign of their difference. But, in Britain, camps could also be sites of intimate interaction—a place where citizens and refugees who had experienced different forms of dislocation came together. Designed for "foreign" populations, they actually served a diverse set of people in motion.

Refugee camps created unique—and uniquely transformative—intimacies and frictions, bringing a startling variety of people into proximity. They allow us to see the closeness of individuals and groups that scholars have traditionally kept separate—not only "citizens" and "refugees," but also refugee populations from diverse countries and conflicts. Camps prompted uneasy ties between refugees of different ethnicities and generations, as well as between refugees and Britons— not only sexual or romantic relationships, but also the complex terrain of friendship, mentorship, and casual social contact. The interactions that took place in these camps cannot be easily characterized in terms of hostility or benevolence, prejudice or tolerance. The camps afforded opportunities for both selfishness and service, enabling us to tell a morally complicated story about empathy, solidarity, and activism.

Multiculturalism in Britain has often been narrated as a numbers game that privileges larger "minority" populations, such as South Asians or West Indians, and ranks these groups by assessing how easy or difficult they are for Britons to digest. This book offers a new genealogy and geography of multiculturalism, as well as new questions about where, when, and to whom multiculturalism happens. Focusing on a space such as Daglingworth, the Polish camp in Gloucestershire, or Tonfanau, the Ugandan Asian camp in North Wales, can shift our sense of the key players in the history of the multicultural, as well as its locales. Interethnic and interracial encounters took place not only in Britain's cities and seaports, but also in remote army bases and rural outposts: hiding in plain sight.

These camps occupied a distinctive role in the history of encounters across cultures—a crucial, if unacknowledged, site in the making of today's multicultural Britain. At the same time, the camps served as a larger project of social engineering. From the state's perspective, camps offered a unique opportunity to shape racial and ethnic patterns of settlement. Under the guise of "resettlement," camps allowed the state to imagine the ideal map of multicultural Britain. Ultimately, the state could never fully control the movements of refugees or citizens; its goals were never achieved. But its efforts to manage the trajectory of the wide variety of people who moved through refugee camps had their own unpredictable effects.

The diverse populations that flowed in and out of British refugee camps demonstrate that multiculturalism in Britain was not only a postcolonial story, but also a global one. The colonial past was just one of many strands of transnational connectivity for refugees, migrants, and citizens. This book integrates the spaces and stories of refugees from different ethnicities and generations, refusing to segregate "European" and "Third World" refugees.[76] Uniting the stories of British subjects and those whose relationship to Britain was less secure is one way to disrupt the stratified categories of immigration law. These camps reveal how little is captured by thinking about difference in contemporary Britain only in terms of "immigrants" or "minorities."[77] The interaction of refugees, migrants, and citizens was much more profound than we have ever understood.

For all of these reasons, refugee history cannot just be about refugees.[78] The history of refugees in Britain is also the story of the transformations of the state in the twentieth century. The notion of what one deserved in life—what specific kind of home or family or food—underwent constant revision by British policymakers, from liberals to social democrats to neoliberals.[79] The care of refugees was one of the first major tasks of the welfare state. As the Home Office put it, the problem of refugees was no less than the problem of welfare itself.[80] There was no specialist unit in Britain that was responsible for refugee care.[81] Rather, refugee work in Britain involved a welter of state actors and volunteers. They forged their interactions with refugees while they parsed the meaning of new benefits for all Britons. Their rapidly changing expectations—how they thought about the categories of need, of happiness, of community—shaped how refugees were viewed: as self or other.

CAMPS IN THE ARCHIVE: SCALING UP AND DOWN

This book is about camps in Britain, but also about their erasure from public memory.[82] This amnesia is selective. Some refugee stories are remembered more than others, and some moments of refugee life are more readily captured or overlooked.[83] But even when the plight of refugees has been highly publicized, their life in camps—the space where they came into closest contact with Britons—is often lost. The fact that there were once dozens of refugee camps operating within Britain has been largely forgotten.

The study of refugees poses distinctive archival problems and possibilities.[84] The historical vocabularies of displacement are constantly shifting, making it all the more difficult to find refugee voices. Tony Kushner notes the slippage between the terms "alien" and "refugee" (and we might add other terms, such as "squatter" or "internee") in the National Archives up until 1971. It is vital to understand the ramifications of the terms the state used to encompass "refugees" and "camps"— as well as "Basques," "Poles," "Anglo-Egyptians," "Ugandan Asians," and so on—and to acknowledge how these terms homogenized diverse populations.

The British state relied on deeply asymmetrical definitions—sometimes national and sometimes not—and false ethnic categories that made little sense in other domains.[85] Here, I both adopt and challenge the state's categories, treating them as starting points that need to be disaggregated or dismantled.[86]

One goal here is to place refugees at the center—rather than at the margins—of the national narrative. Yet there are aspects of refugee experience that cannot be captured by national narratives at all. Refugee camps were located on metropolitan soil, but prompted by overseas disruptions—many of which, in turn, were orchestrated from the metropole. The politics of the camp is both deeply local and profoundly global, underscoring Britain's debts, obligations, and vulnerability both to the far away and the very close.[87]

The amnesia around camps in Britain is linked to this question of scale: namely, the archives in which refugees have been most visible. At the National Archives, we see the production of new genres—petitions and letters of complaint from residents' committees, disciplinary action against camp workers, efforts to regulate interactions between refugees and locals. Other files capture interviews with Anglo-Egyptians or Ugandan Asians who sought business loans, generating a fascinating archive of loss and dispossession. From British caterers' recipes for Hungarian food to angry petitions from Ugandan Asian wives who were separated from their husbands, these documents tell us much about daily life in camps—how refugees felt about their wardens, their neighbors, even their own families.

The National Archives files alone, however, cannot capture the diverse histories of encampment.[88] Refugees and Britons interacted in camps in very different ways than had been planned from the center. Indeed, the impact of refugees may have been felt most powerfully at the local level.[89] Because of the remote locations of many camps, their daily workings took place largely outside the view of the central state—often ignoring or thwarting its policies.[90] In order to capture alternative perspectives, I have delved into largely unexamined archives for camps in East Sussex, West Sussex, Hampshire, and Surrey. These archives offer detailed portraits of the relationships between camp residents and nearby towns, revealing an intensity of interaction that is not always apparent elsewhere. From this vantage point, we can see how refugee camps transformed the lives of ordinary Britons as well as refugees.

The rise of the Internet has helped to generate fresh testimony from refugee voices.[91] For example, the Heritage Lottery Fund has recently supported initiatives to record the histories of Ugandan Asians and refugees from Vietnam, such as the Vietnamese Oral History Project at the British Library's Sound Archive, the North West Sound Archive in Lancashire, and the BBC Asian Network's Millennium Memory Bank interviews.[92] This book is enabled by these new "heritage" sources, as well as my own interviews with people who lived in or worked in refugee camps. I incorporate refugee memoirs, poems, and photographs to give fuller expression to refugees themselves.

From Britain's many refugee stories, I have chosen these cases because their camps proved especially transformative for refugees and Britons alike. I track shifts in encampment through both world wars, the Cold War, the last gasp of formal imperialism, and a new internationalism that was both embraced and constrained by Thatcherism. Here, we can see how these stories were intertwined, but also how policies changed over time—for example, favoring family reunions for refugees from Vietnam, but not for Poles, or indemnifying the property of Anglo-Egyptians, but not of Ugandan Asians. My narrative reflects the camps' complex demography and social ecology. Individuals intersect and reappear in different chapters, weaving in and out of the narrative. The book places its key players in conversation, just as the experience of encampment did.

The book's organization is guided by my argument that refugees should not be isolated from one another, nor should they be siloed off from the key themes of British history. Rather, they can prompt a reconsideration of these themes. This is a story not only of "foreign" refugees, but of the ways in which Britons felt themselves to be unhoused, displaced, unsettled. In refusing to ghettoize refugee camps—and charting the complex interactions that took place within them—I argue that these sites cannot be reduced to a simple story of heroes and victims, nor of successes and failures. The ethical stakes and structure of this book are to work against precisely that ghettoization.

The book begins by narrating the diverse, and often harrowing, stories of how refugees arrived in Britain during the twentieth century. People had very different experiences of British camps depending on when and where they landed, as well as the historical lenses through which they viewed their experiences. The camps were romanticized or vilified at different moments, and by different historical actors. We see camps in all of their material aspects—from the structures of buildings to the practices of mass feeding—as well as the relationships and resistance that were brought into being by these distinctive built environments. In the next chapters, I turn to the material aspects of refugee camps, from military bases to stately homes to prisons. I trace the prehistories of the refugee camp from detention camps in South Africa to plague and famine camps in India and internment camps in Europe. Specific elements of camp architecture—from barbed wire to the Nissen hut to the communal mess hall—gave rise to unique physical and social routines.

I ask how refugee camps transformed people as well as spaces, altering the identities of the people who lived in and near them. Specifically, camps forged and fractured economic, religious, and ethnic identities, as well as new forms of family life and sexual norms. In camps, we can see both tremendous intrusions into the intimate lives of refugees, and fierce resistance to these interventions, from hunger strikes to acts of violence. I explore how camps functioned as sites of daily rebellion, particularly around the issue of where refugees were allowed to settle. Finally, I chart the fates and futures of Britain's refugee camps: the chaotic and incomplete process of camp closures, and their conversion to other uses. I try to make sense of the cacophonies and silences that have surrounded these sites, reflecting on the multiple—and massive—uses of encampment around the world today.

The aim of this book is not to redeem camps—nor, indeed, to condemn them. It is to refuse to ignore them. Now more than ever, these spaces must not be isolated from history, nor from civic life. They are crucial sites of encounters and entanglements that have had profoundly transformative effects, without which certain inequalities will remain opaque. Some individuals suffered terribly in these camps, while others would remember them with gratitude and affection. It is no more helpful to valorize the camps as sites of tolerance or selflessness than simply to denounce them as spaces of racism and abuse, though episodes of both kinds surely took place. They witnessed births and deaths, love affairs and violent conflicts, strikes and protests, comedy and tragedy, without which the making of modern Britain cannot be understood. Their story is one of complicated intentions that played out in unpredictable ways. We cannot allow them to stay buried in the landscape.

Interlude
Before the Camps

On August 4, 1914, German troops crossed the Belgian border and attacked the fortified town of Liège. Britain, which had guaranteed armed support to Belgium if Germany violated its neutrality, suddenly found itself at war. At first, only a few wealthy Belgians sailed to England, paying their own way, relying on personal contacts, and slipping in largely unnoticed. After the fall of Antwerp in early October, Belgian refugees rushed into Britain, crowding on every floating thing that could possibly be put out to sea—channel steamers, yachts, coal boats, barges, and fishing smacks.[1] All told, more than a million people left Belgium during the Great War—nearly one-sixth of its population. Over 250,000 came to Britain: the largest refugee movement in British history.[2] Never—with the exception of the post-Famine Irish—had so many people entered England as refugees or immigrants in such a short time.[3]

By October of 1914, Folkestone—the most popular landing site—had become "a town of refugees."[4] Thirteen boats landed in Folkestone on just one day in October; 35,000 refugees arrived there between September 20 and October 24.[5] Refugee workers drew on a network of private homes in England that had been identified for a different theater of war. As the shadow of civil war hung over Northern Ireland, women's organizations in Ulster had quietly arranged sympathetic homes in England for Protestant civilians who might flee the fighting. When the Belgian crisis began, ironically, these homes were used for Catholic Belgians instead.[6] Belgian refugees lived in workhouses, asylums, and hostels for English vagrants, as well as two of London's greatest pleasure palaces: Earl's Court and Alexandra Palace. Opened on October 15, 1914, the Earl's Court Camp did not close until July 1919.

On May 21, 1937, the luxury ocean liners *Habaña* and *Goizeka Izarra* sailed from Bilbao to Britain, guarded by two Royal Navy ships. The ships carried 3,889 children, 219 women teachers, and 15 priests. These passengers were in flight from the Spanish Civil War (1936–9), the great clash between democracy and fascism. In the north of Spain, as General Franco's right-wing forces strove to oust the popularly elected Republican government, the Basques offered entrenched resistance. Strict rationing, starvation, and mass evacuations followed. Britain's official policy in Spain was nonintervention. But with the bombing of Guernica, popular support in Britain for the Basques spiked. More than 2,000 Britons joined the International Brigade to fight in Spain, and tens of thousands protested and raised funds—around £2 million—to support the Republicans and send medical supplies and food.[7] Under public pressure, the Home Office agreed to accept 2,000 Basque children in Britain, later upping the quota to 4,000.

On the night of departure, the quay "was a thick, black mass of parents, defying bombs as the children, some happy and excited, some in tears, were taken aboard."[8] Many children gorged once they boarded the ship on the luxurious treats they were offered after weeks or months of privation—white bread, chorizo, boiled eggs, and sponge cakes—only to become horribly ill as they entered the choppy Bay of Biscay.[9] Leah Manning, the Labour politician who accompanied the children from Spain to Southampton, recalled the mass hysteria that took place for two "dreadful" days and nights, as she "slipped and slithered from one pool of diarrhea and vomit to another," assuring the children that it wasn't the fascists who had stirred up the troubled waters against them.[10]

The ships arrived in Southampton on May 23. The port was covered with flags and bunting to celebrate King George VI's coronation, though many children believed the festivities were in their honor. The children were greeted at the docks with ice cream and a marching band. They were then tagged with colored ribbons for specific medical problems; many of them swapped ribbons, which meant that children with no lice might have their hair cut off.[11] In the pouring rain, the children were transferred by the busload to a tented camp at North Stoneham, just outside Southampton in Eastleigh. A local farmer, G.H. Brown, had loaned seven of his fields for the campsite. The (wildly unrealistic) plan was that the children would stay in camp for no more than one week.

Just as Basque children started to leave Britain to rejoin their families in Spain, Jewish child refugees—or *Kinder*—began to arrive. As the condition of Jews in Europe deteriorated after the horrors of *Kristallnacht*, the British government (lobbied by Jewish refugee agencies) agreed to accept unaccompanied refugee children under the age of 17. The original aim was to transport 5,000 children out of Germany, Austria, and Czechoslovakia, but after the Colonial Office refused to allow 10,000 refugee children to enter Palestine, the Home Office agreed to bring 10,000 children to Britain instead.

The first train left Berlin in the freezing cold on December 1, 1938, carrying 200 children.[12] The train stations were soon packed with heartbroken parents and anxious, excited children aged 4 to 17. All of the children were given a number to wear around their necks. Many parents were not allowed to say goodbye on the platform for fear they would faint.[13] Indeed, Lory Cahn's father was so distraught that he pulled her off the train through the window and took her home. Lore Segal remembered boarding the train in the dark, surrounded by flashlights, as children were arranged in columns of four. She told herself, "This is terrific, I'm going to England. What a lark! How exciting!" to numb herself to the bedlam and the trauma of leaving her parents.[14]

The *Kindertransporte* lasted for nine months. They peaked with daily transports to Britain in June and July of 1939, and ended with the outbreak of war in September. As the trains crossed into the Netherlands, German border guards routinely plundered the children's carefully packed suitcases. In Holland, the children were cheered by anti-Nazi songs along with cocoa and Dutch zwieback. From the Hook of Holland, the children were shuttled onto ferries, and sailed overnight across the North Sea to Harwich or Southampton. Children who arrived without a specific contact were placed at summer holiday camps on the windy coast of East Anglia: Dovercourt (near Harwich) and Pakefield (near Lowestoft). Pakefield quickly flooded, and was abandoned; Dovercourt filled up with 1,000 children and teen-agers, more than twice its normal capacity.

Jewish adult refugees were also entering Britain.[15] The German authorities agreed to release up to 30,000 men from Nazi concentration camps if the men obtained entry visas for a foreign country and left immediately. The Central British Fund for German Jewry enabled 4,000 German and Austrian Jewish men, selected by Jewish organizations in Europe, to come to Britain on transit visas. The men were supposed to be between the ages of 18 and 40, though this restriction was not always followed, and they must plan to re-emigrate. From February to September of 1939, these refugees were joined by Jews from Belgium, Italy, and Czechoslovakia at Kitchener Camp, an abandoned training camp left over from the Great War. Thus, Dovercourt and Kitchener became—at least for a brief time—focal points of camp life in Britain for Jewish children and adults.

The Poles would seem to be an anomaly in this story. They were not in "flight" from their homeland when they entered Britain, and were designated as "refugees" only by specific acts of legislation.[16] The Second World War had been demograph-ically devastating for Poland. Roughly 6,000,000 Poles were killed, and more than 5,000,000 were scattered abroad: in the Polish armed forces in the west, in DP camps, and in other countries (including Britain) as refugees.[17] At the war's end, 54,234 Polish officers and other military personnel were in Britain.[18] Over the next three years, 130,000 more Poles arrived in Britain from other theaters of war around the world.

The Poles in Britain were a heterogeneous mass. They included the government and armed forces that had fled Poland with the Nazi invasion, arriving after the fall of France in 1940. Polish soldiers played a crucial role in the Battle of Britain; 26,200 Poles were killed under British command. After Russia entered the war in 1941, General Władysław Anders raised a Polish army in Russia of some 100,000 men to fight the Nazis. The surviving members of this army arrived in Britain in 1946.[19] Also in Britain were 90,000 Polish deserters from the Wehrmacht and Todt Org (the Nazi armed forces and engineers), plus 21,000 POWs liberated from German concentration camps, and 2,000 political prisoners. Another 33,000 Poles—the soldiers' dependents—entered Britain between 1945 and 1950.

In 1945, the British government still hoped that most Poles would return to Poland. But when Poland fell to the Soviets, Prime Minister Winston Churchill pledged that Poles who had fought under the British flag would "dwell among us as if they were men of our own blood."[20] By October 1946, close to 120,000 Polish troops were quartered in 265 camps, mostly British and Allied service camps in rural areas. In 1948, there were 16,500 Poles housed in 43 British camps.[21] On March 27, 1947, the Polish Resettlement Act offered British citizenship to exiled

Poles.[22] The promises of the Polish Resettlement Act would be recalibrated for many decades to come.

Over the next decade, Soviet offensives across Europe generated more refugees for Britain. After the Soviet invasion of Hungary in October of 1956, 200,000 Hungarians fled their country—the largest spontaneous movement of a civilian population in Europe since the Spanish Civil War.[23] At first, the Home Office selected Hungarian refugees who had made their way on foot to Austrian camps, and transported them to Britain. But on November 23, the British government removed restrictions on Hungarian immigration, and refugees were admitted (mostly through Blackbushe Airport in Surrey) without immigration controls. The flow was then stopped until January, and resumed much more slowly. After April 1957, entry was restricted to Hungarians who were joining their family members. The initial plan was to take only 2,500 refugees from Hungary. Ultimately, Britain accepted 21,692 Hungarians.[24] Of this number, 11,000 passed through 150 reception camps in south and southeastern England.

Like the Basques and the *Kinder*, the Hungarians and the Anglo-Egyptians arrived in Britain within weeks of each other. On November 5, 1956, British and French paratroopers landed in Egypt as part of a bid (with Israel) to oust President Nasser and regain control of the Suez Canal. The Egyptian forces were defeated, but not before blocking access to the canal for shipping. Under pressure from the United States and Soviet Union, the British withdrew from Egypt in disgrace. The Suez Crisis damaged Britain's prestige abroad, sparking political splits on both the Left and the Right, and demonstrated Britain's vulnerability to what had been thought to be less powerful states. It was followed by oil pipelines sabotaged throughout the Gulf region, strikes and riots in Bahrain and Kuwait, the ousting of the pro-British Iraqi monarchy, and guerrilla activity in Yemen. More broadly, Suez boosted demands for decolonization in Africa, the Caribbean, and the Far East.[25] After Suez, Enoch Powell said, nothing could ever be quite the same again.[26]

At ten minutes to five o'clock on Friday, November 23, 1956, the Egyptian government announced that it intended to expel all British subjects (known as Anglo-Egyptians) from Egypt. The British government feared large numbers of people might cross into Libya and fly to Britain from there, which would mean only twelve hours' notice before they arrived.[27]

The category "Anglo-Egyptian" included a wide variety of people who left Egypt under very different circumstances. The Anglo-Egyptians (also sometimes known as "Nasser refugees") were British subjects, but mostly not English-speaking. The majority spoke French, Greek, Italian, or Arabic. Of the 7,000 or 8,000 who arrived in Britain, about half were Maltese, and most—whether Maltese or not—had never been to Britain before.[28] They arrived by various routes in small family groups (with a high proportion of elderly people), traveling in unpredictable patterns. By August of 1957, it cost nearly £200,000 per month to keep the Anglo-Egyptians housed and fed in Britain.[29]

Throughout 1956–7, the Anglo-Egyptians provided a largely silent backdrop to the highly publicized Hungarian story. Government files described the

Anglo-Egyptians as having few skilled workers.[30] They were frequently contrasted with the Hungarians, who were typed as young, healthy, and virile—political heroes rather than frail and fragile reminders of a political embarrassment. Hungarians and Anglo-Egyptians competed for space in camps and hostels, though they were rarely housed together.[31] Both Hungarians and Anglo-Egyptians crossed paths with British troops, who were leaving for or returning to Suez, on their way in and out of camp.[32]

Like war, decolonization generated many refugees. On August 5, 1972, the Ugandan leader Idi Amin announced that—based on a dream he had guiding him to expel "bloodsucking" Asians from Uganda—all Asian holders of British passports would be expelled from Uganda within ninety days. Over the next three months, 28,000 Ugandan Asians were speedily "repatriated" to Britain. But the fear that African countries might expel their Asian populations is evident in Home Office documents much earlier. British officials conceded that they would have to shelter the descendants of the same Asians they had led from India to Africa in the eighteenth century. In the age of imperial collapse, this was "only the latest of a series of unavoidable capitulations."[33] The Ugandan Asian expulsion was not a sudden revelation or short-term crisis born of the incoherent ravings of Idi Amin, though the British press presented it as such. It was a much-dreaded consequence of independence, British awareness of which had developed over several decades.[34]

No one knew how many Ugandan Asians would arrive in Britain; some estimates were as high as 60,000. In the worst-case scenario—that is, that other East African countries would expel their Asian populations and Britain would receive 100,000 people in two or three months—the Ministry of Defence thought that staging posts in the Mediterranean might be useful. Most officials predicted a "sudden surge," and considered setting up an island territory—either in the Solomon Islands or the Falklands—to absorb Ugandan Asians. Starting in September, Ugandan Asians began traveling on specially chartered flights from Entebbe to Stansted and Heathrow. Many were brutally attacked and robbed by Amin's soldiers on their way to the airport in Uganda; they were allowed to bring no more than £55 and a suitcase. Of the first 193 Ugandan Asian arrivals at Stansted on September 17, 1972, 101 had nowhere to go.[35] Ultimately, 21,000 Ugandan Asians went through sixteen resettlement camps in Britain.

As with the Ugandan Asian expulsion, the "crisis" of refugees from Vietnam was not a sudden or unanticipated emergency. Its history unfolded over years, not weeks, although the popular press—which portrayed Britain as an altruistic bystander to the Vietnam War—ignored this longer narrative.[36] In fact, Britain had secretly sold arms and napalm to the United States, and provided military training for the South Vietnamese in Malaysia and signals intelligence from Hong Kong.[37] In Britain, the New Left saw the conflict in Vietnam as a springboard for working-class mobilization, and the Labour Party debated the war's role as a struggle for national liberation.[38] Camps for refugees from Vietnam were an epilogue to the long story of Britain's ambivalence about the war.

In 1975, when American troops withdrew from Vietnam, more than 130,000 refugees entered the United States within two weeks. That year, Britain took in only thirty-two refugees from Vietnam, but Home Secretary Roy Jenkins pledged to admit an unspecified number of people from Vietnam who had a "previous connection" to the United Kingdom.[39] International attention focused on the plight of hundreds of thousands of Vietnamese "boat people," who risked drowning and pirates as they fled their country. Up to 250,000 people lost their lives at sea.[40] In October 1978, the British ship *Wellpark* rescued 346 refugees off the coast of Taiwan. When Taiwan refused to let them land unless they would promptly board a plane for Britain, the British government conceded. These first 346 arrivals were "gratefully" put up in Kensington Barracks, which had housed Ugandan Asians in 1972.[41]

On May 21, 1979, the *Sibonga*, a British ship, responded to distress calls from two boats in the South China Sea, and took on board 1,003 refugees. One week later, Prime Minister Margaret Thatcher agreed to fly this group to Heathrow.[42] At the United Nations Conference in Geneva in July 1979, Britain agreed to expand its very modest initial quota of 1,500 refugees, and accept another 10,000 "boat people," 6,000 of whom arrived in Britain by the end of that year. Refugees were already pouring into Hong Kong—Britain's most valuable remaining colony—and the Hong Kong authorities wanted Britain to relieve the pressure on its camps. Between 1978 and 1982, Britain admitted 22,500 individuals from Vietnam.[43] At the height of the Vietnamese program, there were forty-six camps for refugees from Vietnam operating throughout Britain.

Arrivals by boat and by plane, expulsions spurred by war or imperial crisis. Some of the most widely circulated images of refugees are of the chaos of mass embarkations and debarkations: people crowding on or off boats and trains, or stranded in airports. These fetishized moments of escape and arrival are heavily photographed and televised. But scenes of arrival—iconic though they have become—cut the story short. They tell us how refugees got to their country of refuge, but not what happened afterwards. The longer era of encampment is more often forgotten.[44] Scholars, too, have generally glossed over the era of encampment in their narratives, moving directly from arrival to stories of refugee success or failure. But the camps were not simply a blank space between the trauma of flight and the happy ending of integration. The story of what happened next—the untold history of encampment—is the true subject of this book.

A word about the images in this book: pictures of camp life are not, of course, necessarily any more "authentic" than those of flight. The Austrian refugee photographer Edith Tudor-Hart took hundreds of photos of children playing and exploring the world independent of adults. Her striking photographs of Basque children at the North Stoneham Camp (one of which appears in Chapter 5) focused more on the children's freedom than their plight, depicting the camp as a site of cheerfully uninhibited spontaneity. Such images have their own staginess, and their own politically charged claims about "heroic" refugees and "benevolent" camps.

Still, the images in this book offer a different perspective from the traditional iconography of expulsion and arrival. Images of flight suggest that refugees were in constant motion. But what happened when that motion was stalled? What kinds of lives were lived in these spaces of apparent immobility? The photographs here reveal the ordinary daily routines in camp that countered or were part of the unordinariness of being a refugee. They help to chart the complex physical and emotional terrain of the camps, and to offer new narratives about refugees and citizens. Focusing on the space of the camp (rather than scenes of arrival) brings new players—and the interactions between them—into view.

All diasporas are unhappy, the literary critic Vijay Mishra has said, but every diaspora is unhappy in its own way.[45] This book seeks to capture both the universality of that unhappiness as well as its historical specificity. There are many differences between these stories, as well as resonances and points of convergence. The Basques and the *Kinder*, for example, were child refugees, whose flights were closely linked in time. The Hungarians and the Anglo-Egyptians, too, arrived in Britain at nearly the same moment, crossing paths in (and competing for) space. There are also insights to be gained from other, more unexpected juxtapositions, which could take place within a single moment in historical time, or cut across it.

We must ask whose interests have been served by treating refugee crises as discontinuous and disconnected episodes—in short, as emergencies. The idea of "emergency" is driven by particular ways of thinking about the world, as well as distinctive moral orientations. Emergencies are understood as sudden, unpredictable, brief exceptions to the normal order. The concept has its absurdities: the situation of displaced Palestinians is often still termed an "emergency" after more than sixty years. Such reasoning severs any historical connections between different groups of refugees, while also ignoring the long-term structural issues that make people vulnerable to disaster.[46]

There are high stakes to these arguments. The refusal to plan for refugees whose arrival is in fact very much anticipated—that is, the manufacturing of emergency—has worked against the creation of permanent structures of aid.[47] The state has regarded each refugee influx as a unique, non-recurring event, linked only by British generosity.[48] Timothy Raison, the Conservative Minister of State for Immigration during the Vietnamese refugee program, claimed there was no connection between the refugees from Vietnam and earlier arrivals. It would be "inappropriate" to impose a pattern on refugee experiences, or to set up any ongoing machinery to deal with "separate and unrelated" situations.[49]

The state's insistence on all refugee movements as episodic and unrelated emergencies has been a key strand of political argument: a deliberate strategy of refusing to see connections between refugees in order to reject more robust structures of aid. Stories of arrival have a high value precisely because they uphold the fiction that each situation was new, unprecedented, and the result of a temporary crisis that was foreign and external to Britain. In focusing on the chaos of short-term displacement, they sustain the myth of emergency. The British state's insistence on this image of refugeedom as unanticipated chaos in turn generated a lot of very real chaos for refugees—and continues to do so. This book offers an alternative. Here, comparative history is a rejoinder to the corrosive discourse of emergency.[50] What happens if we see these camps not as emergencies—severed from Britain's own history—but as deeply rooted in that history? What happens if they are not emergencies at all?

Rather than thinking of each refugee crisis as having a discrete, unrelated beginning and ending, this book thinks instead in terms of webs, networks, and nodes. It uses the long history of encampment—in which refugees and citizens mixed together— to challenge the state's rubric in which every refugee crisis was invented anew, upending the framework of emergency that haunts so many refugee stories.

1

Making Camp

At first glance, the map of encampment makes no sense at all. Camps are scattered across England, Scotland, Ireland, and Wales seemingly at random, ranging from large urban centers to isolated rural locales. Some camps were repurposed for multiple groups of refugees over several decades, while others were deployed only for a single moment, never to be used again. How might we begin to make sense of this map, this representation of the strange relationship between refugees and place?[1]

These camps were not blank spaces, though they might initially appear to be. They were sites with deeply local (and sometimes global) histories. Whether the camps were abandoned or active when refugees arrived, they were socially and politically charged with the freight of their past. They bore very particular relationships to the environment—urban or rural—and the communities in which they were situated. Refugee camps gave a tangible dimension to what might otherwise have been abstractions—empathy, but also prejudice and racism—and rendered these abstractions deeply and vividly material. They existed in dialogue with debates about space and power in Britain: modernization and urban planning, tower blocks and New Towns, demilitarization and remilitarization, squatting, slums and ghettoization, and homes and homelessness. Refugee camps were a largely unseen, unrecognized element in the crafting of the physical environment in which Britons and others lived. They were a vital part of the twentieth-century British landscape.

One of the most dominant structures for housing refugees in Britain was the army or air force base. Military bases were not only a model for civilian encampment, but also a space where this encampment actually took place.[2] These bases had complex histories, which were galvanized anew by each refugee crisis. Some bases had been empty for decades. In other cases, refugees actually crossed paths with soldiers on active duty. Taken together, these camps were places where the lessons of war were both learned and lost. The material cultures of war and refugeedom were intertwined—not only through the obvious historical fact that war generated refugees, but also because the physical structures of war were revived in order to shelter them. In refugee camps, the machinery of war was brought back to life for new purposes.[3]

This chapter explores the physical stuff of which refugee camps were made, and looks closely at the spaces of refugee housing. In this sense, the built environment operates as a crucial archive of camp life—a way to capture people in motion. But refugees did not unquestioningly accept the environments in which they found themselves.[4] They imprinted their own identities on the camp, transforming the camp's physical space and imposing individuality upon it. Here, we can see how refugees altered the cityscape and countryside, and how the spaces where they were housed governed their inclusion or rejection.[5]

THE STUFF OF WAR: NISSEN HUTS AND THE LANDSCAPE OF MODERN BRITAIN

For refugees who lived on military bases, the most common and recognizable element of refugee camps in Britain was the Nissen hut: the prefabricated half-barrel-shaped structure that dotted the military landscapes of Britain and Europe. Here, I zero in on this single element of camp life to understand its role in war and peace, and how it bridged the lives of refugees and citizens. The Nissen hut housed refugees, but also Britons: working-class families displaced by the Blitz, demobbed servicemen, university students, and paramilitary prisoners. The huts provided a material tie between these groups, aligning their experiences of mobility and displacement. At different moments, the Nissen hut was characterized as the ideal working-class home or as a sign of the state's failure. I trace the hut's wartime histories in order to understand its multiple uses in the modern world and how refugees shaped and were shaped by the rapidly changing built environment of twentieth-century Britain.

The creator of the Nissen hut, Peter Nissen, was an American-born engineer who emigrated to Canada and was ultimately naturalized as a UK citizen. In 1916, the bloodiest year of the Great War, Nissen was stationed at Ypres. Because many French villages had been destroyed, it was impossible to billet soldiers in private homes. Nissen sketched out plans for semicircular huts based on his memories of the skating rink at Queen's University. By September of 1916, huts based on Nissen's design were widely available on the battlefront. The advent of the Nissen hut coincided with the war's unleashing of tanks and heavy artillery. Filson Young, a journalist for the *Daily Mail*, described the hut as a sign of these broader transformations. As the tanks were rolled out for the first time,

> Another creature, almost equally primeval of aspect, began to appear in conquered areas. No one ever saw it on the move, or met it on the roads. It just appeared! Overnight you would see a blank space of ground. In the morning it would be occupied by an immense creature of the tortoise species, settled down solidly and permanently on the earth, and emitting green smoke from a right angled system at one end, where its mouth might be, as though it were smoking a morning pipe. And when such a pioneer found that the situation was good and the land habitable, it would pass the word, for by twos and threes, by tens and hundreds, its fellow monsters would appear, so that in a week or two you would find a valley covered with them that had been nothing but pulverized earth before.[6]

The Nissen hut, this useful "monster," resolved one of the problems of modern warfare: how to house an unprecedented number of troops. The hut devised a

Fig. 1.1. Queen Mary of Teck inspecting Nissen huts at Hesdin, July 7, 1917. The officer on the Queen's right is Lieutenant Colonel Peter Nissen, DSO. Reproduced by permission of the Imperial War Museum.

cheap, portable dwelling place. Four men could easily put up a Nissen hut in four hours (the record was one hour and twenty-seven minutes), and the only tool required—a spanner—was included with it. The roof was made of an arch of corrugated iron with no eaves or gables to fit and no nails to drive. The huts supposedly had no drafts, staying warm in the winter and relatively cool in the summer.

By November 1918, over 100,000 Nissen huts had been erected behind Allied lines, sheltering 2.5 million servicemen.[7] These huts were credited with improving the morale of British troops on the Western Front, providing "the new homes for which many a solider on the Somme thanked his stars." During the day, beds could be rolled up against the sides of the hut, and the middle space used for games, reading, and writing. The hut's round back provided "the most artistic camouflage" to protect the residents from shelling. In short, "among the creatures to which the War has given birth, [the Nissen hut] has already earned a high character as a useful, tractable, kindly domestic beast."[8]

In wartime, then, the Nissen hut was a hero. Its role in peacetime was more controversial. As the Great War drew to a close, the British government ordered 100,000 huts. During the 1920s and 1930s, Nissen huts dotted the British landscape as factories and churches.[9] But it was in the domain of private housing that the Nissen hut proved most divisive. The notion of the Nissen hut as the ideal

Fig. 1.2. Members of the Women's Army Auxiliary Corps amidst the ruins of some Nissen huts in their camp at Abbeville destroyed in an air raid, May 22, 1918. Reproduced by permission of the Imperial War Museum.

British home took on new force during the Second World War. Toward the end of the war, a member of the British Expeditionary Force in France wrote to the *Spectator* to address the looming task of reconstruction. Millions of men had lived for years in Nissen huts, and had been so comfortable that they were no longer willing to spend up to a quarter of their income on an overpriced rental. Many British soldiers who had served in Europe might say, "I never want to bother about a house again, when I can have something like this and save a great deal of my money." The writer assumed that the average British homeowner had been converted by military service to the trappings of war, abandoning the "old-fashioned" bias toward stone or brick houses. The *Spectator*'s editors were less optimistic: "after all, house pride is part of the art of life that cannot be cultivated in a British hut... not to mention the appalled reactions of Mrs. Tommy"![10]

Between 1939 and 1942, the Ministry of Works erected more than 250,000 Nissen huts in Britain.[11] For some political leaders, Nissen huts were the home of the future, a compelling solution to the overcrowding and homelessness that plagued Britons in war's wake.[12] In the winter of 1944, 40,000 homeless Londoners were housed in huts.[13] Many private citizens proposed that local councils take over these huts and "make small communities of them," rather than allowing them to go to rack and ruin.[14] Mrs. Greta Clench, who had been bombed out during the Blitz, pleaded with Aneurin Bevan to "let these excellent camps which are now deserted—and so deteriorating—be used as temporary dwelling places for the homeless. They could pay a reasonable rent (some people expect something for nothing!) and could be <u>extremely</u> comfortable." Having lived "from pillar to post" after her London home was destroyed, she yearned for a hut at the disused Dorney Common Camp: "had I had the chance of one of those huts at that time I should have been <u>overjoyed</u>. Well-built, red tiled roofs, sanitation, <u>all</u> domestic conveniences, electricity, even to the telephones still being laid on. I would <u>prefer</u> a hut to a prefab house." Hutted camps were "almost luxurious with billiard tables etc. If people are <u>really</u> homeless or over crowded <u>and not just grumbling</u> they would jump at the chance of a good army hut." She concluded, "I am longing to buy one of those huts to fit on to my present house which is inadequate for our needs!"[15] Any British citizen who wished to purchase a Nissen hut could apply to the Ministry of Works.[16]

Here, the Nissen hut was valorized as "comfortable," even "attractive" for ordinary civilians.[17] In 1947, David Renton, Labour MP for Huntingdon, described how

Fig. 1.3. The kitchen in a completed temporary house converted from an army Nissen hut. Reproduced by permission of the Imperial War Museum.

Nissen huts—which came with surplus furniture and bedding—could prevent squatting.[18] These "once despised" huts, where British soldiers had spent long periods of "varying degrees of discomfort and happiness," were easily renovated by demobilized men.[19] Soldiers had lived communally in the huts. But if the huts were taken over by young married couples, they could provide families a private place to strike out on their own.

British civilians often had highly positive memories of their time in Nissen huts. In 1945, Betty Kellar moved with her family to a Nissen hut at Borough Gun site, just 2 miles outside of Torpoint. The family had been renting a flat in Torpoint, from which her mother could travel to work as a driller in Devonport. Betty's family was asked to quit the flat to make room for the landlord's daughter, who had been bombed out during the Blitz. They were promised a council house within two years if they would accept a hut in the meantime. While still in her Torpoint flat, Betty had often heard the guns firing from this same ack-ack (anti-aircraft) battery site during air raids. When the soldiers moved out, Cornwall County Council converted hundreds of Nissen huts on this site for families. Each hut was divided into two bedrooms plus a kitchen, which also served as a living room. There was a sink, but no hot water; the family heated water in pans on the range, and paid for metered electricity. Each family had a small, grassy area behind and in front of the huts for growing vegetables. The communal washing area was seldom used because the pipes were often frozen.

From 1945 to 1947, Betty and her family lived in one such Nissen hut. Home life in the Nissen huts was very different to what it had been in their flat. Betty's abiding memory was the struggle to keep warm during the bitterly cold winter of 1946–7. Everyone huddled together in the bedroom closest to the kitchen, which was the hut's only source of heat. Relationships between her family and others in nearby huts were cordial, but casual and temporary. But Betty says, "we were never aware of any adverse opinions about the status of Nissen hut dwellers when we were among them. This was because all our neighbours were respectable like us, who had been put in this position by the war." Still, when Betty's sister received a box of stationery from a relative with the return address "12, Borough Gun-site," she exclaimed, "'I hope no one thinks we are living with the soldiers!"[20]

For Betty's family, "although life was hard while we were there, we were so thankful the war was over . . . and a very nice new home at the end of it. We just felt very lucky." But such rosy memories of respectability were confronted by harsher realities. The Nissen huts were pilloried when squatters took over huts that were awaiting demolition. At one point, a squatter family moved into the site, in a small hut at the entrance that had never been converted. The conditions in this hut were appalling, with no facilities for heat or cooking, and Betty remembered that "there was a loud shriek from this hut one night when a tramp moved in on them."

Not all Britons embraced the idea that a hut could be a home. The Conservative politician Major Harry Legge-Bourke found it "very disconcerting to think of England being dotted with tin boxes which apparently will not be fit to live in."[21] Sir Percy Harris, the Liberal Chief Whip, described Nissen huts in 1945 as "an apology for a home"; the huts were, in his view, cold and drafty "caricatures of homes."[22]

One Ministry of Works official saw the "hutting" of Britain as fundamentally at odds with the imperative to eliminate "problem" housing: "eventually we shall be driven ... to acquiesce in homeless individuals putting up shacks of any sort anywhere."[23] Substandard shacks would become a plague, and it would be "most embarrassing" if the government provided the shacks.[24] The Ministry of Health also deemed the huts "very unsatisfactory." At Heathfield Camp in Honiton—a future site for housing Ugandan Asian refugees—the soldiers woke up in their Nissen huts one morning in 1947 to find their boots frozen to the floor.[25]

The Labour politician Billy Blyton proclaimed that the government must build better homes, rather than relying on huts as standard working-class housing.[26] But these objections crossed party lines. In 1953, Bill Deedes, Conservative MP for Ashford, claimed that the huts were worse than any slum. He described the "vicious dew" that formed inside the huts each night, soaking the carpets, the cupboards, the furniture, and the bedding. The huts could never be "decent" or "healthy"; their inhabitants would inevitably fall into squalor and become "social misfits." Now that the war was over, the huts were simply "human traps."[27] Despite these protests, 37,000 huts were used as dwelling houses in 1951.[28]

If the overcrowded flat typified the urban slum, then the Nissen hut was a visible sign of rural poverty and failed welfare. In 1954, the aristocrat Sherman Stonor wrote to the Ministry of Housing to insist that local authorities abolish hutted camps, which housed thousands of English families. Stonor called these huts "rural slums of the worst possible kind." He acknowledged that many of the families who lived in huts "could have done more to help themselves," and might not be "the most desirable section of the population." But such camps constituted an ethical dilemma for a government trying to eradicate substandard housing. Stonor proposed clearing the huts, and building council houses to accommodate all of the hut dwellers.[29]

No one could accurately calculate the lifespan of a Nissen hut, but they had clearly been planned for obsolescence. Some said the huts became uninhabitable after two years, but many were occupied far longer than that.[30] They risked becoming a permanent feature of postwar life. If British families moved into them, "we will never get shot of the camps at all."[31] The huts had an environmental impact as well as a human one. In 1955, William Hoskins decried how soldiers and politicians had devastated Britain's "immemorial" landscape, now "flayed bare" by airfields and other signs of militarism:

> Those long gentle lines of the dip-slope of the Cotswolds, those misty uplands of the sheep-grey oolite, how they have lent themselves to the villainous requirements of the new age! Over them drones, day after day, the obscene shape of the atom-bomber, laying a trail like a filthy slug upon Constable's and Gainsborough's sky, England of the Nissen hut, the "pre-fab," and the electric fence, of the high barbed wire of some unmentionable devilment.[32]

With battle-training sites on former heaths, and tanks crashing through empty, ruined villages, Hoskins portrayed a truly barbarized vision of the "new" landscape of Britain. Within this vision, Nissen huts served as markers of a militarized past and present. Ultimately, refugee camps were integrated into this "ruined" landscape, taking part in the devastation Hoskins described.

It was not only bombed-out families and ex-servicemen who found themselves in Nissen huts. After the Second World War, the populations who lived in Nissen huts diversified. More than 2 million men were conscripted into National Service between 1945 and 1960; hundreds of thousands more volunteered. Many of these men trained at icy Nissen huts on enormous RAF bases, which horrified many of the conscripts. Catterick, in North Yorkshire, which housed 16,000 servicemen, was so large and chaotic that a signalman who deserted survived for six months by stealing food and hiding in the toilets.[33]

In the landscape of higher education, too, the Nissen hut materialized. Students and staff at Keele University were housed in Nissen huts well into the 1960s. The university had been a transit camp for refugees and military personnel from 1939 to 1945.[34] When the university opened in 1950, the estate was extremely neglected. A mass of sixty dilapidated huts, with wooden walls and asbestos compound roofs, were clustered on the "barren wind-swept scrubland." The "pride and glory" of the university were two large Nissen-style huts that housed the Students' Union and the chapel.

Keele's Pioneers (as the hut dwellers were called) loved their uniquely makeshift "Hut Life." Brian Vale reminisced about the "freedom" he experienced in Keele's huts in 1960. As he noted, "talk of 'pioneers' and 'huts' gave the impression of rugged discomfort. Far from it!" His childhood home had been so cold that he had to put his clothes on in bed, while icicles formed on the inside of his windows. But at Keele he luxuriated in his heated hut with enough hot water that he could bathe every day! The mixing of social classes, living "almost as a family," was a crucial element. Martin Tuncliffe came to Keele straight from the army, and found in his hut "something of the barrack-room camaraderie." Tony Powell recalled that each hut at Keele "was an active little community. I shared in one with a guy of completely different background and personality of my own—quite an education." Penny Jones Blackmore, who lived in a hut at Keele in 1963, described this experience as "a privilege...fun and friendly." She used the huts to evade the discipline of university rules: "You could get in and out of the front door and the windows of the room at any time of night. It was the best time."[35]

Glorified in wartime, the Nissen hut would be devalued in the field of refugee work. Ultimately, the Nissen hut came to stand for everything that was wrong with the treatment of refugees. But these huts were ubiquitous—and highly visible—in many aspects of modern British life. There is no simple chronology of the rise and fall of the Nissen hut, nor is there a clear trajectory for when it was embraced or rejected. Hutted camps were coveted or denigrated at different moments, and it was difficult to predict how the press or the public would perceive them.

By the 1970s, some British politicians began to look back at postwar huts with nostalgia, arguing that British squatters had turned Nissen huts into "first-class homes...to be proud of, homes that were a credit to them."[36] Faced with a new generation of squatters, who did not seek a home for their families, but only to extract resources from unoccupied properties, the earlier era of Nissen huts seemed positively romantic. Several councils were still using huts for homeless Britons in the early 1970s, while wartime squatters shared their memories of the hutted camps of their childhood as vast adventure playgrounds. As more draconian proposals for the homeless emerged—putting Bengalis from Tower Hamlets on a disused passenger liner on the Thames, for example—the Nissen hut was speedily cloaked in the golden haze of memory.[37] Confronted with the new realities of urban blight and ghettoization, British politicians reevaluated the Nissen hut as a marker of the heroic (and blameless) homeless of the past.

As Britons "read" the physical environment of refugee camps, they brought their own diverse experiences of British housing in the twentieth century, and their knowledge of other forms of encampment. Public and governmental responses to the Nissen hut were shaped not only by when it was being used, but also by whom and for what purpose. The notion that white, working-class British families were constantly being "resettled" (both from the dislocations of war and, later on, from slum clearances)—and that this process of "resettlement" caused specific mental-health issues—pervaded the social science of the day.[38] Life in huts offered shared, though unequal, experiences between Britons and refugees dealing with temporary housing, periods of military service, and an intimacy with the problems of how to live with the aftermath of war.

These responses remind us that refugee camps were part of the history of domestic displacements as well as foreign crises. Given the recent and urgent history of many Britons' own experience of encampment, we would be wrong to think that refugees who lived in huts were necessarily stigmatized. Rather, the multiple uses of the Nissen hut can reveal the intimacy and convergence of Britons and refugees rather than their isolation from one another. This complex history helps to explain the uneven trajectory of the Nissen hut in Britain, and its alternating phases of praise and criticism in individual and collective memory. By the 1970s, as the home and the camp diverged, this sense of kinship between the material experiences of Britons and refugees largely disappeared. The material culture of the refugee became more distinctive, marking a new gulf between citizens and refugees.

PREHISTORIES: COLONIAL CRISES, LABOR, AND INTERNMENT

Throughout the twentieth century, refugees faced seemingly incompatible accusations that the spaces in which they lived were too opulent or too barbarous. These competing visions were generated by the long colonial history of encampment, as well as the blurred boundaries between refuge and internment. Refugee camps in Britain were hybrids of many other structures of welfare and social control that sought to relocate overly "mobile" bodies.[39] Colonial and metropolitan rule generated multiple spaces that combined aid, penal servitude, and detention. All of these funneled into the making of the modern refugee camp.

In Britain, the experience of encampment was widespread. Salvation Army and labor camps in the 1890s demonstrated what would become a characteristically

British combination of aid and coercion. The British poor were compelled into these camps by the threat of being denied benefits.[40] Metropolitan workhouses—plus a system of passes, permits, and police registration to control the movements of "dangerous classes"—provided the template for camps in Britain and elsewhere by demarcating special spaces for the needy.[41] Later on, the Unemployment Assistance Act of 1934 introduced compulsory "retraining" for unemployed men. In these army-style camps, men grew food, cleared scrubland, drained marshes, and built sea defenses. Many critics denounced the camps as quasi-fascist; Anthony Divers, a Liverpudlian who stayed at one such camp, had heard the sites described as "concentration camps." But he praised the sense of community he gained there. In the camp, "we don't feel set apart no longer."[42]

Colonial settings offered even greater scope for encampment. Colonial locales—most notably, India and South Africa—justified the creation of camps by a "gardening" model, in which the "weeds" were rooted out in the name of order and prosperity. Such camps were legitimated by the discourses of social welfare, uplift, and sanitary reform.[43] Military leaders often claimed that these temporary facilities were liberal, reformist measures to protect detainees, even as they violated detainees' rights within camp boundaries.[44] Colonial camps extended the military practice of care and confinement of mass populations to civilians. In the 1890s, famine sufferers in British India were rounded up into a vast system of closed camps, where they were compelled to work in return for food.[45] At the same time, colonial health acts justified the use of plague segregation camps in British India. With their bamboo huts and barbed-wire fences, these camps constituted a new intervention into the lives of the destitute.[46] The project of famine relief legitimated corralling "dangerous" or "suspect" persons apart from the rest of society.[47]

During the South African War (1899–1902), the mass confinement of civilians under British rule expanded dramatically. British officials were not the first to resettle populations in fortified enclosures.[48] The South African camps marked an extension of Spanish General Valeriano Weyler's 1897 campaign to gather Cuba's rural population in fortified towns to isolate them from insurgents and prevent civilians from aiding guerrilla fighters.[49] In South Africa, the "refugee camps" provided poor relief, of a sort, but also incarceration for destitute Boers whose land had been destroyed by Britain's scorched earth policy.[50] The British policy was to denude the country of "everything moveable," using camps as a mechanism of containment.[51] British forces in South Africa presided over more than 100 camps, detaining a quarter of a million Boer and African civilians. The Colonial Office's inspectors compared the South African camps to workhouses for the poor in Britain, calling in experts from India to lower camp mortality rates (to no avail—it is estimated that 20,000 black South Africans and 28,000 Boer civilians died in the camps, mostly children).[52]

Contemporaries used the terms "refugee camp" and "concentration camp" interchangeably in South Africa. Surrounded by barbed wire, the hastily erected and shockingly unsanitary camps were used both to contain political threats and to offer "protection" or "refuge" to those in need.[53] Such camps were sites of aid, but were also used for surveillance and control.[54] Above all, the camps allowed British officials to classify the population of their newly annexed colony into "bona fide" refugees or "undesirables."[55] Here, the entanglement of aid and detention—of the prisoner and the refugee—deepened.[56]

Although refugee workers in Britain rarely acknowledged these connections, there were important ties between how camps were made in Britain and in the global South. The tension between aid and detention in refugee camps originated in this fraught imperial history, especially as many refugees arrived in Britain from colonial (or former colonial) locales. Camps for refugees, displaced persons, and internees that emerged during the First and Second World Wars drew from all of these precedents, forged through the intersection of military and medical principles.[57] For this reason, camps in Britain cannot be easily reduced to accusations of luxury or barbarity. Rather, the existence of these twinned, contradictory narratives alerts us to the more complex conditions that camps produced.

One feature of many (though not all) refugee camps in Britain was barbed wire. Barbed wire served diverse uses from the American prairie to the trenches of the First World War. It also became a central element of camp architecture. Easily installed or dismantled, and cheap, barbed wire was a sign of the camp's temporary nature. By the end of the Second World War, barbed wire began to be viewed as clumsy and outdated—and as a universal sign of oppression. But it lived on as a ubiquitous material in refugee camps, where barracks were still surrounded by chain-link fences and barbed wire.[58] In Britain, barbed wire created important links between internment and refuge.[59]

The Great War's internment camps established physical norms that were later incorporated into refugee camps. Also, the internment camps of the Second World War swept many refugees into their orbit. In wartime, the relationship between refugees and internees could be difficult to disentangle. Many individuals moved speedily between these two categories: someone who was designated a refugee upon arrival in Britain could be interned with alarming haste. Spaces that had been designed for internees were repurposed (or sometimes simply upcycled) for refugees. The Springhill Lodges for displaced Poles, for example, was originally used for German POWs, and still had barbed-wire fencing off the top part of the camp when the Poles arrived.[60] For this reason, internment camps are part of the larger story here. They were not typically described as "refugee camps," and yet they housed people who were—or had been—refugees.[61]

Internment camps were generally closely modeled on army camps, with the barrack as their archetypal structure. This architectural relationship may have been formalized through the Hague Convention of 1899 that stated that POWs must be held under conditions similar to those for soldiers of the jailing nation. Internment facilities were cramped and unsanitary, but often not very different from the housing used by regular troops. They reflected the social hierarchies of the day, in which officers were provided with better food, furniture, and leisure activities than rank-and-file soldiers.[62] Thus, internment camps helped to create one of the key tropes of encampment in twentieth-century Britain: the tension between luxury and brutality.

During the Great War, internment camps existed in all combatant countries, as well as neutral ones (and many colonial possessions). Close to a million civilians spent part of their war behind barbed wire.[63] In Britain, tens of thousands of ordinary individuals were interned.[64] In August 1914, the War Office ordered the arrest of all German and Austrian men of military age. This order was quickly rescinded, partly because there was no place to house them. After the sinking of the *Lusitania*, the War Office and the Home Office interned more than 30,000 Germans and other "enemy aliens," many of whom had lived in Britain for years.[65]

Internees were housed in an assortment of structures that had fallen out of use—a deserted skating rink in Southampton, a former factory in Lancaster. Here, the architecture of camps evolved: barbed wire outside, wooden barracks or Nissen huts inside.[66] Barbed wire was often the sole physical feature that marked these structures as being designated for detention rather than holidays or pleasure. Indeed, internees described internment as "going behind the wire."[67] Like the South African camps, these internment camps in Britain purported to offer "protection" for civilians who might be the targets of British rage, as well as shielding the British public from people with uncertain loyalties.[68]

The first internment camp in Britain was set up in Douglas at Cunningham's holiday camp (advertised in peacetime under the slogan "good clean fun for young men"), quickly supplemented by the vast, purpose-built establishment at Knockaloe.[69] During the Great War, the Isle of Man was the largest detention center in the British Isles. From 1914 to 1919, it housed some 25,000 male internees, a stunning number considering the island's own population was only 52,000. Some men were confined on the Isle of Man for more than four years.[70]

Camps for internees varied widely in terms of their physical environment and privileges. Some First World War internment camps had gymnasia, and inmates played football, cricket, and tennis.[71] At Newbury, a racecourse, internees were housed in horseboxes with neither heat nor light, whereas others lived in Lofthouse Park, near Wakefield, on the site of an unsuccessful "pleasure park," a country house with fine grounds. The Lofthouse internees were wealthier, and paid 10 shillings a week to stay there. Prisons and workhouses provided additional beds, and some German women were interned at an inebriate reformatory in Aylesbury.

During the Second World War, internment was far more chaotic. In 1939, the government established tribunals to assess the risk of German and Austrian nationals residing in Britain. Every individual was assigned a security category: Category A (clear security risks), Category B (those whose loyalties were in doubt), and Category C (who were clearly loyal and exempt from all restrictions). Of the 73,000 cases heard, around 66,000 were classed as "Category C." Most Jewish refugees were classed as Category C and thus should have been exempt from internment. But as Hitler's invasions gained devastating speed in Europe, this project of sorting refugees was abandoned. Wholesale internment of "enemy aliens" (including German and Austrian Jewish refugees) began in May 1940.[72] Altogether, around 27,000 people were interned. At the height of the internment program, 14,000 individuals were interned on the Isle of Man.[73]

Fig. 1.4. Tennis at an internment camp for German residents at Knockaloe, Isle of Man. Reproduced by permission of the Imperial War Museum.

On the Isle of Man, the "camps" were primarily boarding houses and hotels. Two rings of barbed wire were hastily thrown up around the buildings, which British occupants were ordered to vacate within the week. The women interned at Port Erin and Port St. Mary swept through the Manx shops to buy sunglasses and sweets. The Isle of Man camps offered a "holiday atmosphere" where internees could frolic in the sea or play miniature golf (though under military guard).[74]

These camps—which housed many composers and professional artists—had a high level of cultural activity. The Popular University at Onchan offered classes in clay modeling, portrait and mural painting, interior decorating, and fashion design. At Huyton, internees treated the "emptiness" of the camp experience with the "spiritual vitamins" of classical music; Hans Gál composed his *Huyton Suite* trio here.[75] At Hutchinson, which housed the Dadaist Kurt Schwitters and the Expressionist painter Ludwig Meidner, the camp commander provided art supplies and studio space. The émigré artist Hellmuth Weissenborn used a washing

ACTIVITIES AND INACTIVITIES.

Fig. 1.5. "Activities and Inactivities." Drawing of Huyton internment camp, near Liverpool, by Alfred Lomnitz, *Never Mind, Mr. Lom! Or the Uses of Adversity* (London: Macmillan, 1941).

mangle as a printing press, and produced an ersatz ink from graphite and margarine; vegetable juices were turned into colored inks, and brown paper from parcels was used for drawing. The internees' art exhibitions were critically reviewed in the camp newspapers.[76] For Weissenborn, there was barely enough time to enjoy all the "outstanding" cultural offerings, though he happily skipped the "boring" talks on immigration law.[77]

Many internees viewed the camp as superior to the "real world." The art historian Klaus Ernst Hinrichsen claimed that artists could work "much better" at Hutchinson than in London. Their physical safety was ensured, and they had no need to earn money, plus they could enjoy the close companionship of an artistic community.[78] As Rudolph Munster put it, "fire and death" were all around them, but "we were in absolute safety."[79] Eugen Spier described his life in the Lingfield internment camp as a time of "complete ataraxia" in which he felt free from all danger. The camp had been created by the demands of war, but was strangely immune to the war itself. The German artist Peter Midgley remembered internment as a time when "things I couldn't afford today [were] offered to me on a plate... getting everything (culture, art) I had wanted all my life for nothing." Midgley believed that his identity as an artist was forged in internment: "I was made—it was the beginning of my life, the making of my life."[80]

But these camps were not always creative utopias.[81] As the era of internment persisted, the intellectual activity of the camp's early months declined: the paranormal sciences flourished, and fringe religious sects sprang up. Internees might be found reading their tea leaves instead of attending concerts. Although the camps themselves seemed physically secure, the Isle of Man internees could hear and see Liverpool being bombed, which intensified their fears about their families' fates.

The British press frequently complained that internees were housed in luxury resorts, while many British workers lived in poverty. Many locals resented that "aliens" were kept in hotels—surrounded by barbed wire or not—at the cost of a guinea per week, while the wives of ordinary British soldiers must make do with 17 shillings, plus 7 shillings docked from their husband's pay. One internee, Moishe Bomzer, wrote to his wife, "Hannah, get yourself interned. You've never had it so good."[82]

Those who were labeled Nazi sympathizers were placed at the Swanwick Camp in Derbyshire. There, internees enjoyed a stately manor that housed its own chapel, a park with a kitchen garden, and greenhouses. Older internees had their own rooms with central heating, while younger men bunked together in the great hall.[83] The Swanwick internees bragged that their manor was vastly superior to the dilapidated chalets, racetracks, cotton mills, and canvas tents suffered by Jewish internees. Fred Uhlman, a German-Jewish refugee, began his internment at Bertram Mills Circus quarters at Ascot, sleeping in the elephants' and lions' stalls on straw-filled mattresses, and eating burned porridge and kippers for days on end: "it was a glorious muddle."[84] The guards at Ascot placed sacks of flour and water before the internees and told them "to get on with it."[85]

At Hutchinson, Uhlman had his own room, the privacy of which seemed "more beautiful than Blenheim Palace."[86] To save black-out material, the windows had been painted blue and the light bulbs were red; Uhlman said it looked like an aquarium in the daytime, and a brothel at night. The internees used razor blades to cut flowers and trees into the painted windows. Although Uhlman missed his pregnant wife, and the men were entirely surrounded by barbed wire, he enjoyed the camp's cultural life, and "even sometimes the fun and the realization that this was a unique experience and that one could be proud to belong to an elite of the human race."[87]

Uhlman was grateful to have escaped the worst fate: the infamous Warth Mills Camp. In a derelict cotton mill in Bury, near Manchester, Warth Mills's reputation was "worse than any concentration camp."[88] With vermin-ridden blankets, one bathtub, and only six buckets as toilets for nearly 2,000 people, Warth Mills made the racecourse camps—where men slept on stone floors with only a thin mattress—look appealing. Internees urinated in cooking pots, thermos flasks, and hats.[89] Peter Midgley described Warth Mills as a "nightmare camp," with hundreds of internees sleeping on floors covered with grease from abandoned machinery. Paul Jacobsthal, another Warth Mills internee, recounted how British guards stole medicine from the sickly residents.[90] Violence and mental breakdowns were common.

Myths about internment in World War I shaped individual experiences in World War II along with the fraught realities of the present. Walter Igersheimer, a German Jewish refugee, recalled a tall, well-dressed, and elegant man knocking at his door to say, "I have come to take you for a short holiday, sir." A "cold and empty feeling" surged through him, as he shouted, "I am interned!" Igersheimer was driven off in a posh car to Chelsea Barracks. He speculated about the "lovely internment camps" that he had read about during the Great War, but found himself instead at Huyton Camp near Liverpool, a recently completed housing estate that had a watchtower and barbed wire hastily thrown up for its unhappy first inhabitants. When Huyton's internees asked for tables and chairs, the War Office responded that prisoners of war were forbidden to have moveable furniture. "So we're prisoners of war, are we?" one internee recalled. "The thought was too bewildering."[91] Igersheimer continued to pine for the good food, tennis, and swimming he had heard of on the Isle of Man, that "fairytale island" for internees.[92]

Other internees stayed at Butlin's holiday camps, originally designed to provide cheap holidays for British workers; their motto was "a week's holiday for a week's pay." Karl Wehner described one such camp in Clacton. Internees were housed in pairs in the huts, which were neatly equipped with two-tiered bunks, wardrobes, mirrors, and washbasins. The wooden huts, Wehner recalled, had a "vestige of newness" in 1939, with flower beds, tennis courts, a soccer pitch, an open-air swimming pool, and an arcade of shops. As one internee sardonically commented, it was "everything the exuberant imagination of a bank-clerk could dream of."[93] The camp still looked like a holiday abode, except for the hastily erected barbed wire and soldiers with fixed bayonets.

When Eugen Spier arrived as an internee at Butlin's, he was delighted to find comfortable chairs and fine beds with white, woolen blankets, along with hot and cold running water, a mirror, and open windows that gave the illusion of being free men. Barbed wire was visible, but otherwise all was enjoyable.[94] At Lingfield, Spier enjoyed "the atmosphere of democracy." Although the men were not allowed to leave the grounds, they suffered "no undue regimentation or interference" with their daily activities. They were interrupted only twice a day for roll call. The internees were allowed visitors for two hours twice a week. They hosted fancy teas with real china, and other internees served as waiters.

Spier's account points to the range of experiences that one individual could have in hurtling through the British landscape of internment. As we will see, this diversity of experience was even more powerfully emblematized in refugee camps. Like internees, many refugees experienced multiple forms of camp life that generated contradictory memories. Internment camps were one important influence on refugee camps, as were rapidly shifting expectations of the private home.

The tension between accusations of luxury and barbarity continued as well. Furthermore, there were competing accounts of particular camps, highlighting the ways in which arguments about the "luxury" or "barbarity" of specific sites served as political argument about what constituted the ideal camp. Assertions about "good" or "bad" camps played an important role in the political and social landscape of twentieth-century Britain. Throughout the twentieth century, there were competing practices of encampment.

MAKING THE REFUGEE CAMP: HOMELIKENESS
AND HOMELESSNESS

Camps were always in dialogue with private homes and the specter of homelessness. The average British home underwent tremendous changes during the era of encampment, especially after the Second World War. Under the Labour governments of 1945–51, working-class housing improved significantly, and much dilapidated housing was cleared. In this context, the continued problem of unsettled Britons demanded new explanations and solutions. The National Assistance Act 1948 replaced workhouses with "reception centers" (a term that was also used for refugee camps after World War II) to rehabilitate homeless Britons, on the assumption that homelessness was only a temporary problem spurred by the war.[95] By the mid-1950s, working-class families enjoyed relatively comfortable new homes flooded with consumer goods and modern conveniences: 86 percent of British households were wired for electricity.[96] The percentage of households in England and Wales with exclusive use of piped water, toilet, and bath jumped from 52 percent in 1951 to 70 percent in 1961.[97] By the mid-1970s, more than half the population owned a home. Britain appeared to be well on the way to fulfilling the dream of a property-owning democracy.[98]

Due to these material transformations, Britons' expectations of how they would and should be housed was changing. In 1914, when the Belgian refugees arrived, Britons were just becoming aware of a growing housing shortage in their own country, an unresolved problem that intensified dramatically in the next world war. Although British displacement during the Great War did not reach anything like its later levels, several sites for Belgian refugees were converted into emergency accommodation for Britons after the Belgians had left.[99] By the time that refugees from Vietnam began to arrive in the late 1970s, the Housing (Homeless Persons) Act 1977 elaborated the right to have a home. The act compelled local authorities to house homeless families, though single persons were still excluded. These shifting ambitions about housing Britons threw the condition of refugees into sharper relief.

The Belgians were the first refugees in Britain to face mass encampment.[100] Indeed, camps for Belgians were the first refugee camps in Europe. As such, the camps for Belgians introduced key expectations about what kind of physical and psychological environment such sites must offer. Britons often narrated the Belgian experience in tragicomic terms, focusing on the strangeness of the refugee camp, its fundamental unrecognizability. This sense of the "bizarreness" of the spaces in which refugees lived—and the heroic efforts required to make these spaces domestic and respectable—would shift several times over the next decades. What seemed outlandish during the Great War would be normalized during the Second World War as Britons moved in and out of their own states of need. As citizens' expectations of their own housing rose, the refugee camp once again receded into the realm of the strange, the unfamiliar, and the foreign.

Foiled in their original plan to use the Crystal Palace for Belgian refugees, aid workers turned instead to two other massive pleasure palaces in London. The largest camp sites—Alexandra Palace and Earl's Court—were in the heart of the capital city, to which refugees had unrestricted access. At the great pleasure resort of Alexandra Palace, in North London (near the Wood Green rail station), the spacious Exhibition Halls were converted to airy dormitories, with spotlessly clean sheets. Lady Flora Lugard described an atmosphere of "grace" and "charm."[101] Refugee children freely explored the buildings and grounds, delighting in the swings, merry-go-rounds, and hobbyhorses. Refugee women gossiped in the foliage of the Winter Gardens.[102] Crucifixes were mounted on the walls, and lace curtains (always a hallmark of civilization) on the windows. British observers described a rowdy scene in the camp, which gave the impression that "a great assemblage of very jolly children was indulging in a peculiarly exciting picnic."[103]

Earl's Court—which had a capacity of 4,000—housed 98,654 Belgian refugees from 1914 to 1919. One report described the Earl's Court camp as a "Belgian village in miniature, reflecting the daily life of an industrious people."[104] The site covered 35 acres of decaying temporary structures between the Underground stations of Earl's Court, West Brompton, and West Kensington. The outside was decorated with facsimiles of the Doge's Palace in Venice and pagoda cafes; an exhibition on "Sunny Spain" was in full swing when the Belgian refugees arrived. The exhibition was shut down on October 13, 1914, and the camp staff appeared the next morning at 10 a.m. Within the hour, mattresses, blankets, and spotless white linens were delivered by the thousands; 1,387 refugees arrived that night, sleeping behind a bar, or under a showcase.

The great Empress Hall, which had the largest single-span roof in the country, housed 1,000 beds on one side and 400 on the other. For the first week or two, the residents enjoyed the company of a large menagerie of animals left behind in the old ballroom. Belgian children "wandered amongst the elephants' legs and kicked the bars of the cages containing as fine a collection of lions and tigers as one could wish to see."[105] Out of the "ridiculous medley" of German beer gardens, aerial railways, restaurants, and theatres came "the curiously British institution, 'home,' with its peace-giving feeling of security."[106] Even in this most unlikely setting, Belgian refugees were expected to be "at home" in camp.

The question of whether camps could indeed function as homes would shift many times during the twentieth century. Of all of the camps in Britain, the North Stoneham Camp for Basque child refugees was perhaps the least homelike. Only 2,000 children had been expected, and volunteers rushed to prepare places for the 4,000 children who actually arrived. H.W.H. Sams, who had worked with Russian famine refugees, was named the camp commandant. Students, trade unionists, guides, and scouts all rallied to prepare the camp. The camp was assembled in less than two weeks, with communist dockers hastily digging latrines.[107] Hundreds of canvas tents with no artificial lighting were erected over 30 acres of fields, surrounded by a barbed-wire fence.

From its inception, the culture of the camp at North Stoneham was one of planned obsolescence.[108] So as not to violate the principle of British neutrality, the Treasury bore no costs for the children's care. The War Office loaned tents and field kitchens, charging 5 percent on £6,900 for the first thirty days, and 2.5 percent for each thirty days thereafter.[109] The initial hope was that the children would stay at North Stoneham for no more than a week, at the cost of one shilling a head per day.[110] The time at North Stoneham would be used to treat any cases of shock and malnutrition, and "acclimatize" the Basques to Britain. The Basques would then be distributed in "colonies," or smaller institutions throughout the country. But the period of encampment turned out to be much longer and more expensive than anticipated, costing 15s 9d per child per week.[111]

The first sight of the camp was forever etched on many of the Basque children's memories: 500 bell tents blanketing the flat Hampshire countryside. José and his brother Martín had never seen a tent before, much less slept in one. As far as the boys knew, tents were for Red Indians in cowboy films.[112] One child remarked that it might be all right for the English, who probably lived in tents all their lives, but hard on the Basques, who were used to houses.[113] The sisters Josephina and Carmen Antolin recalled their time at camp was "terrible," with 4,000 children fighting with one another to sleep on a little sheet over some straw.[114] The queues— especially for Horlicks—were "literally never ending: once you got your cup, you drank it quickly and rejoined the end of the line."[115] The ubiquitous loudspeakers dictated the rhythm of life in camp. The children were woken each morning by a martial tune—"Land of Hope and Glory" was a particular favorite. Daily instructions came over the loudspeaker as well, as did a regime of exercises conducted to amplified music. The loudspeaker also—tragically—delivered the news of the fall of Bilbao on June 19, 1937. English planes routinely flew low overhead, terrifying the Basque children who had fled bomber planes in Spain.[116]

Fig. 1.6. Early days of the Basque camp, Eastleigh. From "Arrival at the Camp," Papers of Eleanor Hickman, volunteer at North Stoneham Camp for Basque Children, Modern Records Centre, University of Warwick, MSS.393/1/1/8. Reproduced by permission of the University of Warwick Library.

The sanitary conditions at North Stoneham were disastrous. The latrines were incorrectly labeled "Girls" and the urinals labeled "Boys," so the boys had no latrines; as one sanitary inspector reported, "small boys could be seen squatting about all over the place. Children were dropping their pants and evacuating right under my very nose...It was impossible to walk about the place without treading in excreta." Urinals were used "indiscriminately by either sex and for any purpose." Mugs and spoons were tossed in the latrines and ditches. Thoroughly disgusted, the inspector fled the camp, concluding, "I have never seen such complete chaos in all my life."[117] When he returned the next day, he was outraged to find that, on a beautiful sunny day, all the tent curtains were down and the palliasses were wet, with the children lying about on them. He tried to get the children to move outside, "but I could not make them understand me." The kitchen floor was full of mud, rotten oranges, onion peelings, and bread. The kitchen was crowded with volunteers who were "drinking tea and jabbering away until the place seemed like Bedlam."[118]

The children's assignments to different colonies after they left North Stoneham depended largely on chance. Once the señoritas received their assignments, they could invite individual children to join them. Holiday camps, local authority properties, and Ministry of Labour sites were all pressed into service. Children might find themselves in a stately home, or a Salvation Army hostel.[119] The Catholic Church agreed to look after 1,200 children in its orphanages and convents. The Cambridge colony was deemed "most fortunate," while Margate was widely considered "shocking."[120] The Labour politician Fenner Brockway had a colony of his own. At Tunbridge Wells, there were ponies and child psychologists. Félix Amat Irazola recalled arriving at Basque House in Langham, near Colchester, to find astounding gardens: "We had never seen anything like it, and it's no wonder one of the boys shouted: 'This is paradise!' There were tennis courts, a full cricket pitch, rose gardens, lawns and borders with beautiful flowers, greenhouses, a gardener's cottage and stables." In Irazola's memory, all he did at Langham was play football "all day, every day."[121]

Just as the Basque children began to return to Spain, the *Kinder* started to disembark in Britain.[122] The first reception center opened for Jewish child refugees was Dovercourt Bay Holiday Camp, located in an Essex coastal village. Billy Butlin had built Dovercourt in 1937 as an inexpensive holiday camp for the local townspeople, who paid £2 a week in the summer to rent the huts.[123] When the Jewish children arrived in 1938, Dovercourt had been open for just one season as a holiday camp, and had never been used in the winter. Most of the wooden huts were unheated. Lore Segal, a refugee from Vienna, recalled the 200 identical one-room wooden cottages built along straight intersecting paths, from which she could see the flat, black North Sea over the mud flats. The tiny chalets were fronted by pebble-dash walls and mock Tudor porches, echoing the trends of middle-class British suburbia.[124] Her own little cottage had curtained windows that looked out onto a miniature veranda; "we thought it was sweet." She and the other children breakfasted with unwashed faces, since the water in the sink was often frozen into a solid block of ice, but "it seemed right that the weather should be as unnatural as

Fig. 1.7. Chalets for Jewish children at Dovercourt. Courtesy of The Wiener Library.

our circumstances."[125] Karen Gershon wrote of wandering in the bitter cold in a large central hall at Dovercourt, something like an airplane hangar with a loud-speaker broadcasting messages in English.[126]

After the BBC Home Service's broadcast about Dovercourt, "Children in Flight," local butchers donated meat, and a greengrocer sent a dozen cases of fruit every week. Marks & Spencer fitted out Dovercourt's children with free clothing, right down to gumboots. In 1939, Anna Essinger—who had run a prominent Jewish school in Germany—took over the leadership of Dovercourt, and staffed it with former refugees. She set up language classes, group singing, and exercises to boost morale, but the "cattle market" of foster parents visiting the camp weekly continued to upset the children.

The camps for Jewish children bore little resemblance to the filthy, unsupervised tents of North Stoneham. One visitor to Dovercourt noted how different it was from the Basque camp, even allowing for "national characteristics." The Jewish children at Dovercourt worked in organized groups, and were "well managed," unlike the anarchic spirit of North Stoneham.[127] Ministry of Health officials described Dovercourt as orderly and happy.[128] The differences between the dis-ordered environment of the Basques and the highly structured camps for the *Kinder* were often projected onto the two groups of children themselves, and their imagined differences of moral and political development.[129]

Obviously, neither the Basque nor the Jewish children had created their camps. At Kitchener, the adult Jewish male residents actually participated in the camp's reconstruction. The men were housed at the derelict army camp at Richborough, 3 miles from the port of Sandwich, in January 1939. The site had been used to train Lord Kitchener's army during the First World War, and was then abandoned. The remaking of Kitchener Camp—and in particular its revival after a long period of disuse—was part of the camp's own lore. When the Jewish refugees arrived, the Union Jack was hoisted for the first time since the Great War.

The camp was under the leadership of three young English Jews: Mr. Banks, and the brothers Jonas May and Phineas May, who were born to an Orthodox Jewish family in North London, and worked with the Jewish Lads Brigade.[130] Phineas May's diary describes his first impression of Kitchener's "drab greyness—the perfect concentration Camp." Despite this disturbing comparison, May was struck by "the amazing possibilities of the place."[131] By February of 1939, 100 Jewish refugees—all skilled workmen, mostly joiners or carpenters—had arrived from Germany to begin the work of renovating the camp.

Peter Mansbacher was a German Jewish refugee who arrived in England as part of the *Kindertransport* and later volunteered to work at Kitchener. Used to the "fun, food, and entertainment" at Dovercourt, Mansbacher was shocked when he peered into one disused hut at Kitchener and startled birds and rabbits rushed out "with much noise." The floorboards had rotted away, and weeds and wildflowers grew in abandon inside. Some huts had no roofs. Bones were left inside what had been the hospital during the Great War. Mansbacher labored for weeks under primitive conditions. The faster he worked, May promised, the sooner hundreds of Jews could be released from concentration camps to join him at Kitchener.[132]

Within a few weeks, the residents had organized a newsletter, the *Kitchener Camp Review*. As refugees arrived, they were quickly funneled into the endless work of preparing the camp for others. In an essay titled, "I Saw It Grow," one author described his feeling of "electric expectancy" as he waited for the first arrivals:

> Out of this chaos of old boilers, rubbish dumps, partly distempered walls, ladders, wet green paint, and every day, the debris resulting from such rapidly accumulating items as 200 blue and green mattresses, or 2,000 blankets, there gradually arose a sense of orderliness. The time came when the confusing huts and the ramifications of their interiors became sorted out, growing speedily cleaner and brighter; when the dining hall held an imposing array of very new, and very clean, white wooden tables and chairs; when the Store swelled and swelled with double-decker beds, and enamel jugs, and zinc buckets, and coco-matting rugs—all lavishly numbered in hundreds.

The *Review* instructed the men about "making your homes happy," focusing on the huts as a source of domestic satisfaction. By May of 1939, Kitchener had been transformed from a desolate collection of deserted huts into a "haven, if not a heaven for 1,000 happy men." The back areas of the huts, formerly a wasteland, were turned into beautifully tilled crops, with "delightful little gardens," and fat radishes growing in roughly constructed glasshouses.[133] The huts' interiors were personalized with pictures of the nearby town of Sandwich, or portraits of the royal family, and inscriptions such as "England expects every man to do his duty—You are not an Englishman, but nevertheless do your duty here."[134]

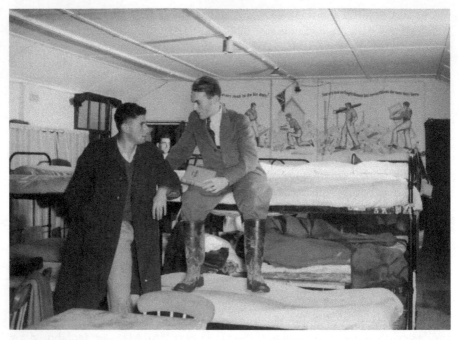

Fig. 1.8. Jewish refugees in their room at Kitchener. The mural was designed and painted by members of the hut, depicting the tasks they performed in the camp, and instructing the residents that "England expects every man to do his duty—You are not an Englishman, but nevertheless do your duty here." Chronicle/Alamy Stock Photo.

Kitchener's leaders emphasized its fundamentally transitory nature. At North Stoneham and Dovercourt, too, child refugees were expected to move quickly out of the camps. The situation with the Polish camps was strikingly different. Due to the housing shortage in Britain, even the government admitted that Poles were likely to stay in camps "for some years."[135] Furthermore, Poles were offered British citizenship under the Polish Resettlement Act and were not expected to emigrate elsewhere. For other refugees, the hope that encampment would be brief shaped their built environment. The long duration of Polish encampment was more openly acknowledged. Still, even the most pessimistic observer at the end of the Second World War would probably not have predicted just how slow the process of decamping would be.

As British forces began to demobilize, the Labour government faced the daunting task—and expense—of supporting almost a quarter of a million Polish servicemen. On May 26, 1946, the Labour politician Aneurin Bevan (then the Minister of Health) announced the formation of the Polish Resettlement Corps, designed to keep Poles who had been under British command in disciplined units, housed in army camps, and receiving army pay. Nominally a military unit, the PRC was an unarmed, non-combatant formation to ease Poles' transition to civilian life.[136] Enrollment in the Corps was voluntary, but strongly encouraged.[137] Poles who

Fig. 1.9. Airmen of No. 300 Polish Bomber Squadron waiting for a scramble call with their bicycles at the ready outside their Nissen hut mess room at RAF Faldingworth, summer 1944. Ugandan Asians would also be housed at Faldingworth in 1972–3. Reproduced by permission of the Imperial War Museum.

would not accept enlistment into the Corps nor repatriation to Poland were labeled "recalcitrant," and could be deported to Germany.[138]

The rights of Poles in Britain were tied explicitly to their military service. The first camps and hostels for Poles in Britain were run by the War Office, which sent a conflicting message about the project of demobilization. Were the Poles soldiers or citizens? At stake here was a broader tension about the role of military power in refugee aid, and how militarized spaces shaped refugee lives. The Corps was officially wound up in July 1948, but Poles in Britain were clearly far from "settled." At this point, control of the Poles' care passed from the War Office to the National Assistance Board, which was created in 1948 to aid unemployed and impoverished Britons.[139] By the end of 1949, the Board administered thirty-seven Polish camps and hostels with a total population of 16,429.[140] These were expensive institutions, which lost about £250,000 every year.[141]

Dealing with Poles was one of the first major tasks of the National Assistance Board. When the Polish Resettlement Act 1947 became law, it placed "new and uncommon" duties upon the Board that "were of a nature previously outside its sphere." The Board must "provide shelter and all the needs of life for a great body of foreign people who for years have lived a nomadic existence."[142] It was a daunting responsibility, especially as Britain was suffering a tremendous housing shortage.

The work of welfare was fundamentally altered by its close involvement with a culture of military basing and refugee care.

The National Assistance Act 1948 demanded that the Board settle its own citizens—that is, unhoused Britons—as well as Polish refugees. The two groups were constantly intertwined and contrasted in the mind of officialdom. The unsettled Briton was a figure with a much longer history. In the 1930s, *The Times* portrayed the mobility of tens of thousands of ravenous young men in "cheap, thin suits and poor shoes," seeking work and charity.[143] By the 1950s, many officials believed that "tramps" were obsolete: "a dying race."[144] The persistence of the vagrant was shocking proof that, even in an age of affluence, many were still in need.[145] Their numbers had declined dramatically, from 17,000 men sleeping in casual wards on a peak night in 1932 to roughly 2,000 per night in the 1950s. Still, the men in the Board's care revealed just how down and out one could be even in the welfare state.[146]

The act aimed to eliminate the old workhouse, and replace it with new physical, political, and moral structures of aid. Thus, as the Board took over the task of refugee care, it was also engaged in a broader process of invention for all who were unsettled. In this new context, "tramps" were reclassed as "persons with an unsettled way of living."[147] The Board's task was to settle them, and convince them to live in a fixed abode. To achieve this goal, the Board closed more than half of Britain's casual wards, and renamed the rest as "reception centres." The 124 centres—known informally as "Spikes"—were typically "austere" places, though with decent standards of warmth and cleanliness.[148] The Board insisted on certain improvements to the old wards—more space between the beds, better meals, and at least three blankets per person. But elements of the old workhouse routines remained, such as compulsory cleaning tasks. Accusations of luxury were present here too; in 1961, the *Daily Express* detailed the meaty stew the men were fed at Camberwell reception centre, and the smart suits they were given to wear.[149]

Under the old Poor Law, vagrants were to be kept in constant motion—in fact, it was an offence to return to the same ward within a month of being discharged. Under the National Assistance Act, the aim was not to keep tramps moving on, but to settle them down.[150] They were interviewed—repeatedly and at length—to find out their personal problems, and find out when and why they became "unsettled."[151] By the 1950s, interpretations of unhoused Britons focused less on structural explanations, such as poverty and unemployment, and more on individual pathologies and wanderlust.[152]

The Board's reception centres endorsed detention, with the object of convincing men to adopt a more "settled" way of life—a goal that the old casual wards had never undertaken.[153] Those who were physically fit to work could be required to remain for forty-eight hours and to complete specific tasks. Men who were willing to settle might be placed in jobs and retrained through the disciplinary routines of the centre, staying a month or longer.[154] Those who refused could be imprisoned for one month, or fined £10. As men were deemed "fit" for resettlement, they would be moved to a more comfortable part of the centre where they were segregated from ordinary wayfarers. Many came to look upon the centre as a permanent "home." There was a tension between "allowing" men to stay longer in the centres to encourage their resettlement, and insisting that they do so.

In the Assistance Board's vast project of settling the unsettled, both Poles and Britons were targeted. Looking at the War Office's proposed sites for Polish dependents, the Board noted that the standard of accommodation was appalling: "mostly of Nissen hut type with bucket latrine services." Some camps were described as "completely hopeless," with huts that had rotten floorboards and dilapidated interiors.[155] Yet refugee work provided pleasures as well as perils: "the misfortunes of war have thus brought to the Board an opportunity of creating a hopeful future to people who feel that they must accept the shelter which has been offered to them by this country."[156] One Board member wrote, "I certainly retain most pleasant memories of my time with Polish work—it seems to me the most worthwhile job I've ever done."[157] The Board strove to distinguish its own pastoral care from that offered by an unsympathetic military infrastructure, and to set new standards for sanitation and comfort in refugee housing.

R.K. Jago of the National Assistance Board reported that Poles seemed happy even in what were reputed to be the "worst" hostels, enjoying excellent food in pleasant rural surroundings. Sometimes, he admitted, they had to drink from mugs instead of cups and saucers, but "the ordinary citizen has to put up with such things" as well. For Jago, Poles suffered less arduous conditions than many Britons. In fact, "I found the atmosphere definitely Arcadian—as Tennyson put it, 'Summers of the snakeless meadow, unlaborious earth and oarless sea.'"[158] The Resettlement Act aimed to provide the mechanisms for assimilating Poles into "normal civilian life." But "normal" civilian life in Britain after the Second World War was already disrupted or destroyed, and, as Jago pointed out, "no one in postwar Britain is paying an economical rent."[159]

The Board detailed its fantasy of what it could provide for Poles. Ideally, the Board's camps should be located within easy walking distance of a railway station and shopping center. They should be set on porous soil that would dry quickly after rain. The camps' layout should offer ample facilities for relaxation and social interaction, and one bath for every fifteen persons, with abundant hot water.[160] Furthermore, conditions must be equitable for Poles and British soldiers. Poles were, after all, future Britons.

Such fantasies were not easily realized. In 1948, the Cabinet Emergency Accommodation Committee compared camps and hostels for British and foreign civilians.[161] The Committee described how 16,000 Poles—mostly women and children—were living in what "can only be described as refugee conditions": isolated from other communities, with primitive washing facilities, widely dispersed buildings with long treks between the sleeping quarters and the mess halls, and "demoralizing" conditions that thwarted cleanliness and decency. Cabinet concluded that many of the Polish camps were situated in "most unsuitable places... in woods, the parks of country houses, or on common land, and all are unsightly blots on the landscape which should be removed without delay."[162]

At Keevil Polish Hostel, the Board inspector reported in 1949 that six elderly single women were living in an unpartitioned hut in "very poor" condition.[163]

The Poles had "sacrificed everything for the sake of freedom...why should they be condemned to live in these awful camps, year in and year out?" While the Poles languished in camps, "hundreds of houses could have been built to house both English and Polish people."[164] This was not the type of aid the Board wished to provide for anyone, of any nationality.[165]

Who fared better: Poles or Britons? The *Dziennik Polski* (*Polish Daily*) described tidy barracks in camps for Polish soldiers that might be "the object of envy for quite a few residents of British slums."[166] Karol Zbyszewski added that British families who had been displaced by imperial crises in India, Burma, Palestine, and Egypt were living in Assistance Board camps that mimicked the conditions for Poles: "the English treat their own homeless families from overseas just like they do Polish families."[167] Indeed, several socialist MPs objected that Poles were privileged over what they called "DPs of British descent."[168] But many Poles felt that their maintenance charges in camps were "excessive." Hostels for Britons charged 30 shillings a week for a bed in a furnished room with two meals a day (and three meals on Sundays) and a three-course evening meal. Camps for Poles charged at least 25 shillings per week for a bed, often without bed linen or pillow, in an unfurnished and overcrowded, often unheated, hut, with the washrooms and lavatories some distance away.[169] Furthermore, Poles paid the same rates whether they were housed in ex-military barracks or newly built hostels, which were as different as "slums and palaces."[170]

Local observers were often quite impressed by the Polish camps. The Nissen huts at Melton Mowbray reminded Mike Bailey, who lived nearby, of his army days, to which he never wished to return. But the Poles "made homes out of it that I wouldn't have thought," renovating the huts with fabric and paint.[171] As *Dziennik Polski* reported, Poles "love to set up house wherever they go. They aren't going to sit on the bed surrounded by four bare walls, like the English do, and repeat cheerfully, 'How nice! Lovely!' Poles need shelves, cupboards, curtains, and a place to keep things," and they used thrift and care to create their "homes" in camp.[172] The National Assistance Board praised the Poles for creating a "homey atmosphere" in the barracks, and expressing their "national talent" for decorating with white lace curtains and embroidered wall tapestries.[173] One Polish woman recalled of her camp near Southampton, "It was peaceful, there was a very good atmosphere. We were quite proud of ourselves...this was a beautiful part of England and there were nice walks to go on."[174]

Urszula Szulakowska, who lived at Melton Mowbray, had a desperately cold hut, where the cooking stove and paraffin heater "emanated a mournful smell." Water ran freely down the inside walls, and the washing turned Prussian blue from the mold. Still, Szulakowska's bedroom was airy and pleasant, decorated with her mother's hand-embroidered linens, and colored prints of the Sacred Heart of Jesus and Mary. People mixed the original army camp furniture with their own purchases or handmade items; Szulakowska was very proud of the two dark-green upholstered armchairs in her hut. Polish women embellished their huts with embroidered hangings, bed coverings, richly decorated cushions, and dolls. Szulakowska's grandmother excelled at creating paper lilies, daisies, and roses. A few residents owned rugs, an expensive luxury item that Turkish peddlers sold around the camp. Despite the challenges, Melton Mowbray was "never squalid." All the Polish huts were "clean and shiny, despite the awful poverty." Szulakowska described all the doors perpetually left open and women "treating each others houses as their own."[175]

Zosia Hartman, who came to Northwick Hostel when she was five years old, recalled the camp's location in the "beautiful" Cotswold countryside, standing on 70 acres of the Northwick Park Estate in Gloucestershire. The Spencer-Churchill family owned this estate, though they could not have seen the camp from the main house, a grand stone building. The camp was built in 1943 as an American field hospital, later housing German prisoners of war. It was then abandoned until 1947, when the War Department gave the camp to the Ministry of Works for the Poles. The camp included fifty-five unheated Nissen huts, each partitioned by a brick wall to house two families. The camp was surrounded by barbed wire and wooden watchtowers from its POW days.[176]

Hartman's family arrived at Northwick from the transit camp at Daglingworth, a drab army camp for American soldiers composed of rows upon rows of black metal corrugated Nissen huts. The adults gasped with horror when they saw the barbed-wire fences at Northwick, thinking that they had arrived at a concentration camp.[177] In 1958, the Board undertook improvements at Northwick to give the camp "a very neat and colourful appearance."[178] Zosia noted that many families had to walk 50 meters in order to use the toilet or fill a kettle. But the "unsightly" Nissen huts were soon disguised with climbing roses. Zosia lived with her family in half a Nissen hut until 1963, when she married a man she met in camp. To this day, she keeps a chest of drawers that was issued to her family in Northwick.

One of the largest Polish camps was Fairford, a former American field hospital on the fringes of the Cotswold Hills. According to Celina Kabala Wojciechowska, who arrived at Fairford in 1949, Poles in camps had a higher standard of living than those who settled directly in town: "At first we had one room, then two, then three."[179] Raising children, she said, was "good in the hostel. There was fresh air and there were places you could go for a walk; there was plenty of hot and cold water and nobody complained that a child was annoying them. The hostel was very safe."[180] Fairford's mortality rates could be high—at times, five people died in a week—but people clung to what they saw as a place of "safety and security."[181]

During the 1950s, the Board renovated many of its Polish hostels to make them more "domestic." In 1951, Fairford was converted to a housing estate, where residents paid rent. The warden reported that residents felt more independent and more invested in the space of the hostel. They became "house proud," and eagerly cultivated the grounds. Yet these physical improvements had a drawback. As Poles became more immersed in tending their own garden, Fairford's cultural activities waned. The warden wrote, "the Pole after many years of communal living has again become a home lover." Instead of enjoying the collective life of the hostel, the Pole would now "find his pleasure in the atmosphere of his home and the company of his family."[182]

Describing his "happy childhood" at Kelvedon, which began when his family moved to the camp in 1952, Kaz Janowski's memories focused on modest material comforts: "Our chairs, tables, and wardrobes were classic examples of British-made Utility furniture. Simple, yet robust. This furniture was functional and comfortable and our little hut was snug and cozy. I loved living there." Indeed, all of the Polish camps shared identical furniture, so one saw the same wicker armchairs and uncomfortable folding chairs everywhere inside the Nissen huts—which the Poles described as "*Beczki*" (or "barrels").[183] Janowski recalled huddling around the stove to listen to Polish fairytales. On Sundays, "the structure reverberated to the sung words of '*Ojczyznę wolną racz nam wrócić Panie*'—'O Lord return to us a free Fatherland.'"[184]

Janowski thought that Kelvedon had an air of exciting "mystery and secrecy" around it, due to the rumor that Special Forces Units had trained there during the Second World War. Kelvedon had been used by the Royal Air Force and the United States Air Force, and was inhabited by the Polish 5th and 6th Battalions of Carpathian Rifles until their demobilization in 1948; it was then taken over by the National Assistance Board. The land was requisitioned from local farmers, and was largely cut off from the surrounding villages. After the Poles moved in, the physical reminders of the site's original function remained: airplane hangars, and air-raid shelters. For Janowski, the isolation of Kelvedon created "the illusion of a tiny Polish state, nestled within a benevolent but alien English landscape."[185]

Barbara Fisher (née Białozorska) also had idyllic memories of her childhood at Doddington, near Cheshire—one of the largest Polish camps, housing around 1,000 Poles. The camp was built to house the Free French and then the American Army. Fisher wrote lyrically:

> I remember the beautiful countryside and green fields around the camp and the variety of beautiful wild flowers and grasses which grew around them. As children, we had the freedom to roam the countryside and to ride our bikes around it. It was exciting, but most exciting of all was the little wood where, during springtime, there grew hundreds of bluebells of the English variety creating a blue carpet with an exhilarating scent which filled the air around the wood and beyond. The children called it The Magic Bluebell Wood. It had a narrow meandering stream which during the summer months we would try to jump across. We built dens and pretend houses out of pieces of dead twigs and leaves which were lying around. These dens and homes were magical to us and we would engage in all kinds of creative play. We were so lucky that we were able to have the freedom and feel safe and secure in this environment.[186]

As a youngster at Tweedsmuir Camp near Surrey (formerly a transit camp for Canadian troops), Piotr Pietrusiewicz ran freely over the spectacular War Department land: "We would sneak over to the Dropping Zone and watch parachute training from a giant balloon and then the real thing as planes flew above us and deposited scores of parachute jumpers into the vast valley below. It was like watching an epic war film and very exciting as we had to stay low and hidden so as not to be caught by the authorities. Just walking across the road from the main entrance to the camp would find us in deep bracken and pine forest. On one occasion a whole regiment of camouflaged faces appeared around us. We were frozen scared but luckily they ignored us and continued with their manoeuvres." Despite

Fig. 1.10. Polish children at Foxley. Photograph by Zbigniew Pawlowicz, by kind permission of his son, Henry Pavlovich (http://foxley.org).

the "hard and basic lifestyle...the sense of solidarity and social cohesion that existed in the camp made our childhood idyllic and trouble free."[187]

Such happy recollections speak to a generational divide in Polish memories of encampment. While parents struggled to shield children from the harsher realities of camp life, children often thought of the camps as sites of freedom and adventure. At Foxley, Polish children "whizzed around dangerously on home-made trolleys, carts, skates, or tripped about on crooked stilts and pogo sticks."[188]

For the National Assistance Board, the Poles were akin to British soldiers or industrial workers, not to other refugees. But refugee work evoked many other comparisons. The nearly simultaneous arrival of Hungarian refugees and Anglo-Egyptians—and the competition for spaces that ensued—meant that these groups were constantly compared to each other. The Hungarians were housed in a combination of hostels and army camps, but the "delicate" Anglo-Egyptians were thought to be unsuited to life in Nissen huts. Both groups were keenly aware of any disparity in their material conditions, which they took as a sign of the sympathy Britons had for their plight.

In November and December of 1956, when Hungarians began to flood into Britain, most were housed in War Office barracks. The British government gave £50,000 to the British Red Cross to aid the Hungarians, plus £10,000 to the British Council for Aid to Refugees (BCAR), which had helped refugees settle in

Britain since 1950.[189] The Lord Mayor's Fund in London raised another £2.5 million. A special Hungarian Department was set up under the chairmanship of Sir Arthur Rucker, a former civil servant. This department, staffed by retired civil servants and voluntary workers, grew rapidly to more than 200 people.[190] At the peak of the operation, BCAR was running 150 camps and hostels for Hungarian refugees. BCAR met Hungarian refugees on arrival, and escorted them to camps to register with the police.[191] Busloads of women volunteers were brought in daily to some of the more isolated camps, and 1,300 Women's Voluntary Service (WVS) centers participated in clothing the Hungarian refugees.[192]

Different populations mixed within the "Hungarian" camps. Chiseldon, for example, was occupied by British troops as well as Hungarian refugees. Some army camps were still occupied by Poles, though most were due to be cleared or scheduled for demolition. Many camps were "indescribably filthy" and in need of expensive repairs.[193] The Hungarian humorist Albert Vajda had daydreamed about being warmly welcomed to Britain by Prime Minister Eden. Instead, he and his compatriots were met by the police and sent by bus to a large, disused military camp near Colchester surrounded by barbed wire. Vajda recalled, "As a refugee, I expected that in my new country I was going to live in the enchanting forest of Shakespeare's 'A Midsummer Night's Dream' only to find out later that in the life of a refugee there are more 'Madsummer Nightmares.'"[194]

In 1957, BCAR opened a large center for 3,000 Hungarian refugees at the RAF camp at Hednesford, near Rugeley in Staffordshire. The camp was in an uninviting location 2 miles from the Hednesford train station, on the edge of Cannock Chase. There was no bus to Rugeley, which was the nearest town, 5 miles away.[195] The camp was established in great haste; the location was so remote that the WVS had to be shown the place on the map, and turned up just half an hour before the refugees, as the RAF was moving out. One volunteer described Hednesford as "the shell of a vast RAF camp . . . very bleak and windswept, poor people."[196] The refugees usually arrived in the early morning while it was still dark. Vera Sheridan, who came to this disused English army barracks with her Red Cross doll, was given twenty items of clothing and a bilingual dictionary.[197] Children were greeted at Hednesford with Hungarian songs and dances even as they were encouraged to learn English. The camp's school was established by a South African woman who was reputedly a member of the anti-apartheid Black Sash Movement.[198]

The physical labor of caring for the Hungarians was daunting. At Crimicar Lane, the boiler had to be fired twenty-four hours a day, using a ton of coal per day; four people were hired just to keep the boiler going.[199] In order to adapt Thorney Pits Hostel in Wiltshire—which was the largest hostel, holding up to 2,000 Hungarians—the Office of Works provisioned 8 electric kettles, 17 electric irons, 4 radio sets, and 16 electric fires. Also needed were 200 iron folding beds, 6 oak beds, 25 easy chairs, 30 fireside chairs, 200 oak chests, 2 flower vase stands, 39 mirrors, 1 grand piano, 45 vinegar bottles, 29 tea cups, 303 dessert forks, 2 potato mashers, 733 plates, 2,000 colored blankets, 450 pairs of curtains, 2,000 single sheets, and 250 ashtrays.[200] This eclectic list reveals much about how life in a refugee camp was envisioned. It also serves as a useful reminder that there were many groups living within the camp at one time, and experiencing them quite differently. The WVS threatened to leave Thorney Pits unless conditions were improved. The six oak beds, one presumes, were for staff; the "improvements" demanded by the WVS were for their own workers, and not for refugees.

Descriptions of the conditions in British camps for Hungarians made their way into Soviet propaganda. A broadcast on Budapest Radio about the plight of Hungarians in Britain referred to 10,000 Hungarians living in disused "military barracks" instead of the flats they had been promised. At Crookham, 200 Hungarians lived in the summer barracks made of plywood, where the wind blew in through the cracks and the roof leaked. The broadcast claimed that refugees were so frustrated with the camp that they were wending their way back to their homeland, which would happily receive its "misguided sons."[201] The Home Office admitted that Crookham was "a rather primitive place with very little comfort." Yet some of the 5,000 Hungarians who passed through Crookham wrote later of their "happy time" in camp. Magda Czigány recalled receiving her first cup of English tea and first bowl of cereal at Crookham—both of which shocked her. She was issued a pair of men's blue and white striped pajamas, tied with a string, which she kept out of sentimentality for many years afterwards.[202]

Many Anglo-Egyptians—who saw themselves as the "blameless" refugees—assumed that they would be situated in more "homelike" sites. Some arrived with surprisingly specific expectations. Mrs. Soncino, an Anglo-Egyptian woman assigned to a hostel in Harrow, sent a detailed inquiry to the Board about her accommodations. She asked, "Is there a single room a bit larger than the usual? I would like a room on my own as I suffer from nerves and noise disturbs me a great deal, I also suffer from sleepless nights." She asked to have her own bed from Egypt transported to the hostel, and to be allowed to choose her own room "as I do not support noise as noise makes me ill." Finally, she asked for the names of the other people who would live in the hostel, "just to see if I know any of them. Excuse me if I ask these questions but as you know this hostel will be the final place I'll live in and end my days."[203]

Still, the Anglo-Egyptians were hardly living in luxury, nor did they escape the fate of the Nissen hut altogether. Eastwood Hostel, near Nottingham, had been constructed for British miners, and had been empty for eight months before its deployment for Anglo-Egyptian evacuees.[204] The Nissen huts at Eastwood were criticized not only for being difficult to heat, but also for encouraging an unnatural segregation of the sexes.[205] Because the Maltese residents preferred not to use different huts for men and women, they typically shared the huts with two or more families, leading to hazardous overcrowding.[206] The hostel offered little privacy, but the Board claimed that the evacuees spent their time in comfortable communal rooms, and were "reasonably happy."[207]

During and immediately after the Second World War, many Britons found themselves living in Nissen huts, or spaces that resembled them. In these decades, when British memories of war were strongest, huts and barbed wire may have united citizens and refugees more than divided them. By the 1970s, when the Ugandan Asians arrived, this was no longer true. The press reports on the Ugandan

Asian camps veered between horror and excessive luxury. The only Asian member of the Uganda Resettlement Board (URB), Praful Patel, toured the camps, saying, "life there is comfortable and I am urging people not to get too comfortable."[208] Yet others compared the Ugandan Asian camps to concentration camps, or sites of totalitarian oppression. Amrit, a student, remarked, "No one in their right sense likes camps. If everything had been generous and good, then we would have had instant houses, jobs, and loans. But without that, well it was camps or nothing."[209]

These conflicting views can be explained by differences between individual camps, but also how camps and homes changed over time. By the 1970s, Britons were rethinking their own ideals of homes, extending the term "homeless" to those who lived in unsanitary or overcrowded conditions: for example, anyone who lived without hot water or an indoor toilet. Without such amenities, one could not be expected to participate fully in British civic life and society.[210] New standards of welfare had shifted Britons' expectations about their homes, and the parameters of privacy and intrusion.

The Ugandan Asians were housed in sixteen camps—all former army and air force bases—ranging from the heart of London to the most remote areas of rural Wales. Some camps were physically attractive, with married quarters and plentiful supplies of games, while others were chaotic and unhygienic. The most striking element of Ugandan Asians' memories of encampment is the sheer diversity of the experience. Arun Sakaria, a taxi driver, spoke fondly of Maresfield, a "lovely camp" in Sussex, he said, where English families took him out every weekend. At Hemswell, his next camp, he was bored and lonely.[211] Residents remembered specific features of individual camps; for example, Plaisterdown, on the slopes of Dartmoor, had a "creepy" barrier at its entrance and a sign that said "Ministry of Defence" on its gates.[212]

Many of the camps that housed Ugandan Asians had played vital roles in the Second World War and in the Cold War. These bases had their own complex pre-history in British society and politics, which shaped local reactions to refugees. For Poles, the wartime history of bases had been much more immediate. The bases were barely converted, if at all, when the Poles arrived, and that recent history is evident in many refugee memories. In 1972, the Ugandan Asians were arriving in a very different context. The bases that housed Ugandan Asians had undergone long stretches of inactivity, though they were still focal points of Cold War and antiwar controversies.

After the Second World War, military sites came under pressure from several directions. Some of these sites were converted to agricultural stores or light-industrial workshops. Many were destroyed by human forces; others were removed by natural processes, such as coastal erosion.[213] Bases were even more controversial in the context of Labour's debate about the universal right to housing. Squatters argued that all spaces that had been commandeered for war should be returned to the people.[214] The bases—where they were still occupied—were often acclaimed for their role in the Cold War, and some were open to the public. At Stradishall in 1958, when Wing Commander R.W. Leggett was reminiscing about "the last war," he was asked by a young fighter pilot, "Excuse me, sir, do you mean Korea or Suez?"[215] In this sense, many of these bases were not really "closed" in the way that Kitchener Camp had been when the Jewish refugees arrived. Rather, the bases served new functions of deterrence, commemoration, and training.[216]

The arrival of the Ugandan Asians was preceded by more than a decade of anxiety about basing—in particular, the nineteen American bases in Britain—and concern that Britain was becoming a "10th rate Banana Republic," a puppet of American nuclear policy.[217] During the Suez Crisis, British opposition to American bases widened to include not only the traditional critics from the Left, but also Conservatives who resented America's lack of support in Egypt. Both parties called for American forces to withdraw from Britain.[218] Thousands of Britons had been displaced from their homes in order to make way for American forces during the war. These Britons—who were described as "evacuees"—were treated as if they had been bombed out, and some felt they deserved higher levels of compensation for being resettled.[219] Public opinion in Britain about American bases vacillated over the next several decades, subject to the ebbs and flows of American military power.

Greenham Common, for example, which would become a key site of Ugandan Asian camp life, had been an important site of wartime and Cold War activity. Located about 2 miles from Newbury (population 20,000), the common served as a traditional recreational area of roughly 880 acres until it was requisitioned as an airfield in 1941. During the war, Greenham Common served as the headquarters for Operation Torch (the invasion of North Africa), and was involved in 1944 in the preparations for and execution of D-Day landings. General Eisenhower visited Greenham Common personally, and there delivered his famous "eyes of the world" speech to the 101st Airborne Division.[220] It reverted to the Royal Air Force in 1945, and was closed in 1946. Following increased East–West tensions after the blockade of Berlin in 1948 and the start of the Korean War, the Air Ministry sought to reacquire the site, and it was taken over by the United States Air Force; American servicemen began to arrive on the base in 1951.[221]

The period during which Greenham Common was used as a Ugandan Asian refugee camp was bracketed by two periods of anti-basing protests, first in the 1960s and then (on a larger scale) in the 1980s.[222] The requisitioning of this land for the USAF took place over the objections of the Newbury Town Council, which collected 10,000 signatures against the base. Public criticism focused on the loss of common rights and agricultural land, noisy aircraft, and the dangers of having a bomber aircraft so close to town.[223] Anthony Hurd, Conservative MP for Newbury, described the sound of low-flying B47s as "Hell . . . let loose over town." Greenham Common was the site of a Campaign for Nuclear Disarmament protest in 1960, with CND members carrying signs that read "No U.S. Bases Here."[224] The base was reconstructed at a cost of £7.5 million (shared by the British Air Ministry and the USAF), and possessed one of the longest military runways in Europe. From 1958 to 1964, Greenham was part of the Reflex Alert Scheme, where B47s armed with nuclear weapons were housed. The base was deactivated in 1964, and reopened as a USAF base in 1968.[225]

When Greenham Common was converted to house the Ugandan Asians in 1972, one Women's Royal Voluntary Service (WRVS) worker warned, "these are not Army Camps and cannot be organized as such. They are like nothing on earth that we have ever seen before."[226] Some Ugandan Asians at Greenham Common were alarmed by the militarized environment of the refugee camp. Ranchhod Badeshia arrived at Heathrow with his family late at night, was shown a map, and put on a bus to what he thought was a house. When he and his family woke up at Greenham Common in the morning, and looked out the windows, they found Britain resembled Uganda more than they would have hoped: "We were shocked...We had come from a country where everywhere were soldiers. And everywhere we looked were soldiers still."[227] For Badeshia, refuge in Britain looked more like war than like peace.

The Piddlehinton Camp (about 4 miles from Dorchester) was built during the Second World War to house 1,500 troops and subsequently became surplus to the Ministry of Defence. During the war, Piddlehinton was also used to house British evacuees displaced by the Blitz.[228] In 1972, the government spent £50,000 renovating Piddlehinton for Ugandan Asians. Conservative MP Simon Wingfield Digby asked in the House of Commons whether £50,000 was not a lot of money "for a camp which had not been occupied for seven years, which was totally unsuited to people coming from a tropical country, which is about to be demolished any time?"[229] Home Secretary Robert Carr responded that camp expenditures in Britain would be offset by reducing aid to Uganda. One WRVS worker described the freezing barracks at Piddlehinton as "quite fantastically awful," aside from the bleak and isolated location.[230] The administrative buildings were splendid and the staff's dining room bright and warm, but the refugees themselves were doomed to cold rooms and widely dispersed lavatories.

By the time the Ugandan Asians arrived, several of these camps had already become sites of struggle or contention.[231] In 1967, private citizens protested the expanded military usage of Dartmoor (which was soon to become a Ugandan Asian camp). As the government prepared to build new barracks to house servicemen returning from the Far East and Aden, the "unique wild character and beauty" of the surrounding national park was threatened. Some locals found Dartmoor's use for training troops "intolerable," with rusty barbed wire and live ammunition left all over the moor.[232] For their part, American soldiers remembered Dartmoor with loathing: treeless wastes of spongy soil where the wind blew constantly. One American captain wrote a parody of John Masefield's poem "Sea Fever" to describe his experiences at the base:

> I want to go out to the moors again,
> To the fog and the rocks and the rain,
> To the gorse and the marsh and the muddy pools,
> Wherein the boys have lain...
> Oh, I'll go out to the moors again,
> But mind you and mark me well:
> I'll carry enough explosives,
> To blow the place to hell.[233]

Hemswell had not been operational since 1966, although the married quarters were still used as overflow for RAF families. According to *The Times*, the camp had a deserted air, with many vast, dark rooms. Some rooms were "completely empty where one's footsteps echo—and yet others containing piles of long-forgotten wastepaper bins and desk lamps."[234] One WRVS worker said that because there was a shortage of housing for RAF couples, there would be no houses at Hemswell made available to the Asian refugees; the RAF wives would have been too resentful if refugees got houses instead of them. Instead, Ugandan Asians would be housed in the barracks, sixteen to a room on camp beds, without so much as a screen for privacy.

Stradishall was one of the oldest bases used for Ugandan Asians, built in 1937 and closed down in 1970. Stradishall's name was derived from the Old English Straetgesell, meaning "shelter on the roads." Stradishall's new life as a refugee camp, *The Times* suggested, proved how history repeated itself.[235] Located close to Stansted Airport, the camp was headed by Captain Frederick Rothwell, recently retired from the Royal Air Force. Rothwell said the first days at Stradishall had gone well, though they still needed flowers and decorations to make things "homely," and the heating and sewage systems were overtaxed.[236] The facilities began "cracking up" within a few weeks, as 1,600 people were rapidly squeezed into the camp.[237] The *Evening Echo* reported, "The runways that once shook to the deafening roar of aircraft still point to the distant horizon—though now unnaturally silent. The flat, endless emptiness of runways, grass and hangars hold no romance for the Asians, though."[238] Rothwell denied reports that Asians were compelled to sleep two to a bed, insisting that "Asian children like to sleep together." One married couple shared a barrack room with fourteen bachelors.[239]

Brian Jackson, a camp volunteer, saw Stradishall in much rosier terms. He recalled bringing treats—balloons, bubbles, chocolates, and a football made in Pakistan—to children at Stradishall. He described the "lovely drive" to the camp from Cambridge, which reveals how the camps fit in (or not) to the postwar landscape. Journeying past sleek racehorses on the rising common beyond Newmarket, and passing gigantic scarlet agricultural machines on "curly-wurly" Essex lanes, they finally reached the abandoned air force camp:

> Long runways with sprays of scarlet poppies pushing through; empty control tower; concrete guard room, and a neo-Georgian office block thickly covered with ivy, and surrounded by white ambulances, green "Meals on Wheels" minivans, BBC camera crews and a stately double decker bus that had brought some of the refugees to tea and a new world.[240]

Vinod Tailor, who stayed in Stradishall for ten days, described the big rooms with lots of beds and no privacy as "typical of the way the military lives ... very comfortable." Furthermore, he recalled that most of the 200 people from his flight were sent together to Stradishall, where he felt they became like a big family or a small community.[241]

At Doniford, new arrivals were greeted after their twenty-six-hour journey from Kampala with a cartoon that showed them how to use the toilet. Just a little over a

Fig. 1.11. Gohel Parshotta, aged 18, arrived in Britain with only 2p. He is shown at the RAF camp at Stradishall in September 1972. Keystone Pictures USA/Alamy Stock Photo.

week before, the camp had been a bare shell, with no beds and no heating. The camp administrator, Gregory Bentley, formerly a civil servant in Malaysia, installed gas heaters, and partitioned the barracks into small rooms for each family.[242] All residents received "Tommies Holiday Camp Bugle," a newsletter that publicized the camp's constantly shifting rules. From the "Bugle," residents learned that the URB planned to begin charging for food and accommodation for those who had "resources of their own." The "Bugle" also reminded residents to notify the camp forty-eight hours before they wished to leave, and to enjoy the discotheque with a "rapidly expanding collection of sounds." Instructions about tidiness were constant; Doniford was "not the most beautiful place at the best of times, and at the present rate we'll be buried in litter before spring."[243]

Still, many Ugandan Asians spoke fondly of their time in camp. According to the Trinidadian writer Shiva Naipaul (brother of the novelist V.S. Naipaul), Plaisterdown would shock anyone who expected scenes of collective despair. He described a "festive atmosphere," where children darted gaily and boys studied for their O levels with happy faces that proclaimed, "England is better than Uganda." Both Diwali and Eid were celebrated, and the Muslim residents were hosting a holiday dinner for camp staff. A Hindi version of *Romeo and Juliet* had just been successfully performed. In Naipaul's view, it was "all very jolly."[244]

Similarly, Manu Lakhani recalled his stay at Honiton in Devon as "superb. I am not going to regret that time... I really enjoyed it." Arriving in autumn, the season

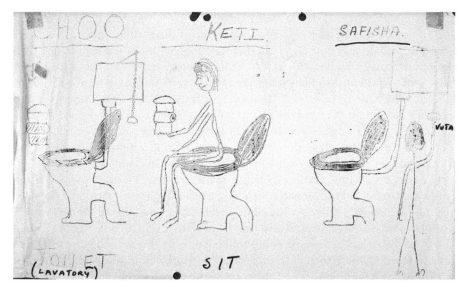

Fig. 1.12. Drawing showing how to use the lavatory at the Ugandan Asian camp at Doniford. Reproduced by permission of the Somerset Archives and Local Studies Service (South West Heritage Trust), DD\X\NAS/1.

Fig. 1.13. Photograph of Tavistock Scouts visiting Plaisterdown by Jim Thorington. Reproduced by permission of the Thorington Archive, Tavistock Museum.

of Diwali and Navaratri, Lakhani remembered playing the stick dance, Dandiya, and having "a wonderful time." Although most of the families in the camp were Hindus, Lakhani said that those of other faiths—even locals—joined in and "did not mind to play Dandias with us."[245] Although he stayed in camp for only two or three months, the British helped his family "in a very, very good way" with clothing and warm overcoats, and "I have still got one jacket which I have kept as a souvenir that I have got from the Honiton Camp." Here, Lakhani echoed the sentiment expressed by earlier Polish and Hungarian refugees such as Zosia Hartman and Magda Czigány—that the physical objects of the camp were important to them, and they would keep them long after their time in camp had ended.

Even a single family could experience many different kinds of camps. When Atul Patel landed at Heathrow Airport, he spoke with a woman sweeping the floor and told her he was going to the camp at Honiton. She replied that it was the warmest place in England, and also that it was famous for lace. He remembered, "I had no idea what lace meant. And I told my mother that we are going to a place called Honiton where they make shoelaces." In truth, Honiton had already been scheduled for demolition. When the costs of the resettlement centres became too high, and the URB began to close some of them, Patel's fortunes took a turn for the better. The URB chartered a train to take Ugandan Asians from Honiton to the small village at Faldingworth where there was a vacant American air force base. Patel recalled:

> Of course, them being Americans, this was posh. We were living in wooden huts in Honiton and here was concrete and cement. Fantastic colours, fantastic facilities, bars, canteens—that we hadn't seen before, snooker tables. But again, no school. So you can imagine what Faldingworth was like, it was like a Butlins holiday. Throughout our stay in these services we were fed well, got clothed well; got really well looked after. And one of the best experiences of being relocated, I guess, that new peoples arriving in this country have had, after us and even before us I don't think anybody had had that kind of experience.[246]

Luxury was evident everywhere at Faldingworth, from the comfortably padded chairs, to the higher quality crockery and cutlery and the central heating, "like a hotel." Whereas Honiton was dully lit, painted in gray and green, Faldingworth was bright, with the rooms painted all different colors.[247] After refusing a housing offer in Fife, Patel's family continued to move from camp to camp for two years, a period he recalls as "nomadic." In this way, his family encapsulated the diversity of the camp experience in Britain, as they moved rapidly between states of plenty and poverty.

One of the strangest sites of encampment for Ugandan Asians was Tonfanau. Located in a bleakly remote corner of Welsh-speaking North Wales, hundreds of Ugandan Asians at Tonfanau huddled over heaters amid "authentic wartime" wooden sheds, Nissen huts, and hangars, all of which had been deserted by the army three years earlier.[248] Miles away from any industrial center, with a high rate of unemployment, squeezed between mountains and the stormy Irish Sea, the camp seemed extremely unpromising, with a barbed-wire fence and a sign that said, "Beware of the firing range."[249] The camp's location was so remote that the URB held it in reserve for many weeks, hoping not to use it at all. Once it became apparent that Tonfanau would be opened, a URB spokesman told *The Times* that it was "something of an exclusive holiday resort."[250]

Adding to the bizarre atmosphere, most of the clothes donated to Tonfanau through the WRVS were from the 1960s. Chandrika Joshi, whose family stayed at Tonfanau for five or six months when she was 14 years old, found herself garbed in a brown rubber minidress. Such outfits went largely unnoticed in the camp, where everyone was similarly attired, but were "so out of place" when she went to school a few weeks later.[251] James Hamilton-Paterson, who reported on Tonfanau for *Nova*, recalls seeing "miserable people in their gorgeous saris," huddling in the "horrid" town's only two fish and chip shops to stay warm. To him, Tonfanau looked "more like something from a concentration camp than a welcoming asylum from a mad African dictator."[252]

"Julie" recalled her difficult stay at Tonfanau: "I just couldn't say anything, I would just stand, I just couldn't talk."[253] For job interviews, residents of Tonfanau often traveled six hours by train. With hardly any chairs, most residents sat on the floors of their huts. The women insisted that though it was "a little chilly" (as their hut rocked in the wind), they were "very happy" and the camp was well run. The camp leader, Captain Freddy Fuller, had spent twenty-five years as a warden of an Outward Bound school. He claimed the residents had "the advantages of a rural life... they are not overtaken by the milling masses. This furniture is limited but this

Fig. 1.14. Photograph of Ugandan Asian family at Tonfanau by Jim Arnould, *Nova* (April 1973).

isn't a permanent camp. We want them out as soon as possible." His critics, he argued, focused only on bricks and mortar, and overlooked the "joy" of the place.[254]

But whose joy was it? At Tonfanau, most of the town's 4,500 inhabitants turned out to greet the Ugandans upon arrival; it was, as one journalist said, "the most exciting thing to have happened for years."[255] Young Community Service Volunteers worked with uniformed WRVS ladies and police cadets to start a camp newspaper called *Communicor*, which the Asian residents neither contributed to nor read, while the staff mysteriously refused to provide the daily newspapers that carried job advertisements. The library, which was open for ninety minutes daily (except Sundays) housed an eclectic selection: a memoir of Modigliani, an 1856 French edition of La Fontaine's fables, J. Paul Getty's autobiography, *My Life and Fortune*. Volunteers gave lectures on "Entertainment," which explained in detail how to book a West End theatre ticket.[256]

Dawood Patel, a Tonfanau resident whose daughter had been murdered in Kampala, noted that the volunteers (compared to the locals) largely kept their distance: "Oh, they are very enthusiastic and friendly: they are always trying to make me play football or write a poem for their newspaper or join a club. They are always ringing the bell and showing people round my room, too. I am tame, I don't mind. It is all the same to me. But they don't want to get too *close*, you understand?"[257]

For many refugees, of course, Britain was not their first site of encampment. Like the Jews and the Poles, refugees from Vietnam had already spent time—in some cases, a year or more—in camps elsewhere. British journalists exposed brutal conditions in the Hong Kong camps, especially the terrifying "closed" centers. Refugees were referred to by numbers instead of individual names, and were "managed" with surveillance cameras, intelligence-gathering networks, and tear gas. At Tai Ah Chau, the private security company that oversaw the camp was trained in industrial security rather than refugee care.[258] The British press described the "closed" Hong Kong centers as little better than concentration camps.[259] Even in the "open" centers, the conditions were alarming. Kai Tak, for example, located in a disused forces camp in a highly urbanized part of the city, surrounded by high-rise public housing estates, was dirty and neglected. It had "the artifacts of community, but not the spirit," and kept refugees in a state of what R.D. Laing had called "ontological uncertainty."[260] Refugee workers feared that such an existence prompted a fugue-like state of learned helplessness, which British camps would have to undo.

In Britain, refugees from Vietnam met very different fates depending on where they landed. The Joint Committee for Refugees from Vietnam (JCRV) arranged for three voluntary agencies—BCAR, Save the Children, and Ockenden—to divide the responsibility of refugee care into geographical zones. BCAR handled South Wales plus the southern third of England, Ockenden took charge of the Midlands, plus North Wales, and Save the Children oversaw Scotland, Northern Ireland, the Northeast, and East Anglia, plus a small sector of the Midlands. Some camps were very isolated; others allowed close interaction with locals. Some allowed refugees to have their own houses, while others required sharing rooms.[261] Refugees were quarantined for a month in some camps, but others had no health requirements at all. The Home Office initially funded refugees' stays in reception centers for twelve to fourteen weeks, but the true average was closer to twenty-three weeks.[262] Again, these expectations of short stays would be thwarted, and most of the centers were extended far beyond their originally anticipated date of closure.

Many aid workers criticized the resettlement centers for providing "an unreal and therefore misleading environment in which refugees can become infantilized."[263] One health visitor, Rachel Whitham, argued that the "protected and isolated" atmosphere of most reception centers was "not ego-strengthening," a devastating critique given that the refugees from Vietnam were fleeing a communist regime and were presumed to be in need of environments that would help them rebuild their sense of individuality. She warned that the centers provided a false sense of security that pushed some refugees into "a state of euphoria" and an "imbalance of reason and judgment" or even "exaggerated nationalistic pride and custom."[264] The centers, Whitham suggested, should aim to provoke "optimal stress," which would prod refugees into active engagement with life in Britain, rather than "paralytic stress" that might lead them to withdraw.

The agencies involved in Vietnamese reception approached refugee care very differently. BCAR centers were more tightly regulated, and focused on providing basic shelter and food. Of the BCAR refugees, 10 percent stayed in its centers for more than one year.[265] BCAR mostly hired Vietnamese staff or Britons who had lived in Southeast Asia. Regional expertise was valued over social work experience in Britain. BCAR operated two of the most publicized centers: Kensington Barracks (which had also housed Ugandan Asians in the 1970s), and Sopley Centre. Whereas Sopley operated in rural peace and semi-isolation near Dorset, on the edge of the New Forest, Kensington Barracks adjoined the bustle of Kensington High Street. Despite Mahmood Mamdani's searing condemnation of Kensington in 1972, many refugees from Vietnam described their time here positively. Tam Ly, who stayed at Kensington for eight or nine months, recalled, "It was a very nice place indeed. When we first arrived, they washed our bed sheets once a week. So every week we just put them outside the door, and they would come and took them away for washing... exactly like a hotel."[266] Cuu Luc also described Kensington, where he stayed for eight to ten months, as "a very beautiful place and very central... Life was great."[267]

The Vietnam War led to a rapid expansion for Ockenden Venture, from a tiny charity for Continental refugees after the Second World War to an agency with 200 staff members running twenty-six reception centers. Ockenden was established in 1951 to provide holidays for young East Europeans in DP camps. The organization grew to give education and care to refugee children, as well as disadvantaged British children, and it provided aid during the Hungarian crisis of 1956.[268] Ockenden also had deep roots in Vietnam, where it ran an orphanage before the fall of Saigon. In 1971, the children from that orphanage were airlifted to Britain, and Ockenden continued their care. Ockenden's centers for Vietnamese refugees in Britain were mostly small and intimate with a "homelike" ambiance; the largest, in Staffordshire, held forty-five people.[269] At Ockenden centers, refugees past and present intermingled. In 1975, *The Times* reported on Ockenden's oldest inhabitant, Maria, a Hungarian refugee. At a large, rambling house in Surrey, the white-haired

Maria stooped over a huge pot of mince she was cooking for Vietnamese orphans.[270] Despite Home Office financing, the (mostly affluent) staff was paid at subsistence level, and was expected to follow an ethic of selfless voluntary work. Its reputation among refugees was paternalistic, inflexible, and authoritarian.[271]

Save the Children's centers averaged seventy to eighty people each, typically with a staff ratio of 1:12. Many of its staff members—mostly younger women—were social workers or teachers, on full salaries. More than professional qualifications, though, the SCF centers emphasized personal qualities of "democratic" leadership, and those who could work in partnership with the Vietnamese. In an effort to move refugee work out of what SCF managers saw as a "postcolonial" mode, they rarely hired ex-colonials.[272] Controversially, SCF also trained Vietnamese and Chinese "parasocial" workers for refugee aid. The Save the Children centers, which mostly housed the North Vietnamese coming in from Hong Kong camps (rather than "boat people" from South Vietnam) were highly decentralized; center leaders had a lot of autonomy, and the individual centers operated quite differently from one another.

Sopley, a former RAF Station near Bournemouth, had been disused for some time: in fact, the government was trying to sell it just before the Vietnamese refugees arrived. Between June 1979 and September 1982, Sopley served 2,855 refugees, including 860 children, in thirty-three military huts. Over this period, eighty-nine babies were born at Sopley, and thirty weddings were celebrated.[273] The population of the tiny village of Sopley increased by 500 percent.[274] Sopley's staff of forty-seven people was led by Brigadier Michael Harbottle, formerly the UN Commander in Cyprus. Vu Khanh Thanh, a refugee fieldworker, recalled that "Sopley was not what I expected. I thought everything in the UK was modern, made of steel and shiny metal—especially places built by the military." In truth, there was little that was shiny about Sopley, located in a flat field with rows and rows of wartime wooden huts, and a discarded radar listening station.[275] With twenty-eight crude housing units, including converted stables, the units were divided into rooms of 12 x 24 feet, each containing six to eight people in closely crowded bunks. Married couples shared rooms with strangers. One refugee worker saw a couple entering the camp with live chickens tucked in their jackets, and commented, "We might be in Hong Kong, though in Hong Kong the camps are closer to civilization."[276]

During winter, the outdoor attractions of rural Hampshire palled and life at Sopley became more difficult.[277] Two hours of English-language tuition every day was compulsory, as was a weekly two-hour session on Housecraft. At one point, language instruction was increased to three or four hours a day; the staff thought the Home Office's demand for five hours a day was "unrealistic."[278] Social Skills classes were held four times a week. According to its staff, Sopley was run "like a village," in which the Vietnamese enjoyed a "normal" family life. Aside from classwork, refugees were left on their own. The center's official aim was to encourage—as Vietnam's communist regime did not—individual choice and responsibility, though Sopley's refugees did not necessarily experience the camp in this way.[279]

Fig. 1.15. Portrait of man and child at Sopley, 1980, by John Perivolaris. Reproduced by kind permission of John Perivolaris.

The Thorney Island center in West Sussex, which was run by BCAR, attracted virulent criticism from its inception. The refugees here were largely segregated from the local population, and experienced a great deal of overcrowding and restrictions on their personal freedom. The choice to use Thorney Island also proved very expensive. The center (previously a Royal Air Force base) was leased from the Ministry of Defence, and access to the camp was allowed only through a restricted security barrier, which was manned twenty-four hours a day. A bomb-dispersal unit was still employed to manage the bombs left behind by the Second World War. As Vu Khanh Thanh suggested, "We were free to come and go, but it was easy to forget this" because of the intimidating prisonlike environment created by uniformed (and often racist) guards.[280] Although aid workers criticized the overly institutional environment, Thorney Island's educational program was renowned. There were seventeen qualified teachers in the primary school, and fifty-five in adult education.[281] Residents undertook five hours of English-language instruction per day. Many of the classes were comprised of family units so that families were educated together. The class stayed with the same teacher throughout their time on the island, becoming "very good friends."[282]

The staff at Thorney Island described it as a "peaceful, open" place, where the scent of seaweed and boats was pervasive at low tide. The island was populated by

Fig. 1.16. Portrait of Thanh Chuong Ly at Sopley, March 1980, by John Perivolaris. Reproduced by kind permission of John Perivolaris and Vinh Ly.

Fig. 1.17. Vietnamese children behind the barbed wire at Sopley. Photograph by Tim Page.

war graves, including those of German airmen. One report described how Thorney Island was "heavily haunted, and the Vietnamese wanted to sleep all night with the lights on, to deter their own variety of ghosts—probably ancestors— but the electricity bills would have been frantic." Ghosts of RAF airmen were said to come and go on this island of "unsurpassing beauty," which offered beautiful cherry trees and magnolias along with opportunities for hunting, fishing, sailing, and swimming. Such English perspectives on Thorney Island were robustly idyllic. One volunteer, Daphne Byrne, recalled how she and her co-workers often paddled out on the water at lunch hour and found the Vietnamese busily picking blackberries despite the "DANGER OUT OF BOUNDS UNEXPLODED BOMBS notices."[283] Byrne described sitting at a yacht club near the camp, observing "the blue blue sea and green and white sails of yachts." She viewed the island as one of the most superbly peaceful places on earth, and thought the refugees were "so lucky" to be there.[284]

Yet beneath this placid surface, there were remnants of violence. Wartime maps showed that pipe mines were buried at both sides of the airport runways at Thorney Island, where Vietnamese children flew their kites. The Royal Navy drove in and out on mysterious missions that were never explained.[285] In September of 1981, a bomb went off unexpectedly near the main road, proving that some of the unexploded bombs were unstable and still dangerous; another bomb was left near the main residential building until the Vietnamese had left the island.[286] The juxtaposition of Byrne's blissful description of Thorney Island with these considerably

At Thorney Island reception centre: 1980

Fig. 1.18. The barrier at Thorney Island.

less peaceful scenes—which were linked to the prehistory of the refugee camp as a military base—point toward the different ways that those who lived in the camps perceived and experienced them. While Byrne enjoyed her verdant strolls around the island, the refugees from Vietnam who inhabited the camp protested what felt like a dangerous imprisonment.

Like British homes, British camps transformed over time. But life in camp took many twists and turns, with no simple trajectory of "improvement" or "decline." Refugee camps served as a nexus of the home and the state, disrupting narratives about the forward march of affluence and domesticity. Refugee camps were experienced against this backdrop of constantly changing perceptions of homes and homelessness. For many refugee workers, the camp could be homelike, but never a home.

This chapter has explored the diverse cultures of encampment in Britain, and the specific built environments for the refugee—from the Nissen hut to the holiday chalet. Again, the physical environment and daily routines of the camps gave rise to new interactions both within and across cultures. As the British home was fundamentally transformed, the material experiences of refugees and citizens diverged. The life of the refugee became more physically distinctive, and more difficult for citizens to imagine themselves inhabiting.

Next, I delve more deeply into one of the most contentious aspects of daily life in British camps: that is, how to feed refugees. The complex process of mass feeding illuminated how material conditions in camps shaped the lives of refugees, but also how camp residents were transforming the way volunteers and locals lived. Camp leaders and refugees continually forged connections between feeding and identity, especially through hunger strikes and other food protests. Refugee camps brought new foods and ways of feeding that formed important constellations of conflict and community. As we have begun to see, refugee camps changed the landscape of modern Britain in a variety of ways, bringing new expectations and daily practices for refugees and citizens.

2

Feeding and Hungering

Many refugees perceived food (and the spaces in which it was served) as a reminder of what they had lost. But food in camp could also be a way to uphold social life and kinship networks that had been disrupted by war and exile: a means of sustaining identity in an uncertain new environment. Making food was one way that refugees in Britain demonstrated their choices, and responded to the camp's constraints. Within the world of the camp, food was both a sign of caretaking and a focal point of resistance.[1]

Wherever refugees ate—whether in communal "mess" halls or cooking in their own huts—food was a highly publicized point of contact and contention between refugees and those who governed them. These choices were linked to camp leaders' ideas about envisioning refugees' futures as citizens or emigrants. They also revealed much about the camp's objectives: that is, whether camps should operate as temporary "homes" that offered a "normal" family life, or as militarized institutions that treated refugees as a mass population. For those who strove to create the trappings of a home within the camp, food was a useful way to enhance that illusion.

The archival sources pertaining to food and feeding in refugee camps are vividly detailed. During the Hungarian refugee crisis, the Ministry of Housing and Local Government drafted a "Notes for Guidance in the Preparation of Various Hungarian Dishes." The file contained detailed notes on "gipsy stew," which was described as "very tasty," and could be prepared of any odd pieces of meat, as well as recipes for pork and cabbage pie, and *szeged* goulash. Of goulash, the Ministry noted, "this famous dish is seldom prepared the correct way outside Hungary, although quite easy to cook, if the directions are closely followed."[2] Government officials thought about the task of feeding refugees as a necessary act of care, but also a feat of cultural translation.

For Britons, the practices of feeding refugees brought locals into contact with new tastes and experiences. At the same time, complaints about food were endemic in refugee camps. Hunger strikes were one of the most crucial political weapons of the refugee. As James Vernon has noted, being fed entailed new sets of obligations and social responsibilities: a project full of failed experiments as well as seeming successes.[3] This chapter considers how refugees were fed, and how they chose to feed themselves. Tensions over food—and, ultimately, the refusal to eat—formed an important axis of political protest during an era of encampment.

ON THE MENU: FOOD AND IDENTITY
IN REFUGEE CAMPS

Generally speaking, refugees were fed according to a national standard of living. These "standards," however, were very much in flux. Government officials used the shifting guidelines of nutritional science to establish a calculus of what refugees should eat. But camp authorities sought to provide refugees with much more than basic nutrition. They recognized that food and identity might be more deeply linked for refugees—who were nostalgic for their lost homelands—than for Britons. In this sense, the hunger of refugees was distinctive. Camps must offer foods that would provide comfort and a sense of "home."

Internment camps offered one early experience of mass feeding. Although the Great War internees were never in danger of starvation, their food was often unappealing. Food rations, which relied heavily on the widely detested salt-herring, were determined by "scientific" means, often calculated by the number of calories consumed without regard for taste or variety. Still, not all internees ate the same thing. Knockaloe, which housed 26,000 internees, offered a canteen where men who could afford it purchased more luxurious foods. The canteen carried spices and baking ingredients—such as cream of tartar and baking powder—as well as honey, pickles, and sauerkraut. Cigarettes, cigars, and tobacco were also available. Older men could ask to tend garden allotments, which enabled them to produce their own food and spend time outdoors.[4] Still, internees often subsisted on a diet of herring, cabbage, and potatoes.[5] During the Second World War, the men of each house at the Isle of Man camps received food rations and did their own cooking. Since the men were "naturally inexpert at cooking, this arrangement caused considerable hardship and wastage of food," but many internees still preferred this more domestic system to mass feeding.[6]

During the Great War, Belgian refugees at Earl's Court were fed with magnificent gifts from abroad: 50,000 tins of salmon from British Columbia, hundredweights of cheese and tons of potatoes from Canada, thousands of pounds of tea from the Indian Tea Planters Association, ham from Australia, Uruguayan beef, and—unappetizingly—swans from New Zealand.[7] The camp restaurant, the Café Royal, served delicacies to those refugees who could afford to supplement the official diet.[8] Alexandra Palace hired a Belgian cook to prepare the foods the refugees liked. Not everyone was impressed: two Belgian men complained that they were fed solely on carrots and cabbages. Pigs in Belgium, they said, ate better than refugees in Britain.[9]

The Belgian refugees brought new foods and recipes to Britain—chicory, for example, was quickly grown and stocked in Covent Garden. Though English cooks scarcely knew it when the war began, its high nutritional value led the government to urge its production after the war; Belgian growers handed out small booklets of recipes to English buyers to teach them how to prepare these new vegetables.[10] *The Belgian Cookbook* was published in 1915, with many recipes from refugees. Described as being suited for Britons of "moderate means," the book included "starvation soup" made with Brussels sprouts, waterzooi, endives, poor man's sauce (milk and shallots), apricot soufflé (good enough for an English dinner party), hawthorn cordial, and military prunes.

The tension between scarcity and plenty was constant in refugee camps. The press watched the camps carefully for any signs of special treatment for refugees, especially during moments of rationing in Britain. During the "hungry 30s," perhaps half the population of Britain (more than 20 million people) were malnourished.[11] Nutritional knowledge—and the personal experience of the hungry—were increasingly at the forefront of political debate.[12] In this context, the ample provisions for many refugees contrasted sharply with the scarcity that many Britons experienced.

For many Basque children at North Stoneham, British food was a great treat. Helvecia Hidalgo recalled that rationing in Bilbao had led to the bread getting darker and darker: "We used to say they swept the floor to make it. It tasted horrible."[13] Yvonne Kapp (pseud. Cloud), a journalist who worked with Basque and Jewish refugees, reported that the Basque children's delight in English white bread was so great that many of them crammed as much of it as they could into their pockets, under their jackets, and into their palliasses. One little boy reported, "I never knew there was so much white bread in the world. We are going to eat all of it!"[14] Many children hoarded their food rations, believing they could take them back to their families in Spain.[15] Because children often queued up for multiple servings of food, the camp leadership instituted colored armbands; the children's armbands were removed after they received a single serving of food, so that they could not be served again. Those who were given yellow armbands (Franco's color) went without their dinner, as they had torn them off and preferred to miss the meal rather than bear this stigma.

Though many Basque children had experienced terrible privation in Spain, their physical health was highly praised in Britain. According to Kapp, Basque refugees were not plagued by the rickety legs, weak eyes, distended abdomens, and decayed teeth of hungry Britons. Instead, she claimed, "these children are beautiful." Working-class English children might have been forced to rely on a diet of margarine, tea, and fog. But even the poorer Basques, she suggested, had enjoyed ample sunshine, olive oil, and fruit. Their parents' efforts were rewarded with "straight brown limbs, even white teeth, glossy hair and clear eyes, even when clothes are ragged and every moment is informed with the agility and sharpness of street life."[16]

Camp workers assumed that Basque children would require special diets—all the more so because they must be ready to return "home" to Spain at a moment's notice. But the initial plan to provide only Spanish foodstuffs in all Basque colonies was abandoned, as Basque children acclimated quickly to English styles of eating. Although many of the children had never eaten at table before, and preferred to take their food in both hands and run outside, they were said to adapt well to "the stilted customs of the board" and learned to sit and eat heartily.[17] At Nazareth House colony in Southampton, the fifty Basque boys ate English food, but were fed separately, after the English orphans also housed there had eaten.[18] The Basque children at Wattermillock in Lancashire also seemed to be "very happy" to abandon Spanish dishes, and reportedly came to enjoy ordinary English fare of meat, mutton, fish, and vegetables.[19]

The Basque children often illicitly "supplemented" their camp rations. At one colony in Brampton, Valentín Sagasti Torrano remembered how "we used to raid a local field and steal potatoes, which we roasted on an open fire. At other times we toasted whatever bread we managed to procure. How we always enjoyed the bounty!" Some boys chased chickens in a nearby garden, and were subsequently chased by the chickens' owners.[20] Herminio, who lived at the notoriously unhappy colony at Margate during the freezing winter of 1939–40, recalled, "Food? We used to steal from another big, nearby house, full of East European Jewish refugees. They were very well organized and provided for."[21] For Herminio, the state of plenty that Jewish child refugees enjoyed contrasted unfairly with his own privation.

The Jewish children at Dovercourt echoed this image of bounty—even extravagance. One child recalled encountering "the delicious novelties of tea with milk, kippers and, best of all, bread with a thick layer of margarine" at her camp. Anticipating skeptical readers, she added, "no sarcasm intended, I really did enjoy these strange new flavors."[22] In fact, one visitor thought that the children at Dovercourt were fed *too* lavishly, and that the cake they were served every night was excessively rich. The staff decided to replace the cake with fruit so that the children would sleep better and "will better appreciate having a luxury treat."[23] All of the children (including those who were not practicing Jews) were served kosher food, which was much more expensive.

At Kitchener Camp, a publicity pamphlet called "Home Town for the Homeless" included photographs of hale and hearty refugees and noted that the men of Kitchener consumed 2,000 pounds of potatoes, 124 pounds of porridge, 200 pounds of jam, 700 pounds of meat, and 1,800 pounds of bread daily. The camp's food bill was £25,000 per year. Still, Kitchener residents objected to the monotony of the camp diet. After the men were fed pea soup forty-nine times in a row for dinner, one resident arranged a protest: ten men marched into the dining hall carrying a shield with the text, "Pea soup for the 50th time." That day, however, they had "excellent sardines," and the demonstration became an enormous joke.[24] Fred Dunston, an Austrian Jew at Kitchener, recalled how when the Viennese residents did not like the food, they would refuse to eat it, banging their spoons on the table in protest. The Germans always obediently spooned up whatever they were served, which Dunston thought reflected their superior discipline.[25] The Kitchener men were encouraged (and at times required) to grow their own vegetables: lettuces, cabbages, potatoes, cauliflowers, peas, carrots, spinach, beets, and tomatoes.[26]

Camp leaders saw Basque and Jewish refugees as eager to adapt to English foods and ways of eating. They were much less optimistic about changing the Polish diet. Especially for Polish women (many of whom had already journeyed to the Middle East and Africa before reaching Britain), food played a crucial role in sustaining Polish identity. At Melton Mowbray, Urszula Szulakowska ate English food for school lunch, but adored her delicious, Polish-style evening meals cooked with her grandmother on the black stove in their hut. Together, they ate *golabki* and *pierogi*, or fried Polish sausage and eggs, and pancakes with apples and cherries. Szulakowska

Fig. 2.1. A typical meal at Kitchener, which included soup, a vegetable, tapioca pudding, wholemeal bread, and a banana. Chronicle/Alamy Stock Photo.

attributed the enviable health of the older Poles in camp to their "excellent organic food," with vegetables grown in their own gardens, eggs from their own hens, fresh fish, and dark black bread.[27] For those who had survived the hunger of Siberia, camps in England represented a dramatic improvement.

Like the Basque children, Poles in camps did not eat only what the camp authorities provided. At Kelvedon Camp in Essex, Polish foods were "imported" by Mr. Janko, a Polish delicatessen owner in London who arrived every Saturday in his VW van. Kaz Janowski, who spent his childhood at Kelvedon, saw Janko's van as just "another of the wonders to be found in the strange land beyond the camp perimeter."[28] Henry Pavlovich remembered the "paradise" of Foxley Valley, where children could forage for mushrooms, sorrel, horseradish, and berries, and fallen timber for the barracks stoves. At Foxley, poorer refugees lived in barracks that smelled of frying onions and boiling cabbages. The huts where residents had a little more money gave off the enticing scent of pricier cakes and chickens, "enough to drive the others insane with bitterness, anger, envy."[29]

Camp leaders sought to control how Poles ate. Food-related infractions were common, though camp authorities disagreed about whether refugees should be allowed to grow their own food. At Northwick, a scheme for a hostel garden was abandoned when the strawberry plants failed. The hostel children had raided the fruit, and only a few berries could be obtained for the kitchen's use.[30] At Stover, one Board member urged that fruit should be grown on the hostel grounds in order for the residents to feast on blackcurrants, gooseberries, strawberries, rhubarb, and tomatoes—but the residents did not volunteer for this work. At the Nettlebed South Hostel for Poles in Henley, residents were warned that they were not allowed to keep pigs, goats, rabbits, geese, or ducks, and must limit themselves only to such indoor domestic pets "as are commonly kept in this country."[31] Ultimately, most residents developed their own allotments for growing vegetables (and tobacco, which was discouraged by the camp authorities).[32]

The National Assistance Board meticulously regulated meals in its Polish camps.[33] A malnourished refugee was a tremendous embarrassment to the Board. After the catering advisor at Stover suggested that the meals were unsatisfying, the warden was required to issue regular progress reports. The warden noted, "this matter has been very carefully watched." Residents were given a "rather larger" helping of potatoes and each person was asked whether they had received enough food.[34] The warden claimed that because many of Stover's residents were old and frail, they did not require as much food as "vigorous persons." Most residents were "elderly peasant stock whose interests are mainly concerned with their meals, Church and garden," and they preferred to make their food "in their own particular way."[35] The Board acknowledged, "we have not insisted that these people should have their meals cooked in the English way and some dishes are being served which seem strange to us."[36] Still, the Board instructed Stover's catering staff to entice the Poles with plentiful, attractive meals. Delicacies like jellies should be served in individual dishes, and not plated up in bulk. The Board also urged caterers to introduce as much variety as possible in the refugee diet. Nutrition was prized over acculturation. The extra expense was justified by healthier, happier refugees.[37]

For Poles in British camps, food provided an important link to the past. During the Ugandan Asian expulsion, too, memories of the flight from Uganda, the arrival in Britain, and the trauma of encampment were linked through food. In earlier decades, refugees were emblematic of the plight of the hungry. By the 1970s, the government assumed—rightly or wrongly—that most Britons no longer suffered from hunger; hunger was a problem for the global South.[38] From the official perspective, the refugee was potentially the last hungry person in Britain.

Most Ugandan Asians ate their first meal in England in a camp. At Stradishall, a large Indian lunch was prepared for the arrival of the first Ugandan Asians: "where only two years ago airmen had dined on bacon and eggs and a roast on Sunday, wafted the cloying aroma of curry."[39] But the Asians preferred fish and chips; British volunteers, who had not eaten a square meal for several days, happily consumed the meal. One volunteer cheerfully commented about her Ugandan Asian work, "I am sure I will never forget the super curry!"[40] Camp residents were often fed in shifts, because the canteens could not cope with such large numbers. People arrived for meals at specified times, but there were long queues outside in the cold. Shirin Abdul Hussein remembered reaching Gaydon at 3 a.m., and being served breakfast— the first time she had ever eaten English food. She described servers piling eggs, which went mostly uneaten, onto a plate, and how older people just "sat there crying, with blank faces crying—really sad to see it."[41]

The Uganda Resettlement Board may have doomed itself on the food question early on when it hired Royal Navy cooks for its sixteen camps and gave them a book of Indian recipes.[42] One note from an Asian camp resident to the staff read, "Please it is of inconvenience to Muslims the serving of Pork and of inconvenience [to Hindus] the serving of cow meat. If possible could these be eliminated. Instead chicken, goat or mutton meat would serve both these communities very well."[43] Eventually, the same London catering firm, Taylorplan (which had also catered in many Hungarian camps), was employed in all of the Ugandan Asian camps. In time, the firm created a standard menu "to give the newcomers the type of food they enjoy most." But caterers were not always sure what that ideal food might be. One of the Doniford chefs studied at an Indian restaurant learning how to cook certain specialties.[44]

Officially, most camps did not allow Ugandan Asian families to cook their own food.[45] But this rule was widely disobeyed. For two mothers at Tonfanau, their most striking memory of the camp was of a shop opened by two enterprising brothers to sell "authentic" Indian spices. There was, they remembered, much illicit cookery, and eventually each family at Tonfanau was given £5 to buy electric plates. Preparing food allowed women to express cultural preferences and keep up household roles. One woman recalled, "As long as I could cook one meal, I was still a mother looking after my family."[46] A local shopkeeper, Mr. Markham, also traveled to Asian neighborhoods in Birmingham and bought foods to sell at camp from his van.[47]

Volunteers who worked with Ugandan Asians were exposed to new tastes. Margretta Young-Jones, a Welsh woman who volunteered at Tonfanau, was invited to join one family's meal; her son Edwin was shocked to be fed a raw chili pepper, which he had never eaten (nor even heard of) before. Margretta and Edwin viewed this meal as the basis of their "beautiful friendship" with Tonfanau residents.[48]

Over time, Asians began to assist the camp caterers in food preparation. Atul Patel recalled that the food at Honiton was not "ethnically appropriate," though the caterers tried to be sensitive to vegetarians. The residents' committee, which included Patel's mother, met with the camp leaders and offered to take over the kitchen. She was taken on outings to Exeter to buy spices and food, and earned a salary as a cook. The camp food improved dramatically.[49] At Faldingworth, each block had its own kitchen, which became a place for the young people of the camp to congregate and have snacks of tea and toast with garlic chili spread. Patel's parents bought small electric plates, and made themselves chai every day at 4 p.m.: a small act of self-sufficiency and independence.

By the 1970s, nutritional scientists were at work in the Ugandan Asian camps. The expulsion provided unique opportunities to study how social and political disruptions influenced diet. Sandra Hunt surveyed 848 Ugandan Asians as her Ph.D. thesis in Nutrition at the University of London, funded by the Department of Health and Social Security.[50] Almost 70 percent of the families in her study had owned at least one car in Uganda, and 92 percent had employed Africans as servants. Their diet in Uganda had been free of economic constraints. When asked what foods they would buy in Uganda if they wanted to eat cheaply, the interviewees all replied that this situation never arose. Hunt concluded that those who stayed longest in camps eventually reported liking English food better than those who resettled quickly. In dietary terms, camps seemed to be a powerful tool of assimilation.

Hunt's research focused on two camps: West Malling, which housed 840 Ugandan Asians, and Greenham Common, a larger camp for 1,500. The two camps had entirely different approaches to feeding refugees. At Greenham Common, which employed an "efficiency expert," the whites were fed British food in a separate room with no queue. The Asians received rice and dal and curry. If the Asian residents wanted British food, they had to submit a special request. Refugees were forbidden to take food to their rooms. Nutritionally, the Asian meals were poor; fresh vegetables and fruit were served only once a week. There were many reports of malnutrition at Greenham Common; forty Ugandan Asian women were treated for anemia.

At West Malling, the staff shared food and the mess hall with refugees, but the staff skipped the queue. Rice and curry were always present, but the rest of the menu was traditional British food. Fresh fruits and vegetables were served daily, and older refugees were allowed to take food back to their rooms. The catering manager, Charles Buckett, was praised for his varied and thoughtful menus. In December of 1972, Buckett prepared a traditional Scottish meal of haggis to entice Ugandan Asians to resettle in Scotland; he also played Father Christmas, and rode into camp on a "sleigh" converted from an airfield trolley. No curry was served that day, and *The Times* reported that the Asian vegetarians were "very excited" about sampling the turkey. Many residents were invited to celebrate Christmas in local homes, but the camp administrator urged them to eat their holiday meal in camp: "we're not stopping them going out, but I think they will have a better time all together here."[51]

For Ugandan Asians, food symbolized the disruption of class and ethnic identities that had taken place during expulsion. Maz Mashru, a Ugandan Asian photojournalist, recalled arriving at an army camp at Yeovil in Somerset, and finding the communal mess halls particularly traumatic:

> It reminds me of the scene which we see in the movies like "Goldies" and things like that. We had to stand with the tray, they would give us two pieces of bread some beans and that…at least we enjoyed that freedom that you know we are not living in a sort of fear of Amin's terrors but in the other way we were all enterprising people in Africa and we were quite proud and I didn't want to live in that camp for a long time.[52]

Akbar Hassan, a resident at Southall, said that he would have stayed in camp longer if there had not been so many problems with the cafeteria. He claimed that some Asians left Southall the very moment they saw the dining room, which was run in the style of a military mess hall, "because Asians consider it shameful to stand in line with trays, asking for their food." In fact, one young man at Hemswell remarked on the queues as a social equalizer: "It is quite good to find yourself standing next to a man who was very rich in Kampala in the food queue, knowing that he has to queue, too."[53] In Uganda, Akbar proclaimed, only beggars would stand in a line with their plates outstretched, and even the homeless would find it disgraceful to queue for food:

> I am not thinking, in all my life, to see myself to ask for food…By my last day, I feel too much, too much shame. You see, I am big capitalist man, and I am thinking that in Uganda, at big hotels, there is always much waiters to serve me. I think, Oh, Lord, I never see this day for Akbar Hassan. I not taking any more food here. It is better to be leaving before I lose my last confidence.[54]

What had been lost in expulsion was not only the special dishes associated with life in Uganda, but also the convivial mode of eating, the indulgence of being served, the open expression of joy in food. At Tonfanau in North Wales, one camp resident composed a poem full of praise for his new life in Britain. But food was the one exception to this otherwise rosy depiction. He contrasted the pleasures and luxuries of eating in Uganda with the paltry substitutes he suffered in his adopted land:

> Are you asking me what I cared about in the old life?
> I've seen neither cream sauce nor dahl
> And no one eats with their fingers
> Or sucks them clean to show their enjoyment of the meal
> (The business of eating with so-called sophisticated cutlery
> Excludes all such expressions of pleasure).
> We can no longer tell our servants to "get a move on"
> And there are no more African faces to be seen.
> Gone are the days of the Mercedes Benz![55]

In this informal elegy, ambivalence about life in Britain is expressed first through food. The recognition that both specific foods and ways of eating have vanished leads to a lamentation about a deeper loss of class and racial status. The author moves from more traditional expressions of regret about the beloved "home-land" to nostalgia for extraordinary privileges that cannot be replicated in Britain. At times, the resistance expressed in this poem about not simply taking what one is given—about refusing to eat at the British table—was formalized into collective protests.

LEAVING THE TABLE: FOOD PROTESTS AND HUNGER STRIKES

As we have seen, food was an axis of contact and care between refugees and Britons. But it was also a source of discontent.[56] Refugees objected to the quality and the quantity of food they ate in camps, how the food was served, and the segregations or inequalities the camps' feeding practices entailed. Protests around food were key to the kind of community that was being created (or fractured) in camp.[57] For refugees who had few forms of effective political expression, food protests and hunger strikes proved critically important.

The experience of internment sparked several food protests. On November 19, 1914, a food riot broke out at Douglas on the Isle of Man after the men were served spoiled meat and wormy potatoes. The internees refused to eat, and allegedly rushed the guards at dinner time, throwing food, furniture, and utensils. The panicked guards opened fire, killing five internees and wounding nineteen. The ensuing inquest found the deaths "justifiable," but the incident led to greater scrutiny of camp conditions. As a result, internees gained more control over their food.[58]

The first sustained protests around food in refugee camps took place in the War Office's camps for Poles. In February 1947, at Fairfield near Prestwick in Scotland, 380 Polish servicemen and their wives (some of whom were British) staged a hunger strike to protest the conditions of their camp and the woeful delays in their resettlement. The strike lasted nearly a week; some of the women were pregnant and desperately ill. Brigadier Frith argued that the camp conditions were not the War Office's fault; rather, Poles needed to use their rations more carefully. He chastised Polish women for refusing to attend the Ministry of Food's cooking classes, and urged them to pool their milk to help needier families during the national milk shortage.[59]

That same year, seventy-two Polish men at the Weston Green Camp in Surrey complained of "circumstances absolutely abnormal" in which they were forced to live. They petitioned the Board to visit the camp and "taste our breakfast and dinner."[60] They acknowledged the need for "rationalized foods" (that is, food rationing), but believed their current diet—mildewed bread, sandwich fillings full of worms, a slice of meat only once a week—rendered them unfit for physical labor. Nutritional advisors viewed the calorific value of camp meals (2,250–2,500 calories per day) as insufficient for working men, who required at least 3,500 calories.[61] Thus, those who worked outside the camps had to pay extra—up to 9 shillings per week—to buy a lunch that would provide the extra 1,000 calories.[62] Likewise, a 1948 petition from twenty-two Polish residents of Petworth Camp in Sussex lamented, "I don't know what for we pay, we are getting just bread and fish and everything like that, nothing we may get better."[63]

When the National Assistance Board took over the care of Polish refugees, it brought new expectations about how refugees might thrive. The Board aimed to surpass the War Office's "emergency" provisions and provide higher levels of sustenance. As we have seen, the Board was deeply committed to seeing that no one went hungry in its camps. The Board offered a detailed response to every single complaint about food, and rebuked individual wardens who failed to nourish their residents. The National Assistance Board offered new styles of feeding as well as new diets. In military camps, Poles were encouraged to eat as one large "family."[64] But by the 1950s, communal feeding became more controversial.

Collective feeding had a longer history in Britain. Originally focused on paupers and criminals, the practice of collective feeding was extended to the rest of British society through wartime rationing. Many Britons experienced mass feeding through school meals and factory canteens. For its champions, communal feeding was a mechanism for producing healthy, productive, socially adapted citizens. Group-feeding situations introduced people to the physical accoutrements of civility that were often lacking in poor homes (tablecloths, plates, cutlery) and to a richer social life. In practice, the poor quality of canteens and school meals seriously compromised the new vision of society they were supposed to produce, often feeling more like a punishment than an entitlement.[65] For Britons, communal feeding was largely a failed experiment.

Communal feeding and self-feeding represented two very different visions of the Poles' future. For the National Assistance Board, communal feeding was laden with the hopes of earlier decades in which mass feeding could serve as a tool of education and social bonding. But it also acknowledged how communal feeding had disenchanted ordinary Britons. Furthermore, communal feeding was associated with a culture of "institutionalization" that might make Poles unfit for resettlement. The Board debated investing in communal dining rooms to make them more attractive, but decided it was more important to cultivate the spirit of the individual householder.[66] At Stover, the Board allowed families to eat together in the dining hall at smaller tables, hoping to alleviate the families' desire to retreat into their "private" living quarters.[67] Ultimately, as families (rather than soldiers) came to dominate hostel life, communal eating facilities were withdrawn.

In September of 1949, the Board experimented with returning ration books to individual heads of household at Melton Mowbray.[68] This process was known by the Poles as being "*na raszynie*" (on rations).[69] This shift was part of a larger effort to transform some of the Board's hostels into housing estates, where refugees would pay rent. The change to "renter's status" was voluntary, but most Poles embraced the chance to run their own household.[70] The Board expected to boost the local economy, as Polish wives would now buy food from British shopkeepers.[71] Furthermore, the Poles would "take up normal family life as their English neighbors," become more independent, and cease "living lives of regimentation." Wardens who had ordered Polish women to cook "the English way" in hostel kitchens—causing great resentment—could no longer make such demands.[72] One Pole reported that "I have been waiting for this moment for 10 years, for my wife to buy the food I like, cook it as we like, and when we like; in short to take up the duties of a housewife once again."[73]

Similar measures followed at Kelvedon, where Polish women reported that they saved money—at least £1 a week—by cooking their own food. One mother declared zealously, "I wouldn't give away [my] *razenbuk* for any amount of treasure!"[74] At Fairford, communal kitchens closed in 1951, and a food shop opened in the hostel. Celina Kabala Wojciechowska was delighted; her husband liked the communal kitchen, "but, when I saw how the food was served and how the server's sweat dripped into the potatoes, I said, '*We are going on rations.*'"[75] Many women saw an opportunity to regain their identity as Poles who ate exclusively Polish food. For the Board, these changes marked a key transition for the Poles from soldiers to civilians—and perhaps citizens.[76]

By 1956, when the Anglo-Egyptians arrived, rationing had just ended in Britain. Refugee work now took place in a context of heightened expectations, with rising rates of consumption among Britons. Significantly, the arrival of the Anglo-Egyptians and the Hungarians in 1956 brought to an end the residence test for welfare foods in Britain. Faced with two groups of refugees—frail Anglo-Egyptian evacuees, and heroic Hungarian Cold Warriors—these groups exposed the difficulties in enforcing a residence test. The government decided to abolish the test. After this point, there were no distinctions in welfare feeding between visitors and permanent residents in the UK. As a result, the population that was eligible for welfare foods in Britain expanded: an unforeseen outcome of refugee work.[77]

Many Anglo-Egyptians protested to the Home Office about their food.[78] The residents' committee at Eastwood Hostel in Nottingham complained that a cockroach had been found on a resident's plate, and that the fruit served at the hostel was not fresh. The residents asked for more meat, and one asked whether some dishes could be fried in the cottonseed oils used in Egypt.[79] Residents defiantly cooked in their rooms, despite the fire hazard.[80] At Summerfield Hostel, near Kidderminster, a protest erupted when the residents complained that they had been served "stinking food," and the residents' committee resigned in protest. The warden blamed the catering manager's lack of "sufficient imagination" and the Anglo-Egyptian tendency toward "continued enlargement of their troubles by constant reiteration of their trials and tribulations."[81] The Home Office accused the residents' committee of failing to provide menus or female advisors; British caterers could not be expected to cook unfamiliar foods without guidance.[82] Privately, the warden admitted that, though the food at Summerfield was "well up to hostel standards," this did not mean it was "acceptable to all the members of a heterogeneous Community accustomed to quite another cuisine and diet—to meals eaten in privacy."[83] Indeed, the ability to eat in private was often more important than the quality of the food itself. Shortly thereafter, 400 Anglo-Egyptians at Summerfield went on hunger strike, protesting the staff's alleged discrimination in selecting residents for emigration.[84] Here, we can see how a food protest merged with larger concerns about labor and migration, enabling refugees to express their anxieties and lobby for specific policy changes.

By the 1970s, the focal point of food protests had shifted, as they were increasingly racialized. In the Ugandan Asian camps, protests targeted the problem of where food was served and to whom. When Mahmood Mamdani asked for milk at Kensington Barracks, he was told that milk "is drunk only by a small minority of wealthy people in this country. This is not East Africa. Perhaps you should go to Leicester and Southall and see what people drink down there."[85] Again, the poor Briton became the foil to the refugee. A health inspector visited the camp and agreed that the vegetarian diet was nutritionally deficient; a pint of milk for children and a half pint for adults was added, plus two ounces of cheese, dry or tinned fruit, and greens. The camp rules dictated that only camp residents were allowed to eat there. Visitors must request permission to eat in camp, and were charged 25p per meal. Mamdani acknowledged the pettiness of these struggles, as camp residents quickly became obsessed by whether anyone consumed more milk than they were owed.

In December of 1972, the Asian residents at Stradishall circulated a petition to protest the quality of food they received: "We recognize that as part of the whole programme of resettlement our meals are provided at the expense of the Government. We therefore believe that there is an obligation on us to consume this food and not to waste it."[86] The petitioners asked to observe the cooking process so they could ensure that nothing was mixed with beef or pork. They also asked for stronger tea, and higher-quality rice. They admitted that some residents took more than their share of food, but they would like to "stop greed" themselves instead of being policed by camp staff. The catering company responded by appointing two Asian food advisors, and providing *halal* meat, Indian pickles and chutneys, fresh fruits and salads, and new mealtimes.

Many Ugandan Asian camps had separate dining facilities for staff, which usually meant that the dining halls were racially segregated. At Tonfanau, the Welsh middle classes adopted the camp shop as their local delicatessen, while the camp staff dined apart from the Asians. The volunteers ate their meat and two veg in their own canteen, earnestly discussing the problem of racial integration. Some residents at Newbury threatened hunger strikes, which were highly publicized, to protest unsatisfactory food and the division of Asians and Europeans in the canteen. The 1,500 Ugandan Asians at Greenham Common shared their canteen with 300 staff members, but complained that they were forced to crowd into half of the canteen because they were not allowed to eat in the "European" section. The *Telegraph* described this situation as "a form of apartheid."[87] At the same time, one caterer reported that "the Asians threw and spilled food onto the floor quite deliberately," and that because they never queued, there was a mad rush when the cafeteria opened and a "complete shambles."[88] Many Greenham Common residents refused all of the food.[89]

Communal feeding practices were controversial for the Poles and the Ugandan Asians. They were even more so for refugees from Vietnam, for whom food was politically charged in different ways. Many Britons linked the practices of mass feeding to the sufferings of communism. Refugee workers praised the centers that had self-catering arrangements, and decried those that offered only institutional meals. One refugee described it as "grossly insensitive" to make Vietnamese refugees eat in a huge communal dining room, though this had been common practice for many earlier groups.[90] For refugees from Vietnam, any way in which the camp experience could—counterintuitively—cultivate a sense of privacy and individual ownership was desirable. But some camp organizers argued that communal feeding was beneficial in freeing refugees—especially women—from responsibility for meals, so that they could focus on the tasks of resettlement.[91]

The larger camps typically used communal catering systems with paid staff, while the smaller centers often let refugees purchase food within a specified budget. Save the Children centers typically encouraged refugees to cook for themselves. The food cupboards were kept open in an effort to avoid treating the refugees "like children," and encouraging them to get out of the institutional mode of life they had inhabited in Hong Kong camps.[92] At Sopley, some refugees (those who lived in small houses instead of the larger dormitories) were initially permitted to cook in the houses and received a weekly food ration. When the camp authorities decided that all refugees should eat in the main dining hall, they removed the tables and chairs from the houses, thinking—quite wrongly—that this would prevent refugees from cooking their own food.[93] British nutritionists warned that the Vietnamese would only feel truly well fed by the culturally familiar (and, in Britain, more expensive) starch: rice. After a typical British meal at Sopley, where the main food was potatoes, the refugees said "they feel full and hunger has been subdued, but their appetite has not been satisfied."[94]

Still, some refugees from Vietnam praised the camp food. At Kensington Barracks, where Mamdani had condemned the stingy provisions and racially seg-regated dining spaces, a refugee from Vietnam, Cuu Luc, described the food as "very good, a lot better than the food we ate at home...chicken legs, pork chops, more than we could eat. There was also a lot of milk, more than we could drink."[95] Tam Ly, too, recalled eating at Kensington as a luxurious experience, with "so much meat, spareribs, pork chops, etc. as much as we could eat. It was just so good there."[96]

At Thorney Island, the largest Vietnamese center, food became a particular point of contention between camp administrators and refugees.[97] The chef had a staff of six: two English cooks and six Vietnamese. One volunteer, Daphne Byrne, felt they were fed "royally," and that the meals in the officers' mess surpassed those in good hotels; the "curries, with all the coconut and other trimmings, were superb," and holiday meals were outstanding.[98] In 1980, the camp hosted a dinner to honor local volunteers, serving braised chicken in oyster sauce, pork spareribs with pimento and black beans, sweet and sour pork, pickled salad, and fried rice.[99] At one point, the chef brought the Vietnamese Committee a selection of vegetables so that they could point out which ones they liked and disliked: a "very useful exercise."

But not everyone was so impressed by Thorney Island's diverse menus. One Thorney Island worker thought that the British staff "smelled terrible" to the refu-gees "because we are milk drinkers and to us the whole place reeked of Chinese food." When the residents' committee protested that the chef "reused" uneaten food, he replied that this was common practice in England; they were not in the tropics, and the food was still fresh.[100] Even efforts to be culturally sensitive could go awry. Unlike the Ugandan Asians, the refugees from Vietnam were informed that they would have duck at Christmas, but no other special food given that a celebration would likely be more appreciated at Tet or Chinese New Year: a deci-sion that overlooked Thorney Island's Christian residents.[101] Although cooking in rooms was forbidden at Thorney Island, many residents made their own appliances by using an electric ring from a stove or old hot pot on top of a tin can, then plug-ging in an exposed wire. These illicit devices horrified the staff, but families would simply make new devices if the old ones were confiscated.[102]

Many of the Vietnamese Sub-Committee's meetings at Thorney Island pertained to food, including a long debate about how to cook rice properly. Major B.J. Arrowsmith, the camp director, responded to food protests by griping that the residents were not performing their cleaning tasks. The staff was providing nourishing food, and "we want the hand of friendship back...if all we ask for is cleaning to be done, this should be done—if people refuse to do the cleaning, then staff won-der why we should work so hard." Arrowsmith also complained that the refugees at Thorney Island were not eating the crusts on their bread, even though "bread was expensive and crusts were perfectly good to eat and that it was extremely wasteful" to leave the crusts. He admonished, "they would find it very expensive to waste food in this manner when they were resettled, and therefore should be encouraged to eat the crusts."[103]

Such outbursts tell us much about how food mediated relationships between refugees and the state. Quite apart from the remarkable level of micromanagement they reveal—where even a crust of bread could not be refused—these debates reflect how food could both uphold refugee identity and establish lines of protest. Not only specific foodstuffs, but also different styles of cooking and eating could signal the refugee's interest in assimilation to British norms or a rejection of them.

There was a wide spectrum of interactions that took place around food in camps, from the cultivation of ethnic foods to the hunger strike. One thinks of the gulf of experience between Edwin, the Welsh boy who was entranced by his first taste of chili pepper on a visit to Tonfanau Camp, and the struggles of Mahmood Mamdani at Kensington Barracks, who asked for milk and was told that needy Britons survived on less. Citizens and refugees both experienced feeding in camps as an exchange across cultures, but unevenly so.

As this chapter suggests, refugee camps played a vital role in transformations of identity—not only for refugees, but also for those who worked in and lived near the camps. Chapter 3 explores these transformations of selves in greater detail, focusing on how the distinctive built environment and daily routines of the camps contributed to the remaking of class, ethnic, and religious identities within the camp. The specific modes of housing and feeding in British camps brought citizens and refugees into closer contact, and changed how they thought about themselves.

3

In Need

Within the camp, identities of class, religion, and ethnicity took new shape, and not always in expected directions. This chapter explores how the camps constructed different kinds of unity and disunity for refugees and Britons alike. What kind of person did camps in Britain seek to create? What kinds of interactions took place within them? In camps, refugees and Britons learned to see themselves—and the possibilities for remaking themselves—in new ways.[1]

Refugee care in Britain was structured around analogies and comparisons. Who were refugees like and unlike? Were they displaced wanderers, or future British citizens? Did they demand their own regimes of aid? Or were they fundamentally like needy Britons (the elderly, the homeless, the poor)? Was neediness culturally specific? Did displacement generate the same problems as poverty? In theory, the benefits of social democracy were universal: need was need. In practice, as the chaos of war had made many Britons homeless, the state debated how different kinds of mobility affected vulnerable individuals. As Britons transformed the ways they thought about the needy, camps became focal points of experimentation.

Immigration history abounds with stories and images of reversals of fortune, and the frustrations of downward mobility suffered through all kinds of diasporas—degrees not recognized, work experiences devalued, skills ignored due to prejudice and protectionism. This story is different. The British state played a complex role in crafting new identities in refugee camps, not as an inevitable byproduct of the realities of displacement, but as a deliberate staging of mobility (both upwards and downwards) for different groups.

Camps functioned as dynamic experiments with identity, producing encounters that would have been unthinkable elsewhere.[2] The refugee camp was not just a device of containment and enclosure. Rather, it grew into a locus of creative subversion and transformation.[3] It became a site for the self-knowledge of the refugee.[4] Refugee camps did not always foster cultural collapse, nor did they lead solely to economic stagnation and loss. Rather, they generated new forms of activity and solidarity, as well as division.[5]

SORTING AND MIXING: THE POLITICS OF ETHNICITY IN CAMP LIFE

From their inception, refugee camps in Britain operated as machines of ethnic mixing and sorting. This process began when refugees arrived in camp, and never really came to an end. Life in camp brought out the tensions between ethnic segregation—which was often the aim of camp authorities—and the cross-cultural interactions that took place in practice. This section explores the camp's competing drives toward sameness and difference, and its two (seemingly contradictory) impulses of sorting and mixing its populations.

During the First World War, social scientists perceived camps as sites for large-scale research projects about ethnicity. Camps could reinforce ethnicity through their everyday routines, and provide a place to study the enemy. Internees and prisoners of war were often separated (sometimes against their will) into what camp authorities recognized as ethnic or national groups.[6] In Britain, some camps were dedicated to the preservation of ethnic and religious identity, whereas others promoted assimilation. These differences depended on whether the state imagined refugees as future citizens, and how it understood the "ethnic purity" of specific refugees. But individual camps often also thwarted or countered the government's policies.

The "Belgian" camp at Earl's Court was not for Belgians alone. Around 90 percent of the residents were Belgians, but the other 10 percent were the "flotsam and jetsam" of the refugee world—Armenians, Danes, Moroccans, and "swarthy gypsies of the genuine nomadic type." The camp leader, G.A. Powell, described a party that was "dumped" on the camp one Sunday at 2 a.m.—allegedly "British subjects," Powell complained, they turned out to be "coloured men of various hues," who were sheltered at Earl's Court, but slept apart from the other residents.[7] The strange rococo buildings sheltered

almost every coloured people, swarthy even to blackness, pale to pink…Coloured men born under the British flag, and Poles coming to join the French Polish Legion were, perhaps, the most differing types, but the lint-haired, fresh-complexioned Belgian has predominated.[8]

Others who shared space with the Belgian refugees at Earl's Court included escaped prisoners from Germany, refugees from Russia, French soldiers and civilians, and Serbians. As one camp official said, "practically every Italian soldier from Germany or Russia and every destitute Italian civilian" had stayed in Earl's Court during these years.[9]

Even when camp populations appeared to be more homogeneous—for example, at Kitchener Camp—camp life both promoted and complicated ethnic and religious identities. At Kitchener, many refugees experienced their Jewishness in new ways. The *Kitchener Camp Review* quoted one refugee as saying that Kitchener would be a "permanent document" in Jewish history, a "haven for the oppressed."[10] The director, Phineas May, gave a rousing speech about how the camp embodied "the unconquerable spirit of Our People in the face of persecution…Yes! It is this unbeatable spirit which has created at Richborough, not merely a camp for refugees, but a happy home." The camp had "become a small town," thanks to the energetic residents who "constructed an entire new community almost from nothing."[11] Boys from Dovercourt visited and formed close friendships with the

Kitchener men, recreating an intergenerational Jewish network that had been fractured by war.[12]

A doctor at Kitchener wrote in "Our Motley Community" that this was the first
time he had lived in "purely Jewish" surroundings. But his friend did not feel that
Kitchener was solely a Jewish camp:

> Do not misunderstand me: we are all Jews, but in this camp we see that that is just one
> part of our individual being. We form a beautiful mixture of human beings, everyone
> of us different from the other, everyone of us a creation happening but once, worth
> studying, preserving, cultivating. There is so much happy individuality in all of us that
> the type of standard "comic journal Jew" does not show up at all.

There were many different modes of being Jewish at Kitchener. The camp visibly
supported Jewish rituals—the camp's synagogue was consecrated in June 1939—
but without linking Jewishness to specific traits.[13] Here, it was possible for Jews
to be what they were no longer allowed to be in Germany: German Jews. May
proclaimed that Kitchener Camp could reshape the image of the Jew, proving to
the world that the Jew was a worker rather than a money-grabber.[14] The *Review*
published a stirring (and strongly masculinist) poem about the Kitchener men's
physical labors:

> Campmen, take your tools and try
> Making tremble earth and sky
> At the power of your blow,
> Let all round the people know
> That no might will ever kill
> Our courage, our will
> Huts will rise from stony ground,
> Our people's lifeboats, bound
> For a better shore of peace;
> When some day the Flood will cease,
> Firmly will their basis stand
> God will bless this hold land.
> Lo, good men are everywhere,
> Fellow-travelers, your fare
> Is your fellow-feeling. Hark!
> Brother-voices in the dark,
> Brother-hands to you will cling,
> Campmen, take your tools and sing![15]

At Kitchener, religious practice was always subordinated to the need for physical
labor. As the director said, the camp's motto should be "We Sacrifice All to Sacrifice
None."[16] On Passover, residents were reminded that they were building a home for
"our brethren who will come sooner or later, out from the Egypt of our days": that
is, the concentration camps of Europe.[17] As Orthodox Jews arrived, May exhorted
them to look upon any work they performed on the Sabbath as a *mitzvah* to save
more Jewish lives. After his appeal, May claimed, "even the most ultra-orthodox
was working in their dungarees."[18] Expressions of Jewish faith at Kitchener had an

assimilationist bent. For Shavuot (which the *Review* likened to the Christian Pentecost), the camp residents decorated the synagogue with hawthorn and geraniums, and gathered "in glorious sunshine" to sing English folk songs.[19]

Building English identity was also part of life at Kitchener Camp, even though the men were scheduled to emigrate elsewhere. In the April 1939 issue of the *Kitchener Camp Review*, an article titled "Get to Know the English Mentality!" included helpful tips such as "do not speak loudly, be polite, do not dress conspicuously, smile and be thankful—BE ENGLISH!" One day a week was set aside when speaking German was "strictly *verboten*." Those who spoke only English received a Union Jack pin.[20] By September of 1939, all men who spoke English were invited to wear special badges, and the *Review* warned that it was "better to be silent in English than to speak German."[21] After the war broke out in October, no German newspapers were allowed at Kitchener.

Refugees at Kitchener narrated their experiences through English plays or songs. May instructed the refugees about "the meaning of 'God Save the King' and that we must stand to attention when we sing it and remove our hats. They sang it and I have never heard it with much more feeling."[22] In an adaptation of the popular English tune "The Lambeth Walk," the refugees sang together, "Any time you're Richboro' way, / Any evening, any day, You'll find us all / Working the English way." The song offered a cheerful vision of "bright and breezy" life at Kitchener, and concluded happily: "Every man and every boy / Helps to make the Camp a joy / You'll find us all / Working the English way, OI!" At a camp musical, the men performed a song of their own composition, which May mocked as sentimental "sob stuff": "Under England's flag for a while / Working happy we are all free men, / In our freedom now we smile."[23] As men left the camp for new homes in Canada or Australia, their fellow residents escorted them to the train station, singing, "It's a Long, Long Way to Tipperary."

Not everyone took such a rosy view of Kitchener Camp's vision of Anglo-Jewish community. Zionists clashed with other political groups within the camp.[24] Furthermore, Fred Dunston, a Viennese Jew, was distressed to hear so many German accents at Kitchener. He found the Germans in camp too rough, too much like the Nazis he had left behind.[25] The Austrian writer Alfred Perles described the atmosphere at Kitchener as "bizarre...made up, I felt, of a series of contradictory emotional currents: of psychological stress and psychological relief; of mental strain and mental exuberance; of physical well-being and the dread of physical suffering." As Perles wrote, most men at Kitchener had not recovered from the horrors of the concentration camps they had recently escaped: "accustomed to think of their lives in terms of hell on earth, the heaven of the Southeast coast of England was too bright to be true. There had been no transition from one form of existence to the other."[26]

In May 1940, as mass internment began, the army took control of Kitchener Camp. Seven tribunals examined 3,500 Kitchener refugees in seven weeks. More than half of Kitchener's residents volunteered to join the Pioneer Corps, the non-combatant unit of the army for aliens. But after Dunkirk, Kitchener men who had not yet joined the Pioneer Corps were interned in camps on the Isle of Man.[27] With little warning, refugees had been transformed into internees. Edgar Sarton recalled the "terrible state" these men were in: "They were completely passive, utterly depressed. I shall never forget the picture of helplessness."[28] The social policy analyst François Lafitte claimed that at least four-fifths of the "enemy aliens" facing internment were actually Jewish refugees.[29]

The machinery for sorting out refugees and other internees was primitive. Prisoners of war, Nazi sympathizers, and anti-Nazis were all thrown together. In some internment camps, "scores of arrogant, jubilant, swaggering Nazis" were housed with "a handful of sorrow-stricken downhearted homeless Jews."[30] At Huyton Camp in Liverpool, George W. Brandt recalled, "What a mixed bunch of people we were behind the barbed wire!" The Huyton internees included:

> Recent and not so recent Jewish refugees from Nazism, affluent or down-and-out, orthodox or atheist, anti-Fascists involved in the anti-Hitler struggle, including some International Brigadiers; and random stragglers in this country's population shifts—Czechs, Dutchmen, stateless persons; flotsam like that pathetic group of little old German barbers who had been working in England for decades but never bothered to get themselves naturalized.[31]

Indeed, Jewish internees in British camps shared not only living space, but also sometimes even closer quarters with avowed Nazis. Lord Farringdon complained in the House of Lords about a terrified 16-year-old Jewish girl on the Isle of Man who was compelled to share her bed with a "bullying Nazi maiden."

Such "unholy fellowships" were presumably rare.[32] Still, Eugen Spier, a Jewish activist, was horrified to wake up one morning while interned at Olympia "surrounded" by Nazis. When Home Secretary Herbert Morrison was asked whether Nazis were bullying Jewish refugees in British camps, he replied that he tried to keep these populations separate, but "I hope the anti-Nazis will be strong enough not to be intimidated and not conduct themselves as if they were afraid of the Nazis."[33] The Duke of Devonshire described the mixing of Nazi and Jewish populations at Port Erin and Port St. Mary as impossible to prevent, as the internees were free to move about the villages and could only be segregated if they were penned into compounds.[34]

Jewish internees were sometimes physically attacked in these camps, and were devastated when British guards did little to intervene.[35] At Kempton Park Racecourse, the refugee Walter Igersheimer was distraught to overhear the Grenadier Guards complaining about the internees, "What a sissy, blabbering lot, eh? Must be all Jews."[36] Jewish internees also feared being mistaken for Nazis. One Jewish internee encouraged his peers to sing "'We are refugees, thanks for your hospitality,' to the tune of 'God Save the King,' just in order to inform the onlookers that we had nothing to do with Hitlerism."[37] On the Isle of Man, Fred Uhlman and other Jews carefully doffed their hats at every war memorial, showing their allegiance to Britain's dead.[38]

The Isle of Man's internment camps jumbled together not only Germans, Poles, and Austrians, but also Jews from Galicia. Rudolph Munster described the Galicians as "totally different from all the others...even Central European Jews felt strange when they were with the Galicians." One Jewish internee said of a Galician,

"I shan't sleep in a bed with that dirty Jew!"[39] In one ghastly blunder, twins who grew up in Scotland and had no idea until they found their birth certificate that they had in fact been born in Germany were interned at Hutchinson and were "completely lost."[40] Many internees had spent their lives in England, and spoke no German. Others who were born in Germany refused to speak German in camp. Most of Hutchinson's classes were conducted in German, but the camp newspaper was written in English. Some internees believed that speaking English in camp— no matter how imperfectly—would strengthen their claim for release, though Hellmuth Weissenborn warned his housemates that their "pidgin English" would ruin them for proper English forever.[41] Internees developed their own camp language of "Emigranto," a mixture of German and English words.[42]

Child refugees perhaps felt the complexity of Jewish identity in camp life even more deeply than adults. At Dovercourt, the aim was for the children to be anglicized as quickly as possible. Every child was greeted with a letter from Chief Rabbi Hertz, instructing them to show gratitude to their English sponsors, and not to congregate together or talk loudly in public places.[43] One poem, "The Children's Exodus," explored the spiritual and personal limbo in which the children of Dovercourt existed:

> At Dovercourt the winter sea
> Was like God's mercy vast and wild
> A fever to a land-locked child
> It seemed fire and cloud to me
> The world's blood and my blood were cold
> The exiled Jew in me was old
> And thoughts of my death appalled me less
> Than knowledge of my loneliness
> People in Dovercourt were gay
> As if they thought we could forget our homes in alien play
> As if we were not German Jews
> But mealtimes were a market-place
> When sudden visitors could choose
> Although we were not orphaned yet
> A son or daughter by their face
> My childhood smoulders in the name
> Of the town which was my home
> All we were became no more
> Than answers on each questionnaire
> At Dovercourt we were taught that our share of the Jewish fate
> Had not been left behind but was
> The refugee life facing us.[44]

For this writer, the camp did not simply mark the start of a new life as a British Jew. Rather, the tragic history of German Jews would continue to unfold at Dovercourt. The German past was to be perpetually present.

At Dovercourt, Hanukkah candlesticks appeared on the tables in December, but there were also Christmas trees, and a grand party on Christmas Eve (Christmas Day was considered too offensive to religious Jews).[45] The *Manchester Guardian* estimated that only half the children at Dovercourt were Jewish; the others were "non-Aryan" Catholics and Protestants.[46] When Lore Segal, an Austrian Jew, wrote to her parents that she was going to leave Dovercourt to live with a "lovely Orthodox family" in Liverpool, she had to ask them to tell her what "Orthodox" meant.[47] Segal recalled being taught to dance the *hora* for the first time at Dovercourt. Segal was instructed to perform this dance for English women who were selecting children for foster care, but she refused. After this failed experiment, the children also learned songs in English: "Ten Green Bottles," "Boomps-a-Daisy," and, of course, "Rule Britannia." Ultimately, the *hora* music caught on, and the children whistled it while they dressed in the morning.

Camps for Jewish children aimed to preserve (or in some cases to create) their religious and ethnic identities. Camps for Basque children, on the other hand, were dedicated to safeguarding their ethnic purity. Not everyone was sure that the Basques in Britain were a true "ethnic" population. Yvonne Kapp claimed that most of the children in camp actually spoke Spanish, not Basque; the majority were from Bilbao, and "they are not even pure Basque types."[48] One refugee, Rafael, described himself as "not that Basque . . . I mean they called us the Basque Children evacuated to England but half of them or more weren't really Basque."[49] Despite these objections, most refugee workers insisted on the notion of Basque ethnic purity. The secretary of the Save the Children Fund, Mr. Golden, initially opposed the Basque children's rescue from Spain, saying that he would "sooner see them die in their own land than rot slowly in exile where they deteriorate physically, morally and mentally."[50] Death was preferable to assimilation.

Because the Basques were supposed to be repatriated to Spain at the earliest possible moment, integration was never desirable. Camp workers at North Stoneham used any mechanism by which the Basques might strengthen their feeling as a group.[51] The Home Secretary would only allow Basque children to be boarded out if they took classes and at least one meal daily with their "fellow nationals."[52] For Jews, he argued, "there was a bond between them and co-religionists in this country" that allowed them to feel part of English life. For the Basque children, no such bond existed—they had no "natural" ethnic allies in Britain, and could only look toward home.[53] Camps must not serve as a tool of anglicization. Herminio, a Basque child refugee, was asked if he was taught to speak English at North Stoneham; he replied with amusement, "Oh my goodness, no . . . you're all the time seeking organization of a civilized sort of way of life."[54] The chaos of the camp— the absence of language instruction, for example—might be seen not just as a failure of planning, but also as a deliberate strategy of anti-assimilation.

Such memories reflect a larger debate about the role of the camp in promoting or suppressing group identity.[55] Refugee workers in Polish camps were deeply concerned about how camps might transform ethnic allegiances. As with the Jews and the Basques, not everyone in the Polish camps was actually Polish. Celina Kalaba Wojciechowska claimed that many of the "Poles" at Fairford were in fact Ukrainians who had served in the Polish Army. Indeed, one whole section of Fairford was called "Little Ukraine."[56] She noted that "we didn't differentiate between Ukrainians and Poles," since they had all been together in the army.[57] Camp authorities, too, invested little in these distinctions, and classified the diverse camp populations as Polish. "Poles" were defined by their wartime service, and not by ethnicity.

There were other lines of fracture as well. At Doddington, there was open conflict about the loyalty of different groups within the camp. Specifically, those who had lived in German territory were accused of being Nazi collaborators. The tensions were so severe that a Board inspector came to investigate in 1947. He found "one or two" former SS men camouflaging themselves among the Poles.[58] At Foxley, too, Henry Pavlovich remembered hearing his father agonize about his encounters in camp with men he recognized as members of the Waffen SS Galicia Division. The men had fought on the Nazi side during the war and were now masquerading as refugees in Britain.[59]

Despite these divisions, there were sources of great pride and unity in Polish camps. Catholic ceremonies forged a powerful tie among camp residents. Zosia Hartman recalled hearing the church bell peal throughout Northwick to call worshippers to Sunday Mass.[60] Christenings, first communions, and funerals were all celebrated at the camp. Britons gathered to watch the Corpus Christi processions and see the shrines that the Poles had built. Residents who lived along the walkway for the procession decorated their barracks with green branches, ribbons, and flowers. Though Hartman described each Polish camp as "a world in itself," knowing little of each other's existence, photographs tell a different, more universal story, with standardized markers of faith.

Fig. 3.1. First communion at Foxley. Photograph by Zbigniew Pawlowicz, by kind permission of his son, Henry Pavlovich (http://foxley.org).

Fig. 3.2. Corpus Christi procession at Northwick Park. Photo from http://www.polishresettlementcampsintheuk.co.uk, by kind permission of Zosia Biegus.

Interestingly, Polish Catholics in camps were exempt from the jurisdiction of British bishops. This was a unique arrangement in the history of the Catholic Church, which heightened the group consciousness of Poles in British camps.[61] Polish priests may have preferred to remain in camps rather than moving to private accommodation, as being counted as the "parish priest" of a camp gave them more power and autonomy than aiding an English priest in the wider community.[62] Still, Catholic practice in camp was not always easy. At the Polish hostel in Wheaton Aston, the residents paid to redecorate the chapel in order to create "a normal and unpretending village church." After learning that the chapel was not considered part of the estate, and could be destroyed, they described their "restlessness and agitation" about the "sacrilegious" destruction of a consecrated space:

> Mothers and fathers, sisters and brothers of Polish airmen killed over these Isles, would never understand the reason which—for the sake of a few acres of agricultural land— asks to level with the ground their pride, their beloved church and their shrine...Our people are truly attached to their religion and places of worship, and most certainly a demolition of their church will be considered by them as an act of religious persecution. The recent brutal and hostile actions of the communist government in Poland, directed against churches and clergy make no doubt our people [are] very sensitive on that point.[63]

The protection of the chapel would be a rightful reward for their wartime sacrifices, an acknowledgment of the Poles as zealous Cold Warriors. But the council replied that the Poles would have to pay £700 per year to save the chapel themselves.[64]

Beyond the realm of Catholicism, camps promoted communal identities in other ways. At Northwick, Zosia Hartman attended classes on Polish history and culture: "The camp to us, was like living in a village where every one knew every one. We were taught to be polite to others and of course if we misbehaved our parents soon knew about it."[65] Residents of different camps banded together for political events. The Polish military leader and politician General Anders visited Polish camps, arriving at Northwick in 1952. Poles from Springhill Lodges, Long Marston, and Daglingworth turned out to greet him in a crowd of around 3,000.[66] Football matches and cultural events also brought the Polish camps together.[67] Indeed, Springhill and Northwick were only 3 miles apart, and it was possible to walk from one camp to another in an hour; the residents of the two camps shared a school and attended each other's dances.[68]

The relative quietude of life in the British camp was juxtaposed with memories of wartime trauma. As Urszula Szulakowska recalled, "the Poles were all free now, sort-of, physically if not psychically, and safe in the idiosyncratic but peaceful haven" of Melton Mowbray. Still, although she had not lived through the horrors of war herself, Szulakowska experienced nightmares in camp, "during which I would walk around in a half-waking condition, a sort of trance, filled with terror, gibbering that 'they' were coming to get me." Despite her limited understanding of the war,

Fig. 3.3. A jazz band at Foxley. Photograph by Zbigniew Pawlowicz, by kind permission of his son, Henry Pavlovich (http://foxley.org).

Fig. 3.4. Rysiek Sozański, Jurek Jałowiecki, Tadek Strach, Jurek Zdanko, and Tadek Gostomski in front of the "Ewidencija," the center of Northwick Park, 1966. Photograph from http://www.polishresettlementcampsintheuk.co.uk, by kind permission of Zosia Biegus.

Szulakowska knew "that I was Polish and different, but not really sure how I had got to be this way."[69]

For the Jews, the Basques, and the Poles, camps promised both to promote identities of ethnicity and religion and to thwart them. For other groups—most especially the Anglo-Egyptians and the Ugandan Asians—it was class identities that were most clearly transformed (and also threatened) by the experience of encampment. Much more so than with other refugee groups, when it came to the perceived victims of the end of empire, the state strove to craft a new bourgeoisie—or to uphold those seen as former colonial elites—with varying degrees of success.

CLASS IN THE CAMPS: MYTHS OF THE MIDDLE-CLASS REFUGEE

What class were refugees expected to be? In the United States, immigration authorities assumed that refugees would become part of the working poor. Refugee camps in Britain took a different approach to how refugees might be "classed." At times, refugees were depicted as model minorities, who were superior to other migrants (especially those of color).[70] During other moments, government officials assumed refugees would "naturally" align with migrants from their own ethnic background, and contribute to the creation of new ghettoes and an urban underclass.

Overwhelmingly, British authorities "typed" refugees by their presumed class—trafficking in images of the Jewish or Hungarian intellectual, the Polish or Vietnamese peasant, the Anglo-Egyptian merchant, the skilled Hungarian laborer, or the bourgeois Ugandan Asian shopkeeper. Yet refugee camps also held the power to transform class positions, operating not only as sites of class formation, but also as didactic environments of correction and uplift. The British state's fantasies about refugees and class clashed with the realities of diverse refugee populations. But these fantasies could be hugely powerful in creating new socioeconomic realities. By providing aid to "restore" some (but not all) refugees to the class positions Britons imagined they had held in their previous lives, the camps became a crucial site for shaping refugees' futures.

As the impoverished Briton emerged more clearly in the imagination of the welfare state, the refugee was his constant companion and critic. Aid workers struggled to determine whether refugees were like or unlike other groups—such as the poor or the homeless—who needed the state's help. Some Britons worried that refugees would compete with other needy populations for scarce resources. When the Jewish girls of Dovercourt picked berries on Rushall Common, the camp received a hostile letter from local residents: "Will you please ask the girls not to eat the raspberries, as they are meant for the English poor."[71]

There was much at stake in these analogies. When the Home Office claimed in the 1960s that the needs of refugees were "obviously" very similar to those of other homeless people, it was trying to remove itself from the task of refugee care.[72] If refugees were like the poor or homeless, then they were the local authority's problem. Alternatively, if refugees were more like immigrants, then the Home Office—which oversaw immigration control—was very much involved. Colin Hodgetts, who worked with homeless Britons before he ran the Save the Children centers for refugees from Vietnam, saw refugees and the homeless as entirely unrelated groups. For him, the homeless were permanently afflicted, mostly psychiatric cases, who could be treated only on an individual basis. The plight of refugees was temporary, and they could be aided as a group.[73] In contrast, Sue Millman, who worked with Vietnamese refugees at Sopley and Hothfield, saw her work with refugees as "absolutely transferable" to the work with the homeless she did later on. Indeed, she often resettled homeless Britons on the same housing estates where she had placed Vietnamese families a few years earlier.[74]

For many Britons, the term "refugee" was linked to economic deprivation. In order to be a refugee, one must be poor. But during the Belgian crisis, Britons encountered a strange phenomenon: middle-class people who had been deprived of their property by war. In this sense, it was not only the habitually poor who were destitute.[75] Aid workers were struck by the socioeconomic diversity of the Belgians: "what never-to-be-forgotten sights were these first arrivals in their cosmopolitan crowds and admixture of classes! Officials and clerks, peasants in their blue overalls and sabots direct from Flemish fields, workmen in their working garb or Sunday best." The refugees carried mattresses, sewing machines, coffee grinders, and parrots; one refugee from a troupe of acrobats brought the cannon out of which he shot his wife.[76] Some Belgians were so smartly dressed, *The Times* suggested, that they could hardly be thought of as "refugees" at all.[77]

In private homes, Belgian refugees were segregated—Fleming from Walloon, Jew from Gentile, and working class from the "better sort."[78] Aristocratic Belgians lived separately in Harrington House, a famous London mansion that overlooked Kensington Gardens, or in other mansions gifted by wealthy Britons.[79] English hosts were warned that they must respect Belgian social prejudices, and not mix the classes together. One schoolteacher complained piteously when she was housed with maids and forced to share their table.[80] Wealthier refugees could simply set themselves up with furnished houses, as many did in Hampstead. They refused to register as refugees, and may never have thought of themselves as such. Many middle-class refugees were sent to furnished flats in model dwellings in Battersea and Brixton so that they could "maintain even in exile the decencies and privacy of home life."[81] Unlike the Ugandan Asians, whose bourgeois traits would later be celebrated, the Belgian middle class was criticized as having "the greatest nostalgia for its lost possessions" and "the greatest difficulty in adapting itself to ways of life not its own."[82]

When the Belgian refugees arrived, the Home Office was in charge of aliens; the Local Government Board was in charge of the destitute. The two departments decided that the Local Government Board would take over refugee care.[83] In practice, this meant that the Belgians would be likened to the poor more readily than to other aliens, as Belgian refugees occupied Poor Law institutions and Salvation Army shelters. Edmonton, for example, was being converted from a workhouse to an asylum when it became a "haven" for refugees, but it was still widely detested in this new guise as a dumping ground for "undesirables."[84] Some Belgian refugees were housed in Poor Law accommodation in London.[85] The use of workhouses for refugee aid was controversial, because it often involved moving the poor to another locality.[86]

At the ports, aid workers gave Belgian refugees either a pink card (to denote middle-class status) or a blue card (working-class). Overwhelmed volunteers often guessed the class of Belgians based on their appearance. In early days, fishermen were sent inland to the heart of England, miners were sent far from England's mining districts, and mechanics were placed in agricultural counties in the south.[87] *The Times* helpfully pointed out that Belgian peasants could be distinguished from their urban working-class compatriots by their wooden shoes, looking like they had stepped out of Millet's *The Sower*.[88] Those with pink cards were offered hotel recommendations, whereas those with blue cards were guided to Earl's Court and Alexandra Palace.[89]

By 1915, Earl's Court had become more uniformly working class. Camp workshops produced army hutments, shell cases, and army clothing. As the residents said, at Earl's Court, "*on travaille* (one works)."[90] Refugees were paid 8–10 shillings per week; as their food and board was free, the payment was "more in the nature of a gift than a wage."[91] *The Times* called Earl's Court a "model community"—a quasi-utopia of eager, industrious workers and happy, healthy families that offered lessons for Britain's future.[92] Mothers at Earl's Court were not expected to do any work beyond caring for their children—a pilot program, perhaps, for mother's pensions for all Britons. The refugee camp could teach Britons how to recover from war and undertake the project of reconstruction, but also how to prepare for the welfare state to come. In this sense, the lessons of the refugee camp were universal. All Britons would eventually live in the world of Earl's Court.

During the First World War, internment camps—like refugee camps—jumbled classes together. When a detective called on Paul Cohen-Portheim to (very politely) tell him that he would be interned, Cohen-Portheim had "not the slightest idea" of what this meant. The officer amiably told him to pack for a holiday, which led to Cohen-Portheim departing for the Isle of Man with his white flannels, bathing things, and evening dress.[93] At Knockaloe, Cohen-Portheim was roundly mocked for wearing those aristocratic white flannels. Many internees considered Knockaloe "distasteful," and urged Cohen-Portheim to move to the "gentlemen's camp" at Wakefield. But Cohen-Portheim embraced Knockaloe as a "curious and interesting place" where he observed an exciting mix of "a great many types I should never have come in contact with under normal conditions." When the camp authorities began allowing wealthier men to draw £1 per week from the camp bank, Cohen-Portheim lamented the false creation of social inequality in this "communist" society.[94] Moving to Lofthouse Park, where "the canteen seemed like Selfridge's," Cohen-Portheim found his new camp colorless and drab. Unlike the restlessly anarchic seething of Knockaloe, Lofthouse Park seemed like a lower-middle-class suburb.

During the Second World War, the mixing of classes continued to be one of the most striking aspects of internment. The German art historian Klaus Ernst Hinrichsen described his experience at Hutchinson as "immensely stimulating," noting that you can "learn an awful lot about yourself" in camp. Some internees were shocked to be sharing their tables—and sometimes their beds—with laborers they would not have met in ordinary life, and had to be persuaded that they "had to mix." Some of the "industrialists" were "arrogant and snobby," and hired other internees to clean their rooms and their shoes. There were also class divisions between internees and their British guards; the internees wished to form a chamber orchestra while the camp commandment wanted a showier, less refined brass band.[95] Leo Kahn complained that although the internees came from different class backgrounds, their anxiety united them in a "fake middle-class respectability" that he strongly disliked.[96]

Like the internment camps, Kitchener Camp was intended to be largely self-governing, and was run communally; the wages of the Jewish refugees who were engaged as agricultural laborers on nearby farms were pooled in a central camp fund.[97] Each refugee received a daily ration of chocolate and cigarettes, and 6d weekly in pocket money. When a small canteen opened in 1939, it was run cooperatively so that those who could afford it contributed to the purchase of chocolate and cigarettes for those who could not.[98] Many middle-class men received agricultural training at Kitchener, which had nearly 10 acres of farmable land. In this sense, Kitchener was designed to eradicate the bourgeois identity its residents held before the camp, and prepare the men for whatever life lay ahead.

During the Second World War, many camp administrators sought to recapture the class position that refugees "naturally" held in their countries of origin. For displaced Poles, such zeal focused on the trope of the Polish peasant. The Stover warden insisted, "the majority of our residents are from peasant stock who are content to be left alone to pursue their gardening, attend church, and celebrate festive occasions."[99] Accordingly, he argued, these residents did not need special grants for warmer clothing. Such claims suggest how the image of the refugee (in this case, as a happy and satisfied peasant) shaped the structures of aid. Of course, not all Poles in British camps were peasants. And the camps played a role in bringing the different classes into contact. At Kelvedon, the residents' committee complained about a particular family "of the intelligentsia" occupying a hut illegally. Regarding the presence of intelligentsia in the camp, the manager replied that, "it is my wish not to have the whole of this class concentrated on site 7, as has been the tendency in the past, but to have them spread throughout the hostel."[100]

Camp leaders debated what constituted a proper economic life for refugees. The Poles had been tossed about for years, and had "lost the will to work inherent in any human being in normal conditions." Now, they must regain their psychic balance through paid labor. The National Assistance Board developed a complex calculus of charges that had little to do with economic imperatives. Rather, these calculations depended on creating economic equality between refugees and Britons. The Labour politician James Chuter Ede acknowledged that the scale of relief for Poles was higher than for British subjects, because the Poles "came as refugees and would not be able to maintain themselves like a person who has some furniture and some household goods already in this country."[101] While "displaced persons of British origin" were charged for housing, it was harder for Poles to find jobs, and thus they needed more generous payments.[102] Refugees, it seemed, could not simply be treated like poor Britons.

Here, we can see how the figure of the refugee offered a test case of whether one could actually survive and thrive on welfare. Even more than with the Poles, the aid regime for Anglo-Egyptians was governed by British expectations about class. And who, exactly, were the Anglo-Egyptians?[103] What, if anything, was "Anglo" about them? Determining the ethnic and class composition of Anglo-Egyptians was an important element of British refugee work.

The term "Anglo-Egyptians" actually encompassed diverse subgroups, including many prominent Jews.[104] In a 1956 article titled "British—But Many Strange to Britain," the *Manchester Guardian* reported on the "bewildered" but genteel populations that composed the "Anglo-Egyptians": a retired English engineer who could not take his assets out of Egypt, a young Maltese accountant, and half a dozen students from the Gold Coast, who had been attending Cairo University at the Egyptian government's invitation before they were expelled. Others included Mrs. E. Gentles, a 66-year-old woman, who was German by birth, employed in Egypt as a secretary. She married a Scotsman who was in the Ministry of Education in Egypt; she, too, now counted as an Anglo-Egyptian.[105] Their Britishness was both a source of their pride and the reason for their plight. Broadly speaking, all were victims of Egyptian retaliation against British military measures. But not all were entitled to the same measures of British aid.

Aid for Anglo-Egyptians was constructed not only in terms of economic need, but also through the idea of "restoring" them to their former position. The Prime Minister was applauded when he called the expulsion an illegal act for which the Anglo-Egyptians must be "compensated." But what did this mean? Could refugees be restored to the same exalted way of life they had enjoyed in Egypt? The idea of

Fig. 3.5. Anglo-Egyptians in Britain were rarely photographed. This unusual picture shows Miss Anna Crooks, who was a model in Cairo, lining up at the Anglo-Egyptian Aid Society in Regent's Park to seek work as a dancer or a model. Keystone Pictures USA/Alamy Stock Photo.

"compensation" appeared nowhere else in British refugee work. Refugee workers tried to calculate precisely the extent of the Anglo-Egyptians' downward mobility, measuring their loss of social status and dignity as well as financial humiliation.[106]

When the Anglo-Egyptians arrived in Britain, they registered their assets with the Foreign Office. Initially, the Home Office was asked to pay out the claimants in full. The Home Office refused, but in July 1957, as a result of heavy pressure in the House of Lords, the government announced a new £4-million scheme of ex gratia loans against registered assets, plus another £2 million in direct payments from the Anglo-Egyptian Resettlement Board for "relief and rehabilitation." These grants included personal allowances for clothing, housing, and furniture, as well as business grants. Clearly, this was much more than emergency aid. The Anglo-Egyptian Resettlement Board defined "hardship" widely to include wealthier recipients who suffered by being deprived access to their assets.[107] Rather than granting all refugees the same lump sum, the board grappled with each individual's needs.[108]

Interestingly, other cases of refugee aid (the Jews, the Basques, the Poles) were never invoked as useful examples for the Anglo-Egyptians to follow. Instead, the AERB cited the precedent of the resettlement grants that had been offered by the Ministry of Labour to ex-servicemen after the Second World War, as well as payments by the National Assistance Board under the War Damage Acts to compensate Britons who lost land, buildings, or personal property during the Blitz. The Anglo-Egyptians were thus likened to Britons who had suffered the horrors of war, and not to "foreign" refugees.

Despite British stereotypes—that is, of the "typical" refugee as an older, affluent executive—about two-thirds of the Anglo-Egyptians arrived with no tangible assets. Only 2,600 had assets that qualified for the loan scheme.[109] Whereas the Hungarians were described in Parliament as young, single, skilled men who would easily find jobs, those coming from Egypt (especially the Maltese) were seen as much more difficult to employ.[110] Those who worked with Anglo-Egyptians complained that the Hungarians had drawn far more cash and sympathy, which is why Anglo-Egyptian care fell on the Treasury. The Anglo-Egyptians may have been just as "blameless" as the Hungarians, but they were certainly not as popular. Indeed, Anglo-Egyptians were humiliated when Hungarian refugees held a concert to raise money for them.[111] *The Times* pleaded with its readers not to neglect the Anglo-Egyptians:

> Compassion for the victims of Soviet crime in Hungary should not veil us from the plight of another body of wretched refugees for whom we in Britain have a special responsibility: the British subjects whom Colonel Nasser has expelled, virtually penniless. Many, perhaps most of them, have no homes or friends or assets save in Egypt: to have British passports is their only offence, to claim Britain's help their undoubted right.[112]

Maurice Orbach, the MP for Willesden East, described Britons as "ominously quiet" about the Egyptians, prone to forget that "we have our own folk, stateless people, not from Hungary." They must be treated as "people who had come home."[113] Orbach attributed this silence to guilt about the role of British military action.[114] In his view, it was precisely because the expulsion of the Anglo-Egyptians was a direct consequence of British action that the British public ignored them.

Originally, the loan scheme for Anglo-Egyptians was only supposed to affect those who had to leave Egypt as a "direct result" of Suez. But it was not easy to determine who had been "directly" affected by this complex crisis. In 1958, the Home Office stated that the scheme must not "encourage persons who can still lead a tolerable life in Egypt to come to the UK just in order to better themselves."[115] As new arrivals continued to receive ex gratia grants, the definition of who counted as a "refugee" expanded.[116] As the Conservative politician Viscount Hailsham noted, "it is not true that all those who have lost assets are refugees; and it is not true that all those who have lost assets are suffering hardship."[117] Many of those who made claims through the loans scheme were very wealthy; sixteen people in one family filed claims of up to £20 million, and speedily received £80,000. Such cases—in which enormous amounts of public money were spent on a single family—highlighted a crucial distinction between claims based on financial hardship versus those based on the moral right to compensation.

Social scientists argued that the Anglo-Egyptians' recovery from their expulsion depended on their economic renewal. G.M. Wilcox, a psychiatric social worker, studied two middle-aged Anglo-Egyptian ladies "whose protected leisured mode of life in Egypt had ill-prepared them for living amongst a mixed crowd of ill-assorted companions, whose language at times they found shocking, and whose habits were repulsive to them." Both women developed neuroses, keeping to their rooms, solitary and afraid; one wept constantly, and the other became mildly delusional. Wilcox claimed their mental health would improve only when "they can return to a mode of life nearly approximating that of their cultural norm." That is, financial compensation would heal psychological trauma.[118]

Anglo-Egyptians were assisted not only as if they deserved more than other refugees, but also as if they were worthy of higher payments than poor Britons. To the extent that they were like the poor, they were superior to them. The Home Office argued that it would be "unseemly" for Anglo-Egyptians to be dealt with by the National Assistance Board (as the Poles had been), as this would equate British subjects with paupers.[119] As Sir Frank Newsam, the Permanent Under-Secretary of State, put it, "The refugees will not be brought into close contact with the poor law."[120] Some pleaded that Anglo-Egyptians should never fall upon the normal machinery for hardship relief "if they formerly enjoyed a high standard of living."[121]

The Anglo-Egyptian Aid Society argued that evacuees could not survive on national assistance because "they were unaccustomed to life in England which does permit natives to live on those rates."[122] They would be paid on a higher scale "so as to temper the wind and give them a chance to save a little money."[123] National assistance was paid according to need. But the Home Office claimed that the needs of Anglo-Egyptians were greater than those of Britons in financial distress. In 1958, the Cabinet agreed to extend the (very expensive) life of the Resettlement Board because there were still "formerly prosperous people whom it would be both harsh and politically embarrassing to reduce abruptly" to national assistance.[124]

Still, some refugee workers objected to the idea of offering aid based on "former standing." Anglo-Egyptians were not unique in falling on hard times through no fault of their own. Most Britons who required national assistance were also blameless, and had to make "mental adjustments" when they experienced financial crises. Why, then, should it be thought of as "humiliating" for Anglo-Egyptians to turn to national assistance? And why should this form of help be seen as "pathetically inadequate" for them, but not for poor Britons?[125]

Perhaps the most eloquent defense of Anglo-Egyptian affluence was in the House of Lords, which was particularly mindful of the downward mobility of elites. Lord Teviot mourned the "faultless" Anglo-Egyptians who used to buy their clothes from Savile Row, and were now outfitted from "any jumble sale to which they can go."[126] As with the Poles, wartime service justified postwar aid. Lord Killearn praised the British community's role in Egypt during the Second World War. The Anglo-Egyptians had not flinched when they had seen the flashes from Rommel's guns. Now, they were hapless victims of British policy. Lord Colyton spoke passionately about the "needs" of Anglo-Egyptians. They required basic material support to stay alive, but they also needed enough money to "hold up their heads." Lord Jeffreys proposed large capital sums for poorer refugees, and "considerable lump sums" for wealthier individuals.[127]

The truth was that only some Anglo-Egyptians were targeted for aid. The Anglo-Egyptian Aid Society focused on preserving the status of older, affluent Anglo-Egyptians, who would have enjoyed prosperous careers and retirements.[128] One recipient of the loan scheme was Mrs. C.C. Samy, aged 63. Mrs. Samy, British by birth, had married an Egyptian, but had never forfeited her British nationality. Her husband, Ahmed Fahmy, was a senior official in the Egyptian Ministry of Agriculture. He died in 1943, long before the Suez Crisis, and left his wife an estate of over £15,000. In 1945, Mrs. Samy left Egypt for her health, and came to Britain. She lived on the interest from her assets in Egypt, plus a widow's pension of £18 a month from the Egyptian government. Her assets were frozen in 1956, leaving her sole income as the £18 that she now received from the Resettlement Board in lieu of her Egyptian pension. Mrs. Samy moved to an unfurnished room in Hove, borrowing a bed, a chair, and one small table. Mrs. Samy's caseworker described her position as "thoroughly humiliating…one surely cannot expect a woman who has held a high social position in Egypt to grovel in a slum for £4 a week."[129] Mrs. Samy had been living in Britain since 1945; she was not a "refugee" in any traditional sense. But neither could she be considered successfully "settled."

The case rested not only on defining who was a refugee, but figuring out who had been socially impacted by Britain's imperial decline and thus deserved special aid. Poorer subjects of Maltese origin were actually seen as better off in Britain (with its free education and the National Health Service) than if they had remained in Egypt, and they received significantly less assistance.[130] Many Maltese were deeply embittered by the loan scheme. Victor Lagnardo, the Chairman of the Eastwood Hostel Residents' Committee, where most of the residents were Maltese, said he felt the government was "responsible towards the plight which we found ourselves in now," and "should compensate morally as well as materially" all refugees with a lump sum of cash. Regarding national assistance, Lagnardo replied "we would rather like to have our own money lost in Egypt than to live in charity." Finally, the rent at Eastwood was too expensive, "not forgetting that our Hostel is more like a concentration camp than anything else."[131]

Lord Colyton, chair of the Anglo-Egyptian Resettlement Board, responded that he could only deal with the issue of immediate distress.[132] The Board was not empowered, Colyton said, to pay refugees a percentage of the assets they had left behind. But in fact the Board often did exactly that. The distinction between resettlement (aid for the future) and compensation (for past riches) broke down all the time, resting on the Board's assessment of former social standing. The Ministry of Labour argued that "the greatest enemy of the Anglo-Egyptian is himself." The high standard of living in Egypt "tended to distort his sense of his own value, and he finds it difficult to reconcile himself to the standard of living he is likely to attain" in Britain. Yet even as government officials lamented that Anglo-Egyptians expected too much, their own policies preserved the status of former elites, aiding the richer rather than the poorer.[133] An ethnic and racial divide emerged; the Maltese might receive "emergency resettlement" aid, but not "compensation." From the state's perspective, the Maltese had not lost as much as white British subjects, if indeed they had lost anything at all. They did not need to be restored to their former position. In fact, precisely because their former position was low, they should not desire to be returned to it.

Being a "refugee" was bounded not only by geography and historical experience, but also by time. By 1959, British subjects leaving Egypt were no longer viewed as "evacuees" or "refugees." Rather, they were recategorized as distressed British subjects.[134] At this point, the Home Office considered transferring the "residual" cases of Anglo-Egyptians to National Assistance.[135] This handover meant a lower level of aid, since Anglo-Egyptians had been paid at higher rates than poor Britons.[136]

There are many points of comparison—and important contrasts—between the Anglo-Egyptians and the Ugandan Asians. Both groups of refugees were created by the collapse of Britain's imperial power and were perceived as being displaced by British action, although that link was much more explicit for the Anglo-Egyptians.[137] Anglo-Egyptians were portrayed as the helpless victims of a very recent British military intervention; Britain's role in the Ugandan crisis was seen in much deeper historical terms, going back to Britain's export of South Asians to Uganda from India in the eighteenth century. Furthermore, the mechanisms of aid were structurally intertwined, as the Ugandan Resettlement Board (the main agency at work in 1972) was modeled on the Anglo-Egyptian Resettlement Board. The vital difference was that the British state indemnified the property of the Anglo-Egyptians and did not do so for the Ugandan Asians. The choice to compensate Anglo-Egyptians (at least some of them) for what they had lost in Egypt was not to be repeated with other refugees, even those generated by other imperial crises.

Before the Ugandan Asians even arrived in Britain, labor specialists were studying their economic utility. One report from 1967 stated that Asians in Uganda ran the garages, the bakeries, the better quality furniture shops, and the profitable sawmills.[138] In the 1969 BBC Third Programme feature "Asians in East Africa," Nemchand Shah declared that his children mixed freely with white Britons in Uganda and experienced "no feeling of social inferiority"; in contrast, they found it difficult to mix with Indians when they visited India. East African Asians were "not offensive...we are level to British, not behind them." Shah suggested that Ugandan Asians could act as a "bridge" between white Britons and other Asians.[139] The interviewer, Christie Davies, emphasized that Ugandan Asians had been living in a "multiracial" country, and had a "broader outlook" and were more highly skilled than those coming directly from India.

Prior to the expulsion, Britons received a reassuring message about Ugandan Asians: they were thoroughly anglicized, and wholly bourgeois. The press insisted that East African Asians should not be confused with Indian and Pakistani "migrants." The Ugandan Asians had not moved directly from their ancestral homeland to Britain; rather, they had undergone a "double" migration. The *Observer* quoted one young Ugandan Asian as saying that he had only ever studied in English: "In fact, I failed Gujerati...I did Macbeth, Dickens, and Tennyson. I wasn't taught Indian history, but the history of the British Empire." An Englishman had trained him in scouting, leaving him "knowing more about the Yorkshire dales than he did about the Himalayas."[140] Compared with Indians and Pakistanis, Ugandan Asians were typed as "progressive and dynamic," proud of having achieved middle-class status.[141] And they had no myth of return; they knew they were never going home.

The media presumed that the bourgeois values that had provoked hostility toward Asians in Africa would actually serve them well in Britain.[142] The press agreed that Ugandan Asians aspired to join Britain's property-owning democracy, with a semi-detached house in the suburbs as their cherished ideal. They would "recoil" from the "ghetto life" into which West Indians had been forced in the 1950s and 1960s. In short, "what is coming now is a middle class invasion."[143]

Here we can see the origins of the stereotype of the Ugandan Asian as anglicized self-starter. These myths underpinned the type of aid that Ugandan Asians received, and would long outlast the expulsion crisis. The URB assumed that Ugandan Asians would leave the camps within one or two days, as they rapidly became economically self-sufficient.[144] The official insistence that all Ugandan Asians spoke perfect English meant that very few interpreters were assigned—in contrast to the extensive translation services for Anglo-Egyptians and Hungarians—and many camps had no Asian-language books or newspapers.[145] In reality, the Department of Employment suggested that about 20 percent of Ugandan Asians who registered for work would require language training. As one journalist wrote, "their English is often not good enough to explain the more complicated problems with which their expulsion has faced them."[146]

Not everyone perceived the "bourgeois" traits of the Ugandan Asians positively. When a doctor's wife complained that Heathfield Camp was squalid, the camp leadership responded that the real problem was the luxurious existence Asians had led in Uganda: "we are not going to spoon feed them in every direction and it would be entirely wrong if we brought in Europeans to clean their lavatories."[147] Many camp workers complained that Asians refused to do manual labor: "employing cheap African labor to do these chores for them in Uganda is one thing—if they think the British taxpayer is going to willingly and meekly foot the bill for their little quirk, then they'll have to think again."[148] Chotalal Vadhia Mohan, who stayed at West Malling, recalled how camp authorities had him "cleaning all the time," making sure to keep "everything spic and span," and how residents were instructed not to spit or urinate in the wrong place.[149]

These tales of the bourgeois refugee were always at odds with the realities of encampment. The WRVS complained that the Ugandan Asians "in no way resembled the group of gifted and genteel professionals that the Home Office had led the English to expect." Instead, they were indistinguishable from the thousands of "shabby Indian and Pakistani workers" already in Britain.[150] When Akbar Hassan arrived at Southall, wearing a long green overcoat from the WRVS, he was swarmed by reporters asking "how it felt to be a big capitalist man sharing the unused barracks of an American Air Force base with 800 other refugees." He did not wish to see his relatives in England when he was "so discouraged," and opted to stay at West Malling instead. Akbar was frustrated that Ugandan Asians (unlike the Anglo-Egyptians) had not been indemnified for their property. Long waits for loans delayed many departures from camp: "If I could have had a loan for house mortgage or to start up business I would have been out of West Malling within a week."[151] Instead, he was offered a job cleaning runways at the airport.

As on the war-torn Continent, refugee camps in Britain served as laboratories for social science. But rather than the army of psychologists, nutritionists, and social workers who typically staffed Continental camps after the Second World War, new experts emerged in the British camps, especially in the field of labor. These brief interactions and collisions with new forms of expertise could prove transformative. Camp leaders analyzed troves of numerical data, trying to "fix" the class position of Ugandan Asians in Britain according to what they thought it had been in Africa. Ugandan Asian businessman C.B. Patel recalled his time in camp as a marvel of statistical knowledge.[152] But translating "African" economic information to be usable in Britain proved challenging. British officials feared that Ugandan Asians exaggerated their incomes, and miscalculated the exchange rates. The difficulty of determining the class position of Ugandan Asians would become one of social science's failures during this period, to be replaced by the equally faulty rubric of the model minority. Indeed, the myth of Ugandan Asians as the model minority became entrenched in the camps, even as the logic of the decisions to aid specific individuals is now difficult to parse.

One refugee explained the "jolly mood" of the camps by saying that life in camp had erased social distinctions among the Ugandan Asians. Whereas in Uganda the richer Asians looked down on the poorer ones, now they all received the same £2 10s every week from social security.[153] For this individual, the camp was the utopia of the welfare state. In truth, though, Ugandan Asian camps entrenched class divisions among their residents. British labor specialists conducted extensive interviews in the camps to identify suitable candidates for small business loans. Such files tell us as much about their creators as their subjects. But they also highlight what was suppressed at the time: the socioeconomic diversity of the refugees. Indeed, one of the revelations of these conversations was precisely how flawed the media perception of Ugandan Asians had been.[154]

These interviews form an important archive of camp life, one of the few records of loss and dispossession that Ugandan Asians had suffered. Interviewees detailed the assets they had left behind as well as their available capital. Very few claims about net worth in Uganda could be verified, which made assessments of character and capability all the more important. They were asked about their relatives and friends in Britain, their education, work history, hobbies (including the newspapers they read), and fluency in English. For example, one 42-year-old West Malling resident was described as having "no really definable skills or knowledge," despite working as a bookkeeper in his father's tailoring shop for twenty years. The interviewer noted under "interests" that the man was "very status conscious." His fear that it would be difficult to establish a business in England without financial backing was derided as a lack of motivation.[155]

Interviewers were more willing to invest in younger men, even if they lacked capital and work experience. For a 57-year-old at Greenham Common who had worked in the family business, the interviewer wrote, "suspect older brother always played leading management role (Difficult to establish). Does not appear to have been involved in establishment/expansion of any aspect of business—bought from older generation." Although the interviewee claimed that his brother would bring money from India, the interviewer wrote, "Vague—sounds like <u>hope</u> only." This man was described as a poor investment prospect, recommended for light factory work and social-security benefits.

Among the Anglo-Egyptians, older men had been singled out for extra aid. But labor specialists in the 1970s tended to see Ugandan Asian men in their 50s and 60s as riskier prospects. One candidate with a successful business selling cloth to Africans was dismissed because he had relied too heavily on the African market; he too was recommended for factory work. Other businessmen were discredited if they had employed cheap African labor, which was unavailable in Britain. Candidates were assessed by the energy they demonstrated in the camps themselves: namely, whether they took part in the camp leadership.

The trope of Ugandan Asians as the model minority gained strength as people left the camps. It took on particular value during Thatcherism, as Conservatives invested in the narrative of rapid economic mobility, and the triumph of the small business owner. Conservative politicians saw Ugandan Asians as sources of middle-class leadership in the inner city, and praised the "innate conservatism" of Asian families.[156] In 1982, an article titled "The Ugandan Asian Success Magic" traced the life of Chandrakant Patel, who stayed in Kensington Barracks for two months and later bought his own news agency. He argued that Ugandan Asians worked harder in Britain than they had in Uganda, "where we had servants and a bloody good life. Here life is difficult, and those who were working class Asians in Uganda have probably moved up here. But then there is nothing else to do but work. That is the secret of our success."[157] According to Praful Patel, the Ugandan Asian community had stupefied its white neighbors with its upward mobility and relentless accumulation of capital.

Many Ugandan Asians complained in the 1980s about misleading press reports: "Sometimes my English neighbours tell me, they say, have you seen the newspaper? Your people are in it again, and look at how much money you all have and the wonderful houses you live in. I tell them, yes some have done well in this country, but some haven't, but they don't listen, they just think about the millionaires in the newspaper."[158] Others insisted that, rather than vast fortunes, Ugandan Asians sought only a "comfortable, middle-class" lifestyle.[159] One interviewee lamented, "So many of our people are still struggling to make ends meet, they're living in council houses, and their families have broken up, the daughters have run off and left all of this because of the struggles they have faced over here, but you never see that in the paper."[160]

Despite these objections, the myth of the bourgeois Ugandan Asian easily gave way to the myth of the Ugandan Asian millionaire.[161] Vaughan Robinson, a geographer with the Migration Unit at Swansea, described Ugandan Asians in 1993 as a "remarkable success story," whose achievements surpassed most other minority groups in Britain.[162] Dominic Sandbrook called the Ugandan Asian arrival "the biggest immigration story" of the 1970s, with a happy ending. He depicted Ugandan Asians settling cheerfully into British life, "brimming with brains, ambition, and commercial enthusiasm." These "immigrants" (not refugees) were, in Sandbrook's view, one of the few success stories of an unhappy decade: a people who had moved from pariah to paragon.[163]

The point here is not to replace a story of success with one of failure. Rather, it is to consider how the model minority narrative obscures the role of the state—and the camp—in privileging some Ugandan Asians and not others in the guise of resettlement.[164] Refugee camps altered future trajectories by selecting individuals for business loans, as well as advantageous placements in homes and schools. As we will see in Chapter 6, camps rarely achieved their objective of guiding refugee settlement patterns; indeed, their efforts to shape the geography of settlement were remarkably unsuccessful. But their designation of some Ugandan Asians as more worthy of aid than others altered the trajectory of many individuals and families. The time that people spent in camps could have a significant (and unpredictable) impact on their future.

Thinking comparatively, this juxtaposition shows the complexity of what was gained and lost at the end of empire, and by whom. The Anglo-Egyptians were characterized as too lofty for the normal provisions of aid; the Ugandan Asians were initially typed as having no need of them, or needing them only briefly in order to regain their "natural" status as bourgeois Anglophiles. In both cases, the decolonizing state worked to create "class" in the camps. Some Anglo-Egyptians appeared to receive much more in terms of financial aid. Perhaps even more striking than the amount of aid was the way it was conceived: that is, as compensation for lost status and what was left behind. And yet, hardly anyone knows who the Anglo-Egyptians are today—and they play virtually no part in contemporary discourses of multicultural Britain. Ugandan Asians have been amalgamated into "normal" migration regimes: a feat of political mobilization and myth-making about unified community that the Anglo-Egyptians did not fulfill. If the Ugandan Asians are now the model minority, then we might say that the Anglo-Egyptians are no longer a minority at all.

As the Anglo-Egyptian and Ugandan Asian cases suggest, one of the most rebellious (and dangerous) things refugees could do is move away from the class positions that Britons had assigned to them. The initial British assumption was that refugees from Vietnam came from the entrepreneurial class. But camp life soon revealed a more politically and socially diverse group. As social workers noted, one might move in a British camp from talking to an ex-officer of the South Vietnamese Army to a one-time soldier of the Vietcong.[165] Whatever the original class position of the refugees, the Ockenden authorities insisted that refugees from Vietnam were fundamentally different from the socially dysfunctional British poor. Refugees were resourceful, capable people who were superior to Britain's "problem families." For this reason, Ockenden's leadership warned that camp staff must not become too possessive of refugees, or hamper their independence. Camp life could cause refugees to become just as "overdependent" as poor Britons.

Many clashes between white Britons and refugees from Vietnam revolved around the violation of class boundaries. Some refugees arrived in camps with extremely smart luggage, "which caused a little envy on the part of not so well off Field

Workers and even more envy over their hi-fi and radio equipment."[166] Fieldworkers interviewed refugees about their socks and underwear, ensuring that only the most destitute refugees would receive clothing vouchers and none would be too luxuriously dressed. It was important to uphold the image of the "poor refugee."[167] At Thorney Island, Major Arrowsmith discouraged refugees from giving "resettlement parties" to thank the staff. The parties left refugees impoverished when they arrived in their new homes; "they are really very poor people and cannot afford to spend this money."[168] Locals complained about DHSS money being spent on party food, and the refugees buying drinks in pubs when "they should not have been able to afford it."[169] Refugees must be introduced to English living conditions, but—Arrowsmith warned—"care must be taken to see it was not too luxurious."[170] He feared that refugees would expect too much, but also that poorer Britons might be jealous. Anglicization, Arrowsmith suggested, should not be tied to upward mobility.

For other refugees, as we have seen, the message had been exactly the opposite. There were many paradoxes in refugee care. Some refugees were cared for by the same agencies that aided the poor, creating institutional links between these groups. Yet state authorities claimed that even destitute refugees were not truly "poor." That is, they were morally and socially distinguishable from Britain's own impoverished families. The problems of refugees were temporary and solvable; their former class positions could be regained. In terms of class, refugee workers sought to create the refugees of their own imaginings. While they could not entirely control the futures of those who were encamped, their insistence on identifying refugees as linked to specific class positions had a profound impact on refugees, conjuring up new economic realities.

In terms of ethnic, religious, and class identities, camps were crucial sites of transformation: places where identity could be made either more fluid or more fixed. As we will see in Chapter 4, camps functioned not only as places of class formation, but also as sites for didacticism and rebellion about gender. Norms of sex and family took new shape in these spaces that were mapped against—and yet decidedly intertwined with—the British home. The intimate lives of refugees were transformed by encampment, though not always as camp leaders predicted or desired.

4

Happy Families?

What counted as a "family" in a refugee camp? Camp authorities strove to instruct refugees about national principles of home and family. But life in camp often threw these ideals into disarray. In particular, refugees were an uneasy fit with the ideal of the nuclear family and the male breadwinner, as displacement often entailed the separation of husbands and wives (or mothers and fathers).[1] Camps were places of possibility for rethinking the notions of family and home, and what these concepts meant to all who lived in Britain.

The experience of encampment is part of the larger story of the reconstruction of family life in wartime and postwar Britain. It is a reminder that the twentieth century witnessed not one emotional regime, but many.[2] Even in what was supposed to be the "golden age" of British marriage, from the 1930s to the 1950s, the very prevalence of marriage and childcare manuals and child counseling agencies suggests that the other side of this family "norm" was awareness of its fragility. Rather than a "golden era" of stability and consensus around gender roles, gender became a site of contestation for wider changes to family and community life.[3] As British ideals of family life shifted, refugees played a distinctive role in this milieu of flux. Not everyone was able to take advantage of new norms of intimacy and domestic life, nor did everyone accept the ideals of the nuclear family unquestioningly. Refugees offered their own definitions of what constituted a home, and a family.

The social ties that refugees forged in camps were vulnerable to the rigidly demanding categories of aid. Camp leaders often insisted that refugees conform to particular domestic arrangements in order to receive benefits. But the camp archives also offer powerful testimony about how refugees in camps fought to preserve their intimacy with their families, and how they resisted camp officials' unwelcome interference with their private lives. Over eight decades of encampment, we can see both tremendous intrusions into the emotional lives of refugees, and fierce resistance to these interventions.

MAKING AND BREAKING FAMILIES: SINGLE MEN AND STATELESS HUSBANDS

One of the defining characteristics of refugee life was the fracturing of families that accompanied displacement.[4] The government's policies on family reunification were opaque and uneven. Some camp authorities saw the task of uniting refugee families as their highest objective. Yet many individual camps actually separated families instead. Family separations were deeply traumatic. But they also offered an outlet for refugees to resist the state's definition of what it meant to be a family.

Initially, Polish camps had little to do with family. The War Office's warrant was to focus on the resettlement of Polish men from the armed forces. But the Polish Resettlement Act, which included soldiers' dependents, brought tens of thousands of Polish women and children flooding into Britain from the far-flung POW and refugee camps of the Middle East, Europe, India, and Africa. With their arrival, the War Office (and later, the National Assistance Board) confronted new problems of family life in its camps and hostels.[5] As one Board member put it, "we are now fairly and squarely faced with the problem of the married Polish soldier."[6] At this point, the question of what could be expected from camp life—and how to create privacy and intimacy within the camp—were fundamentally transformed.

Who were these dependents? In 1948, Gwilym Ivor Thomas, Administrator for the Polish Forces under British Command, proposed, "What I have in mind is that a man should be allowed to take his wife and children and possibly a few of the more aged and decrepit relatives."[7] Ultimately, the Polish Resettlement Act embraced a much wider definition of "dependents." Under the act, dependents who held the right to settle in Britain included wives, fiancées (if they were of Polish nationality), all blood relations, natural or adopted children and stepchildren of Polish armed forces under British command. It also included widows and orphans of former members of these same armed forces, if the widows were of Polish nationality. If the wives or widows were Polish, then all of their blood relations counted as dependents as well.[8]

Some dependents were prized more than others. Polish dependents from Lebanon arrived in the summer of 1950, reassuringly well clothed and healthy with a "prosperous" air. They settled in their hostel quickly, with the children happily playing on the green grass they had not seen in years. In contrast, the Poles arriving from Kenya and Tanzania seemed primarily "of the peasant type." They turned up wearing homemade clothes that betrayed their poverty.[9] The Board representative at Tengeru lamented that "the poor old UK is going to get a pretty poor bundle of assets out of this lot." He described the Poles in Kenya as "mainly lumps of bovine flesh"—lazy, apathetic, and plagued by immorality and drunkenness.[10] Nearly half were between the ages of 40 and 60, and—he believed—too old to adjust to civilian life in Britain. The vast majority, he predicted, would remain in camps forever, as "completely useless members of British society."[11]

The dependents of Polish soldiers were not allowed to choose the camp in which they wished to live. Rather, they were posted to vacancies, following the order in which camps were earmarked for transfer from the War Office to the National Assistance Board. Once posted to a camp, they could not leave without permission. If, by luck, they happened to land in the same camp as their family members—defined for this purpose as "blood or close relations"—then they were allowed to live together at the discretion of the camp's commanding officer.[12] Polish wives protested that they were "unofficially" encouraged to squat in the Board's camps in squalor.

Most Polish dependents were placed in camps in "outlandish" places with barely any job prospects.[13] As Polish men quit their jobs to join their wives in these "isolated" camps, the Board debated whether it was more important for these men to find work or to live with their wives. After many ministerial promises that Polish men would be reunited with their families, it seemed politically undesirable to compel these "wretched husbands" to seek work away from their wives. The Board concluded that Polish men were "most reluctant to be separated from their wives and children under <u>any</u> circumstances," and that separate camps for husbands and wives would be viewed with "utmost dissatisfaction."[14]

At Keevil Hostel, some husbands were told they could not join their wives unless they relinquished their places in their current hostel; when they did so, some were told there was no place for them at Keevil either, rendering them homeless.[15] Keevil was technically a "family" hostel, but many husbands and wives continued to endure long separations until the men could be transferred to Keevil. In an angry letter to *Dziennik Polski*, Polish men who were still waiting to join their wives and children at Keevil asked: "How can it be like this? We have enough of this gypsy life, don't women need the help of their husbands after so many years of demeaning themselves?"[16]

Officially, the Board wished to achieve the "maximum bringing together of men and their wives and children."[17] But despite the act's expansive definition of dependents, there were always limits to how the Board understood the Polish "family." One vexed problem was how to deal with British women in Polish camps. Home Secretary James Chuter Ede angered the Labour social reformer Leah Manning when he used the term "camp follower" to describe English women who accompanied the Poles, stigmatizing these women as prostitutes and denying the legitimacy of their relationships.[18] By the end of the Second World War, around 4,000 marriages between Britons and Poles had taken place, often arousing great hostility.[19] The National Assistance Board discouraged British-born women from entering its Polish camps. At Chandler's Ford in Hampshire, one English woman was forbidden to join her Polish husband in camp.[20] The aim of family reunification policies—and the broad conception of "dependents" they entailed—was to strengthen ties between Poles, not to create Anglo-Polish families. In the Board's view, British wives of Polish soldiers were already established in Britain with their own networks of support, "while Polish wives are strangers."[21] Thus, a British wife of a Pole should not be in a camp at all.

As refugee workers acknowledged, many Britons experienced their own forms of family fragmentation after the Second World War. Industrial hostels did not usually provide family housing for the hundreds of thousands of British workers who had been transferred away from their homes during the war. The Board lamented, "we have had to harden our hearts," and deny British workers' requests for family reunions.[22] It was risky to value Polish families over British ones; "we could not do for the Poles what we are unable to do for our own people, many of whom have been separated from their wives and families for years."[23] If the Board was going to reunite Polish men with their families, then why should British men be left in lonely solitude?

Such comments served as painful reminders that displacement was a domestic story as well as a foreign one. There was a danger that Poles would be reunited with their families more quickly than Britons displaced by war work. But the Board countered that, "whereas the family of the British worker would normally have a home of some sort to start with the Pole ordinarily has to begin with no roots in this country and no alternative home."[24] But others doubted that any British worker would wish to have his family leave their home and join him in an uncomfortable hostel.[25] Such choices would only be made by the most radically displaced individuals: that is, by refugees.

In Anton Drweski's 1948 article in *Dziennik Polski*, "When the Husband Is Not Allowed to Live with His Wife," a Polish locksmith woefully recounted how he had not seen his wife in seven years. Now, he had finally caught sight of her—waiting at the entrance of a factory office for a ride to Daglingworth. Compelled to stage their intimate reunion in the communal hut-room of the noisy camp, he reported, "It was like calling on a person one used to know. Seven years and not one moment alone with my wife and not able to speak to her quietly." Because Daglingworth was only a transit camp, his wife was scheduled to move again; "she certainly will be in another part of England and our marriage will be again only on the paper." In Drweski's view, the British state was enforcing the separation of Polish husbands and wives. The husband confided, "I am already so tired of this abnormal life without any possibilities to be together with my wife and live again in normal conditions."

Such vivid accounts charted the toll that British camps took on Polish families. Drweski exhorted the British government to abolish "forced celibacy" for the Poles.[26] Despite the cult of family that the Poles saw all around them in Britain—little houses, fireplaces, utterly boring Sundays—Britons seemed to see family separations as normal:

> Perhaps I am mistaken but I had the impression that the Warden was surprised in his inner heart about our continental habit to attach such great importance to the problem of marriage. He had too good manners to speak about this matter, but he mentioned, by the way, that he himself has already lived 9 years without his wife.

In one sense, Drweski was correct; poor and displaced Britons were likely to experience family separations even during the welfare state's most expansionist era.[27] Many local authorities continued to use sex-segregated Poor Law hostels for homeless British families long after the National Assistance Act 1948 formally repealed the Poor Laws.

The Board's family reunion policies were never uniform. One warden allowed family accommodation in his hostel for Poles, without the Board's approval. He allowed some hostel residents to marry, and created a day nursery for babies.[28] But this was far from the norm. At Stonehouse, married Polish couples were not allowed to live together even though double bedrooms were available: "the husband is accommodated with another man and the wife with another woman. If they commit the horrible crime to spend one night together they are turned out immediately." Many Poles complained that the Board's policies—and the built environment of the camps—were antithetical to "normal" family life. Mr. Perun wrote to Kelvedon Hostel's manager that in his one-roomed hut it would be "actually impossible to move normally and this would remind me of Soviet-Russia where I was staying as a forced deportee with no human rights." In a "cultured country" such as Great Britain, confining five people in this way was "a disgrace to the good name of this country and people and I being a loyal resident do not intend to contribute to it."[29] Forcing those who had rejected communism into communal living, Perun asserted, was clearly unjust. The right to live with one's family in privacy was part of life in a liberal democracy.

Other residents pleaded for privacy within the space of the camps. Mrs. Kiczorowska of Kelvedon wrote to her warden shortly after her wedding to ask for permission to use the other half of her hut: "really I got no patience to wait any longer...I have got married and still I have to live with my husband in the same half hut where my parents live. Besides the uncomfort of cooking, having four beds in such small room that is not very nice and comfortable for us young people to live together with parents."[30] The estate manager refused, because Mrs. Kiczorowska's husband had already been settled outside the hostel when they married, and "it would seem to be the husband's responsibility to find accommodation for his wife outside the hostel." Mr. Kiczorowska's illicit presence in the hostel placed the family at risk of losing the half a hut that they currently had.[31]

In the 1950s, Polish hostels began evicting "single people." The plan was to reduce costs by allowing married couples and families to stay on and cater for themselves. At Northwick Hostel, this project galvanized a fierce protest. F. Hajduczek wrote to the Ministry of Pensions to object that he did not want to leave Northwick. He implored, "it is not my fault that I am a 70% invalid (amputation right leg and injury to right eye) and that I am single."[32] Stefan Kuchta sent his eloquent plea to stay at Northwick directly to the Queen. Under British command during the Second World War, Kuchta had sustained injuries to his left leg, left hand, and pelvis. As a result of these war wounds, Kuchta lamented, "I cannot have a family of my own it means a wife and children." The Board's plan was to move Kuchta to the Long Marston barracks. Kuchta was horrified. Long Marston was "the places for old people waiting for worst to come 'DEATH.'" Furthermore, the barracks were too cold for Kuchta to "keep warm my wounded limbs," and there was not enough privacy to keep his injuries confidential.

At Northwick, Kuchta claimed, he could live communally with other Poles who had viewed him as part of their family for nearly a decade. These friends would provide him with a surrogate for the biological family he could not create on his own. His service to the British state had deprived him of the chance to have children. The state now owed him the chance to forge whatever social ties he could, even if these connections did not conform to the Board's own ideals of "family":

> So the war for the cause to all people deprived me of the human rights and priviledges [*sic*] and the human understanding from the authorities of the N.A. Board. Because of having no capacity to have a wife and own children, it means a family life with a family warm which I need badly to strengthen me phisically [*sic*] and mentally I have begun my life with some families since my come to Northwick Park and it happened

nearly 10 years ago. My life with the families with whom I live on very relative good terms seems to me that it gives me not so sad thoughts of being so useless and alone in this work so bad to me in my luck.

Kuchta claimed that, although he was officially single, "I have families who want me to stick to them." These families, he promised, would feed him when the communal kitchen at Northwick closed, "so it is no worry of me being unnourished." He evoked his wartime service, concluding, "I think that I have deserved a bit of human understanding... By sending me elsewhere from these families with whom I have lived so long feeling in their bevies as if I were their member it would be a very big wrong done to me alike a weapon to kill me prematurely."[33] The Board ordered Kuchta to leave Northwick.

Edward Holownia also petitioned the Queen to stay at Northwick, stating that the injuries he had sustained under British command had made it impossible for him to marry. Being "highly disabled," he noted, it was a "very difficult thing to find a woman who would like to marry a man with artificial limbs and other appliances which have to be put off when a time comes to go to bed." But, he added, he was entitled to "human rights on the same level as those who have families and can much easier have families of their own." During Holownia's eight years at Northwick, "I acquainted with some families to feel myself not so completely alone. Those families surround me with warmth and friendship and by these things I get some moral strength to go forth on the way of my bad luck life." To tear him away from these families, who had received him with open hearts as if he were a biological relative, would be "an unforgettable wrong." As disabled veterans, Kuchta and Holownia claimed, "what we need is a warm dorm and not a nissen hut. We need a place where we shall have some privacy as some times during the night we have to get up several times and put on our orthopedic instruments."[34]

Like Kuchta, Holownia was ordered to leave his camp.[35] For the Board, treating Kuchta and Holownia as part of the "families" at Northwick was not an option. Single residents were ordered to limit their luggage when they moved to the new hostel; they were not allowed to take furniture, fuel, firewood, or any livestock. The Northwick Park Hostel Residents Single Persons Group objected that they had paid rent for many years at a place where they found themselves "not by our own volition or personal endeavor," and deserved to stay until they found a true home.[36] The Single Persons Group advocated a more inclusive notion of "family." The aftermath of war demanded a more expansive understanding of social ties:

> The notion of "family" in regard to many who now live in the hostel is relative in respect of many of them. There are, namely, many such families who fathers or fortuitous guardians are single men too, they just live with women and children. There are also people who registered quickly in the Registrar's Office as soon as they found out about the notice to leave the hostel. In this way two single people gain the privileges of a family. Do these categories of people enjoy greater rights in Great Britain[?] It seems to us that it is single people, advanced in age and disabled who deserve protection from a social welfare institution, while in reality these odd families take advantage of these privileges.

The protestors concluded, "we do wish to explain that each of us has some family in Poland who we help financially."[37] Such petitions served as powerful reminders that "single" refugees were often part of larger social networks, even if the state refused to recognize these relationships.

In refugee camps, where housing and other forms of aid were strongly linked to family units, being "single" was a major disadvantage. Single people were targeted in evictions because the National Assistance Board claimed they could find housing more easily. Those who resisted eviction were brought to court. Kazimierz Zozial (a concentration camp survivor) told the judge that he was not truly a single man—he had a family to support in Poland, with an aging mother, a wife and son, and a fatherless niece. He produced receipts to show the parcels he sent to this family out of his meager earnings, and showed photographs of his family members. Nevertheless, the judge ordered Zozial to vacate his hut within twenty-eight days.[38] For the purposes of camp life, he was defined as single.

Beyond the "single persons" protests, Polish camps and hostels were the sites of other family dramas. Wardens often intervened in the marital and family affairs of their residents. In 1949, a Polish woman with two infant children arrived at a Board hostel under cover of darkness and squatted in an empty hut. The woman had fought with her husband, a Polish miner living at Clifton, about 2 miles away, and had decided with her "boyfriend" to take up an abode in the camp. She was described in the Board's report as being "suspected of being somewhat loose, morally." The hostel's efforts to get rid of her were in vain. The hostel's chief inspector used "all his ammunition" to get her to reunite with her husband (even calling the police to evict her), but he failed. A Polish doctor in camp finally persuaded her to return "home" to her husband, and she was sent off with a warning about her future conduct.[39]

In a subsequent case, Mrs. Jozefa Lipowska of Northwick was accused of inventing excuses to avoid joining her husband, who had found a job in a nearby town. She was interviewed many times to encourage her to leave the hostel and live with her husband, but to no avail. Her husband came to visit, bringing written proof that he had purchased a house in Wolverhampton, but "it was known that the woman was too comfortable here and she had a 'boy friend.'" The warden informed Mrs. Lipowska that her rightful place was with her husband, and she must leave with her husband the next day or face eviction. Mrs. Lipowska won an extension, but ultimately left the hostel as ordered. Her husband thanked the warden for his efforts to "urge the wife to join him."[40] Such interactions revealed both the scope of the Board's intrusions with refugee families, and the limits on its powers.

The Board also intervened in relationships between parents and children. The Northwick warden wrote to one Polish woman, whose father had left the hostel and was living with her in town, that he was disturbed that her mother still remained at Northwick. He urged the daughter to "induce" her mother to join them, as "we consider that her natural place is with her family."[41] In 1955, the same warden wrote to Jan Ozga that his mother was being sued because she refused to pay maintenance charges. The suit was withdrawn when the hostel doctor certified that she was unfit for work. She refused meals from the dining hall, because she said none of the food was tasty—"a view," the warden hastened to add, "which is not held by any of the other 500 residents served." Increasingly desperate, the warden asked, "I wonder whether it is possible for you to cooperate and help in getting your Mother to live as a normal resident and take her meals in the normal manner?" The warden suspected that Ozga's mother was a prostitute, and he suggested housing her with a female roommate to curtail any illicit activities.[42]

The Poles had entered Britain with their families already fragmented by war. The camp's task was to consider how to put Polish families back together or—in some cases—how to justify their continued separation. In the 1950s, the Anglo-Egyptians experienced a different set of interventions in their family lives, and a new set of policies about family reunification. Unlike the Poles, Anglo-Egyptians were mostly evacuated with intact family groups. The Anglo-Egyptian Resettlement Board's intention was to keep families together in its hostels, noting that refugees were too "unhappy" when family groups—even the larger ones—were divided.[43]

The Anglo-Egyptian Resettlement Board paid careful attention to Anglo-Egyptian family ties in crafting resettlement plans. Prior experiences of Britain were heavily weighted. For one elderly refugee who had spent his boyhood in Brighton, the Board proposed returning him there. The Board also approved the transfer of Mr. and Mrs. Buhagiar, who had a daughter in Hampstead, to Golders Green, as "they do not want to be too near each other, but would like to be near enough to visit."[44] The Board considered restructuring the hostels to offer more family units, since there was "very great reluctance on the part of Husbands in Camps" to take jobs until they could find housing for their whole family. In the spring of 1957, the Board introduced a house purchase scheme to induce Anglo-Egyptians to leave the camps and hostels. Preference for home purchases would be given to large families with three generations.[45]

The Board worked to reunite Anglo-Egyptian families even when some family members were foreign or stateless. The Home Office's policy toward admission of foreign husbands was based on the wife's birth and parentage and her connections with the United Kingdom. The fact that a woman held a British passport did not automatically give her husband a claim to live in Britain with her. Many women from Egypt who were British subjects had been born in the Levant or the Mediterranean, and had no obvious connection with the United Kingdom. When the husbands of these women were stateless, the Home Office admitted the husbands. But if they held passports to other countries, they were expected to claim admittance in that other country and then apply for admission to Britain on the grounds of hardship.[46] The Home Office ultimately relaxed its policy in order to admit 166 stateless husbands from Egypt, but still urged these couples to settle in the husband's country, since "in nine such cases out of ten the woman has no more connection with this country than the husband has with his own."[47] One peer proposed sending the wives and children of stateless husbands to Ecuador or Bolivia.[48]

The Board was authorized to offer maintenance payments only if the family was "predominantly British": that is, if the male breadwinner was a British subject.[49] This "problem," which had surfaced for the Poles as well, was never discussed for the Ugandan Asians or the Vietnamese, who were assumed to marry only within their own group. At Greenbanks Hostel, a man who married another Anglo-Egyptian was eligible for a £500 housing grant. But if he married a British subject, who was normally resident in the United Kingdom, the grant was reduced to £250.[50] Under Standing Instruction 1119—which aided people whose marriage prospects had been disrupted by the Suez Crisis—male refugees who married British women, foreigners, or other refugees were entitled to receive a housing and furnishing grant.[51] Anglo-Egyptian women who married Britons received half the normal furnishing grant in order to enable them to contribute to the marriage. The Board emphasized that this grant did *not* nullify the principle that all husbands (regardless of their nationality) should be expected to provide for their wives.

As with the Poles, aid workers for Anglo-Egyptians devalued the single refugee. The Board debated whether single people were entitled to grants to purchase their own homes. The chief officer for Anglo-Egyptians, S.J. Dibble, argued that single refugees could adjust more easily to changed circumstances, though they had still lost the savings that made it easier to marry.[52] Overall, the Board did not wish to support single men keeping house on their own. Resettlement grants were designed for families.

The issue of family separation and reunification—and the state's role in both processes—became highly politically charged with the arrival of the Ugandan Asians. The Ugandan Asian expulsion prompted a flurry of efforts to mobilize social-scientific knowledge around the Asian family. Aid workers were cautioned that most arrivals would be clustered in the "typical" Asian family group: that is, three or four generations living together, with married sons living with their wives, children, and parents.[53] It was not clear, however, whether Ugandan Asians would be resettled in intergenerational ("Asian") family groups or nuclear ("British") ones. British politicians routinely praised Asian families, who "could often teach many of our indigenous families a thing or two about family responsibility."[54] But camp administrators' understandings of Asian family structures were often confused and confusing. Their assumptions benefited Ugandan Asian families in unpredictable ways.

In December 1972, a group of Ugandan Asian wives in Britain began a highly effective campaign to persuade the government to admit their stateless husbands. The husbands were considered "stateless" because they had become Ugandan citizens prior to Amin's expulsion order, and were held in camps in Belgium, Austria, and Italy. Their wives argued that they would never be able to get off welfare without their husbands to "support us and make our lives worth living again."[55] These Ugandan Asian wives were strikingly successful in crafting British rhetoric about family—and turning British "knowledge" about Asian family structures—to their own advantage.

The left-wing Anglican priest Canon L. John Collins pleaded with the prime minister to admit stateless husbands to Britain. Their wives, trapped in British camps, "have led sheltered, domestic, middle-class lives, accustomed to leave all decisions to the male head of the family; they are completely bewildered by the present situation."[56] These tragically dependent women were "forced" to live off the state, he suggested, although their husbands were eager to care for them. In a sermon at St. Paul's Cathedral, Collins read a powerful letter from Mrs. Sunibalu Modhwadia and twenty-three other Ugandan Asian wives of stateless husbands. The signatories urged British women to imagine the misery of Ugandan Asian wives "wondering what will ever happen to us, and when we will ever see our husbands again, when our children will know that they still have a father." Modhwadia wrote, "We do not wish to live off the state any longer, but while our husbands are refused admission to Britain, there is little hope of most of us being able to work. Only some of us are competent in English, and most of us are trying to raise families of young children. Our husbands on the other hands [*sic*] are working men of all skills and professions." Collins castigated the sexism of family separations: "Why do we so discriminate against these women? Why is it that an immigrant husband with a British passport may bring his wife and children to live with him here in Britain but a wife with a British passport is denied a similar right?"

The personal tragedies of these "split" or "divided" families were detailed in the British press, which ran photographs of lonely Ugandan Asian wives in camps.[57] Prabha G. Probat of the West Malling Camp, whose husband was detained in Vienna, described to the *Sunday Times* how "my son is always crying and asking when his Daddy will come home. I need my husband here with my family in Britain."[58] One welfare officer described a Ugandan Asian man in detention who had never seen his baby, born in a camp in England.[59] In one awful case, a 3-year-old Ugandan Asian boy in England died pining for his father, who was trapped in a stateless persons camp in Europe.[60] In 1973, thirty stateless wives at West Malling performed an ode that pleaded with Queen Elizabeth ("Mother") to allow their husbands to enter Britain:

> Listen to our difficulties, oh, our mother.
> Children without father are crying
> Have mercy, oh, our mother
> Bring children and father together, oh, our mother
> Amindada [Idi Amin] has kicked us out, and
> Heathdada [Edward Heath] caught us.[61]

The Ugandan Asian crisis brought the male breadwinner ideal into direct conflict with immigration law. Baroness Eirene White spoke in the House of Lords about Ugandan Asian mothers becoming so distraught due to their enforced separation from their husbands that they could not take care of their children. In the "tight knit unit" of the Asian family, women who were left without support from male breadwinners might "go to pieces." Asian men should not be kept in "useless detention" abroad when they could be supporting their families in Britain.[62] Mary Dines, a founder of the Joint Council for the Welfare of Immigrants, described the Ugandan Asian wives of stateless husbands as mentally ill and taking drugs in order to cope with their plight. "Fatherless" children were unruly and withdrawn. Instead of reuniting families, the Home Office had created a special group of deprived families in Britain, with its own distinctive pathologies. Dines argued that family separations were a "special torment" for Gujeratis, and refugee workers termed the pathologies of family separation "la malaise Gujerati."[63] Other British observers noted that

South Asian women might attempt suicide if they were deprived of male care. Without their husbands, these women would find it impossible to focus on rehousing. Resettlement without reunion was impossible.[64]

The image of the helpless Ugandan Asian wife—abandoned not by her husband, but by British immigration law—recurred in both British and Asian sources. Yasmin Alibhai-Brown's powerful autobiography, *No Place Like Home*, recalled that the most traumatized person she met in a Ugandan Asian refugee camp near Oxford was one of these wives of stateless husbands. Wandering around the camp aimlessly, with *tasbi* (Muslim prayer beads) in her hand, Mithi pleaded with Alibhai-Brown to help her prepare a feast for seven virgins in order to purify herself so that her husband might reunite with her in Britain. Alibhai-Brown explained:

> I said it was probably not going to be easy in the camp. This is a last-resort ritual used by the desperate in our community when troubles seem too much to bear. You gather seven pubescent girls, preferably from less well-off families, you feed them, fuss over them, and send them off with lovely white lacy handkerchiefs and rose water. It was always a very popular choice back home. Mithi would not be persuaded that in the cold, damp camps with dormitories and institutionalized conditions, she could not purge her sins in this way and get her husband to join her. It was fifteen years before they could be together again. By that time, Mithi had turned grey and sour.[65]

As camps for Ugandan Asians emptied, residents were often relocated without their consent. But, crucially, women who were separated from their male bread-winner could refuse to move without his permission. Some Ugandan Asian wives used this technique to pressure the government to allow their husbands to enter Britain.[66] In this way, the wives of stateless husbands found a powerful technique of resistance to camp authorities. For example, a West Malling administrator complained of Mrs. S.B. Samani, whose husband was in India waiting for his entry permit, and who refused to consider living in any area other than Kent. She also insisted that she must stay with her widowed friend, Mrs. Koteeha. Interestingly, the camp leadership agreed to place the friends together, adding that, "although Mrs. Samani is 38 she is a slim and attractive woman, her two dependent children are 1 and 14, if the husband is not admitted I would expect her to remarry in due course if there are Asians in the area."[67]

One Ugandan Asian woman stayed in camp until late 1973, purely to campaign for her stateless husband's admission to the UK. She moved camp three times, helped in each case by the liaison officer in her campaign. Although her case might appear to be a resettlement failure, she was actually using the camps to obtain support and legal advice that would not have been available elsewhere.[68] One social worker wondered whether Ugandan Asian women with stateless husbands actually enjoyed their newfound freedom in camps, and might resent having to readjust to a more passive role when their husbands were admitted to Britain.[69]

Family reunions did not always lead to the "happy ending" of resettlement. In 1973, *The Times* reported on the case of Mohamed Mughal, a game warden and garage owner who finally rejoined his family at Greenham Common after a stint in an Austrian camp. Mughal was described as a proud man who was unhappy

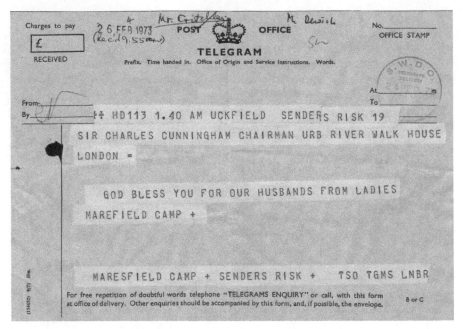

Fig. 4.1. Telegram from the Ugandan Asian wives of stateless husbands at Maresfield Camp to Sir Charles Cunningham of the Ugandan Resettlement Board, thanking him for allowing their husbands to enter Britain in 1973. Courtesy of the National Archives, Kew.

about taking charity. He had once owned five cars, but his only remaining valuable possession was a jacket made of leopard skins. Mughal had two wives, who lived in separate blocks of the camp, and thirteen children, ranging in age from 2 to 17. Mughal insisted that his wives must be resettled in houses within a few hundred yards of each other: a request that the URB did not feel compelled to honor. Thus, the whole family remained in camp. Mughal divided his time at Greenham Common between playing billiards and reading Gujerati newspapers, having given up on finding a suitable house for his reunited family.[70]

As with the Poles, many Ugandan Asian camp residents who were classified as "single" persons were not actually single at all. Joseph De Souza deposited his wife and three children in India after their escape from Uganda, and continued on to Britain alone; he was placed in the West Malling Camp. He found work, but refused to leave the camp, announcing that he was entitled to stay there until he had saved enough money to bring his family to England and set up a home for them. If he went into private accommodation as a single person, he would not be able to save money at the same rate, since the camp cost him only £4.40 per week.[71] In a desperate (and punitive) bid to expel De Souza, the camp authorities proposed that such individuals would be refused admission to the dining hall and have their blankets withdrawn.[72]

Ugandan Asian families were constantly reshaped not only by the traumas of expulsion, but also by the demands of resettlement.[73] For the Husen family at

Gaydon Camp, the father found a job at British Rail, but the only house available was a three-bedroom, and the local housing authority would not allow more than five people to live there. In order to get the house and job, he had to "farm out" two of his daughters to foster care.[74]

Family separations were a focal point of Ugandan Asian discontent. S.A. Dharamshi wrote to the Uganda Resettlement Board to protest the trauma his family had suffered due to constant transfers and camp closures. When Dharamshi's mother, brother, and sister arrived in England, they were all sent to Stradishall. At the same time, Dharamshi was transferred to Plaisterdown against his will. His requests to be reunited with his family were denied. When Plaisterdown was scheduled for closure in 1973, he tried again to get to Stradishall, but he was sent instead to Doniford. His brother was moved to Gaydon. Dharamshi wrote about the emotional impact of these events, but also about how family separations actually delayed the ultimate goal of resettlement:

> The fact that we have been separated for a very long time has brought us a lot of heartache and heart-break. On several occasions, we missed opportunities to resettle because we couldn't arrive at any conclusion through lack of person to person discussion. Honestly speaking, we would have been resettled long ago if we were reunited... this idea of keeping us separate has helped neither me nor the Resettlement Board, I am afraid. The idle and parasitical life at camps has nearly brainwashed us of any initiative and enterprising ideas we came to this country with and the longer we remain at camps the greater are the possibilities that we will find normal life too difficult to adjust to.

Dharamshi asked for a transfer to Gaydon, noting that "as we are going to live as a joint family in this country as well, you must realize that my request is fair... Please, help me."[75] The authorities' rejection of his claims contrasts sharply with the situation of the Anglo-Egyptians, in which large, intergenerational families had been favored for home purchase schemes. Jan Romijn, a social worker in London, noted the contradictions of resettlement policies for Ugandan Asians, and the strains they placed on the extended family: "When we don't know what to do with the old and needy people we call it the responsibility of the extended family. When they want to reunite their families we tell them that their children are old enough to stand on their own feet."[76] Many elderly Ugandan Asians were hastily rehoused—often on their own—when the camps closed down.[77] The intergenerational family was alternately valued and devalued in the sphere of refugee work.

As with the Poles and the Ugandan Asians, those who worked with refugees from Vietnam worried that refugees might define "family" differently from Britons. These differences were unevenly enshrined in immigration law. The government's family reunion policy for refugees from Vietnam was initially quite liberal. Married siblings were allowed to come over with their families, for example. As the number of Vietnamese refugees in Britain rose to more than 14,000, the state became increasingly stringent in its criteria for "family," and narrowed the definition to include only spouses, unmarried children under the age of 21, and aged parents who were living alone in Vietnam.[78] Relatives who were not normally considered "dependent" in Britain were less sympathetically viewed, especially adult siblings who had been included in earlier phases.[79] The Home Office instructed refugee workers to assess Vietnamese claims about relatives very carefully: "It is essential to establish that if a Vietnamese says 'a sister' he does not really mean 'a cousin'!"[80]

Of the refugees from Vietnam in Britain, 20 percent were under 15 years of age, and a large percentage of the women were of reproductive age. The Family Planning Association of Hong Kong reported that only 15 percent of the refugees had ever used birth control, and English social workers urged the expansion of family planning services for refugees in Britain.[81] At Thorney Island, refugees were given lectures on family planning, but Vu Khanh Thanh of the Vietnamese Sub-Committee complained that "people have not yet applied the contraceptive practice properly," and there had been as many as ten abortions afterwards.[82] The Pill was made available at Thorney Island in the autumn of 1979.[83] Health visitors who screened the Vietnamese arrivals at Devizes, a Save the Children camp in Wiltshire, described "clear medical signs" of sexual frustration among the refugees, mostly "eligible bachelors." Unlike the Poles, Vietnamese men were assumed to be unlikely to marry, or even speak to, white English women. This demographic misalignment was expected to cause major social problems in resettlement centers.[84] One health worker took the fact that refugees from Vietnam "were unable to share food" with family members as a sign of the dysfunctions and pathologies that camps wrought.[85]

Refugee workers reported that women from Vietnam seemed to learn English more quickly than men, and women often ceased their studies in order to avoid embarrassing their husbands. At the same time, camp workers at Thorney Island were affronted that Vietnamese women were "so keen" to learn English that they would leave their babies up in their bedrooms, which was "the last thing we wanted them to do."[86] One volunteer described the children at Thorney Island as "immensely destructive," eating the flowers, and ransacking the orchards; "beautiful toys were given to the children by kind local people but the mothers were never too interested."[87] The director complained that "Vietnamese parents do not seem to realize that they should be responsible for their children," and threatened to close the playroom if the mothers continued to abuse the staff's generosity.[88] The daily routines of the camp—and in particular the emphasis on language training—were seen as promoting the family's upward mobility for the future, but also thwarting the family's ties during their period of encampment.

Camps generated their own tensions between husbands and wives from Vietnam. Hoang Thuy Mai, a 25-year-old Vietnamese woman at Sopley, was found dead in her hut after a drug overdose. Her husband and two children lived at Sopley with her, but her parents and six siblings were still trapped in Hong Kong. Her husband, Loi Binh Quach, appeared in court with tears streaming down his face, wearing a black armband. He recounted the strains of life in camp for the young couple: "since we arrived at Sopley, we quarreled a lot as she missed her family. We never used to quarrel in Vietnam."[89]

As with the Polish refugees, aid workers for refugees from Vietnam often became intimately involved with their residents' marital problems. Many social workers perceived wife-battering as a "normal" feature of Vietnamese life, which would

Fig. 4.2. Vietnamese boy with gun at Sopley. Photograph by Tim Page.

inevitably occur in the camps.[90] At Thorney Island, one wife from Vietnam was reluctant to be resettled with her husband because of their "domestic problems" (typically a euphemism for violence). The staff concluded that these problems would have to be sorted out after the couple left the camp.[91] Just before that meeting, a staff member was assaulted by a resident with a 7-foot pole for trying to intervene in a matrimonial dispute.[92] There were multiple references to women in the camp being afraid of their husbands—one man had threatened to attack his wife with a hatchet. The Centre leadership advocated informing women about their legal rights in Britain. But even in cases of domestic violence, Vietnamese fieldworkers often encouraged refugee couples to stay together. They perceived the population as too vulnerable to withstand divorce.[93] When one Thorney Island couple wanted a divorce, the Vietnamese Committee acted as "marriage counselor," and the couple eventually abandoned the idea.[94]

Overwhelmingly, the state saw the single refugee—or those who wished to be single—as a threat to the project of resettlement. For Polish ex-soldiers or Ugandan Asian wives whose husbands were detained outside of Britain, camp authorities viewed "single" residents as those who should leave the camp first, who were least worthy of aid. But with varying degrees of success, the "single" refugees pushed back against the state's definition of what counted as a family, urging camp authorities to consider that refugees required different definitions of kinship. In the realm of sexual behavior, too, many refugees refused to adopt the camp's norms.

SEX, INTIMACY, AND "IMMORALITY" IN CAMP LIFE

Refugee camps figured in the British press as places where families were tragically separated or happily reunited. But government documents also depicted the camps as sites of sexual misbehavior that required intervention. Camp officials believed that some refugees were morally teachable, while others were prone to sexual immorality. Despite careful attention by refugee workers to teaching gendered behavior—and the investment of governmental resources in reinforcing these norms—refugees constantly threatened to reject the camp's ideals.

At times, concerns about immorality in refugee camps became a matter of life and death. Such was the case with the British debate about who counted as a "child" in a refugee camp, which focused on the age limit for Basque refugees. The stakes for defining Basque refugees as "children" were incredibly high. It was their status as children that allowed the Basques to enter Britain, even as the government clung to its position of neutrality and nonintervention. But the definition of a "child" shifted throughout the Spanish Civil War. While very young children signaled hope for the future, the broader category of "youth" and adolescence was tinged with anxiety. Increased protection for children was also linked to increased monitoring and surveillance.[95]

Sir Wilfred Roberts, Secretary of the National Joint Committee for Spanish Relief, initially vowed that no children under the age of 9 would be allowed to enter Britain.[96] But as the bombing of civilians escalated in Spain, British authorities debated whether the parameters for entry should be set at ages 6 to 12, or 5 to 15. Leah Manning, who oversaw the trip from Spain to Southampton, castigated the British government for its initial refusal to accept any Basque child under 8 or over 14, which "undermined all our ideas about families staying together...Were these tiny children to be left behind in a city about to fall into the hands of the enemy, the young girls to be raped by the *tercio* [a division of the Spanish Army], and their brothers shot as traitors?"[97] For most of the crisis, Britain allowed Basques between the ages of 5 and 15 to enter Britain as refugees. The Home Office preferred girls in the higher age range, and sent an urgent telegram to Bilbao expressing its preference for girls.[98] In practice, the age restrictions were more fluid. Many parents lied about their sons' age in order to get them safely to England. The Ministry of Health believed that boys over the age of 12 might be intensely politicized, as they were approaching military age.[99]

One widespread concern was that older children would have to be separated by sex in camp to avoid "immoral" mixing.[100] One sanitary inspector complained that the Basques had no sense of decency or modesty, and the boys and girls used the latrine together "in the same filthy manner."[101] Numerous documents stressed the need for constant, effective supervision of Basque adolescents, whose status as "child" refugees was precarious. Camp leaders lamented that they could not keep the Basques in their beds at night, nor prevent boys and girls from sleeping together.[102] Adolescent Basque girls were characterized as "seductive" to (or in need of protection from) local men. At the Oakley Park colony, English girls were allowed to visit the camp if their mothers were with them, but the Basque boys were forbidden to be alone with them; "it would not do as the English people are watching the behavior of the Spanish boys."[103]

At times, the aims of family unity and sexual morality conflicted.[104] British authorities had pledged to keep children from the same family together in camp. But the demands of propriety thwarted the goal of keeping refugee siblings together. One sanitary inspector described how the Basques were separated by sex when they arrived at North Stoneham—the boys going to one person and the girls to another—and were put to bed in separate tents, but "finally ended up by running wild all over the field."[105] Older girls were given a special dressing tent for privacy. At the Tunbridge Wells colony, the North Stoneham authorities instructed the matron that siblings must not be separated; thus, boys of 11 were placed to sleep in the dorm with girls of 14. The matron agreed, but once the children had "settled down happily, she is sure there will be no hardship in separating brothers and sisters." All the children were, fortunately, "clean in their habits."[106]

Elsewhere, too, camp authorities were preoccupied with the sexual behavior of their residents. Single-sex camps, such as internment camps during the Second World War, were plagued by reports of homosexual behavior. Klaus Hinrichsen viewed homosexuality at Hutchinson as a "problem among younger men," and a reason why it was important to give each man his own bed; he also suggested that internees who were "latent homosexuals" would experience their identity in new ways in the camp environment.[107] Leo Kahn described two kinds of homosexual behavior in Onchan. He differentiated what he called the "lower" or "despised" kind of homosexual, akin to a prostitute, who came into the open in the disrupted environment of internment, from the "decent and civilized homosexual," for whom Kahn gained empathy and respect.[108]

Sexual behavior was closely monitored in Polish camps, especially when the Poles were under military rule. The War Office issued strict orders that girls—and indeed all visitors—were forbidden in camp except on authorized days. But it was logistically impossible to monitor everyone who was entering and leaving. In 1946, the police raided a Polish camp at Watton, near Driffield, after complaints from local residents about the camp's illicit activities. No girls were found on the first raid, but a surprise visit the next night revealed eighty girls hiding in the huts, and in the soldiers' beds.[109] Most of the girls were between the ages of 14 and 18; they were rounded up and put on buses back to Hull. One volunteer described young English girls sleeping with Poles at two different camps in Northumberland, estimating that "60–70% of the blame lay with the girls."[110] *Dziennik Polski* reported in 1946 that Anglo-Polish relations at a military camp in Newcastle were "downright hot," as all the soldiers were "simply enchanted" by local women. The camp commander complained, "we are constantly besieged by English women...I even had to double the guards in the camp, because English women started wandering around the area where the [soldiers'] quarters are, and one mummy has already lodged a complaint."[111]

Faced with immoral or even criminal behavior, most wardens simply moved troublesome refugees to other hostels, or even out of the country. They avoided the courts, which were expensive and drew unwanted scandal. In 1948, the warden of Stowell Park wrote to the Ministry of Labour and National Service about Maria Kondratiew, who had been taken away from her mother because of the mother's "unsatisfactory" way of life. The girl was now also demonstrating her own "leanings towards immorality," and was a bad influence. He proposed moving Kondratiew to a different hostel.[112] In another case at Northwick, a Polish family was scheduled to emigrate to Canada, but the father was also due to appear in court for charges of indecent assault on young girl residents at the hostel. The warden lobbied the police to drop the case so that it would not interfere with the emigration. The charges were dropped, and the family proceeded to Canada.[113]

The National Assistance Board debated what standards of sexual morality to employ in its Polish camps. For example, should unmarried couples be allowed to live together? The Board treated unmarried British couples who lived together (and received national assistance) as if they were husband and wife. In Polish camps, relationships between unmarried men and women were typically accepted unless they appeared "lightly entered into," or otherwise immoral. Wardens were informed that "the Poles are considered to be a moral people."[114] But one Board member argued that these couples hurt the Board's reputation. Existing cases should be left undisturbed, but "fresh cases should not be allowed to flourish." Those who violated this rule should be made to terminate their association or leave the hostel. The fact that cohabitation was allowed amongst Britons "does not commit us to permitting it in hostels."[115] Here, the Board raised the prospect that Britons and Poles might be compelled into different standards of sexual behavior. These standards, however, were constantly changing, making it all the more difficult for refugees to conform to British norms.

In one hostel, a couple who went by the name of Czak was known to be cohabiting. Mr. Czak was willing to pay charges for Miss Czak's illegitimate children as long as he was assessed as a married man for income tax purposes. The warden reported that Miss Czak worked to support herself and her children, and that Mr. Czak was "honest and desirous" of marrying her. The Board concluded that the case should be treated as if the residents were British, because there were so many "abnormal conditions of doubts" regarding the survival of spouses in Poland, which deprived the Poles of "a normal married life." The warden helped Mr. Czak obtain proof of his first wife's death so that he could remarry in camp.[116] Cases in which a Pole refused to maintain an unmarried partner were more complicated. The Board acknowledged that it could not require Mr. Muraszko, the head cook at Hiltingbury, to pay for the woman with whom he cohabited, "but he has a moral obligation to do so and he is aware that we expect him to honor this obligation" if he were to avoid being seen as an "undesirable."[117] The main disciplinary technique was moral suasion; legal options (such as eviction or criminal proceedings) were avoided.

For the Poles, camps became a site for instructing women about appropriate feminine behavior. Wardens selected "suitable" Polish women—youthful, with good English, and motivated to leave the hostels quickly—to undergo "severely practical" domestic training courses. These women would reside briefly in English homes, where they would be in close contact with English women's routines: coping with rationing, shopping, looking after children, and "making the best use of all the social service facilities." These women, who were paid 15 shillings per week to undergo training, would then act as "guides" for other Polish women in the camps, offering advice about "how best they can slip into English way of social and domestic life to which it is our duty to assimilate them."[118] Thus, encamped Polish women would be trained in the economies and social norms of the ordinary English housewife. They would "domesticate" the space of the camp, and properly manage their own future homes.

With the Anglo-Egyptians, British expectations were thwarted not through sexual misbehavior, but through fears about "backward" Anglo-Egyptian women who stubbornly refused to modernize. The WVS urged these women to transform the hostels into "homely" environments, and to make the spaces "brighter and more attractive" through the use of "gay posters, flowers, bright curtains." The WVS also encouraged Anglo-Egyptians to make their own clothes, and sent seeds to all the hostels, though the women refused to garden. WVS helpers complained that the average Anglo-Egyptian woman did not know how to use a broom, and must be trained in domestic labor.

The WVS set up nurseries in Anglo-Egyptian hostels "so that the children are not endlessly trailed round by their mothers and kept cooped up in bedrooms for a large part of the day." Mothers who kept their children with them in "small rooms" were seen as unhealthy. Some WVS helpers at Summerfield did not believe a nursery was necessary, as children in the hostel should be their mother's responsibility. But Lady Stella Reading, then the chair of WVS, instructed the staff that "we must act as mothers to them all and do little things for them." She concluded that Anglo-Egyptian children were happier and healthier when they were "spared" constant contact with their mothers.[119]

The WVS had another agenda, which was to urge all refugee women to take up paid employment: "these Anglo-Egyptian repatriates are unaccustomed to having their women folk work, and in many cases will consider this a very undignified proceeding." The WVS intended to "make them realize what a large proportion of British women are in employment including married women and mothers when their children are at school."[120] WVS helpers complained that Anglo-Egyptian girls at Summerfield thought it was "infra dig" (that is, beneath their dignity) to work, and refused to enter the labor force. The WVS deployed lecturers to discuss wages with Anglo-Egyptian women, exhorting them that "women have to work, and that they work equally with men."[121]

Such conflicting messages for refugees emerged at a moment of ambivalence in British culture about whether married women's work would promote the values of equality or operate as a destabilizing force.[122] Just as the Anglo-Egyptians arrived in 1957, married women's share of the British workforce passed 50 percent.

Refugee women were incorporated into this optimistic narrative of the democratized family.[123] The male breadwinner ideal came under stress—but was never eradicated—by the situation of families in flight. Rather, refugee families exposed the flaws and obstacles that emerged with this ideal in practice.

Life in the Anglo-Egyptian hostels involved a regime of enforced domesticity, in which women were instructed to uphold the increasingly high standards of the British housewife. Indeed, the material aid these women received depended on how well they proved that they had absorbed these lessons, and were ready for their own private home. In 1957, the *Kidderminster Shuttle* reported that while many Anglo-Egyptian women had servants in Egypt, they had completely changed their attitude, and were now happily doing "the usual domestic work." But, the newspaper warned, "until you get them into their own four walls this change won't happen. As long as they are in the hostel they will lean on their husbands."[124] Yet camp leaders also urged Anglo-Egyptian women into paid work—often against the wishes of their male family members. The AERB invited women's organizations to teach Anglo-Egyptians "how women in Britain desire to make careers for themselves independently of their menfolk."[125] Refugee women must learn to be perfect housewives, but they must be ideal workers as well.

The campaign to convert Anglo-Egyptian women to the "modern" norms of working womanhood in the 1950s offers a striking contrast with British responses to Ugandan Asian women in the 1970s. Although one would expect that Ugandan Asian women would come under more pressure to work outside the home, as they arrived in a moment in which women's paid labor was more accepted, the opposite was true. Ugandan Asian women were expected to be more dependent on their male breadwinner in the 1970s than were Anglo-Egyptian women in the 1950s. Indeed, as we have seen in the stateless husbands campaign, Ugandan Asian women successfully negotiated British expectations of their dependency on male breadwinners in order to circumvent immigration controls. For the Anglo-Egyptians, true resettlement was to be heralded by women taking up paid employment. For Ugandan Asians, reunion with a male breadwinner was the sign that resettlement was complete. Some refugee women were left strictly alone, while others were seen as in need of intervention.

Here, we can see the contradictory messages about gender, work, and home that refugees faced, and how these messages oscillated over time. Such cases illustrate that the consequences of encampment differed for men and women. Women faced more powerful (and contradictory) demands that they conform to shifting expectations of gender roles for "modern" Britons. Ugandan Asian men and women also had different experiences of the camp, with uneven points of contact with locals. Men at Stradishall spent their days in job interviews or walking the tree-lined paths in small groups, while their wives visited with local families. Residents of Haverhill, 7 miles away, called frequently to take Ugandan Asian women to the market.[126] In Vietnamese camps, too, refugee men and women experienced resettlement very differently. Men were urged into speedy employment, while women were deliberately delayed. The camp authorities at Sopley claimed that Vietnamese women "are not suited to taking up domestic work until they have lived in this country for some time and got used to our way of life." For this reason, Vietnamese women were not supposed to look for paid work until they were resettled.[127]

The geographic isolation of many camps placed refugees and aid workers in intimate proximity, which sparked some interracial romances. Lee Allane (a volunteer at the Ugandan Asian camp at Raleigh Hall, who had studied Islamic and Oriental art at Oxford and Manchester) recalled his time in camp as "exciting," and full of "handsome boys and pretty girls." Whereas the civil servants from the Department of Employment and DHSS went home every night, the young volunteers actually lived in the camp with the Ugandan Asian residents. The remote location of the camp—6 or 7 miles to the nearest pub—increased the closeness of volunteers and residents, who held parties in their huts together. Allane perceived the largely Ismaili residents at Raleigh Hall as "very Westernized" and approving of the liaisons that took place in camp.[128] Some of these romances (including Allane's own with a camp resident, and several relationships or marriages between white British fieldworkers and Vietnamese refugees) outlasted the camp closures.[129] But Allane was also aware that the camp did not reflect the real world; it was like a "little island in a country," an "unnatural scenario" where normal pressures and expectations did not exist.

Camp residents had different recollections of this kind of intimacy. Atul Patel recalled that because the local schools in Devon "just did not want to know us," Honiton was full of teenagers "running free around this very compact area. The

Fig. 4.3. Volunteers tidying up Raleigh Hall for Ugandan Asians. Photograph courtesy of *Staffordshire Newsletter*.

Fig. 4.4. Ugandan Asians at Stradishall Camp in Suffolk take part in a rock 'n' roll session with members of the local Youth Aid. Keystone Pictures USA/Alamy Stock Photo.

proximity of living was something that they had never experienced before." From Patel's perspective, the camp posed a tremendous opportunity for young Asian men who had hardly any contact with young women until that point. At Honiton, teenagers were "jumping in and out of beds! We had nothing to do." Patel's testimony is startling for what it reveals next: "So you can imagine closeness. And, of course, one other outcome or by-product of this kind of proximity for teenagers are relationships. And so unwanted pregnancies were a phenomenon, which is unreported in this history because nobody talks about it."[130] Many relationships among young people in camps were unsanctioned by parents. The camps offered no way to enact barriers: for example, between Hindus and Muslims. For this reason, Patel suggested, parents of girls especially wanted to leave the camps quickly to protect their daughters. Some interracial relationships between residents and staff continued after the camps closed, though Patel noted that the rumor that white girls were "easy" only led to some very disappointing experiences for him at the local disco.

For Patel, the camp offered not only romantic and sexual opportunities, but also a reconfiguration of his nuclear family. Disenchanted with what he saw as an increasingly unsavory atmosphere in the camp, he began working in Exeter as a machine operator, making rotary blades for aircraft engines: "here I was operating this machine and I began to understand the British working life and the British working people with whom I had connections. And they were a very different group of people."¹³¹ Patel lied about his age to get the job, and began paying national insurance at 17. He had a salary, and gave money to his relatives.¹³² During this time, Patel's father was not with the family. Every day, his family would look through the list of new arrivals until one day they saw his father's name: "And I thought, you know, that's my father. I said where is this guy? And the admin people looked at the record and said 'he's in Wales.' And I thought, sorry, where is Wales?" As it turned out, his father had "drunk himself sick" during the separation from his family. He was taken directly from the airport to a Welsh hospital for detox, "because he couldn't even articulate a sentence to say." Patel's father eventually reunited with his relatives at Honiton, "so then now there was four of us, we were a family again." After this traumatic episode, his father stopped drinking and became the spouse his mother had always wanted: emotionally accessible, and interested in forging new social networks in camp. For the Patels, encampment played a crucial role in shaping the family's new emotional life in Britain.

Patel's story, with its many twists and turns, highlights the unpredictable impact of encampment on family life. As the individual stories of this chapter suggest, camps shaped refugee families in myriad ways, not only extending their separation and division, but also bringing about their (often troubled) reunions. Furthermore, camps and hostels often made their aid dependent on meeting certain expectations of behavior, many of which were covertly or openly resisted by refugees. The dictates of emergency could either heighten—or eradicate—the inequalities between refugee men and women.

Depending on the context, refugees could advance their own agendas by either rejecting or embracing British norms of gender and family. "Family" was defined differently for each refugee population, and traditional gender roles were not so easy to enforce within the camp. In the 1940s and 1950s, Poles sought to revamp British definitions of the nuclear family in order to encompass the (often tragic) realities of lives that had been structured and transformed by the war. By contrast, Ugandan Asian men and women in camps actually drew on conventional British beliefs about Asian family structure in Britain to deploy their own resistance.

By the time refugees emerged from their camps, they had been taught many lessons about roles for men and women—and husbands and wives—in Britain. But there was no guarantee that they would conform to these expectations, either in camp or in the community.

This chapter has looked at intimacy within the camp. But what about beyond it? What kinds of interactions and relationships did refugees forge with the world outside the camp? Chapter 5 explores how refugee camps brought diverse populations—specifically, camp residents and the locals who surrounded them—into close, personal contact.

5

Mixing Up

In Continental Europe, refugees were often violently resented by the locals who lived near their camps, especially after the Second World War. The sociologist Maria Pfister-Ammende recorded how one villager near a Swiss camp said of the refugees, "To tell the truth, we wish they were all dead."[1] British interactions with refugees were rarely so openly hostile. But they had their own antagonisms, perils, and pleasures. Depending on the historical moment, refugees in Britain could be imagined in opposition to both citizens and migrants, or as closer to one than the other.[2]

Refugee spaces have always been in fluid interactions with the cities and nations of which they are part.[3] The refugee camp was a spatial practice as well as a temporal one.[4] The term "camp" is derived from the Latin term *campus*, an open space for military exercise that was set apart from other areas. Many refugee camps extended this distinction with clearly demarcated boundaries (such as fences or barbed wire), while others promoted the free circulation of people, goods, and ideas. In Britain, refugee camps bore complex relationships to the cities and towns they bordered. Here, I examine how camps interacted with local populations, including communities of color, generating new intimacies and frictions.

Camps are typically imagined to emphasize the differences between those who lived inside and outside more than any differences among the residents. But thinking of refugee camps as being only for "foreign" refugees misses the complexity of their demography. Licitly or not, many Britons lived in refugee camps—not only giving aid, but also receiving it. This was especially true in times of war, when the displacement of Britons spiked dramatically, and the possibility of mass encampment seemed urgently local. But even in peacetime, Britain was still full of people who were in need and on the move.

BREAKING BOUNDS: LOCALS AND THE REFUGEE CAMP

Camps varied in their openness to the surrounding community, but also in whether this openness was positively or negatively perceived. Camp leaders in Britain might work to isolate the residents from locals, or to mix them together. Refugee camps aimed to instill particular kinds of feelings as well as specific behaviors—feelings of kinship with other refugees, or with different groups of Britons. These aims were never easily achieved. Even when camps were focal points of intense media and local interest, these interactions did not necessarily alter refugees' sense that they were cut off from the larger community.

The Belgian refugee crisis was noteworthy not only because of the scale of the refugee influx, but also because of the scale of British volunteerism. Few Britons had zero contact with Belgian refugees, and walking to one of the camps to see "the Beljums" was popular entertainment.[5] At the peak of the operation, 2,000 local committees were working on Belgian aid.[6] Yet aid workers were warned that relations between Britons and Belgians should be no more than cordial. Friendly intimacy might easily become disorder.[7] One hostess's refugees were miserable, despite their handsome rooms and good meals, because she tried to press them into closer contact, giving them tea when they longed for coffee, and expensive beef instead of the "cheap, savory dishes...dear to their souls."[8]

Camp authorities for Basque children took a much more extreme attitude of isolationism. The children were met by a huge outpouring of public sympathy, especially from those who had opposed Britain's policy of neutrality in Spain. Various celebrities visited the children in camp: Paul Robeson, the heavyweight boxing champion Joe Beckett, and the Hungarian war correspondent Arthur Koestler, who had himself been imprisoned by Franco's regime.[9] But despite this enthusiasm, British officials sought to limit contact between locals and the Basque children. The rationale for segregating the child refugees shifted over time—from protecting the Basques from communist indoctrination to shielding Britons from unpredictable "foreign" youths.

Officially, the Basque children were in the hands of a network of volunteers, not the British government. The Basque Children's Committee, organized by the National Joint Committee for Spanish Relief (an umbrella organization for 150 different groups) had overseen their passage from Spain to England. Still, once the children landed at North Stoneham, British officials treated these volunteers with skepticism. Turning up in their best clothes, they seemed misguided and unhelpful.[10] In some colonies, volunteers were rejected altogether in order to reduce interactions between the Basques and locals.[11] E.P. Harries of the Trades Union Congress complained that once the "rough work" of setting up the camp was done, British workers were squeezed out and "middle-class persons" were imported to take their place. He remarked that there were more sightseers at the camp than refugees.[12] Hundreds of local children were "in camp playing with the refugees."[13] The camp authorities had to broadcast an appeal for all visitors to leave the camp at 10:15 p.m. so that the Basque children could go to bed.

Trespassers were a constant problem at North Stoneham. When a sanitary inspector asked visitors for their passes, he was "quite surprised...We did not know that the camp enjoyed the services of such an aristocratic looking sanitary squad complete with button holes and cameras." He feared that many people were using the "passes" as meal tickets, trying to eat enough to last them for the week-end. The head cook complained that volunteers "had a damn good breakfast, loafed about all day, had a good dinner at night and then went home." The Basque boys "were lounging in the tents and swinging in the trees."[14] The camp was "infested

Fig. 5.1. The photographer Edith Tudor-Hart, herself a Jewish refugee from Austria, was a supporter of the Republican cause. A former Montessori teacher, she often portrayed Basque and English children playing or working together. Edith Tudor-Hart, "Basque and English School Boys, North Stoneham Camp." Courtesy of the National Galleries of Scotland.

with sightseers and photographers," who generated more chaos.[15] The state's vision of aid without assimilation—or even interaction—was a constant challenge. The goal of total isolation for the Basques was never achieved.

Other refugee camps also drew intense local interest. Celia Lee, a Jewish child refugee, found the media attention at Dovercourt very wearying. Although she appreciated the "very nice camp," with its big garden and a view of the sea, "all day long we get no peace. Wherever we went we met reporter. At first it was fun and we liked it, but afterwards we got tired of: standing, jumping, dancing and sitting, of talking to and shaking hands."[16] Kitchener Camp, too, was frequented by reporters; its opening was a major media event. Keystone Press came to Kitchener in 1939, photographing the tallest refugee next to the smallest. Phineas May thought these visits were "a nuisance," and yet felt he must be polite in order to gain positive press.[17]

On Sundays, Londoners "flocked" to Kitchener to see the reconstruction of the camp, attend concerts, and speak with the residents. The sleepy country road leading into the camp became "just like 'downtown,'" and police were required to direct the multitude of cars, buses, and bicycles." Young Britons came to Kitchener to play

Fig. 5.2. A group of visitors walking down a street at Kitchener. Courtesy of The Wiener Library.

darts, excluding the camp residents, which led to stricter rules about the admission of visitors.[18] Some locals, at least, expected total access to the camp. In July 1939, two entire motor-coachloads of "trippers" drove into Kitchener. When May asked who they were, the visitors replied that they "were from some convalescent home and were going to see round the camp." May said they required written permission, as "this was a private camp and we would not have large parties of people going round as it was not a place of entertainment." In his view, the visitors were "the rough and very common type who thought they were fully entitled to do what they liked in the Camp." The visitors were outraged, and threatened to contact the press about the camp's "inhospitality."

The *Kitchener Camp Review* printed many paeans to the nearby town of Sandwich, "with its lovely places, its cozy corners, its mosaic-like walls of timber and bricks, laid in manifold patterns." The populations of Kitchener and Sandwich were roughly equal in size, which made for an interesting balance of camp and town. Sandwich was a small, but fashionable watering hole for the wealthy and powerful, replete with golf courses and private clubs. Refugees contrasted the peace of the countryside with the camp itself, which was described as being very "Continental" in mood, filled with traumatized refugees whose nerves were "oscillating wildly." As one article suggested, one must go outside the camp's gates to come to England, even though "the Camp is becoming England too."[19] One refugee's poem dedicated to Sandwich juxtaposed the Jews' tumultuous history with the calm pastures and winding streets of this old English town:

"I, son of an old people feel the scent / Of history, feel lucky that my tent / Is far now from the dangers of the sea."[20]

Camp authorities worried about anti-Semitic forces in town; blackshirts came by the camp with their flag, and Kitchener men were not allowed to go to Sandwich on days when fascists were holding meetings.[21] One Kitchener resident described Sandwich's population as "markedly reserved" at first. Refugees from Nazism often had to explain at a very basic level the reasons why they had fled their homes.[22] Peter Mansbacher, who had toiled to renovate the camp, was annoyed by visitors who exclaimed over Kitchener's loveliness, and assumed that the state had provided everything. As they admired the paved roads and the flower gardens, they said, "Bet you are glad you came to such a nice camp, aren't you? These men must be very happy!"[23] Mansbacher resented that locals knew nothing of the hardships the refugees had suffered, nor of the physical labor they had performed at Kitchener.

Over time, the locals of Sandwich grew more sympathetic, offering small gifts of sweets, cigarettes, and shoelaces. Kitchener hosted large concerts—performed in English—for friends of the camp. The *Kitchener Camp Review* reported that the Jewish refugees cycled with the locals. The refugees recounted how they played "like children" on these expeditions; as they recalled, "we are cheerful and happy like them." After a sack race and riding blindfolded, the group stopped for tea at a

Fig. 5.3. Float from Kitchener Camp with Kitchener residents on top and banner saying "Our Thanks to England" in a parade in 1939. Courtesy of The Wiener Library.

British Legion hut where the tables were bright with flowers, everything was "gay and cheerful," and "happy English girls" served the treats.[24]

Ultimately, Kitchener Camp aimed at forging close relationships between its own residents, not between camp dwellers and locals. Phineas May described the friendships that developed at Kitchener as "far different from those of ordinary life." The men of Kitchener enjoyed "the comradeship of the trenches, where men facing the unknown future, formed attachments deep and unbreakable."[25] Alfred Lomnitz, who was interned at Huyton, also thought the friendships he made in camp were superior to those outside: "life in Town is too rational, materialistic and superficial." Outside the camp, "one misses a great deal, both in life and in friendship."[26]

At North Stoneham and Kitchener, Britons were primarily visitors and spectators. But in refugee camps, Britons were not only observers. Sometimes, they were inhabitants as well. In Polish camps, Poles encountered working-class Britons, who were experiencing their own forms of displacement. Britons and Poles moved through these camps together, though the British presence was often unacknowledged or denied.

This mixing of Britons and refugees in the "refugee" camp took place at a moment when such camps were increasingly represented in British popular culture. Under the Camp Clearance Programme, which started in 1958, British towns could "adopt" a whole Continental European camp and take responsibility for its clearance. A "refugee camp" was exhibited at the Crystal Palace in 1960, complete with a faux border guard. Fake refugee camps in London and Manchester were enormously popular.[27] That same year, sixty people at St. Leonard's Church in Hove paid 2s 6d to eat a real "refugee meal." This event, a fundraiser for World Refugee Year, was designed to give Britons a sense of the hardships refugees endured. They were served bread, cheese, and coffee—but no butter with the bread, no milk or sugar with the coffee, and the cheese was deliberately "old and stale."[28] Plays about refugees were also staged in British theatres: *The Price of Freedom*, *Sorry for Them*, and James Brabazon's *People of Nowhere*.[29]

The plight of refugees was thus both literally and figuratively "staged" in highly public ways. All of these representations, though, denied the presence of refugee camps in Britain itself—as well as the presence of Britons in these camps. In popular exhibitions and plays, Britons were selfless heroes who occupied a position of wealth and strength, and rescued victims of injustice abroad. The role of Britons as camp residents was ignored.

BRITONS IN NEED: CITIZENS IN THE REFUGEE CAMP

Refugee camps were an important site of exchange across cultures. Refugees and citizens interacted in camps not only as tragic victims and heroic saviors. Rather, they were twinned populations in need. The mixing of Poles and Britons, specifically, was an important part of the increased diversity of populations galvanized by the Second World War.[30] In 1941, the novelist Rose Macaulay in the *Listener* described how "the pageant of life is enormously enriched by the presence of so many foreigners in our midst... the uniforms of Polish soldiers mingle with those of Czechs, Norwegians, Dutch and Free French."[31] The British media charted the arrival of Polish troops in 1940, and films such as *Dangerous Moonlight* and Eugeniusz Cekalski's *Diary of a Polish Airman* (1942) celebrated Polish aviators. Such mingling prompted interallied friendships and frictions.

Still, when the war ended, these alliances were strained. Harold Macmillan had always worried that the Polish troops in Britain would "disintegrate into a rabble of refugees." He was proved wrong by the Poles' bravery in battle, but Anglo-Polish tensions spiked after the war.[32] In a public-relations fiasco, Poles were excluded from the 1946 Victory Parade in London at the Soviet Union's request. A Gallup Poll of June 1946 showed that 56 percent of Britons surveyed favored deporting the Poles.[33] Stefan Knapp, a Pole who fought in the Battle of Britain, remembered "choking with bitterness" about his rejection after the war: "Not so long ago I had enjoyed the exaggerated prestige of a fighter pilot and the hysterical adulation that surrounded him. Suddenly I was turned into the slag everybody wanted to be rid of, a thing useless, burdensome, even noxious. It was very hard to bear."[34] Some West Indians, who had also fought for the British, envied the resettlement aid that Polish soldiers received.[35] Both of these histories—of valorizing Poles during the war, and resenting them thereafter—would shape the culture of encampment for Poles and Britons in the late 1940s and 1950s.

Most camp leaders assumed that interactions between Britons and Poles were minimal. At Ashby Hostel, just a few locals attended the Polish Independence Day celebrations. The warden described the English villagers as "mostly simple country folk... not the type who go in for social events in a big way."[36] At Marsworth, the warden rated relations with locals as "satisfactory" to "good," but acknowledged that the villagers and hostel residents led separate lives.[37] At the Keevil Polish Hostel, local feeling was still "not as good as it might be."[38] On occasion, Poles and Britons did socialize together in the camps. In 1949, 100 British guests attended a party at Burton-on-the-Wolds Hostel, the old RAF camp in North Leicestershire, with fiddlers and folk dancers performing for hours. Here, "the thin, prosaic asbestos walls sheltered a small corner of happy pre-war Poland from the keen wind that blew over the gentle rolls of the English countryside outside."[39] At Tweedsmuir camp, the Rogalski brothers attended bonfires on Thursley Green for Guy Fawkes Day. But their visits with English children were rare, perhaps once a year.[40]

Schools provided an opportunity for some Poles and Britons to socialize, though not always happily. Local schools often forbade children from the camps to speak Polish.[41] Zosia and Jurek Biegus recalled how Polish parents often withdrew their children from English schools, so that they could attend a camp school "to learn good Polish and broken English."[42] Urszula Szulakowska saw her English school as "peripheral to my real life which was literally miles away in the fields around the camp and with the Polish community." She felt no connection to the town of Melton Mowbray, of which "I saw very little. I was impressed by the leafy trees around the school and it seemed to me, what little I saw of it at the age of seven from the school bus, as a place of wealth and glamour, removed from my own realities."[43]

There was, however, another story to be told about Britons and Poles, and how they mixed in camps together. After the Second World War, local authorities took over a large number of camps as temporary housing. During the summer and autumn of 1946, tens of thousands of Britons—at least 40,000 in England and Wales, and 7,000 more in Scotland—occupied these army camps: a desperate, unauthorized response to a growing housing crisis.[44] Aerial bombardment had destroyed over 200,000 houses in Britain. Profiteering and overcrowding spurred further displacements. For the most part, the media portrayed the squatters sympathetically. Squatters created an air of homeliness and respectability in hutted camps (hanging curtains and wallpaper, putting in plumbing and electricity, renaming the camps as "estates," and improvising street names and numbers on their hut doors). As they improved derelict spaces, they heightened their own moral claim to these properties.[45]

British squatters thwarted official efforts to control camp sites and populations. Some of these squatters were precisely those families that councils were not willing to place in brand-new houses because they were seen as unsatisfactory tenants. The Department of Housing and Local Government preferred to isolate these families in camps instead of evicting them.[46] For local authorities, refugee camps could be places to stash British "problem families." They provided a place to hide those citizens who were not adequately served by the state.

Many squatters referred to themselves as "refugees" from overcrowding. But this was more than just a metaphor.[47] British squatters often took over camps that had been earmarked for (or already occupied by) Poles, prompting difficulties for the War Office.[48] In August 1946, a deserted camp in Buckinghamshire that had been slated for Polish soldiers' wives was taken over by British ex-servicemen and their families. The thirty families who moved into the camp refused to vacate until suitable housing was found for them.[49] It would take 3,000 men to protect the camp. British troops were not available, and Polish guards could not be used since "awkward political questions" might arise if Poles kept homeless Britons from entering empty camps. The Poles had the stronger legal claim, but evicting homeless Britons in favor of foreigners would alienate the public. The Cabinet decided to send the Poles to other camps. Ultimately, the Cabinet was willing to pay for new construction rather than evicting the local squatters to make way for Poles.[50] Few Britons were prosecuted or evicted.[51]

Elsewhere, too, Polish and British families squatted in camps together. At the Tilstock Anglo-Polish Housing Units, forty huts were occupied by British families, and fifty-six by Poles, plus sixteen squatter families, of which six were Polish. The National Assistance Board said that British and Polish families lived together "amicably" on these sites, but planned to segregate them in a new conversion.[52] At the large Polish camp at Bicester, north Oxfordshire, which housed 600 Polish men, the scholar Maud Bülbring advocated using any vacant huts for homeless Britons.[53]

Local councils advised the National Assistance Board on how Britons and Poles should interact within camps. They explicitly designed several camps to house both British and Polish families. When one council took over a camp, it reserved specific sites for Poles, others for Britons, and one site for both nationalities together. A councilor concluded, "the advantage of intermixing is of course hardly local, but lies in a better understanding between the two nations, through appreciation of each other's way of life and outlook."[54]

By 1949, the National Assistance Board had developed a scheme to build village communities on former camp sites throughout Britain. Here, Poles would live side by side with Britons and learn "the British way of life." The *Birmingham Gazette* offered the headline, "The 'Phlegmatic British' will help to end hostel disturbances." The *Gazette* claimed that the regimentation of the hostel system tended to "disrupt the Slavonic temperament and inspire an irresponsibility which has been blamed for 'Polish troubles.'" Polish hostels and camps in the Midlands were converted into experimental villages in which British and Polish families would share the responsibility for their "mixed" community.[55]

Experiments with Anglo-Polish communities took place on a larger scale at Delamere in Cheshire. Delamere was one of the biggest camps in northwest England, which had housed up to 50,000 American troops. Polish troops began to arrive from Italy in the summer of 1946, and the American "street" names in the camp were changed to Polish ones (such as Sikorski Avenue). In 1949, Delamere was taken over by the Ministry of Housing and Local Government. At this point, 400 bombed-out British families were moved to Delamere. The huts were modernized: partitions created two flats per hut, each with a sitting room, two bedrooms, and a kitchen. Running water, stoves, and sanitation facilities were also installed. The British families generally left more quickly as they received council houses.[56] One Briton recalled living at Delamere after a family crisis, and although "we were not Polish," the Polish residents treated the family "as one of their own."[57]

Poles and Britons also lived together at the Wheaton Aston aerodrome, near the former bomber station at Seighford. The 180 Polish families were housed in the station's living quarters; 18 British families squatted in outlying units. The Ministry of Health took over the camp from the National Assistance Board in 1950. In 1951, the aerodrome was scheduled to reopen under a Royal Air Force expansion scheme. The local press emphasized the plight of displaced British families. One official said, "I suppose we shall have to find somewhere for the squatters though I cannot think where. It is much easier for the RAF to build huts than it is for us to build houses."[58] An English housewife who had been squatting at Wheaton Aston for four years said she would be "glad to get out of it." The *Staffordshire Advertiser* praised the squatters' efforts to create beauty and respectability:

> There are signs of brave attempts to turn the crude Service huts into homes. A rustic porch with roses growing on it has been incongruously added to one building, and the inhabited huts have bright curtains at the windows. But there are also signs of the council's attempts to discourage squatting; piles of rubble where huts have been demolished when the lucky families have found proper accommodation.[59]

From the outside, the former military huts were unattractive. But one priest had "a nice surprise" when he stepped into the huts, and saw holy pictures hanging on the wall, intricate Polish embroidery, and warm welcomes.[60] He noted that Wheaton Aston was not a Polish "ghetto"; hostel residents routinely played sports with their

English neighbors. By September of 1951, the English squatters had won the right to stay when the Air Ministry reopened the airfield.[61] In 1954, Wheaton Aston became known as Little Onn, an Anglo-Polish housing estate of converted huts managed by the local authority.[62] Polish families took 60 percent of the camp, and British families 40 percent.[63] By 1956, the camp—a short-lived experiment—had closed altogether, and the land had reverted to agriculture.

Transients and transience, then, were not limited to the Polish population. Kaz Janowski, who spent his childhood at Kelvedon Polish Hostel in Essex, recalled how his parents bought encyclopedias, a vacuum cleaner, and colorful rugs to brighten up their Nissen hut, all purchased from "men in turbans" who visited the camp as salesmen. Also in the mix was "the steady flow of disheveled-looking (English) rustics," as some of the airfield buildings were set up as wayfarers' centers. Janowski remembered seeing "gypsy" caravans moving through this part of camp, and ashamedly recalled one of his friends dropping a clod of dirt on the chest of a wayfarer who was sleeping in a camp ditch.[64]

Henry Pavlovich, who lived at Foxley Camp in Herefordshire as a child, recalled that when Poles left the camp, poor (often Irish) families took their place.[65] Mixed communities sprang up in what was still officially a "Polish" camp. In Pavlovich's memoir, he described the diverse populations that inhabited the camp: homeless Irish laborers, "Gypsies," Italians, and a few African Caribbean families who arrived in the mid-1950s "with catchy Calypso records." Pavlovich's father, a trumpet player, was intrigued by the new music and drums made from large oil or food cans. The "closet Mosaicists" and "Mohamedans" mournfully watched the Catholic processions at Foxley without participating. In Pavlovich's account, these "new-comers" were largely shunned in the camp: Polish children were "warned against straying or beaten for inappropriate friendships." In particular, the English and Irish residents in the camp were "totally unpredictable and uncomprehending about everything."[66]

At times, the projects of settling refugees and Britons collided. When the National Assistance Board took over the project of settling "casuals" (also known as vagrants or wayfarers), it was already responsible for scores of Polish hostels. These projects were typically kept separate, as most Polish hostels were deemed too remote to be used as shelters for poor Britons. But there were movements of convergence that reveal the mind of the state in dealing with unsettled peoples. At the Kelvedon Polish Hostel, the work of settling citizens and settling refugees came together in a single camp.

In 1950, the Board opened a reception center for British wayfarers at Kelvedon, which also served (since 1946) as a family camp for Poles in Essex. Poles and Britons were physically separated on the site, but they shared clothing, a warden, and a doctor; two Polish women also cooked for the British "vagrants." The task of caring for Poles and Britons together exhausted Kelvedon's warden, L.W. Moore. He pleaded for more staff and worried that he was "in danger of dissatisfying both populations."[67] As the British sector of the hostel became far more popular than expected, refugees and homeless Britons were drawn into closer contact.[68] Moore claimed that Poles and British wayfarers were conspiring against the state's authority. For example, the Polish doctors at Kelvedon were all too happy to give British wayfarers a certificate stating that they were unfit to work—the common room was "cluttered up" with idle men.[69]

In dealing with these two unsettled groups—Poles and Britons—the state's assumption was that refugeedom was temporary, but British vagrancy was permanent. The Polish hostel might eventually close, but the need for a place to shelter unsettled Britons seemed never-ending.[70] Worse yet, West Indians and the Irish might become "unsettled" in the future as well.[71] The Board's officials found refugee work more gratifying than work with poor or homeless Britons, perhaps feeling that refugee problems had solutions. As we will see, the expectation that Polish hostels would close quickly was not borne out, and so the imagined difference between refugees and homeless Britons began to break down.

Like the Poles, Hungarian refugees were also often housed alongside British residents: for example, refugees lived at Thorney Pits in Corsham at the same time as British industrial workers from local factories. Typically, though, Britons and Hungarians were segregated into separate blocks of the camp. After several anti-Semitic episodes in the Hungarian camps, Hungarian Jewish refugees were moved elsewhere. The National Assistance Board did not consider itself responsible for the Britons in the hostel. As the Hungarians planned to vacate, the fate of the British residents was uncertain.

Such mixing between Britons and Poles or Hungarians was not always immediately discernible. But the presence of 22,000 Ugandan Asians on Britain's military bases changed the demography of many small towns in a much more visible way. It became a common sight in many English country lanes to meet Asians taking walks to get away from the boredom of the camps.[72] But, for Ugandan Asians, interactions with "locals" had another layer of complexity. Because of the strong presence of other Asians in Britain, the relationship between "hosts" and "refugees" was complicated by the third category of "migrants."

VOLUNTEERS IN THE CAMPS: RACE, EMPATHY, AND ENCAMPMENT

Refugee work in the 1970s and 1980s, which was undertaken by an increasingly diverse constellation of people, was a means of remaking identities for Britons as well as refugees. Through refugee work, Britons experienced the connections between the local and the global, as well as the tensions between their era's optimistic and pessimistic strains. In particular, refugee work galvanized new debates about migrant loyalties, and whether migrants were in fact citizens. Who truly cared for the refugee? Many migrants of color aided Ugandan Asians and Vietnamese refugees, forging complicated ties of feeling and mutual responsibility. Communities of color were both "inside" and "outside" the camp.[73]

The 1970s have been lambasted as a dismal, ungovernable decade of strikes, racial conflict, unemployment, and moral panics about the apparent hollowing out of government capability and public authority.[74] The decade became shorthand for a set of nightmarish images of dilapidation, neglect, and decay, when the dead went unburied, and the rubbish piled up in the streets.[75] The prevailing narrative was that these were the worst of times—uniquely drab, more cantankerous and less compassionate than earlier decades.[76] But this version of the 1970s misses the era's undercurrents of creative, demotic egalitarianism and inclusiveness.[77] Ordinary Britons came to see their everyday actions as connected to crises abroad, contributing to a growing culture of aid.[78]

Similarly, refugee work offers an opportunity to rethink the 1980s as an age of activism (rather than apathy), countering the image of selfishness that has characterized the late twentieth century.[79] The aim here is not to suggest a hidden vein of generosity within Thatcherism, but to complicate our understanding of Britain's global commitments. The image of egotistical Thatcherites turning their backs on society is too simplistic. Indeed, the state's refusal to provide adequate refugee care meant that more of this work fell on ordinary citizens. Voluntary action continued to exist in a complementary—though not always harmonious—relationship to the state.[80] One 1984 survey found that one in five people did voluntary work, and the number of Community Service Volunteers rose by six times during the 1980s.[81] Andy McSmith's description of the 1980s as "The Decade of Greed and Live Aid" evokes the period's contradictions, in which shared notions of community were devalued just as new forms of civic engagement, such as NGOs, proliferated.[82]

Refugee camps in Britain were decidedly not the province of experts. Some camp workers (certainly not all) had experience in the refugees' languages or countries of origin. A background in security or experience with overseeing mass populations—for example, in military barracks—was often considered more valuable than culturally specific knowledge. Camp commanders might be former colonial civil servants, employees of multinational corporations, or military officers. As we will see in Chapter 6, such backgrounds made for uneasy relationships between camp leaders and (often anti-military and anti-corporate) volunteers. Radical young volunteers and staff could be deeply critical of the decolonizing state and its initiatives.[83]

The Ugandan Asian camp at Tonfanau was led by Dr. Dymond, a lifetime employee of Shell Oil who had served in the navy.[84] Sir Charles Cunningham, who chaired the Ugandan Resettlement Board, was permanent undersecretary of state at the Home Office from 1957 to 1966, and had served as deputy chairman of the UK Atomic Energy Authority.[85] Lord Colyton, chair of the Anglo-Egyptian Resettlement Board and Conservative MP for Taunton, had been Minister of State for the Colonies during the "emergencies" in Malaya and Cyprus; he was thus considered an expert in dealing with the disasters of decolonization. Some camp leaders circulated from crisis to crisis; the warden at Bridgend Hostel for Anglo-Egyptians was on loan from the Polish camp at Daglingworth. Before he was appointed to oversee the Thorney Island Camp for refugees from Vietnam, Major Arrowsmith spent fifteen years in the Territorial Regular Army, twenty-one years in the colonial police service in British North Borneo and Sabah, Malaysia, a year as a security advisor in Botswana, and two years on the Uganda Resettlement Board.

But refugee workers looked very different beyond the camp leadership. Over twenty voluntary organizations clustered to aid Ugandan Asian resettlement, including some of the Board's most outspoken critics. *The Times* described the Ugandan Asian camps as bustling with "ex-Army and RAF officers who have come out of retirement...an example of British wartime spirit at its good-humoured best."[86] Thousands of Britons revived the practice of mass volunteerism that had bridged classes and cultures during the Second World War. The Red Cross estimated that its volunteers provided 45,000 hours during the expulsion crisis, and at least 20,000 WRVS volunteers served in Ugandan Asian operations.[87] For middle-class women bored with the monotony of meals on wheels, the Ugandan Asian arrival was, as one volunteer said, "the best thing that could have happened to us."[88] Bunty Charles, a WRVS organizer in Honiton, recalled of the Ugandan Asian crisis, "It's an awful thing to say, but it was probably the happiest time of life."[89]

Volunteers at Ugandan Asian camps often treated refugee work as a noble form of anthropological research. When an elderly Muslim man died at Faldingworth, a WRVS representative attended the funeral. Her report described this "most moving and unique experience":

> Inside the Crematorium, the women sat on the left, the men on the right—the open coffin, placed in the centre. The ceremony began with several men chanting, whilst the women, heavily veiled, rose from their seats and with bowed heads and clasped hands circled the coffin several times. The lid was placed on the coffin and coconuts put on each corner, and two small grandsons walked round it several times—this was fol- lowed by a male and female mourner circling round the coffin several times sprinkling it with, what appeared to be, red peppers before it finally disappeared. A cine film of the whole proceedings was made by a member of the family.[90]

Another WRVS volunteer at Plaisterdown reported that she attended the funeral of a Ugandan Asian child, who had died of pneumonia (the WRVS claimed the parents had waited too long to visit the doctor). She was present as the child's body was prepared for cremation, and wrote excitedly, "I wonder if I will ever have the opportunity of attending a Hindu funeral again!"[91]

The race relations expert Nadine Peppard proposed that social scientists take refugee camps as a case study of fruitful interaction across cultures. For her, the camps signified much more than Asian success or failure. Rather, they represented "the positive interaction between such divergent groups of people who in many cases would not expect to cross each other's path, let alone work together for a common cause."[92] In bringing together a diverse group of citizens and refugees, Peppard claimed, the refugee camp represented "mixing" at its best: a multicultural triumph.

For many volunteers, working with Ugandan Asians was "a revelation." Charlie Bartlett, who lived near Tonfanau in North Wales, recollects that the chance of seeing an Asian in town before 1972 was "one in ten thousand." When the Ugandan Asians arrived by train, most volunteers had never spoken to anyone from outside their own culture. ITV Wales described the opening of Tonfanau as an "extraordinary moment" in Welsh history. Margretta Young-Jones, who "adopted" a Ugandan Asian family at Tonfanau, was proud to recall how she and the matriarch of the family pricked their fingers and mixed blood. She was then considered another "daughter." In a story that hit the national press, her son, Edwin, and his friend Dylan ran away after school one day laden with soccer balls, toys, and dolls for "the little black children in the camp."[93]

Brenda Kidman, who volunteered with Ugandan Asians in Tunbridge Wells, credited this work with detaching from her racist husband. She described herself as a "moral refugee," who was disenchanted with her stultifying life: "I needed displacement, an opportunity to discover if there was an honest individual beneath all those onion layers of middle-class conditioning." She accompanied a Ugandan Asian family to India, and her husband told her not to bother coming back—"so I experienced my first taste of what it meant to be a refugee."[94] One is struck here by Kidman's easy overidentification with the refugee experience. Rather than valuing her refugee work for exposing her to the exotic and the faraway (which other volunteers certainly did), Kidman found echoes of her own isolation and, ultimately, a sense of liberation.

For locals, there could be unexpected benefits to having a camp nearby. Camp directors worried that impoverished white Britons could pose as volunteers, eating free meals "at the public expense." A badge system was instituted in order to distinguish camp residents—both refugees and volunteers—from the white and Asian locals.[95] Sean O'Garvaigh (a URB worker) recalled that the Ugandan Asian influx prompted hiring in social services, and boosted the local economy. Tonfanau gave many Welsh people back their employment, which had disappeared with the closure of army and RAF bases.[96] Unlike many other camps, Tonfanau operated an open-door policy, and Ugandan Asians mixed freely with locals at pubs.[97] The presence of Asians at Tonfanau prompted the opening of the bridge over the River Dysynni. Villagers were also allowed to use the bridge, which cut the distance between Towyn and Tonfanau from 8 miles to 2.[98]

Brian Jackson, a teacher (who had also volunteered at Stradishall), described his work at Tonfanau in idyllic terms. With other young volunteers, he hosted a "scruffy 'welcome to Britain' party, with pop records, incomprehensible dirty jokes from the seventeen-stone Scots at the microphone; and a flickering film show of the Royal Ballet in *Coppelia* shown by an Oxford undergraduate in bow tie and college blazer."[99] At this strange event, Jackson quoted a poem written by a Ugandan Asian refugee. Composed in Hindi, and translated first into Gujerati and then into English, the poem began:

> When we were in Uganda
> We heard a lot about British kindness and humanity.
> When we arrived in England
> We saw with our own eyes all that there was to see.
> The young were carried
> And the old people given a helping hand.
> Everyone gave their love in such a way that we were overwhelmed.

The poem included themes of loss and nostalgia—"Of course, my friends, it is no one's fault / That things like this have slipped away from us. / Old friendships have been severed— / Promises forgotten. / But that is all past." But it marveled at the "magnificent forty-eight string Welsh harp!" that now accompanied the sitar and sarangi. The poem concluded,

> We lack nothing or did we have to ask for anything
> For when we arrived we did not know what to expect,
> But all was ready...
> All that has happened must be put behind us
> And our feelings kept secret.
> The regime we knew took everything—
> Our houses, our possessions, our livelihoods.
> But one thing that they couldn't take from us
> Was the love that we have in our hearts for you.
> We saved that for you.[100]

For Atul Patel, who had lived at both Honiton and Faldingworth, the camps offered a cocoon within the more hostile world of white Britain, a "softness" to return to every day. He credited the camp environment with giving him the confidence to develop his own ethnic identity. He was willing to eat beef, for example, but made sure that he was still able to read and write in Gujerati and Swahili. He also fondly recalled the empathetic volunteers at the camps—university students who were "fantastic, curious people," and he praised the local youth clubs that invited Ugandan Asians to their houses for Sunday roasts as "illuminating and educative" in introducing him to new foods and friends.[101] For Patel's father, the camps acted as crucial buffers to reality, in which he could retreat to the safety of numbers. The "real world" shocked him when he left the camp, and he died almost as soon as he resettled at Tower Hamlets.[102]

Some politicians advocated a wider program of encampment that would encompass the poor as well as refugees. Arthur Lewis, the MP for West Ham North, described a British woman in his constituency who had become homeless. He noted that the halfway settlement homes in his area were physically similar to Ugandan Asian resettlement camps, but there were also important differences. If his constituent were able to find a place in a halfway house,

> She would, rightly, have to pay an economic rent, clean her accommodation, pay for her food and cook her meals. The Ugandan Asians in resettlement camps get a home, furniture, linen, lighting and fuel. They get food, which is cooked for them, and contractors clean their apartments—paid for by the taxpayer. They do nothing to keep their apartments clean. They are also supplied with entertainment and television sets. Good luck to them; God bless them; may they get all this for as long as they want it. All I want is for my constituents to have the same.

But Lewis avoided a predictable critique of refugees as minority "scroungers" on the welfare state. Rather, he proposed, "we often speak of integration...we might start integration in these camps. Some of my old-age pensioners would like the opportunity to live in them. Why can accommodation not be offered to them?"

Lewis envisioned Ugandan Asians (or other refugees) living together with elderly or impoverished Britons in the utopia of the camp.[103]

Lewis's analogy of Ugandan Asians and the British poor was one mode of comparative thinking. Camp leaders were also preoccupied by the relationship between Ugandan Asians and Asian "migrants."[104] At a global level, refugee workers have been at pains to highlight the unique role of the refugee within broader population movements, and refugees have often been treated as unwanted migrants.[105] In Britain, refugees intersected with "normal" migrants in complicated ways. The state's expectations about the success or failure of refugee groups were tied to assumptions about whether the refugees had a "community" of migrants willing to aid them in Britain.[106] Such musings were crucial to British predictions about the upward mobility of Ugandan Asians and the downward mobility of refugees from Vietnam. The fate of the refugee was closely linked to how other forms of mobility and migration were perceived.[107]

Throughout the twentieth century, British officials debated whether refugees should be subsumed under an immigration agenda. Refugee care was bipartisan, but the parties differed on this point. Conservatives typically elided refugees and economic migrants, except in specific cases of refugee aid (as with the Vietnamese) that were sponsored by Conservative leaders.[108] When Margaret Thatcher faced criticism for accepting so few refugees from Vietnam, she responded that Britain had welcomed nearly 2 million immigrants, and she "could not accept" the distinction between immigrants and refugees.[109] Rather than conceiving migrants and refugees as competing populations, we must acknowledge that they were not necessarily different populations at all, but were categorized differently at various moments in time.

Despite the social-scientific insistence that the Ugandan Asians were entirely different from Indians and Pakistanis, *The Times* reported that many Asians in Britain offered to help ready houses for the arrival of their "countrymen."[110] The *Observer* referred to aid preparations taking place "in the Sikh and Hindu temples and the Muslim mosques of Britain."[111] Indeed, the Community Relations Commission reported that many Ugandan Asians left the camps too quickly because they believed they could rely on help from Asian communities.[112] Shirin Abdul Hussein, who stayed at Gaydon, remembered that Asians visited the camp after a tepid initial response.[113] In fact, Lee Allane, a volunteer at Raleigh Hall in Staffordshire, believed that the biggest problem at his camp was Indian and Pakistani "con men" who drifted in from Birmingham, offering to sell gold for the residents or hyping shady investment opportunities. The camp began vetting all visitors before they entered. Allane also worried about African Caribbean activists who promoted a radical political agenda to Ugandan Asians, wanting to stave off extremism of all kinds.[114] Other volunteers spoke of trying to keep "visiting Asians" away from the camp residents.[115]

For migrants of color in Britain—including Asians from Uganda who left the country before expulsion—the Ugandan Asian influx generated complex reactions. When Idi Amin issued the expulsion order, Praful Thakrar was already in Britain as a student. His family was still in Uganda, and when he turned on the television to watch the news, he saw his sister getting out of an airplane. This was how he found out that his family had arrived in Britain. He called ITV to find out his family's location, and traveled to a camp in Devon to see them. He recalls being "very surprised and amazed" to see so many people he knew from Uganda in this camp: "tears came out of my eyes—so many people there, all living together." This, Thakrar suggested, was the model of community that he had once enjoyed in Uganda: solidarity and mutual aid among all Asians.[116]

Chandrika Joshi, whose family lived at Tonfanau when she was a teenager, was fascinated to meet Asian volunteers who had been born in Britain. She was especially intrigued by how different they were from her own family. Time in Britain seemed to have transformed them. One Asian woman volunteer approached Chandrika's father—who was a Hindu priest—and asked him if he would introduce her to nice men in the camp, as she was eager to get married. Chandrika was amazed to hear an Asian woman (who was always clad in English-style wellies) announce her romantic intentions so boldly and forthrightly. From her perspective, British Asians and Ugandan Asians had little in common.[117]

Yasmin Alibhai-Brown, the Ugandan Asian writer, was studying at Oxford when the expulsion order came. She visited one of the camps near Oxford, and praised the refugees' resilience and bravery: "it was extraordinary how a group of people who had lost everything could still sing together when they were cooking and laugh at their own childlike terror of what was going to happen to them." The men were already talking about how to get bank loans, and how to use their connections with people who had settled. But Alibhai-Brown's identification with the encamped refugees quickly dissipated. She complained, "You had to sit and listen endlessly to the tales of loss, always at this time expressed in terms of homes, cars, furniture, gold."[118]

Alibhai-Brown castigated the refugees for their subservience, noting "I did feel guilty when I felt myself shrinking away from my people, especially after I had visited a resettlement camp and seen their degradation."[119] She was embarrassed to see dignified entrepreneurs treated like children by the ex-colonials who ran the camps. With white Britons, Alibhai-Brown insisted, she was nothing like the timid, repressed refugees. For her own part, "it was madly exciting to know that you could turn men on who were once your masters. Is this why I wore that grey and wine-colored miniskirt to the Bodleian and made sure my knickers were pretty so that I could climb the step-ladders with confidence and watch the pallid, bespectacled men looking up at me?"[120]

One of the most powerful (and one of the only) published accounts of camp life, was Mahmood Mamdani's 1973 memoir, *From Citizen to Refugee*. This memoir compellingly situated the Ugandan Asian camps in the constellation of race, class, and radicalism in 1970s Britain. When Idi Amin announced the expulsion order, Mamdani had been back in Uganda for only five months. He had returned recently from a decade as a student in the United States, where he had been active in the civil rights struggles in the South, and anti-war campaigns in the North.[121] Mamdani parsed how the experiences of expulsion and encampment reshaped relationships between Ugandan Asians and white Britons, as well as between Ugandan Asians and other Asians in Britain.

In November 1972, on arrival at Heathrow Airport, Mamdani was greeted by URB officials and joined his parents at Kensington Barracks. He picked up his linen, and entered the room where he would spend the next two and a half months: 30 feet by 10 feet, with eight beds arranged as in a hospital. While at the camp, Mamdani studied colonial records on Uganda. He also (very speedily) wrote *From Citizen to Refugee* for a £200 advance, on the promise that he would write the book in three weeks. Mamdani completed the draft in twenty days, and it was published unedited.

In this polemical book, Mamdani charted his harrowing experiences at this camp, right near the fashionable shops of Kensington. Run by a former colonial servant from Uganda, the camp exemplified to Mamdani the bureaucratic quest for a perfectly ordered universe, omniscience, and a colonialist belief in natural hierarchy. The camp administrator had been a civil servant in Uganda, and thus was perfectly suited to such an endeavor. Job information at the camp was tightly controlled, rather than being freely displayed on the public bulletin boards, which instead were papered with emigration opportunities for Sweden, Chile, and Iran. The camp administrator encouraged residents to report on one another for taking more than their fair share of milk, and housing offers were given only to those who shared such rumors. With the distinction between public and private life obliterated, the camp became a nightmare in totally controlled living—like a prison or an insane asylum. On the face of it, life in the camp, with its surface calm, presented a sharp and favorable contrast to the open terror of living in Uganda. But (Mamdani said) it was the Kensington Camp, and not Amin's Uganda, which was "my first experience in what it would be like to live in a totalitarian society."[122]

For Mamdani, there were important potential alliances between Ugandan Asians and poor Britons. Like English workers, he and his peers had no incentive to save their money. They received their social security benefit on Friday and spent it all by Sunday on drinks and cigarettes. Mamdani described how he and his friends went out for excursions, but "we realized it wasn't such a nice feeling to walk up and down Kensington High Street among people who seemed to be buying things just about all the time. Our resources were limited to social security payments of £2.10 a week. With such a meager income, buying anything was out of the question. But all around us was incessant consumption; staring at us from every window were things just waiting to be bought, to be eaten, to be worn, to be read." Memorably (if profanely), he wrote, "under such circumstances, looking at life on Kensington High Street seemed like seeing the city through its ass-hole."[123]

Camp residents were acutely conscious of British racism. Volunteers at Hobbs Barracks received confidential instructions about how to respond to extremist right-wing demonstrators who might attempt to block the camp gates or enter the camp with Union Jacks, hurling insults. The best antidote was not to respond: "the young and strong must control their tempers and refuse to be involved." They should lock their doors and windows, and calmly retreat.[124] Baroness White was "deeply moved" by an experience at a Ugandan Asian camp near London, in which right-wing "louts" had staged a hostile demonstration. They tried to recruit local homeless families to join their racist protest, but none would participate. One

homeless woman told the demonstrators to get out and leave the Asians alone—
"they are our friends." For White, this was proof that poor Britons could recognize
the universality of the experience of displacement.[125]

Several nasty encounters with British racists were enough to send the Ugandan
Asians back to the "fortress" of the camp. When Mamdani finally left the camp,
and came back to visit friends, they showed him dried blood on the ground—a
sign of a recent attack by skinheads on the refugees, while the camp staff idly
watched. Mamdani's friend concluded, "'we are going to resettle ourselves.' We
walked away from the camp. I looked back. The blood, dried and lifeless, lay on
the tarred driveway, like a question mark." Ultimately, what kept him from "choking in the blanket of prejudice that was the Kensington camp," Mamdani said, was
the refugees' ability to maintain a "semblance of dignity and a modicum of rights"
in the face of absolute authority.

My point is not to reinforce Mamdani's narrative, but to consider how camp
residents faced critiques from multiple directions. Critics included not only
right-wing anti-immigrationists, but also activists of color, who saw the camps
as failed sites of radicalization. Shiva Naipaul denounced Asian camp residents as
ridiculously optimistic, eager to "mix up" with the British, and turn their backs on
Indian and African politics. For Naipaul, the disengagement and fatalism that
had led Asians to accept their British passports culminated in the camps: the
ultimate flowering of their dependence on Britain and acceptance of their own
undesirability.[126]

One Ugandan Asian told Naipaul that having a British passport "excused"
Asians from engaging with Ugandan politics. Of this fetishized passport, Naipaul
wrote, "nestled in the breast-pocket of his jacket, it must have helped to keep
him warm in this refugee camp on the fringes of Dartmoor." As Mr. Shah, an
electrical engineer, said, "'I would always prefer to mix up with people in England'...
Mix up. It is another favoured expression. They all want to mix up." Other observers complained that Asians who received so much "white benefice" developed
harmful ideas. Jenny Bourne of the Institute of Race Relations reported that
young Ugandan Asian men constantly shared with her "their wish to marry
white girls and to show how ready they were to liberate themselves from an
Eastern culture." If Idi Amin had charged Ugandan Asians with being divorced
from African reality, then Bourne suggested that the false security of camp life
cut the Ugandan Asians off from the realities of life in Britain for most "coloured"
people, making them believe that every white person was automatically good,
sensible, and honorable.[127] As the WRVS reflected on problems that were likely
to afflict Ugandan Asians after they left the camps, "integration with other coloured
races" was high on the list.[128]

But were the Ugandan Asians "colored"? With whom, exactly, were they supposed to integrate—white Britons or brown ones? White Britons found the
Ugandan Asians more "Indian" (by which they meant more diverse in terms of
class and education) than they had expected. But activists of color saw Ugandan
Asians as frustratingly assimilationist, lacking radical impulses and more fixated
on upward mobility than racial solidarity. One rationale behind the camps

was that they would prepare Asians for life in British society. Yet, within the camps, "every white face [was] the face of somebody in authority... an unconscious reconstruction of the colonial situation."[129] The camps bore little resemblance to the Asian community in multiracial Britain.[130]

British sources rarely, if ever, characterized Ugandan Asians as Africans.[131] Jagit Singh, a Ugandan Asian at Tonfanau, wrote a poem called "Portrait of an Asian as an East African," which evoked this powerful image of East African Asian disaffection for the cause of African independence: "the past has boiled itself over / and we are the steam that must flee." He vowed to bring about "a resurrection of brown pride" in Britain that would redeem his father's sacrifice in the service of the old empire:

> For i see you now, my father
> fling the victoria cross
> into dung-heap of the british empire
> not for your valour
> was this false honour on your chest.
> but for blood discarded
> and bodies dismembered
> in white wars of yesterday.
> why then, must i, your latter-day blood,
> bow to live content with vouchers and quotas?[132]

Singh proposed that the Ugandan Asians "are the green leaves / that must sprout no more, / for the roots have thrived / on black silence / and false kindness of the white race." Expulsion cemented the identity of Ugandan Asians as part of a South Asian diasporic community rather than an African one.

The Jews, the Poles, and the Ugandan Asians—all were seen as having some kind of ethnic community already in Britain. Refugees from Vietnam were typically described in terms of absolute, unrelenting difference—in relation both to white Britons and to other migrant communities. Enoch Powell described Vietnam as "a country with which we have no connections and towards which we have no obligations."[133] Significantly, Powell's arguments ignored the historical connection between Britain and Hong Kong, one of the key sites of detention for refugees from Vietnam. Refugee care was very much in keeping with Thatcher's vision of a fruitful interaction between state and volunteer, and the need to render aid more personal, informal, and immediate.[134] After agreeing to raise the initial quota, Thatcher sought to minimize state intervention in resettlement.[135] Thatcher herself was quite unmoved by public opinion in favor of admitting refugees. She proposed that if Britain took more refugees from Vietnam, then it should reduce the entry visas for dependent children from other parts of Asia.[136]

The prevailing British assumption was that refugees from Vietnam had no "host" community to serve as their natural allies. In fact, the refugees were up to 80 percent ethnically Chinese, and there were 60,000 ethnic Chinese living in Britain. But this community was widely characterized as too impoverished and fragmented to be useful to refugees. Accurate or not, this perception of an "absent" community contrasted sharply with the Ugandan Asian case. In 1985, a Home Office Research and Planning Unit Report praised the South Asian community in Britain for coming to the aid of Ugandan Asians, but castigated the much smaller British Chinese community for failing to offer the same help to their own.[137] This sense of isolation may have been overstated; at Nelson Hall, Joan Leadley reported that many visitors "came for weekends and also during the week."[138]

In this context, the white British volunteers at the Vietnamese camps became the focal points of praise and adulation. Le Con, a refugee who arrived at Ockenden's reception center at Sunshine House, Gosport, in 1979, wrote the following verses:

> I, a tired and toiled traveller, no longer have any worries because of my joyful reunion.
> It is not yet too late to begin a peaceful carefree life...
> I truly love England from my heart.
> And now all my dreams have come true.
> This house received me with open arms and endless love.
> For my situation was so bad that God pitied me and opened the doors to my freedom...
> Let everybody praise the Queen for her kindness and mercy towards the refugees.[139]

The camp newspaper of Thorney Island, *New Homeland*, published Pham Thanh's poem, "The Memories Have Never Been Forgotten," which also valorized refugee workers:

> We, the refugee bands
> The honest people
> Climbed up the shore like ghosts
> Clothes were ragged
> The skins were becoming black from wind and sun
> And we had circles under our eyes from lack of sleep
> The terrible things were still etched deeply on the sad faces
> Some boat people were drooping down like prisoners
> Or lying full length on the litters unmoving
> Had the Gods seen our plight?
>
> Today,
> The same refugees, also
> Met one another in a British Reception Centre,
> With faces bright
> In good health and well dressed
> Sitting confidently in sunlit classes
> Listening and learning simple sentences
> With nice feelings that had been lost for so long
>
> We have wonderful and powerful faith
> In this country, its people and our bright future.[140]

Also at Thorney Island, Dieu Huong, aged 15, wrote a poem for *New Homeland* about her experience of encampment. Titled "Away from Mum," she acknowledged that BCAR "is looking after me instead of you," but assured her mother that

"Britain has come into my life sweetly / As beautiful as rice stalks / As lovely as branches full of Oranges."

But these same newsletters—which promoted a highly positive image of camp life—revealed complicated interactions between refugees and white volunteers. The Sopley newsletter included a "Sopley Quotes" section replete with jokes about Vietnamese mistakes in English, including refugees who spoke of a "kamikaze course" when they meant "car mechanics," or the Vietnamese fieldworker who said she was going to Bournemouth to get a roast duck (not a "road tax").[141] It is difficult to know what to make of these jokes, or who was supposed to find them funny. At Save the Children, project leaders complained about volunteers who felt they "owned" the refugees, smothering them with inappropriate attention, or trying to delay their settlement in order to prolong their own pleasure in interacting with them.[142]

Sopley was only about half a mile from the town, and an easy walk. Camp officials encouraged locals to "adopt" refugee families—visiting the camp for games and conversation, and taking refugees on outings to teach them how to use public transport. One couple in Bournemouth "adopted" two Vietnamese teenagers from Sopley who were getting married, and baked them a wedding cake; the couple called them "Mummy and Daddy" thereafter. But locals were also invited to bring refugees to their home to "help" with household tasks: mowing the lawn or picking fruit. As BCAR suggested, "no money repayment is sought: only the friendship which comes from working together at a task."[143] At Moyle Tower, a small resettlement center in Hythe (on the south coast of Kent), the co-director Thanh Cherry recalled that locals saw the Vietnamese refugees as "the best thing that ever happened to Hythe." The refugee crisis gave them a chance to meet people from other cultures, but also an "opportunity to be good." Several decades later, Moyle Tower was still fundamental to the identity of the town, and a focal point of local memory.[144]

Daphne Byrne, who worked at Thorney Island, said she and her fellow volunteers "got so used to our Vietnamese friends with their dark, glossy hair and beautiful brown eyes that English people seemed strange to us once we left the Centre."[145] But she also recalled that the nearby town of Emsworth had "mixed feelings" about "the Viets." The local pharmacist complained about Vietnamese girls coming in and opening his bars of soap to see what was inside; many shops had what she called a cynical "WELCOME TO CHINATOWN" approach and put up copies of their signs in Vietnamese. The BBC decided without warning to their regular listeners to broadcast twice a week in Vietnamese.[146]

In the rapidly shifting racial politics of late twentieth-century Britain, refugees were castigated for their own prejudices. One Thorney Island family allegedly refused housing in London because they believed there were too many black people in the area. Major Arrowsmith piously instructed the Vietnamese staff that people in the United Kingdom were expected to live in harmony whatever the color of their skin.[147] He stressed that this family would not be offered any other housing, and that "Britain is becoming a multi-racial society and many good people live in these areas." Arrowsmith also criticized refugees at Thorney Island who refused to resettle next to other Vietnamese, a startling twist on the government's concern that refugees would naturally form a "ghetto."[148]

Arrowsmith's comments speak to a much deeper vein of activism and protest within the refugee camp. Refugees and volunteers both struggled with camp leaders about the limits that the camp placed on their freedom. As we will see, many refugees engaged in multiple forms of resistance—sometimes violently so—both within and outside the camp's confines.

6

Hard Core

Were refugees in Britain free? When they lived in camps, could they come and go as they pleased? When they left the camps, could they settle where they wished? In Britain, struggles over refugees' freedom—freedom of physical movement, freedom of political expression, and freedom of settlement—proved especially contentious. As we will see, refugees were constantly policed and restricted, but never successfully controlled. Refugee camps dramatized the dilemmas of a liberal society, and the tensions around mobility (physical, social, and political) that characterize democratic states and selves.

In some sense, of course, every chapter in this book deals with power and resistance. This chapter zeroes in on individual and collective acts that were based on an emerging notion of refugee rights.[1] Here, I show the roiling underneath the surface of the camps that speaks to refugees' political energies, often in their own voice.[2] Refugee politics often sat uneasily with the language and agendas of liberal democracy, and Britons constantly shifted their demands for refugees to be political or apolitical in particular ways. Camps inspired their own political desires and aspirations, as well as new methods to achieve them.[3] They operated as spaces of activism, where refugees developed powerful critiques of the state.

Some refugees were seen as more rebellious than others. For example, the administrators at Kitchener Camp described Jewish refugees as easily led, compliant, and generally quiescent: the higher purpose of creating shelter for desperate Jews, they suggested, trumped any individual desires for resistance.[4] Camp staff also often described Vietnamese refugees as "quiet" or "giving no trouble": the opposite of the intransigent Poles or militant Ugandan Asians. But camp archives tell a different, more complicated story—one that cuts across ethnic and chronological divides—about daily rebellions and acts of resistance during times of encampment.

This chapter charts myths of "good" and "bad" refugees, but also seeks to look beyond them. It takes as its central theme the notion of the "hard core"—a term that originally described refugees who were difficult to settle, and might be left behind when the camps closed: the elderly, the sick, the disabled. But it was also used for refugees who openly rejected the camp's regimes, and who countered the camp's rules with their own activist agendas.

In considering the fate of the "hard core," this chapter explores many different types of interactions and exchanges between citizens and refugees. The camp operated both as a device for managing refugees and as a means of mobilizing them.[5]

First, I consider the nature of power in the refugee camp. Who had power and of what kind? What disciplinary techniques did camp authorities deploy? And what were the different forms that resistance to this power—including violence— might take?

POWER TRIPS: SELF-GOVERNANCE AND CULTURES OF COMPLAINT

Camp leaders held clashing expectations of how to control and civilize the refugee. In general, camp officials were far more authoritarian and oppressive than the state they were supposed to represent. In turn, refugees offered diverse forms of resistance to this oppression. Volunteers also often explicitly rejected the camp's rules. Whose behavior, exactly, did the camp seek to regulate? The camp's disciplinary regimes targeted both citizens and refugees.

Many of the refugee camp's structures of discipline originated in internment. But the daily lives of internees were often *less* restricted than those of refugees. Security measures on the Isle of Man were surprisingly lax. Barbed-wire fences were often left open, and guards and house fathers took tea together.[6] At Hutchinson, internees enjoyed aimless rambles through the town of Douglas with "no discipline at all," chatting with the guards and borrowing their rifles.[7] Internees were encouraged to establish their own administration, and self-government was prized.[8] Each hut had a "house father." Klaus Hinrichsen recalled that Hutchinson's first house fathers (selected by the British authorities) were "obviously not suitable," as they had been chosen for superficial reasons such as wearing a good blazer. They were "toppled" and new elections held.[9] Right-wing internees preferred more military terms for the camp leadership, such as "house captain," while leftists used the term "father."

For Poles, camp authorities initially advocated the same techniques. The War Office viewed self-government as good for morale and discipline, as well as facilitating the reduction of military staff.[10] As the National Assistance Board took over the Polish camps and hostels, the Board expected that Poles could be "given a free hand to manage their own affairs," much like Britons living in industrial hostels. But the shift from the War Office to the National Assistance Board also raised Polish expectations about the standard of living. When the Board failed to meet these standards, Poles in camps voiced their frustration. In 1947, the Poles at Fowlmere proposed to strike until the amenities at their camp were brought up to civilian levels. Incited by an article in a Polish newspaper about luxurious conditions at British workers' hostels, Poles threatened strikes throughout the camp system. They also refused to pay their full rents, arguing that the accommodation was not worth what the Board was charging.

Should refugees be treated like other populations (soldiers, prisoners, the poor) who were subject to the state's discipline? One Board member felt that refugees needed their own disciplinary regimes, distinct from workhouses or internment camps: "I feel it unfortunate that the well ordering of our Hostels should in any way be related to Home Office orders for internment camps. I cannot conceive that we should want to have anything associated with internment."[11] The problem of rules for Poles was unique: "We are dealing with pockets of people who are of the general community but apart from it."[12]

As Home Secretary James Chuter Ede reminded his fellow MPs in 1947 that he had no disciplinary powers over the Poles other than his general power to deport aliens. Men who left the camp could not be treated as "deserters" from the Polish forces, because the Polish forces had ceased to exist. The Poles were "a collection of private individuals... there is no power to hold them in a camp, there is no power to deal with them if, inside the camp that we have provided for them, they are refractory." Poles could be brought before a civil court, but "frankly, I do not know what a court... could do with a man who was accused of being out of a camp after 'lights out' at night."[13]

Refugees were subject to the general laws of the country. But the Polish Resettlement Act also gave the Board the power to "frame particular rules for their discipline."[14] The Board could craft any regulations it liked for the "well ordering" of Polish camps and hostels. At the Checkendon Hostel near Reading, Berkshire, every resident was warned that they must accept the accommodation allotted to them, that they were not to use water or electricity carelessly, and that officers were allowed to inspect their huts.[15] Camp residents might be required to attend English classes. Music, loud conversation, and noise were forbidden from 11 p.m. to 6 a.m. Beds must be made every day by 10 a.m. Men who were over the age of 16 and under the age of 65 (or 60 for women) must perform twelve hours of unpaid work per week. Residents must comport themselves with "courtesy and dignity so as to foster mutual esteem and friendship."[16]

Those who disobeyed the camp's rules faced various penalties. Anyone who held a meeting without the warden's consent, for example, could be fined £25, or imprisoned for three months.[17] Rebellious residents could be moved to a less attractive hostel, with a stricter warden. The Board might refuse to pay their pocket money, or withhold their meal tickets. Yet financial punishments could backfire; desperate offenders might simply wander off to large towns, where they would become a burden on national assistance. In most cases, administrators prescribed frequent "interviews" (at least once a week) to convince noncompliant residents to behave. Discipline rested on close personal interaction and the powers of suasion.[18]

By the 1950s, life in Polish hostels was characterized by increasingly elaborate rules, and a wider range of behaviors was penalized. Self-rationing introduced new levels of independence, and new disciplinary problems.[19] The installation of unauthorized electrical appliances, the keeping of geese, ducks, and rabbits, and the erection of lean-to sheds were all emerging as commonplaces of camp life. The process of making oneself "at home" in camp—which was encouraged at some moments—was penalized at others. One hostel resident was fined £2 for taking wood to erect his own hen run; another man was sued for allegedly stealing the branches of a tree. Residents were accused of pilfering the lavatory chains, taking the screws from the water taps, blocking gullies with rags and tins, damaging their huts by storing coke and wood against the sides, and engaging in the "uncontrolled keeping of livestock." Trees were "mutilated" by driving nails into them to hang clotheslines.[20] The Board chastised the warden for the hostel's dilapidated condition. But the warden described all of these acts as "pilfering." One imagines that the refugees might have viewed these acts quite differently, as the line between individual and communal property in camp was difficult to discern.

Wardens in refugee camps were given tremendous scope to define their roles.[21] They were instructed to ensure that residents did not "offend against one another" or endanger the moral or physical well-being of young children. Ryszard Kiersnowski, a Polish writer who traveled to more than sixty camps in Britain, described the well-paid wardens as akin to "the colonial officials in the British colonies. The warden is often powerful, unavailable, despondent, churlish, sniffing out abuses everywhere, and suspecting everyone." Such a warden, Kiersnowski lamented, became "a watchdog and a terror" instead of a caretaker and a friend. He did provide a counterexample of a wonderful warden at a camp near York, who had sacrificed his own family life to devote himself to the Poles. His camp was "like an oasis on a desert, and he is like a martyr and apostle in one... This camp is really the camp of camps. White-washed, with flowers, renovated to the last doorknob. And above all this is a camp full of satisfied people. 'Oh! Our warden!' they say." This warden filled his house with Polish books, and served as godfather to the camp's children. He refused to impose strict rules, saying that anyone who understood the Poles' history would stop bothering them and leave them in peace.[22]

Hostel reports offered happy tales of "successful rehabilitation": residents who had been transformed through this system of corrections.[23] One mentally ill man at Northwick had long refused to clean his "exceedingly filthy" room. He was removed against his will, and his room was cleaned and decorated. The warden reported, "the man is now a different person, clean and tidy and his room is kept in excellent condition."[24] Likewise, Mr. Kmita, who had displayed the "worst kind of work shyness" since he arrived at Northwick in 1948, was finally induced in 1955 to start working after a "stormy interview" with the warden. The warden reported that it had been a "long and difficult battle" to "tame" Kmita, but the family was now "completely transformed from the appalling state of laziness, dirt and filth into a self-respecting unit."[25]

Wardens in Polish camps were also authorized to approve exceptional needs grants, such as clothing grants.[26] The warden at Stover painstakingly documented Stanislaw Sikorski's request for clothing. The warden doubted that Sikorski's need for clothing was genuine, but "searching enquiry has been made here over a period of weeks and my conclusion is that his story of the loan of clothing from friends cannot be refuted. I have interviewed each of the individuals concerned."[27] Celezewski Franciszek complained that the warden at Mepal had refused all his requests for a grant to buy a suit and an overcoat. In his three years in Britain, he had received only one pair of shoes, two pairs of underwear, one pair of pajamas, three pairs of socks, one pair of trunks, old trousers, one shirt, and two pairs of galoshes.[28] The warden responded that Franciszek had "violent and drunken" habits, and "dissipated" his pocket money instead of saving it to buy clothes.[29]

Clothing was a visible sign of British aid. The Board insisted that Polish refugees must be well clothed, and not have a shabby appearance.[30] Refugees could not be expected to "make do," as poor Britons might:

> I cannot help feeling that our Polish applicants have not anything like the same reserves of clothing as would a British unemployed family. You will appreciate, I am sure, that the pocket money rate of 5s. is a very rigid sum and cannot be manipulated in any way as it might be done by British families who could so arrange their domestic economy in order to meet periodic expenditure on clothing.[31]

Within this calculus of welfare, refugees and poor Britons were not supposed to learn precisely the same lessons. Refugees were perceived as needier than the poor, and also less able to meet their needs. But many wardens worried that clothing allowances had a detrimental effect. "We must not," one warden from Northwick argued, "kill the incentive to work...to provide more or better clothing and odd luxuries." Even a few more shillings a week, he suggested, would diminish the urge to earn.[32]

Wardens often took harsher, more punitive stances toward refugees than the Board, but refugees could circumvent their wardens by appealing to the Board directly. Jozef Skrzypiniak at Northwick pleaded that his warden kept him "practically naked and bare-footed," and asked the Board to intervene.[33] Also at Northwick, Mr. Szyszko complained to the Board that his £12 grant did not cover his clothing costs: "the cheapest raincoat costs £5 10 s., and a suit £7 10 s., but how am I to buy footwear and underclothing? I also point out that I have not mentioned or requested many other items which I do not possess at all such as cap, braces, pyjamas and handkerchiefs."[34] He promised to leave the hostel as soon as he received proper clothes. His warden argued that Szyszko was too ill to leave the hostel, because he would become a bigger burden on the state. The Board replied that Szyszko was still free to go, even if he would need national assistance. Szyszko won an exceptional needs grant, against his own warden's wishes.[35]

Over time, the structure of control in Polish camps grew more complex, and the strata of power multiplied. Liaisons, for example, were supposed to serve as a link between the warden and the Polish-speaking residents, and to inform on the "pulse of community life" in the hostels. The liaison would educate the warden about issues that "although not in British eyes obviously apparent or in need of remedy, are causing irritation to Polish residents as well as activities among residents which, if unchecked, could disturb the harmony of the hostel."[36] One important mechanism of refugee activism was the residents' committee, which generated its own archive of petitions and grievances. The Polish residents' committees were extremely vocal and active. At Springhill Lodges, the residents' committee was elected by "free and secret ballot." The residents' committee was supposed to maintain "harmony and discipline," promote the hostel's social and cultural life, and lobby the warden on the refugees' behalf.[37]

The National Assistance Board received many letters of complaint from Poles, ranging from concerns about unfair management to accusations that residents were threatening each other physically or hoarding coal and firewood. One resident at

East Moor Hostel noted that their manager (who had been imprisoned several times for trafficking in stolen goods) picked through the donations from English people, keeping the "good things" for his family in Poland, and "gives to us only rags."[38] Many of the letters were anonymous, but the Board conducted handwriting analysis to track down the authors.

One residents' committee at Mepal objected to the National Assistance Board that an "unpleasant atmosphere" had arisen when the new manager, George B. Kidd, tried to "tighten the reins." He restricted the showing of films to once a week, and charged fees for dances. The residents claimed that these charges paralyzed their social lives. They argued that because they paid more for their housing than Britons who lived in council flats, they had the collective right to use the communal services, such as the cinema, without interference. Kidd's threats of eviction "introduced an atmosphere (bad feeling) for which we are unable to foresee the consequences."[39] For his part, Kidd responded that the residents' committee chair had described Mepal as being "not even like borstal, but like Belsen, to which I replied that he wasn't bound to stay here."[40]

As we saw in Chapter 4, wardens intervened in marital and family disputes. They also used disciplinary measures to regulate the camp's social relationships. The Stover warden frequently stopped the payment of pocket money to Mrs. Jozefa Wierszycka, who fought incessantly with other residents, once striking a man so hard that he needed stitches. Because Mrs. Wierszycka repaired clothing at the hostel, she was given a privileged position as a barrack warden. The warden warned that she felt "a measure of immunity from authoritative action and adopted a dictatorial attitude." Far from being a sweet old lady, Wierszycka was "a veritable virago" and an "inveterate liar."[41] Several women petitioned to evict Mrs. Wierszycka, because she was "unbearable, quarrelsome and vulgar."[42] One resident complained that Mrs. Wierszycka had poured dirty water on her laundry and shouted "you Jewish wench!" at her. In response, Mrs. Wierszycka sent the Board a dramatic report titled "The Harmed," claiming that the "appallingly brutal" warden had shoved her, and moved her into a hut where all the other residents were men.[43]

The Board acknowledged that Mrs. Wierszycka was a "thundering nuisance." Yet, "it seems difficult to grasp that it has been necessary on at least four occasions to withdraw the payment of pocket money from a 63 year old widow who has a background of epileptic and nervous troubles." Although "adjustments" of pocket money might be a powerful form of disciplinary action, such punishments were designed for those who voluntarily gave up paid work. The Board warned that wardens should not cancel allowances completely: "to put it bluntly, how does the Warden expect them to clean their teeth?"[44] Wardens who wished to reduce allowances had to report their actions to headquarters, and they were urged to consider other options, such as psychiatric exams.

The Board often cautioned unduly harsh wardens not to abuse their power. At Fairford, the Board's inspector reported that two single women with young children had been refused pocket money (presumably because they had turned down jobs). The inspector reminded the warden that the Ministry of Labour could not force Polish women to work.[45] At the East Moor Hostel, too, the same inspector worried that a "very severe" line had been taken toward women with children who were not employed. The warden had suspended several women's pocket money without the right of appeal. The Board formally chastised the East Moor warden.[46]

The arrival of the Hungarian refugees in British camps brought new disciplinary regimes. Any unmarried person who refused to register for work or to take suitable employment was told that his pocket money would be stopped "until he changes his attitude." Wardens were instructed to "increase pressure" by refusing to issue meal tickets and ensuring that meals were not obtained through other means.[47] Men who refused to pay their maintenance charges could be forced to leave within forty-eight hours.[48] Hostel wardens for Hungarians were reminded that Polish hostels had achieved order through "steady and consistent pressure, largely bluff." These wardens were told to lecture noncompliant Hungarians about how Britons of all classes were contributing to their upkeep, and that they were taking unfair advantage of their new countrymen. As disciplinary techniques expanded, so too did the emerging discourse of refugee rights. BCAR set up an Appeals Committee, so that Hungarian refugees who disagreed with their wardens could appear to an adjudicator. The adjudicators were drawn from the Hardship Committees that had been set up to excuse Britons from National Service, drawing parallels between the plights of impoverished Britons during conscription and disobedient (or oppressed) refugees.[49]

In 1957, the Home Office debated how to keep effective control over "young toughs" in the Hungarian hostels. Thorney Pits Hostel became the target of a joint investigation by BCAR and WVS, focusing on the "moral deterioration" of refugees who were cohabiting or refusing to seek work. One inspector reported that he had found fifteen refugees at Thorney Pits still lying in bed one afternoon, and described these refugees as a "problem family."[50] There was a full-scale riot at Haverton Hill in June 1957, where the residents—mostly young men employed in the steel and chemical industries—routinely committed acts of drunkenness, hooliganism, assault, and malicious damage.[51] At Crimicar Lane Sanitorium for Hungarian refugees, the superintendent reported that, "he had had some trouble with some of the young men and had been obliged to 'tame' them."[52] S.J. Partridge, the county welfare officer at the RAF camp at Catfoss, complained that he had a "pretty rough" time with the Hungarians in his care. The refugees distrusted each other, and "would not help in the running of the Camp, even for their own benefit, unless we paid them." Their thoughts were already turned to emigration, and they only wished to hear when they would leave. Partridge claimed he "did everything possible" to make the Hungarians happy, but "my experience so far has rather hardened my heart a little."[53]

The Home Office considered new sanctions against Hungarian refugees. For example, it could drop the offender's name to the bottom of the emigration list, though this would mean Britain would retain the people "we should like to be rid of the soonest." One promising alternative was simply to return troublesome Hungarian refugees to Austria. Stopping their pocket money was also considered, but, as with the Poles, this strategy "might actually stimulate the offender to wander off to a large town" and demand national assistance.[54] Dorothy Richard of the

WVS reported that Hungarian refugees posed a special disciplinary challenge because they were "impervious" to lectures. They had been subjected to so much wholesale propaganda that they were completely cynical about authority. Their suspicion of the state rendered them less than ideal subjects of refugee care. Richard urged refugee workers to cultivate individual relationships with Hungarians instead of disciplining them as a group: "every effort should be made to increase these personal contacts, when their natural gaiety and charm are given full rein."[55]

The Hungarian refugee operation depended on the close cooperation between camp authorities and the police. Hungarian refugees were supposed to register with the police as soon as they arrived at camp; their first stop at Crookham was at a police registration hut. One Hungarian refugee spoke about the friendliness of English constables:

> You see we haven't known Policemen of this sort. We have been told by our Radio, that when we go to England we will be put into uniform and sent to fight for England or be sent away in forced labour camps. You know we Hungarians are very excitable people, but when we see such calm, happy-looking and cheerful Policemen, working so hard and so patient with us, it helps and influences us.[56]

These practices were said to give Hungarians, who were initially suspicious of all forms of authority, a more positive view of the state.[57] But interactions between refugees and the police were not always so cordial. The Home Office concluded that the only way to make the Hungarian camp completely efficient "would be to run it under police control like a concentration camp," which was "obviously undesirable."[58]

Abusive wardens drew criticism from higher-level policymakers. The warden at Eastwood Hostel, an Anglo-Egyptian hostel near Nottingham, was a Mr. Garden, who had served in the army for thirty-seven years. His organizing capabilities were highly praised, and he had overseen a number of army camps in Germany for Polish and Yugoslavian troops. But, the Board worried, "he has, however, rather an overpowering personality and is inclined to take the view that cooperation can only be secured by everybody coming in line with him." Like the wardens in many Hungarian camps, Garden was described as having "very friendly" relations with the local police superintendent. He arranged for the police constable on the beat to stroll through camp every evening. In his view, this nightly surveillance let the camp inhabitants "see 'the law' in person."[59]

Refugees protested about lax wardens as well as overly strict ones. Michael Micallef, an Anglo-Egyptian, complained to the Board about the weakness of discipline among the hostel staff. The hostel, he wrote, had an "appearance of a farm yard. There is no disciplinary order in any part of the hostel premises, one cannot have any peace from noise either in the TV room or in the big Hall. All this due to children having complete freedom to do what they like, where they like." The staff, he lamented, took no action unless the residents actually came to physical blows. Families were allowed to break the rules against cooking in their sleeping quarters, and gambling was encouraged.[60]

Refugees were not the only ones who engaged in acts of resistance and rebellion in camp. Many disciplinary cases in the Ugandan Asian camps involved volunteers, some of whom were accused of thwarting camp rules. Some volunteers acknowledged that they were monitoring—or obstructing—the state's policies on Ugandan Asian resettlement. Lee Allane, a volunteer at Raleigh Hall, saw his role as ensuring that government plans for refugees were fair and transparent.[61] When Allane received a fax suggesting that any Ugandan Asians who were not back at camp on a Friday would be considered to have left the camp and not allowed to return, he leaked this information to a national newspaper; the government was compelled to disavow the harsh policy.

Volunteers were banned from Greenham Common Camp at least three times.[62] The administrator, Brigadier Geoffrey "Billy" Beyts, had extensive military experience in India and Kenya.[63] Beyts understood the "culture clash" in camp as being between socially conservative Ugandan Asians and "radical" white volunteers. According to Beyts, the Asian committee feared that white volunteers were introducing young Asians too rapidly to Western culture. Furthermore, Beyts felt that volunteers had inflamed the press in speaking to them about a possible hunger strike in the camp.[64] Beyts banished the "bitterly disappointed" volunteers, and replaced them with Asian residents. The WRVS also objected to the morals and politics of the "girl" volunteers at Greenham Common, complaining that Greenham Common was run by "a bunch of left wingers" who were influencing the Asians' behavior: "there is an undercurrent in the Centre which is not attractive."[65]

At the Vietnamese camps, divisions among the staff were heightened by competing views of the Vietnam War. For many camp workers, a crude understanding that the South was "good" and the North was "bad" was as far as their knowledge went.[66] At Sopley, several of the staff—and the camp leader, Brigadier Michael Harbottle—came from the (overwhelmingly left-wing) Peace Studies program at Bradford. Fieldworker Peter Rimmer recalled that students who had worked at Sopley were not welcomed back at Bradford, because they were seen as aiding people who had abandoned communism. At the same time, when one staff member at Thorney Island showed anti-American films about the Vietnam War, he was lambasted by the camp director, Major Arrowsmith, for sharing "communist propaganda."[67] Fieldworkers who were deeply committed to left-wing causes often found themselves in positions of great responsibility in camp work. Sue Millman, for example, a Peace Studies graduate, was only 25 years old when she accepted a fieldworker position at Sopley. Such experiences reveal that encampment was not simply a vast state enterprise that was imposed from the top down. The camps had a strong military and civil service infrastructure, but they were also staffed by young people who often rejected the state's resettlement policies.

Among camp staff, interpreters often played an especially controversial role. Interpreters were supposed to serve as "mediators" between the refugees and the staff, a difficult path to negotiate. The WVS prepared 500,000 phrase sheets in Hungarian and English and worked with the BBC to create long-playing gramophone records about life in England; these records were played throughout the Hungarian camps. But other interpreter services were more fraught. The interpreters at Crookham were said to be "damaging," and one was fired after she counseled a refugee to have an abortion. Some interpreters were accused of threatening refugees, or giving them false information. Many interpreters had come to Britain as European Voluntary Workers, and were jealous that the refugees were not suffering as they had.[68] Such conflicts highlight the mixing of populations within refugee camps that went far beyond a simple division of "host" and "refugee."

Interpreters for refugees from Vietnam were often frustrated by their status within the camps, and how white university students usurped their authority. At one point, the interpreters at Sopley threatened an industrial action to protest their treatment.[69] The Vietnamese and Chinese members of staff who lived in the centers were believed to suffer special stresses—more than the white British staff—because they had no "linguistic immunity" to the anxieties of other refugees. Other interpreters complained that they had little power to act on their own initiative, and that refugees mocked them, "Why are you saying this—you're only a refugee."[70] Interpreters also sometimes derailed resettlement plans by refusing to offer accurate translations. In two different centers, interpreters said that refugees had threatened to murder the project leader because she would not offer them the house they wanted. The interpreter did not translate the threat, the family got a house, and the woman who had made the threat thought she had "won." The other residents felt that they, too, could get the house they wanted by threatening physical violence.

The issue of language training was deeply charged in Vietnamese camps, raising the question of whether unwilling refugees could be compelled to anglicize.[71] Most teachers thought the Home Office's provision of three months of language instruction was inadequate, and lobbied to keep their students encamped for longer periods so they could continue their English classes. In this sense, language instruction could be used to delay departure from the camps. In some cases, refugees were "woken up, turned out of bed, and driven to class."[72] A social worker wrote about truancy in English-language classes, "there can be no compulsion; indeed, there is no comparable social or legal relationship to that of the adult refugee and his or her guardians. It is both voluntary and involuntary."[73] The plight of elderly Poles who had lived in Britain for decades and still did not speak English served as a cautionary tale.[74] In 1980, rumors circulated at Thorney Island that anyone who failed to learn English would be sent back to Vietnam.[75]

Fieldworkers were warned that the Vietnamese would see them as "magical" providers, who could conjure up houses in London, family reunions, and other impossibilities. During the 1980s, refugee work became more diverse. Save the Children reception centers experimented with using refugees from Vietnam to assist in the work of resettlement.[76] Vietnamese fieldworkers believed their British colleagues intervened in problems too quickly, and that most of the time, "the refugee can live with the problem. As for Oriental culture—we are more subtle, the problem is contained inside, they can contain it."[77] Furthermore, these fieldworkers argued that because of the community orientation of refugees from Vietnam, it was useful to draw on gossip to identify problem families in camp, and the fieldworker should feel no ethical dilemma in doing so.

Power in camps was not just imposed from the top down, but flowed in multiple directions. Refugee lives were defined by this ambiguity of compulsion. The authority of policymakers and camp wardens was never absolute. It was limited by the government's reluctance to use a full range of methods of coercion, and also by the residents' committees—particularly active among the Poles, Ugandan Asians, and Vietnamese—and volunteers who rebelled against the camps' regulations. But refugees resisted some forms of compulsion more fiercely—and violently—than others.

One of the durable assumptions of refugee work has been that refugees cannot act on their own behalf, and therefore must be acted upon: they have needs rather than wishes.[78] Liisa Malkki has described how aid workers "leach" history out of refugee life, and how certain representations of refugees "actively displace, muffle, and pulverize history, especially the history linking viewers' own pasts with those of refugees."[79] Refugees can find themselves "quickly rising to a floating world either beyond or above politics and history—a world in which they are simply 'victims' ... it is this floating world without the gravities of history and politics that can ultimately become a deeply dehumanizing environment for refugees, even as it shelters."[80] The next section counters this ahistorical leaching, using the camps to write the people in them (and their politics) back into history.

THE POLITICS OF VIOLENCE: REFUGEE ACTIVISM IN THE CAMPS

At various moments, different political sentiments and behaviors were demanded from refugees—that is, to be more or less politically engaged. But the range of acceptable political actions was always narrowly defined. Camp authorities held many shifting assumptions about the political loyalties of refugees, and structured the camp rules in order to control these political energies. They also devised penalties for exceeding (or failing to meet) these rites of citizenship. Signs of refugee politics were often suppressed, a process that sometimes ended in violence. But this ongoing denial of political engagement is countered in the archives by evidence of refugees' lively and diverse political orientations, which unfolded in Britain in unpredictable ways.[81] The camp's dream of the apolitical (or ideally politicized) refugee was never achieved.

The Basque children posed disciplinary problems from the moment they arrived in Britain. One popular British joke of the time went: "Why has your child become so unruly? Oh, he's been playing with some Basque children."[82] The Labour leader George Lansbury suggested that most Basque children were *too* good—"I like children to be naughty," he proclaimed—but few of his compatriots agreed.[83] The Basque children were "under no definite control." Indeed, camp authorities complained that the Spanish women who had accompanied the children had abdicated all responsibility, and neglected their charges.[84] They were "entirely out of hand and go in and out of the camp as they please." For Yvonne Kapp, this lack of adult supervision actually was one of North Stoneham's strengths, engaging the Basques in unstructured play. In its chaos, the camp operated like a "free" school, allowing the children eagerly and experimentally to cluster around (and destroy) every object.[85] Still, many camp workers complained about the Basques' wild and unregulated behavior, arguably brought on by the physical conditions of the camp itself.

The deepest British fears about the Basques focused on refugee politics. There were two key concerns. First, the "innocent children" might be radicalized by English citizens. English communists tried to contact the boys, one claiming that he had the right to do so because he had given money to the Basque Children's Fund. When refugee children participated in May Day demonstrations in Norwich in 1938, MPs protested that foreigners in Britain were expected to refrain from engaging in political propaganda.[86] Second, camp leaders at North Stoneham and the colonies worried that these "innocent children" were in fact violent, anarchical ideologues. In either case, insisting that the refugees stayed apolitical proved impossible to enforce.

The North Stoneham children had been carefully selected from all creeds, classes, and political opinions.[87] Parents were interviewed in Spain about their political affiliations, and places for evacuation were allotted to each political party in proportion to the voting patterns of the last election. The camp was divided into political sections (communists, socialists, Basque nationalists, fascists) based on these interviews. The fascist children's sleeping quarters were periodically changed, so that no one would be certain where they slept. Yvonne Kapp wrote of the "natural" desire to preserve the "gangs" (i.e. groups of friends) in camp, but acknowledged that this was impossible because such gangs were composed of "officially incompatible" elements.[88] The children's social attachments were trumped by the camp leadership's desire to conform to strict political divisions.

Kapp claimed that the Basque children were deeply—almost naturally—political.[89] Any insistence on neutrality would alienate these young refugees, who scoured the English newspapers for any mention of "Franco" or "Bilbao," and decorated their tents with hammers and sickles or the initials of their parents' political parties: "I have seen two hundred children in a Hampshire lane return the cry of 'Salud!' from a passing car. A forest of fists went up, a chorus of answering salutes rang out and, as the car passed on they stood, two hundred heads turned, and on every face a reassured smile."[90] The political energies of such children, she suggested, must be embraced, not repressed.

After the devastating news of the fall of Bilbao in June of 1937, scores of "hysterical" Basque children fled North Stoneham in despair. The Basques who remained in camp also tore up tent pegs and hedges to threaten their guards and threw stones at the radio van.[91] In July, one sanitary inspector at North Stoneham reported:

> There has been another riot the communist kids tried to burn down the Catholics Chapel and when they were stopped they tried to strike it down. Lovely little Basque Babies... the communist kids in the camp were visiting the tents of the little Catholic girls during the night and telling them that they would be killed before the morning and these poor little kids were packing grub into suitcases and hiding in the woods around the camp.[92]

Here, we can see the contradictions that arose from camp authorities' definition of the Basques as "children." These refugees were not supposed to act as fully politicized adults. We saw in Chapter 4, however, the Basques' status as "children" was never secure.[93] Perhaps precisely because the Basque children served an iconic purpose in Britain as the innocent, vulnerable, and apolitical victims of fascism, public support for them proved quite fragile. Any misbehavior was liable to be construed as "anarchist" activism.[94] While the British press initially emphasized the Basques' vulnerability, individual refugees did not fit neatly into the media's categories.[95]

The notion that the Basque refugees were "children" structured the techniques of discipline used against them. At Wattermillock, the Basques could be sent to bed for one day without bread.[96] One sanitary inspector complained that it was impossible to discipline the Basque refugees, as any punishment of these "innocents" would be widely exaggerated; the camp would be made out to be a prison.[97] Even when several Basques armed with knives threw rocks at an interpreter, the radio van implored the English staff to control their tempers "and not lay a hand on the children."[98] At Hexham, the Basques allegedly plotted to murder one staff member and stabbed another. In the affray, six boys ran away to Brampton, kicking a policeman they met along the way. They caused significant property damage while attacking the couple in charge. But even this report concluded, "apart from these outbreaks... the boys are quite attractive!!!"[99]

Yvonne Kapp acknowledged that older boys constituted a "special element" in camp. These "boys" had played the role of men during the war in Spain, digging trenches on the front lines. Expecting to control them like "children" (even if they fell within the appropriate age limits) could only lead to rebellion. Kapp described how a group of older boys set out from North Stoneham one day for London. When confronted, they announced their intention to see the capital city; "they had not traveled so far merely to live in a field and, since this appeared to be their fate, they had taken matters into their own hands."[100] Kapp concluded that the best way to satisfy these Basque "boys'" longing for a "tougher life" was to give them their own special section of the camp where they might cook for themselves, and allow them to be self-governing.

Physical violence was never far from these discussions. One persistent stereotype was that the Basques all possessed knives, which they would wield with little provocation. At Burmaston House in Derby, the director suggested that Basques should not be allowed to have knives at meals; six boys had already been found with knives in their belts.[101] Basque girls were admonished for fighting with English girls, hitting a matron in the face, and insisting on returning to Spain.[102] The 100 Basque boys at St. Mary's Convent in Southall—some of whom escaped, armed with knives—were described as "full of almost alarming vitality... entirely without any idea of discipline." A visiting Spanish priest said something pro-Franco, and the boys "began smashing beds, door-handles, and school equipment." A Basque priest had to be called to calm them.[103]

In July of 1937, several newspapers reported on seventy-two Basque boys who were "terrifying" Welsh villagers at Cynarth, a Ministry of Labour camp 2 miles south of the village in Brechfa. The Basques were accused of smashing windows, and throwing a knife at a policeman, keeping the camp in a constant state of riot. Locals from the placid village pleaded, "For heaven's sake take them away from here. We are afraid to sleep in our beds at night."[104] But there was another side to the story. The Basques were appalled by the conditions at Brechfa, where the Nissen huts had been used by sick and unemployed miners. Indeed, *The Times* likened the primitive Ministry of Labour camps to concentration camps.[105] One boy said he would prefer to go back to Spain and face the shelling than remain at Brechfa.

The boys at Brechfa, who were between the ages of 8 and 15, were mostly from the industrialized city of Bilbao, where they had lived in apartment blocks in tightly knit, working-class districts. Set down in this remote parish, in a cold and inhospitable camp, with no schooling, no structure to the day, and very little adult supervision, the boys quickly became disruptive. José Armolea recalled arriving at Brechfa when he was 11 years old, and realizing that he and his fellow travelers were on their own:

> It was a beautiful spot, out in the wild and on a slight incline. There was an urn in the middle of the camp full of cocoa and lots of corned beef sandwiches that we ate for days afterwards. We had to fill our mattresses with straw, which we then put over three slats of wood to sleep on. No sheets. In the morning, there was the same cocoa and sandwiches and that was our meal for I don't know how many days. The Brechfa people were snooty and well off. They didn't want us there from day one. Mind you I'm not saying that we were angels...We were in a situation where we had no supervision. We could do anything we wanted. No schooling, no proper meals. After a while kids started venturing out. How do you expect kids to behave?[106]

Franco's apologists seized on these stories, claiming that the children at Brechfa were all from communist backgrounds.[107] The right-wing press branded the Basques as ungrateful and violent, and several MPs criticized their "riotous conduct." Home Secretary Selwyn Lloyd sent twenty-four Basque boys back to Spain for their "attacks on British citizens."[108]

Many British authorities contrasted the anarchic, violent Basques with Jewish child refugees, whom they saw as timid, passive, and well behaved. But oral histories point to a more complicated history. Erich Duschinsky, a Czech refugee who worked at Dovercourt, described how he had to break up knife fights between Jewish children (much like the "disorderly" Basques). Duschinsky also recalled difficulties controlling the older adolescents when they arrived at Harwich, as the boys snuck off to the harbor to meet prostitutes.[109] Some Basque children resented what they saw as the staging of their own "disorder" by unsympathetic reporters. Rafael, a Basque refugee, recalled people throwing chocolate over the fence at North Stoneham and then photographing the chaos: "rumors had gone around about us but of course all we doing is trying to live."[110] Such conflicting accounts suggest the need for caution in adopting British stereotypes of different groups of refugees.

British authorities strove to deny the political energies of Basque and Jewish refugees. Conversely, camp leaders were not overly concerned about the political loyalties of displaced Poles. The British assumed that most Poles in Britain were "staunchly anti-Russian."[111] The politics of Hungarian refugees was more mysterious. Within the pantheon of refugees, Hungarians enjoyed a special international reputation as Cold War heroes: vigorous, courageous, and politically active. Hungarians refugees were not idle DPs, who passively awaited international aid. They had already braved minefields, rivers, and armed guards in order to seek their freedom.[112] Initial Treasury reports described the Hungarians as less likely to have a large "hard core" than the Polish and German (that is, Jewish) refugees.[113] One report on Crookham Camp described the Hungarians as "very intelligent," with a "quick sense for real quality."[114]

These flattering assessments were countered by concerns about the threat that Hungarians posed to public safety and security. Whereas the Poles were largely perceived as immune to communism's allure, the Home Office files contain numerous reports of British authorities "listening in" on conversations between Hungarian refugees at Crookham and their relatives in Budapest. The most vital British fears about Hungarian refugees pertained to the possibility that they were communist spies. The camp administrators determined that the gifts refugees sent to their relatives in Hungary could be a vital form of propaganda for the West. For this reason, they did little to encourage Hungarian refugees to save their money, hoping only "once they get used to seeing plenty of everything, they will be better able to balance their spending." While other refugees might be compelled into frugality, free spending and consumption for the Hungarians was viewed as a Cold War imperative.

Camp leaders may have been wary of Hungarian politics. But Hungarian refugees staged few acts of formal, organized resistance. The arrival of the Ugandan Asians in the 1970s brought new anxieties about grassroots activism in refugee camps. The Ugandan Asian camps were the site of numerous collective protests. Camp leaders veered wildly in their political assessments of Ugandan Asians, sometimes highlighting their comforting social conservatism, and other moments fearing their political radicalization. Camp officers often split up anyone they perceived as an organized "group" and redistributed them to different centers, disrupting the quest for housing and employment.[115]

At Maresfield, six Ugandan Asian men were accused of refusing to perform their cleaning tasks, and spreading "false information" regarding settlement in Scotland (specifically, that Scotland was too cold and that there were no Asians there). The men also allegedly wrote to the Home Office to protest the camp's charges for food and housing. The camp leader described the men as rebellious and possibly violent.[116] A document called "Uncooperative Residents" included the men's own report of this meeting: "This morning you called us in your office, and as we entered, we wished you Good Morning. You did not reply and even did not show courtesy to answer, but kept quiet." According to the residents, the camp leader banged his fist on the table, and threatened to evict them in twenty-four hours. They responded, but "we are most hurt by the insults that we had from you without any reason. We have self respect, and it is very, very dear to us, dearer than our lives. Why such insults should have been inflicted upon us, and that is why we were called in your office? This seems to us quite strange, and most embarrassing.

You had also said 'You people are here with my money...' We would like to know what made you insult us, and why were we deprived of our legitimate right to speak. <u>Is it called DEMOCRACY?</u>"[117] All six men were transferred to other centers.[118]

At the heart of these struggles was the Ugandan Asians' insistence that they were not refugees, but citizens. Mamdani described how a Kensington Barracks administrator gave him a badge and told him he had to wear it at all times, ostensibly to prevent people who did not live in the camp from eating there. No meals would be served to those without badges. Mamdani refused: "We will *carry* cards for the sake of administrative efficiency, but will not *wear* badges." The administrator replied, "Don't be petty, Mr. Mamdani. What is the difference between a card and a badge? One is rectangular, the other is square. That is all." For Mamdani, this protest was significant:

> We had refused to act as refugees, as helpless, well-behaved children, totally devoid of initiative, indiscriminately grateful for anything that may come their way; in other words, dependence personified... It would all have happened according to the text, except that we were *not refugees.*[119]

Camp authorities struggled to control the political actions and affections of the Basques, the Poles, the Hungarians, and the Ugandan Asians. The refugees from Vietnam posed a different problem. Here, the concern was to spark the spirit of independence that led to resistance in the first place.[120] British camp leaders saw the Vietnamese not as natural anarchists, but as passive victims who had been warped by communist oppression. These refugees had been politically paralyzed not only by their tragic and violent encounters with communism, but also with the paternalistic and rigidly authoritarian camps of Hong Kong. Social workers hoped that camps in Britain could offer refugees more scope for individual independence. Full-blooded grassroots participation was, they noted, not truly part of the culture of these refugees. They were used to hierarchy and being "governed"; they were likely to find roles of continued dependency reassuring rather than oppressive.

Most British sources described the Vietnamese as more compliant than other refugees.[121] Indeed, one project leader noted that the Vietnamese would wait on the staff and try to cook their food, clean their shoes, cut their hair, or read the newspaper to them. But archival records tell a different, more troubled story, which suggests that we should be as suspicious of the trope of the "passive" Vietnamese refugee as of the knife-wielding, hot-tempered Basque. As drunkenness, vandalism, and violence increased, the Sopley Centre staff considered a moratorium on bringing young, single men from Hong Kong.[122] In one conflict at Thorney Island in 1979, a child of 14 was stabbed in the neck. While the Vietnamese Sub-Committee suggested that the offender's family should be moved in disgrace to another camp, Major Arrowsmith disagreed. He noted that although the knife was seen as an extremely vicious weapon in England, this was not true in the East. Refugees should be educated about how to handle conflicts peacefully, not punished.[123]

Still, disciplinary measures in the Vietnamese camps could be draconian. Residents who failed to participate in the "communal life" of Thorney Island could have their resettlement suspended, and their house given to another family. They could also lose their fieldworker or interpreter. At that point, DHSS would treat the family "as an English family," who must sort out their problems on their own. Furthermore, these individuals would not be allowed to participate in excursions, and their boilers and radiators would not be serviced. Young men who refused to go to English classes would have their privileges withdrawn "until they began to conform."[124]

Residents who refused to clean at Thorney Island could become ineligible for resettlement altogether. When cockroaches appeared in the Centre, Arrowsmith was incensed: "all we have asked of the Vietnamese is that the Centre should be kept clean. It is NOT clean." Arrowsmith (wrongly) claimed that the refugees were paid social security only on the condition that they performed certain tasks in camp. He translated into Vietnamese an article from the local press about the 81-year-old widow of the oldest serving British soldier, living alone in a cold, one-bedroom flat with no hot water. This old lady, he said, "would love to live here [at Thorney Island] with good food, clothing, heating, hot water—in fact everything."[125] Discussing the electric bill, Arrowsmith cautioned that if residents failed to turn out the lights, Britain would have no money to bring "your friends" from Hong Kong.[126] Another center organizer complained of "a typical situation: a volunteer washing the floor, with all the refugees watching."[127]

The Vietnamese Committee complained that Arrowsmith did not discipline wayward refugees harshly enough. Indeed, the chair of the committee resigned because he felt that Arrowsmith was "too gentle" with guilty residents. Arrowsmith replied tartly that England was not a "Communist Society where quite often innocent people could be convicted and he hoped when the Vietnamese were resettled they would remember that if wronged in the future they should not take the law into their own hands but inform the Police." When the chair tried to establish rules to prevent gambling at Thorney Island (which made him many enemies), Arrowsmith said blithely that it was impossible to stop "Chinese people" from gambling. The staff could not monitor the residents, because "in Britain it is not usual to control people's activities in their own rooms."[128]

Faced with what they saw as a failure of camp leadership, the residents' committee devised its own system of justice. It warned that "there is a messy mixture of social classes in this Centre. Bad and bizarre behavior is expected and must be corrected." The committee's "code" for refugee behavior instructed residents to behave themselves both as good Vietnamese and as good English citizens: "Desirably, we would expect of you all an adaptation to westernization, but not a total westernization, we sincerely mean this." Refugees must work hard to learn English, clean properly, and look after their own children instead of fobbing them off on the staff. Gambling was forbidden, as was taking food from the dining room, fishing in the river, hunting birds, or picking fruit from the trees. Finally, propaganda leaflets, "nonsense letters," and gossip were all disallowed.[129] After one assault at Thorney Island, Vu Khanh Thanh suggested that anyone who behaved violently should be "forced to resettle in remote and undesirable areas where they hardly manage to get on with life."[130] Such rules did not make the residents' committee popular. Indeed, anonymous letters plastered around the camp claimed that someone was planning to stab the committee members.[131]

As we can see here, both discipline and violence spiraled out in several different directions. Camp leaders did not simply impose rules upon helpless refugees. Rather, camp authorities struggled to understand the limits of their own power. Their ability to craft and enforce rules was curtailed by welfare departments who had their own vision of refugee care. Furthermore, refugees themselves opposed injustice with individual and collective acts of protest.

THE CAMP AND THE GHETTO: THE STRANGE HISTORY OF DISPERSAL

One key issue of contention was where refugees would resettle when they left the camps. Camp leaders struggled to ensure that refugees would settle in "appropriate" areas—that they would "disperse" throughout the country. The government's shifting vision of dispersal shaped how people were allowed to leave the camps, and under what conditions. The jagged history of dispersal reveals many ironies and contradictions. Namely, it was precisely those who were most vigorously exhorted to stay out of ethnic enclaves who became the most firmly entrenched within them. Dispersal embodied the most destructive effects of the power of the camp, but also revealed the limits of this power.

The fundamental principle of dispersal was to avoid creating "ghettos" or "enclaves" of refugees. In some cases, camp locations were actually chosen to support dispersal. The often bizarre location of the camps was part of the failed technology of managing and imagining race relations. They reflected competing visions of a planned society, with carefully regulated degrees of ethnic and racial mixing and segregation. Dispersal sought to imagine relationships among refugees, as well as between refugees and citizens, positing idealized and spatially controlled forms of interaction. Thus, strategies of encampment and dispersal were deeply intertwined. The policies of dispersal in Britain were never linear; they shifted frequently and unpredictably. Furthermore, refugees never passively accepted these policies. The choice of where to settle was a focal point of refugee activity and activism.

Dispersal had been piloted in many sites, and failed in all of them. As we saw earlier, colonial-era British officials had experimented with dispersal in Indian famine camps and plague segregation camps. But there were also more recent models to adopt or reject. After partition, the Indian government sent Bengal's Hindu refugees to Nissen-hut camps far away from the metropolis. This program was a colossal failure. The refugees were "stubbornly" unwilling to abandon Calcutta, and the government fell back on the "ugly solution" of restricting relief only to refugees who dispersed. Anthropologists damned the refugees' desire to cluster in Calcutta as irrational "herd" thinking, rather than admitting the impossibility of finding work in remote camp locations. According to this logic, dispersal failed because of the refugees' own failings. Nobody questioned the wisdom of setting up a refugee camp in a malarial swamp miles from the nearest town. The government continued to pursue dispersal avidly, despite its catastrophic results.[132]

The United States provided another model. During the Second World War, Isaiah Bowman, the president of Johns Hopkins University, developed a plan to resettle Europe's Jews outside the United States—mostly in rural areas so that they would move away from the commercial professions that he believed provoked anti-Semitism. Drawing on Bowman's work, President Roosevelt planned to distribute Japanese American internees throughout the country in order to "dissolve" their ethnic characteristics.[133] Resettlers defied this bid for state-engineered assimilation, and settled together where they wished. Still, social scientists continued to treat dispersal as a tremendous opportunity for racial equality and liberation, an explanation for the "success" of Asian Americans.[134] In the 1970s, the Ford administration dispersed Indo-Chinese refugees outside the West Coast as a condition of their release from refugee camps. Again, the policy was a radical failure. Most refugees who agreed to be dispersed soon moved permanently into ethnic enclaves.[135]

Clearly, the larger project of trying to reshape migration patterns through social engineering was widespread. Dispersal was a key element of refugee "care" in multiple locales. What lessons did Britons learn from these South Asian and American histories? On both sides of the Atlantic, social scientists and government officials promoted dispersal despite mounting evidence of its failures. The British case reflects much more vacillation.[136] Even at the height of the state's zeal, dispersal was nearly impossible to enforce. There was little evidence that placing camps in remote locations would lead refugees to settle in those areas, or govern their choice of settlement at all. The state had no consensus on whether dispersal was a social and political good. As a form of constraint on mobility within a free, liberal society, dispersal was always suspect.

The question of how to control the settlement patterns of refugees began in Britain in the Great War, structured by the demands of the security state. Belgian refugees were not allowed to settle in prohibited areas, mostly near areas of national defense.[137] The Home Office debated the boundaries of the restricted areas, as well as the question of whether Belgian refugees should be banned outright in these areas, or merely regulated by verifying their identities and tracking their movements. Those who had arrived in prohibited areas in Norfolk, Suffolk, and Essex were to be "thinned out" whenever opportunities arose.[138]

In the 1930s, dispersal policies moved away from security concerns to debates about cultural integrity. In theory, because Basque and Jewish children were supposed to be destined for repatriation or emigration, there was no need to disperse them in Britain. Still, the Home Office sought to disperse Jewish children widely and prevent the formation of Jewish "enclaves."[139] In contrast, Basque children—concentrated in their "colonies" and often touring the country together to perform Basque dances and songs for English audiences—were subject to a strategy of unambiguous unification.[140] As we saw in Chapter 3, British aid workers were deeply invested in the idea of the ethnic purity of the Basques, and the strength of their collective feeling. These assumptions shaped the fate of dispersal for Basque children in Britain. Basques were to be kept together instead of scattered apart.

With the arrival of the Poles, debates about dispersal intensified. The Ministry of Labour wanted to site the Polish camps near centers of industry, but the Foreign Office wanted to disperse the camps as widely as possible. The Foreign Office prevailed, and the Polish camps were dispersed, both to weaken the grip of the Polish military and to prevent the development of Polish "ghettoes."[141] On the second reading of the Polish Resettlement Bill in 1947, several MPs spoke against the creation of "separate foreign enclaves." Leah Manning argued that if the Poles were to become "one of us," then they required English influence. They must abandon their traditional militarism, which was "alien" to the more democratic British Army.[142] Poles would forget the "bad things" they had learned from Polish officers only by "mixing with honest-to-God British Tommies, miners and agriculturalists and not by being put into groups of their own." She acknowledged that it was "nice to have a pal," and thus settling the Poles in groups of two or three would be acceptable.[143] As Lady Reading of the WVS said in 1949, we wanted "to help foreigners to see with our eyes." Intensive social contact between Britons and Poles was desirable and necessary.[144]

Ultimately, the long life of Polish encampment rendered dispersal irrelevant. But, in the coming decades, the project of dispersal gained traction for other groups.[145] Dispersal was not only used in the "exceptional" circumstances of refugee crises. It was also part of a program of racialized social policy interventions and population redistribution.[146] The state sought at different moments to control the settlement of both migrants and refugees. But refugees—and more specifically, refugee camps—offered special possibilities for population management. The camp functioned as a way for the state to envision the multicultural future. Because the camp provided a means to "hold" refugees until they changed the impulses that drove them to overcrowded cities (and toward each other), refugee settlement could be planned in ways that migrant settlement could not.

During the 1960s, dispersal activists focused their energies not on refugees, but on another highly mobile population: Commonwealth immigrants. These immigrants clustered in urban centers– 60 percent in Greater London, and 30 percent in the Midlands and West Riding.[147] The Home Office considered linking employment vouchers to places that had low immigrant populations, and admitting women and children only if their male heads of household worked in approved locations. But there was no way to prevent men from taking other jobs after they entered Britain. Conservatives proposed keeping rigid controls over Commonwealth citizens for years after their entry, but it "hardly seems justifiable to erect a complicated apparatus of control for the purpose of keeping a few thousand immigrants" out of the cities.[148] Stricter entry controls were not the answer. Rather, suasion was key. Immigrants could be asked what would motivate them to move, and in what kinds of places they wished to live.[149]

Jack Thomas Howard-Drake, assistant secretary to the Home Office, doubted the wisdom of dispersal. He noted that other ethnic or religious groups—Maltese, Greeks, Chinese, Australians, and Jews—were left undisturbed, and asked "why it is wrong for coloured people to live together." He agreed that immigrants were disadvantaged when they were confined to impoverished areas. But the solution was not to induce them to move. If immigrants truly possessed full "freedom of movement," then the Home Office should not interfere.[150] The aim must be to ensure that Commonwealth immigrants enjoyed the same choices—that is, to disperse or to congregate—as "the rest of us."[151]

Ultimately, the Home Office determined that "coloured people" must not be dispersed. Rather, they could be part of a larger population redistribution if they were identified as members of some other group—such as underprivileged urban residents. Anyone in need could be dispersed. On this view, dispersal merely bolstered "the Government's existing intention to increase the mobility of the population as a whole."[152] It was crucial to "make it easy for the immigrant to move about freely." Otherwise, the fact that immigrants had "less mobility than other citizens" might promote ghettoization. Dispersal thus bore a strange relationship to mobility, as it sought to increase certain kinds of population movements and discourage (or ban) others.

State authorities agreed that immigrants of color clustered together because of British racism. Moreover, they were reluctant to interfere with the physical freedoms of immigrants once they had arrived in Britain and braved its increasingly discriminatory entry controls. Even Conservatives—who paired restrictive immigration legislation with programs of aid for immigrants already in Britain—argued that dispersal must not trump the immigrant's own "happiness and contentment."[153] Certainly, the existence of openly racist busing schemes and proposals to entice immigrants to settle in New Towns reveal the state's eagerness to promote "voluntary dispersal" for people of color. But New Town planners stressed that such movements must be "natural"—any "deliberate plantation" would be disastrous.[154] The guiding principle was individual choice, not direct intervention or compulsion.[155]

Refugees were different. State authorities were less willing to accept that refugees in Britain faced prejudice or outright racism. Rather, the problem was the refugee's impulse to settle in the "wrong" place. When refugees picked their own homes, their choices were inevitably misguided: that is, focused on urban centers. The camp was the secret weapon of dispersal, seeming to provide precisely the mechanism of persuasion that was needed to change people's minds about where to settle. It afforded a chance of supervision, without coercion. As camp authorities would learn, this mechanism was deeply imperfect. But it offered new opportunities to create the ideal map of multiethnic Britain.

Dispersal was developed most fully—and became most contentious—with the arrival of the Ugandan Asians. In refugee camps for Ugandan Asians (and later the Vietnamese), the state saw the opportunity for what had so far proved elusive: the chance to control the settlement of people of color in Britain. At the same time, opposition to dispersal policies strengthened in the 1970s and 1980s. Not only refugees, but also many aid workers, viewed dispersal as a racist, colonialist experiment and actively resisted it. In their protests, they raised bigger questions about social engineering in Britain, and the extent to which interaction across cultures could be planned.

Many officials hoped to use Ugandan Asian camps to shape the geography of resettlement. The original description of the resettlement centers was that they were for people "who agreed to take time to reflect and to listen to advice about the best course to follow."[156] That is, camps were designed to channel Ugandan Asians into specific areas of Britain. Ugandan Asians received contradictory messages. They were urged to "join the community" as soon as possible, to avoid becoming "demoralized and isolated."[157] But they must stay in camp until they were persuaded to settle in the "right" place.

The infamous "red/green" policy for Ugandan Asians—which aimed to discourage settlement in "red" areas with large immigrant populations, and to direct camp residents into "green" areas of low immigrant population—amplified strategies that had percolated in earlier decades. Maps of Britain's "red" areas were publicized in Kampala's newspapers and the passport offices in Uganda. But as refugees flooded into "red" areas, camp officials in Britain became intent on changing their minds. The Runnymede Trust, a liberal think tank, lobbied the Foreign Office to send an expert team to Uganda to gather "every imaginable detail" about Asian householders who wished to settle in Britain. Dispersal plans should be organized for each individual before the Asians left Uganda.[158]

On September 17, 1972, *The Times* leaked secret information on the red/green policy.[159] Now in public view, dispersal was immediately controversial. Lord Hawke, the Conservative politician, described Ugandan Asians as "remarkably capable" people, who might help run Britain within a generation or two, "but they cannot do it from these remote camps...I was astonished when I saw that the Government were popping these people into the most remote areas of the country. I do not quite know why."[160] The Polish camps, he suggested, had been much more centrally located. Indeed, some sites seemed too bleak even to the URB. Hemswell and Faldingworth were both terribly isolated; volunteers huddled at these camps when they were off duty, feeling that the nearest villages were too inaccessible.

For advocates of dispersal, the geographical isolation of the camps could "rescue" Asians from racial prejudice. Commander Reay Parkinson of the RAF said that Ugandan Asians were better off in rural communities than if they were "pitchforked into our centres of racial strife."[161] *The Times* urged its readers not to be alarmed by large numbers of Asians flooding into camps; it was much better than if they rushed off to the cities "because they want to be with other Asians."[162] The Lord Chancellor described the camps as places of temporary respite for Ugandan Asians "whilst they make up their minds" where to settle—guided, of course, by reception teams.[163]

The government's designation of "red" and "green" areas had glaring anomalies. Some areas with large Asian populations (such as Barnet, Hounslow, Coventry, and Blackburn) were labeled green.[164] Glasgow, which had a tremendous housing shortage but no sizable Asian community, was declared green, while Leicester, which had a large Asian community but plenty of available housing, was deemed red. Furthermore, "red" areas were not always rejected for Ugandan Asian settlement. Ugandan Asians at West Malling were placed in the "red" area of London in order to facilitate the camp's closure.

The red/green policy was not a foregone conclusion. When the expulsion crisis began, early discussions suggested that it might actually be easier to let new arrivals settle in cities with large Asian populations.[165] But that possibility was soon rejected. Private correspondence suggests that ministers hoped for a spatial and temporal "buffer"—that is, camps—between the arrival of the Ugandan Asians and their site of settlement.[166] The question was how to enforce this policy. The greater the number of Ugandan Asians who went to camps, the more control the government hoped to have over their eventual settlement. One reason that the URB accepted mass encampment as a strategy of refugee care was to meet the demands of dispersal.

The Home Office admitted that it could not compel anyone to live in a particular place, though it did consider seeking a statutory power to keep Ugandan Asians in transit camps for a specified period. Such a power would not be enforceable for very long: "one could not imprison or deport a Ugandan Asian who had moved to Leicester." Rather, the aim must be to devise ways of steering Ugandan Asians into "places they might be expected to remain."[167] Camp authorities had no legal power to make any refugee remain in camp. Indeed, another official felt it necessary to remind his colleague that while they might hope the Asians would disperse into "green" areas, there was "no law which would enable the Government, no matter how fine or elaborate its temporary camps, to hold in them a Uganda Asian against his will."[168]

Ugandan Asians who went straight into the community upon arrival (instead of into one of the sixteen resettlement camps) were not eligible for houses offered to the URB. In order to qualify for these houses, one had to go first to a camp.[169] With this economic enticement, the URB hoped to better control the settlement patterns of Ugandan Asians. Thus, encampment shaped economic opportunity in a variety of ways, making the "choice" to stay in camp much more complicated. The camps offered material benefits that went far beyond the realm of emergency aid.

Again, the URB relied on persuasion.[170] One of its tactics was to have "settled" Ugandan Asians write to camp residents, exhorting them to consider less urban areas. These letters were published in camp newspapers, publicizing the merits of dispersal. Kurban Isaji, who spent his first days in Britain at Maresfield, exhorted camp residents to "Go To a Smaller Town." He described how his children had been admitted to school within three days of their arrival. He and his family were respected by locals, who recognized them as being special refugees rather than ordinary Asian migrants.

Even in the strictest days of dispersal, Ugandan Asians still had choices. While at Tonfanau, Chandrika Joshi's sister urged their father to pick housing in the New Town at Stockport, which was reasonably close to Manchester, and—she hoped—would offer some of the resources of a larger city. She was disappointed when their father (heartsick from his wife's illness) accepted the first house he was offered, which was in South Wales. Nine other families from Tonfanau settled close by, however, and the Joshi family created a "little community" of Sikhs, Muslims, and Hindus who knew each other from camp.[171]

Ultimately, only 38 percent of the Ugandan Asians who moved through Britain's camps settled in so-called "green" areas.[172] Dispersal policies actually produced *more* concentrated enclaves of Ugandan Asians than for Indians and Pakistanis.[173] But dispersal was a remarkably durable policy. As late as 1977, the Ministry of Housing and Local Government said it was difficult to influence where refugees would settle "unless they are compelled to go particular places."[174] By the 1980s, the Home Office admitted that the red/green policy for Ugandan Asians had failed, presumably because "it lacked either a power of compulsion or any effective inducements."[175]

Such sentiments gained strength with the arrival of refugees from Vietnam. The governing principle was that Vietnamese refugees should be grouped to encourage integration, but not assimilation.[176] Paul Rushton, who worked on Vietnamese resettlement in Hampshire, proposed that Vietnamese families who wanted to live near each other should be placed that way if possible, but he advised against housing them on the same street "for reasons of encouraging independence, privacy, and gradual integration in a natural way." The Vietnamese should have the opportunity for integration in the early stages of resettlement, even if they later chose to "draw together as a matter of cultural preferences."[177]

Here, we can see how very finely the idea of "dispersal" was calibrated—thinking not only in terms of cities, but individual streets. Logistically, this meant that Rushton and others advocated distributing Vietnamese families around the country in clusters of four to ten families.[178] But the cluster plan quickly fell apart, and dispersal became more "reactive" to housing offers from local authorities. Some families were split up during the dispersal process; Lam Cong was resettled to Thamesmead in London, but his mother and brother were sent to Inverness in Scotland. Thorney Island settled seven young men in the tiny village of Ottery St Mary in Devon. Within weeks, six of the men had returned to Thorney Island, saying they could not live there. Others were settled in Northern Ireland during the Troubles.[179] By 1982, 50 percent of refugees from Vietnam were in isolated circumstances, often without any facilities for language tuition.[180] The size of the dispersal groups varied from one family to up to 100 people.

By 1985, the Home Office and the Ministry of Housing and Local Government agreed that dispersal for Vietnamese refugees was undesirable. More than half the Vietnamese in Britain ultimately moved to London. Even those refugees who were placed in "good" housing abandoned these homes, and moved to Lambeth or Hackney.[181] Many fieldworkers considered the dispersal policy "a complete disaster," and "really cruel."[182] Indeed, SCF leaders tacitly thwarted dispersal by settling the Vietnamese in remote locations as the Home Office wished, but then advising them how to find housing in London.[183] Ultimately, dispersal was blamed for the high unemployment rate—perhaps as high as 60 percent—among refugees from Vietnam.[184]

Dispersal policies failed spectacularly in terms of achieving their desired ends, but wrought havoc with many refugees' lives in the process. And they continue to do so today. Refugee camps are still often located outside of cities, in demonstrably peripheral sites, with the strategic aim of dispersing of asylum seekers.[185] Recently,

Labour proposed a regionalized immigration policy that would allow higher immigration to London, but tighter restrictions on immigration to the rest of the country.[186] This policy reversed the imagined map of dispersal as it existed in the twentieth century, but spoke to the same impulse that drove those failed social engineering projects of bygone eras.

If dispersal did not transform migration patterns as intended, it still powerfully—and unpredictably—shaped the futures of many individuals. Ostensibly aimed at refugees, dispersal was part of a larger conversation about whether racialized settlement patterns could be usefully controlled. Although dispersal never reshaped migration patterns as intended, it created an imagined map of multicultural Britain that ran alongside the reality of what new settlements actually looked like, continuing to spark fantasies of social engineering that involved citizens, migrants, and refugees.

The strategy of dispersal reflects that one of the most vexed issues for camp leaders was the physical mobility of refugees. Refugees, of course, were defined by the experience of enforced mobility. The camps aimed to transform this mobility, but in precisely calibrated ways, and on a highly structured timeline. Camp authorities wanted to ensure that refugees would not burden local authorities, and thus sought to delay their departure until they had achieved a certain level of self-sufficiency. But overly long stays seemed to cultivate passivity. Refugees were routinely pathologized for leaving camps either too early or too late. As camp authorities deployed conflicting strategies of containment and eviction, leaving and staying could both be important forms of resistance.

LAST ACTS: REFUSING TO STAY, REFUSING TO LEAVE

Even on the very basic point of physical freedom, the camps varied widely. Some camps had fences with a military patrol; others had completely uncontrolled perimeters. Some camps offered unrestricted movement, while others tightly regulated the boundary between the inside and outside. Camp leaders saw some groups as excessively mobile, while others were inadequately so. Bluntly put, some refugees refused to stay in camp, while others refused to leave.

The movement of Belgian refugees was limited even before they arrived in camps, especially in coastal areas. In September of 1914, Belgians lost the right to move freely around Britain, and were subject to official registration from October. In November 1914, all Belgian refugees were compelled to register with the police, and entry or residence in prohibited areas was prevented without a special permit. But *The Times* described Earl's Court itself as free and open: "going and coming is managed so that order may be preserved without too great an infringement of personal liberty."[187] In this sense, Belgian refugees gained more mobility once they were registered in camp.

For many British observers, the Basque child refugees at North Stoneham were entirely too mobile. As unauthorized visitors flooded into the North Stoneham

Camp, the Basque children continued to break out of it. Indeed, the most disruptive act the Basque children could undertake in camp was to leave it. Many gates blocked off the camp, but no one patrolled them. One Basque child, Herminio, described how he easily got out of camp and hid out in the New Forest. The barbed wire around the camp, he claimed, was no impediment at all. One camp official complained that he had seen a gang of Basque children "arranged like a mangled crocodile, i.e. just a mob, walking in the town."[188] There was no real control over the movements of the Basques, who wandered into the villages, missed meals, and even slept out of the camp at times.

The camp authorities considered having the Ministry of Transport shut down the road parallel to the camp, or installing an expensive fence that would be impossible to climb.[189] One road into camp was eventually blocked, and the pass system tightened. Loudspeakers and cinemas were installed to amuse the children, but one official lamented, "We are still busy catching them and bringing them back to Camp."[190] It would be impossible to ensure that all children had been properly placed (and not simply lost) when the camp closed.[191] By June 1937, the children were allowed out of camp in North Stoneham if they were under adult supervision, in hopes that this would forestall "uncontrolled wandering." As we

Fig. 6.1. The imposing gate at the main entrance to Kitchener. In striking contrast to the chaos of North Stoneham, the Kitchener men required a permit to leave camp. Aside from the heavy gate, the men were surrounded by barbed wire and under guard. As the camp leader Phineas May said, "One didn't just walk out." Chronicle/Alamy Stock Photo.

have seen, the state's concern about this kind of "wandering" was not only about child protection. It was also about protecting Britons from an unpredictably radicalized group of unknowns.[192]

Once the children were dispersed from North Stoneham into the "colonies," the rules about their confinement varied widely. At Woolwich, local residents often took the Basque children out to play on the heath. But at Swansea, the children were held behind barbed wire.[193] At the Salvation Army Home in Clapton, which the Ministry of Health admitted was "very cramped," children occasionally broke out of the Home, "encouraged by irresponsible local elements."[194]

The Poles offered a very different mode of resistance. If the Basque children proved difficult to track and corral, then the Polish refugees proved nearly impossible to dislodge. To the chagrin of the British, some Poles never left camp at all.[195]

Surprisingly, the National Assistance Board rarely evicted anyone.[196] The Board warned camp residents that they could be turned out if they refused to work, but ejecting people too quickly would burden local authorities. The Polish camp at Great Bowerwood, located on the property of Lord Portman near Beaconsfield and occupied by a "hard core" of Poles who refused to leave, posed a persistent problem. A mass eviction was likely to be unpopular with the public, as the Poles were "exiles who fought gallantly for us during the war and whose country has been savagely overrun and forcibly drawn behind the Iron Curtain."[197] They were not only wartime, but also Cold War heroes. The government apologized to Lord Portman for failing to clear the camp, but offered no solution beyond moving (at great expense) all of the Nissen huts to one part of the site.

In 1949, the National Assistance Board began to consider eviction more seriously. Wardens were encouraged to evict Poles who had the means to make their own way in life.[198] The police must witness all evictions, and only "reasonable force" should be used. If "very great violence" was encountered, then the warden should desist and resort to the courts.[199] Wardens could appeal to headquarters if they wanted to evict people for cohabitation, being convicted of criminal offences, or engaging in "undesirable activities of a political nature." The Northwick warden argued that evictions encouraged independence, and healthy, single men should be compelled to leave for the outside world. He concluded, "once a Pole does actually make the break from a Hostel he or she invariably soon settles down."[200] But the Board's own chairman still opposed evictions, saying they should be undertaken only if they were in the public interest. The Board's legal right to evict refugees must be balanced with its moral duty to settle them.

The ideal trajectory that the National Assistance Board had imagined—that is, from camp to private home—was often thwarted. Many Poles returned again and again to camp, even if they had been resettled or evicted. The Board could refuse to readmit Poles to its hostels. But the Board believed that people were only willing to risk leaving the hostel's security if they thought they could come back.[201] It also acknowledged that there were "strong reasons of sentiment" to allow Poles to return to camp in cases of family reunion. Wardens were instructed to refuse readmission only to "undesirable" persons. If any Pole lost his job and sought to be readmitted to a camp, or, "having failed to establish himself outside, he still regards it as his 'home,' every effort should be made to find room for him."[202] Such policies acknowledged that resettlement could fail.

Many individuals broke the Board's rules about returning to camp. The barriers to Polish camps were not policed, and entry to vacant huts was quite easy.[203] At Kelvedon, Mr. Platta and Mr. Kubinski asked to stay on at the hostel (where Mr. Platta's mother resided) after they quit their jobs at the Midland Gas Board. Refused permission, they broke into a hut and stayed anyway. All attempts to persuade them to leave failed, and both men obtained work locally. The Colchester County Court heard multiple cases of defendants who remained in camp against the warden's wishes, as well as Poles breaking back into camp after they had settled elsewhere. The judge stated that the National Assistance Board had the right to exclude trespassers, but the court could only enforce obedience by imprisoning the defendants. He concluded that the Board's moral responsibility to the defendants trumped the illegal conduct of the refugees.[204]

The frustrated warden at Northwick noted that residents postponed their departures as long as possible. He proposed overcoming this resistance by "constant pressure and interviews," or taking some "visual action" to spur families to leave, such as pulling down the Nissen huts.[205] The Board responded that people were naturally reluctant to leave Northwick, which was "quite a comfortable place where they get more for their money than they could expect to get in the outside world, and with a Polish community life which they naturally do not want to quit."[206] The warden expected "to have to soften his heart a little when the time comes," and allow a few Poles in the camp to stay on as lodgers, or "pair up to run a little household of their own." The "empty" camp would thus become a home.

Mrs. Maria Pajdzik, a widow with six children (the largest family at Northwick), also resisted being transferred. Mrs. Pajdzik had been asked to move in 1962, but had refused, and was left alone for another six years. In 1968, she was offered a three-bedroom council house in "very good" condition, with an outhouse and a spacious garden. The local authority declined to offer the house to a British family, as the house was in the middle of a Polish "colony." Mrs. Pajdzik rejected the house, claiming that her son would be unable to find work in the new location. After negotiating with Mrs. Pajdzik, the warden concluded that the only means of compulsion would be court proceedings to evict her. Until now, the Board had avoided this drastic measure. But Northwick was down to the "hard core," and harsher measures were necessary.[207] Another Northwick resident refused to apply for council housing because his wife worked in the hostel as a cleaner. She would lose her job if they left. He pleaded, "I don't think that the aim of the National Assistance Board is to force people into greater need."[208] From his perspective, resettlement represented economic loss. The Board denounced this "open resistance," and asked why a refugee should have to be coerced into a council house which a British family would be pleased to accept.[209]

Closures of refugee camps were met with protest by other groups as well. When Summerfield Hostel and Frobisher Hostel for Anglo-Egyptians were scheduled for closure in the spring of 1958, some residents threatened to squat.[210] The Board rejected any punitive action against them. At the same time, wardens confronted those who simply would not be resettled. One warden at an Anglo-Egyptian hostel wrote to the Board to complain about the Abela sisters, who had been slated for a flat in Dursley. The Abelas refused even to look at the flat and measure it for curtains and linoleum. The warden lamented, "their attitude is completely demoralizing and they are hardcore cases of healthy middle-aged women who have become 'hostel-minded.'" He determined, "there can be no doubt at all that they have decided to obstruct their resettlement." The WVS transported the "howling" sisters' belongings to the flat without their consent.[211]

Family ties played their own part in resistance to resettlement. John Abela, an Anglo-Egyptian resident at the Bridgend Hostel, was offered a council house in Swindon. He began working but then left his job and returned to the hostel. He told the hostel staff that his wife was very lonely while he was away and "she had cried so hard" on the Sunday evening when he was supposed to go back to Swindon that he "felt he could not leave her." The staff sent for his wife and "together they were told how stupid they were acting." They were given a furniture grant to prepare for their new home. Abela returned to Swindon, but promptly came back again to the hostel and said he now wished to buy his own house and not rent one; he then quit his job and found work on his own as an electrician in London. He and his wife refused to leave the hostel.[212]

One Home Office file on Anglo-Egyptian refugees, "Residual Cases in Which Resettlement Cannot be Effected by the Board," suggested how refugees could thwart the resettlement process. Angelo Garrana arrived from Egypt with his mother, Yolanda, in 1956 and stayed at Drake Hall. Angelo failed to qualify as a teacher, and suffered a nervous breakdown. He was sent to Stafford Mental Hospital, but refused treatment and returned to London at his own expense. The Anglo-Egyptian Resettlement Board determined that a man in Angelo's fragile condition was unsuited to stay in a hostel. The Board kept Angelo in a hotel in London, but he continued to be "difficult." He was admitted again to hospital, and his mother was moved to Bridgend Hostel. Yolanda was described as being "fairly happy" at Bridgend, but fearful about her son's future. The Board decided that because Angelo was "ultra-susceptible" to his surroundings and missed his mother's company "to an extreme degree," he should be admitted to Bridgend to live with her.[213] Such cases of abortive resettlements plagued refugee workers.

Of course, it was only possible to keep refugees in camp—or move them out—if camp authorities knew where they were. In theory, every Hungarian was met on arrival, and escorted to a camp to register with the police. In practice, registration was chaotic. At Grange Farm, it was difficult to keep track of Hungarian refugees at any given time, and the warden was "nearly hysterical." Refugees were "allowed to roam at will," and some moved out of the camp before they ever registered at all.[214] Even the most efficient warden would be unable to ensure that all refugees collected where and when they were wanted. Furthermore, various people had access to the camp: press photographer, parties of schoolboys anxious to practice their foreign languages, and members of the British Communist Party. Aldershot and Dover were also quite haphazard, with "no secure check on who enters or leaves" the barracks. Once the Hungarians had registered, BCAR insisted that they were free to move about the country like other "foreigners," but if relatives wished to take refugees from the hostels to their own homes, they must sign a form. BCAR kept all the records on Hungarian arrivals even after they left the camps, intending to "maintain contact with them to be sure that they are happily settled in their new life."[215]

The Hungarian humorist Albert Vajda was greatly alarmed by the prisonlike appearance of the military camp in Britain when he arrived with his compatriots. Upon seeing the barbed wire, "the children began to cry and the lines of suffering in our face grew deeper." Vajda was disturbed that the camp's borders were so strictly policed:

> What we Hungarians couldn't understand was why we were being locked up behind barbed wire, not knowing whether we should have to remain there for days, weeks, or months. What the English couldn't understand was why we didn't behave with calm and composure. An English crowd would be perfectly happy as long as everyone had the opportunity to queue up three or four times a day for meals.[216]

Vajda insisted that he be allowed to leave: " 'I go!' I shouted. 'I not like camp! Barbed wire no good! I escape country barbed wire round. Home prison. England prison! I go!' " He ran towards the main gate and was stopped by a policeman and two soldiers, who convinced him that he must wait for his identity documents. Vajda was ashamed at the trouble he had caused—"it was only logical that they couldn't allow us to disperse without identity papers"—and told the policeman the only "nice" expression he knew in English, "I love you." He left the next day with his proper documentation.[217]

The Dover police were also concerned about Hungarian refugees squatting in the disused army camps nearby. Constables were ordered to look out for wayward refugees on their patrols. Once Hungarians left their hostels they were no longer under BCAR's auspices. If no one else would take them, BCAR often acknowledged a moral obligation and took them back—though not to the same hostel where they had stayed before. At one point, three Hungarians who had departed from three different hostels were arrested for "sleeping rough."[218] Clearly, their resettlement had been incomplete.

Everything possible was done to keep Anglo-Egyptians and Hungarians inside the hostels.[219] Residents were allowed to leave their hostels if they had a definite appointment, but were not permitted to go freely from factory to factory to look for work. Such restrictions were also common in Ugandan Asian camps. The Home Office claimed that it never intended (nor was it empowered) to control the movements of Ugandan Asian camp residents, but it did consider employing a "stronger force" of wardens to keep track of who came and left.[220] Camp administrators complained that they had no real idea of the size of their population from day to day. They tried to track residents' movements, but their information was constantly outdated: "clearly a more direct method of control is essential."[221] One official proposed confiscating camp residents' passports, which might "alarm" them into becoming less mobile. Chotalal Mohan Vadhia recalled that at West

Malling, "freedom was there," but the residents had to return to camp by 7 p.m. and "the police would round you up in town if you were out after that."[222]

The boundaries between aid and detention were especially blurry in Ugandan Asian camps. In August of 1970, the Conservative government contracted the private company Securicor (which would provide "security" at many Ugandan Asian and Vietnamese camps) to run Harmondsworth, the detention center for illegal immigrants at Heathrow Airport.[223] As panic mounted in Uganda in 1972, the Home Office anticipated large parties of queue-jumpers—mostly stateless Ugandan Asians, who had not applied for British passports before the expulsion order—arriving without vouchers. The policy was to detain them at Harmondsworth (or other prisons) for two months, and then admit them, though the Home Office predicted that detention might have to be abandoned if the numbers became too vast. J.S. Waddell of the Home Office wrote confidentially that he would prefer to detain *all* Ugandan Asians instead of allowing them to resettle:

> We must stretch the detention possibilities as far as the situation will let us. But there may come a point at which the build up of numbers will oblige us to drop the concept of detention and think instead of a stage towards settlement of refugees.[224]

Local security firms were also hired to man the gates at West Malling, and the civil police were called after a political group there staged an "unsavory demonstration." The Coordinating Committee for the Welfare of Evacuees from Uganda (CCWEU) faulted the "peremptory and unsympathetic treatment" of Ugandan Asians at West Malling. More care should have been taken to explain to Asians that the Securicor guards were to protect the camp, and not to keep people in.[225]

Such decisions reveal much about the development of contemporary detention policies. Camps for refugees were imagined both as alternatives to detention and as bolsters for it. Some officials viewed refugee camps and detention centers as interchangeable. Many Ugandan Asian detainees at Harmondsworth had spouses and parents in resettlement camps. In December 1972, Viscount Colville agreed to transfer stateless Ugandan Asians from Harmondsworth to the main resettlement camps. The point of the transfer was not actually to resettle the stateless Ugandan Asians, but to provide a more humane space in which to continue their detention.[226]

Greenham Common was the camp of choice for stateless Ugandan Asians who had been released from Harmondsworth, because it had a secure perimeter with a gate guarded by American air force police; the whole camp was patrolled by the Ministry of Defence police. The director could offer "parole" for stateless individuals only during the daytime; it was vital to keep track of these "detainees."[227] Thus, stateless Ugandan Asians were basically under house arrest within the camps. Stateless men were not allowed to leave the camp freely to seek work or housing, though their wives and children might do so. In one case, Mrs. Premkunvar Kotecha moved into a house with her children, but her elderly husband—who was stateless—was compelled to stay in camp and could not join them.[228]

More than any other encamped group, Ugandan Asians sought to shape when and where they would be settled. They refused to leave the camps, or agreed to leave on their own, highly conditional terms. Many residents insisted on staying in camp until they found housing in their chosen area, a clear rejection of the government's dispersal plans. The URB assumed that camps were for people who had no other options. But 49 percent of Ugandan Asians who spent at least a week in camps had relatives in Britain.[229] Jayantilae Umrania, a civil engineer, had a sister in North London, but he preferred to go to the camp at Stradishall and take his chances with the Resettlement Board rather than impose on his sister.[230] Some families regretted not having gone to camps—or having left them too abruptly—feeling that they had missed out on crucial assistance with jobs and housing. As Chotalal Mohan Vadhia recalled, the camps provided a tightly knit community of Asians; he felt that it would have been "very, very difficult" if he had gone directly into a house without the material aid and social support of West Malling.[231]

The rules about who could enter—or re-enter—camp shifted over the course of the Ugandan Asian expulsion, though these rules were rarely uniformly enforced. In an attempt to reduce costs and induce independence, free telephones were withdrawn from Ugandan Asian camps in November 1972, and those who had left the camps were not permitted to re-enter.[232] Residents who showed signs of overstaying were "helped on" by being left out of community activities or excluded from sports teams.[233]

The URB was especially troubled by individuals who had been placed in private housing and then abandoned it to return to the "more secure" life of the camps. Hansa Patel, who stayed in a camp in Britain when she was 12 years old, recalled her family's resettlement as an abortive and fitful process. Her family initially left the camp for Southall, where she had an aunt, but "When we came to Southall, I did not like it. My father and mother and I went back to the camp." Once they returned to camp, her father proposed settling in Scotland, but her mother said, "'No, we don't want to go to Scotland. It is very cold there.' So we didn't go to Scotland and we came to Southall" again. This time, they stayed.[234] People did not necessarily move in a straight line from camps to homes, as British authorities had hoped, but made circuits through camps and private housing in a more complex trajectory. Those who had been officially counted as resettled could easily become unsettled once more.

Camp closures and transfers became a focal point of Ugandan Asian resistance. On December 20, 1972, fifty residents at Kensington (including Mahmood Mamdani) were instructed to pack their belongings and move to Greenham Common within thirteen hours. Mamdani met with camp officials to ask if those on the list (most of whom had already found jobs) could be replaced by those who had not yet found employment, but the answer was no. Those on the transfer list crafted a petition—"because the English like petitions"—in which they "respectfully declined" to leave Kensington. They wrote, "we protest at being treated as objects or, at best, as cattle."[235] When the bus arrived the next morning, the residents assigned for transfer refused to board, and the buses left empty. The camp leaders were furious at this act of disobedience. A new order stated that the original fifty plus another fifty residents must leave the next morning; there would be "very serious consequences" if they disobeyed. Mamdani described an "extraordinary attempt at individual intimidation." Senior staff entered the rooms of every protestor and detailed the retaliatory measures they might face. People with families agreed to leave; young couples and single residents decided to stay.[236]

In December 1972, Hobbs Barracks was abruptly—and unexpectedly—scheduled for closure. The news left the Asian residents in a state of "despondency and dismay." Although the official reason for the sudden closure was that the camp was a fire risk, the staff perceived it as a heavy handed political move by the government because its success exposed the racial prejudice in other camps.[237] Although the National Front had done its best to plague the camp, and staff complained of white girls from East Grinstead trying to seduce the Asian boys, the director described a "wonderful" atmosphere at the camp: "something fine and good when a people fleeing from the tyranny of General Idi Amin found, for a short time, peace and friendship."[238] The government's decision to close the camp "has destroyed much valuable work in what was developing as a splendid multiracial society."[239] Protest groups formed at Hobbs Barracks to try to stop the closure, though to no avail.[240]

For refugees from Vietnam, too, evictions were always a last resort. But people who resettled themselves without British permission were also suspect. Options for Vietnamese families who were unhappy with their housing were very limited. In 1980, the Sopley authorities considered evicting refugees who refused their housing offers. Instead, they adopted strategies to persuade these "refuseniks" by cutting their personal allowances, or transferring them to other centers. One Vietnamese family was "resettled" to a flat in Speke that had heaps of rubble outside the front door, dirty concrete floors, and not a single unbroken window. They asked to be taken back to Nelson Hall, but the resettlement officer refused, threatening to leave them on the pavement with their belongings. The family was "very upset and apprehensive about the future."[241]

In urban camps, refugees who had already resettled were largely viewed as disruptive to the camp atmosphere. At Kensington Barracks in London, the *Guardian* reported, on young men from Vietnam who had been resettled in council flats continued to spend all their time at the camp, "visiting friends." Their return to camp, even for brief social calls, was widely stigmatized. The newspaper suggested that Vietnam's Chinese population had been heavily involved in the drug trade during the war, and "there is a fear that Soho Chinese may be seeking to recruit some of the younger refugees as dealers."[242]

In 1981, the Joint Committee for Refugees from Vietnam decided that refugees who had been offered suitable housing and still refused to move could be removed forcibly (by the police, if necessary).[243] The Thorney Island leadership warned that the staff must be "on alert" for people coming back to the Centre after they had been officially resettled, and visitors were not allowed to stay overnight. It was important to be "rigid" and "severe" on this point, or "we could lose control of the Centre."[244] When Thorney Island residents refused to accept their housing assignments, Arrowsmith blamed his own staff (many of whom opposed dispersal) for encouraging the residents to ask for specific areas.

In theory, refugees—like all council tenants—had the right to refuse two offers of accommodation. In practice, camp leaders often insisted that there should be no choice. At Thorney Island, Daphne Byrne recalled that the camp workers were careful never to mention America to the Vietnamese, "as this would have been their Mecca"; they would have been "off like lemmings."[245] One BCAR missive sternly reminded fieldworkers that "there must be <u>no refusals</u>." BCAR was even accused of "punishing" individuals who misbehaved in its centers by sending them to remote locations. One SCF staff member protested that a fellow refugee had been settled against his will in Scotland, and that he had thought Britain was a free country—or wasn't it?[246] Camp officials tried to get refugees to think about resettlement within limited frameworks, placing constraints on how resettlement could be imagined and achieved.

Refugee activism took many different forms, from the evolving genres of the petition or complaint letter to physical violence. But of all the forms of resistance within the refugee camp, refusing to be resettled—and refusing to give up one's physical mobility—was one of the most basic and fundamental. Within a context of very imperfect options, leaving camp and staying inside it could both be power-ful choices.

Today, most of the world's refugee camps are "closed" camps (the classic examples being Kenya and Tanzania), while many others have informal confinement policies. The spaces of contemporary camps can be both open and closed, in the sense that residents are physically able to leave, but inhibited by the camp's remote location or the fear of being prosecuted for vagrancy or illegal border crossings.[247] In this context, the refugee camps of liberal democracies past and present are instructive. None of Britain's camps were formally "closed" to the outside world, but nearly all placed some form of restriction on the movements of the residents. One might ask: to what end? If the ultimate aim of these constraints was to control the (racialized) process of settlement, then they must be deemed a spectacular failure. Even as it wrought havoc with refugees' hopes and wishes, the camp could not create the world it envisioned.

Epilogue
Camps after Encampment

As we are all too aware, there has been no end to the era of encampment. Today, there are more than 1,000 camps in operation for more than 12 million displaced people. Although refugee camps in Britain were supposed to plan their own obsolescence, they were never rendered as fully out of date as their creators might have hoped. There were numerous miscalculations about how long camps needed to exist, and for whom. Ultimately, there were many different endings to the history of encampment in Britain. For some, encampment only ended with death.

This chapter looks at the chaotic and incomplete process of camp closures, and the shifting definition of resettlement. For many refugees, resettlement generated its own kinds of loss and disruption. Who, in the end, had been "resettled"? What did it mean to be "resettled" at different moments in time? Did camps promote resettlement or thwart it? How did refugees and the state remember (or forget) this process?

As refugees left the camps, British fantasies about how these spaces might be deployed for new purposes and populations began to proliferate. Though most of these plans never materialized, they point to the possibilities that were opened up—as well as closed down—by episodes of encampment. Today, spaces for refugees are being reopened or created anew. This chapter explores the diverse fates and futures of refugee camps.

THE LAST REFUGEE CAMP? CAMP "CLOSURES" AND THE ENDS OF ENCAMPMENT

Refugee camps in Britain varied greatly in terms of how quickly they were shut down, or if they were shut down at all. The Belgian camps closed rapidly. In 1915, Alexandra Palace was converted to a camp for interned Germans and other enemy civilians.[1] The Earl's Court camp actually outlasted the war, staying open to refugees until the summer of 1919. Because of rising anti-alienism, the government pressed for speedy removal of the Belgians. By 1921, there were fewer than 10,000 Belgians in Britain.[2] Repatriation was not strictly compulsory, but refugees who refused to return to Belgium did not receive any further assistance from the state.[3] As the camps reverted to pleasure palaces, nearly all the Belgians in Britain "melted away," disappearing from England as quickly as they came.[4]

The Basque camp at North Stoneham seemed to have one of the most straightforward endings imaginable. Hastily assembled in May 1937, the camp was broken down with little fanfare only four months later in September; the field later became part of Southampton Airport. But shutting down the camp by no means marked the end of Basque displacement. The repatriation of Basque children to Spain began in 1938.[5] The Home Office decided that refugees over the age of 14 would be allowed to choose whether to stay in England; younger children had no choice.[6] One little girl on her way to Bilbao continually cried "Viva England"; she wanted to visit her parents in Spain and then come back to her "lovely home" in Bristol to live.[7]

Repatriation was fraught with political and physical dangers. The children returned by boat to Rouen, then took a special train to Irun, and finally walked across the frontier to Bilbao, using the same bridge across which many Basques had fled earlier.[8] Franco's regime coerced many parents into claiming their children back from Britain, and the children faced suspicion about their loyalty to Franco.[9] Many children viewed their return to Spain as a "disaster."[10] Those Basques who stayed in Britain were barred from active duty in the war effort, and faced restrictions on their daily movements—requiring police permission to ride a bike or stay out past midnight. Their status was downgraded from refugees to "aliens": one of the legal signs that one's identity as a refugee could expire. By 1945, only 250 of the former Basque child refugees remained in Britain.[11]

The camps for Jews (both children and adults) also shut down relatively quickly. Dovercourt closed to refugees in March 1939. It briefly returned to its function as a holiday camp after the *Kinder* departed, but was requisitioned as a prisoner-of-war camp in 1942; it reverted to a holiday camp once more in 1947.[12] Hostel life became an ongoing reality for many *Kinder* who had not yet been placed with foster parents. Some Jewish children were eventually housed in Basque colonies, and even went on to marry Basque refugees, perhaps drawn to those from a similarly disrupted background. Rosina Domingo, one of the *Kinder*, recounted how she settled in Belsize Park, not far from a hostel for Spanish Civil War refugees: "One thing led to another. A lot of us married Spaniards. There were language difficulties but we had things in common."[13] Like the Basques, the *Kinder* found that they aged out of refugee status; Annette Saville recalled that when she turned 16 in 1939, she was photographed as an "enemy alien" for the Aliens' Book, still wearing her school uniform and pigtails.[14]

In September 1939, with the outbreak of war, Kitchener Camp closed to refugees. Its inhabitants either joined the British Army or were interned. Here, too, speedy camp closures did not necessarily signal resettlement. The camp residents were swept into other institutional settings. In May 1940, when Sandwich was deemed vulnerable to invasion, camp dwellers were marched out of Kitchener under armed guard, and forced to leave their luggage behind. The Kitchener men who had joined the Pioneer Corps were taken to makeshift army camps in southwest England. Civilians were sent to the Isle of Man for internment. At the end of the war, internees would eventually make their way back to England, with boats leaving the Isle of Man once or twice a week.[15] Kitchener Camp was purchased by Petbow Engineering; its workers were housed in Kitchener's huts during the post-Blitz housing shortage. Only one small hut remains from the original site.[16]

In contrast to the Belgian, Basque, and Jewish cases, the Polish camps and hostels wound down exceedingly slowly. The number of hostels under the National Assistance Board's supervision fell from forty-three in 1948 to nine at the end of 1958, and the number of Poles in Board hostels plummeted from 16,249 in 1948 to 3,711 in 1958.[17] In 1959, the National Assistance Board finally declared itself able to discharge its responsibilities under the Polish Resettlement Act 1947.[18] Still, the problem of Poles was by no means over. Some Poles were simply shifted from "Polish" hostels to Hungarian ones. Even at hostels that had been officially closed, Polish squatters continued to occupy the space, and had to be "broken" by evictions.

The final days of Polish encampment could be eerily quiet and grim. The lively cultural activities of the earlier years came to a halt, as it was no longer profitable to perform or show films in half-empty camps. Children who grew up in Polish camps vividly remembered this moment of closure. The Rogalski brothers, who spent much of their childhood at Tweedsmuir Camp in Surrey, enjoyed the full run of the camp: "As areas of the camp became unoccupied and fell silent, they became large playgrounds for us children." Felt roof tiles became "Frisbees" and old brushes and tins of paint "gave us the chance to practise our painting skills on doors of unoccupied barracks."[19] But Piotr Pietrusiewicz took a more mournful view. His family was one of the last to leave Tweedsmuir, and he witnessed the camp falling into dereliction and becoming "soulless" as families departed for private homes. Pietrusiewicz visited the camp regularly over the next six decades. He relished his pilgrimages to the water tower, the sole surviving landmark of the years he had spent "innocently wrapped up in a magical world."[20]

Many Poles mourned the end of encampment, even as they "successfully" settled elsewhere. In 1958, just before Urszula Szulakowska's eighth birthday, her family was given a council house in Rugby, and they moved away from Melton Mowbray. Certainly, no one would miss the camp's physical discomforts, especially the endless damp. Still, she remembered her childhood in camp as "a very special time." It was "the last of pre-war Poland, the last time all the Poles would share their culture with each other in an integral manner and on a daily basis. Truly, no-one was ever quite so happy again." She recalls, "There was a special sort of atmospheric about the camp...a nostalgia and letting-go, and understanding that it was the end of a unique Polish culture...It was a quite new way of being Polish," which she viewed as appreciably different from the Polishness that was being developed in Soviet-occupied Poland. To this day, she claims, "I still dream of our last Polish home at Melton Mowbray."[21]

This deep sense of loss around the camp is striking, along with Szulakowska's notion of the camp as the last truly Polish "home." In the uncertain future, it was "not the Polish hostel but the Polish family which will be responsible for maintaining the catholic and Polish spiritual life; also to become that which the British define when they speak of their home as 'my castle'—preservation of their Polish origin."²² The private home, and not the camp, would have to become the new source of Polishness. But the era of encampment was not ending for all Poles in Britain. In fact, some camps never closed at all. One of the original camps, Ilford Park, is still open to this day. The long life of Ilford Park tells us much about the persistence of encampment, and how definitions of resettlement in Britain changed over time. Looking more closely at the history of Ilford Park illuminates how refugee camps in Britain generated affection and nostalgia, as well as resentment and shame.

During the Second World War, Stover camp at Ilford Park (about 3 miles from Newton Abbott in Devon) was used as a military hospital for Americans. In 1947, it was taken over as a camp for the relatives of Polish soldiers, and was then adapted as a hostel for Poles "pending their merging into the British community."²³ This 38-acre brick-built camp, set at the edge of Dartmoor in beautiful countryside, initially housed 600 refugees. The English called the settlement "little Poland." Although the residents ranged from age 7 to 98, there was a "substantial majority" of elderly people who were gathered at Ilford.²⁴

Ultimately, Ilford Park evolved into a residential care facility and nursing home for elderly Polish veterans.²⁵ It became the resting place for the "hard core" who would never resettle, and who required ongoing care. During the 1960s, as most other Polish hostels shut down, Ilford Park attracted much media attention. In 1966, Robert Sparke's article, "Still Happy After 20 Years in Huts," featured Ilford Park as the "last refugee camp" in Britain. The BBC Spotlight team from Plymouth studied the site for a story, "A Place Called Home." In their world of Nissen huts and wire fences, Sparke concluded, "these war victims have found an odd sort of melancholy happiness and a security that they will not give up." The producer, Terry Dobson, wanted to show "why these refugees will not leave and what their happiness is...Life in the camp is pathetic and it is moving, but the people are cheerful and they are content."²⁶

Despite these positive media reports, the National Assistance Board found Ilford Park embarrassing. As one Board member said, although the residents were "quite proud of their gardens, I certainly do not feel proud of the accommodation." The "shanty buildings" were a blot on the landscape, as the residents bolstered huts from all sorts of odd material. In the wake of slum clearance, ordinary Britons would never be housed in such subpar conditions. The residents were shabbily dressed and the toilets were "unwholesome." The Poles might be happy, but the Board member insisted, "I really cannot envisage that a Local Authority would have maintained an old people's home in this condition in 1966."²⁷ Residents in single rooms paid £40 per week, though many were probably able to pay more, and were charged 1 d for watching television at night so that the Poles would "know they cannot get something for nothing." The residents lived in single rooms with shared washing facilities. The toilets, washrooms, and corridors were unheated. The conditions were worse than those of many wartime hostels. Materially speaking, refugees looked like the failed beneficiaries of the welfare state.

But physical comforts were not the only factor to consider. As the definition of a "good" old age expanded after the Second World War to include independence, companionship, and opportunities for self-expression, old people in Britain experienced increasingly close contact with the state.[28] As Britons began to think about the needs of the elderly in new ways, the Board considered the distinctive needs of aging refugees. As one report stated in 1968, many of the Ilford Park residents "are similar to native old folk living in their own homes and like these old folk may never need much care and attention."[29] With a cinema and billiards, they should "be able to lead reasonably full and interesting lives. This, coupled with the fact that they receive three full meals daily should put them in a better position than many of the old people living alone in this country."[30] In this sense, Ilford Park highlighted the (sometimes privileged) position of refugees within the larger project of caring for the aged. As old-age homes run by local authorities were critiqued for their failure to create strong communities and social networks, Ilford Park—with its tightly knit society of Poles—could seem like a welcome realization of an ideal.[31]

By 1970, Ilford Park was—with 447 residents—the only Polish camp left, a "last relic" of the era of Polish camps in Britain. In 1971, the Ilford Park management officially converted it from a camp into a "home." Waitress service was introduced so that residents no longer had to queue for meals, and the chapel was refurbished. Laundry and cleaning services were added, and "outsiders" were invited for social events. Many residents took English conversation classes, extending the dream of integration. At this point, Ilford Park became a settled community of elderly Poles. It bore almost no resemblance to the camps originally set up by the Polish Resettlement Act.[32]

In 1979, the Supplementary Benefits Commission noted that, "having turned Ilford Park from a 'camp' into a well-run home with a close-knit community it would be very difficult simply to turn out the residents, many of whom must be expecting to end their days there."[33] But keeping the home open until the last resident died was an equally disturbing prospect. As residents passed away, their rooms were left empty.[34] Any rumor that Ilford Park might close caused panic among the residents, who immediately began packing their bags and weeping. The Board did not trust the local social services to care for elderly Poles. The local authority in Devon claimed that it intended "to preserve the identity and culture of the Poles," but this "is incompatible with their declared aim to fill vacant places with elderly British people."[35]

Ilford Park continued to attract media attention into the 1980s. These reports evoked nostalgia for the camp era, urging Britons to preserve this living memorial to wartime generosity.[36] In 1986, BBC2 ran a program about Ilford Park, *Our Little Poland*, in which one reporter declared, "I was grateful for a cool, calm look at a corner of Devon that's forever Poland." The camera toured the bleak, low army camp buildings, where Poles of all ages cared for the remaining 100 residents. Women sewed together and bartered at the weekly market, while old men drank vodka and played cards, their grandchildren skipping by in folk costumes. The residents "thought of home, of knocks on the door at night, and were content to die in Devon."[37]

The residents of Ilford Park were openly acknowledged to be unassimilable. Indeed, "failure to integrate" was a crucial criterion for admission. Tests of integration included whether the applicant could speak, read, and write in English, and whether they had ever held a job in Britain. Many Poles wrote poignant letters to prove that their elderly relatives should be admitted to Ilford Park. Mrs. M.T. Benford (formerly Mysia Rembowski) wrote that her father had had a difficult, unhappy life in Britain. He had set up a factory in Gillingham that employed Polish ex-servicemen. When this company went bankrupt, he worked in a Polish engineering firm, then a Polish printing press in Paddington, and taught physics in a Polish school. He lived alone in Henley, "making no attempt to integrate." Mrs. Benford believed that her father "desperately" needed to be with other Poles during the final chapter of his life.[38] Returning him to camp, she argued, was the only humane solution.

The case of Stanislaw Zosz-Zuchowski and Halina Zosz-Zuchowska is instructive. During the war, the couple fought for the Polish forces in Italy. When they arrived in Britain, they lived at Deverill camp in Wiltshire. They married, and moved to the hostel at Ilford Park. They lived there for seven years before settling in a nearby council house in 1955; the priest at Ilford Park told them they could always return. Their social life still revolved around Ilford Park, especially its church. Mr. Zosz-Zuchowski worked at Ilford Park as a storeman and driver until he retired in 1972. In 1985, Stanislaw and Halina applied to return to Ilford Park. According to the home's policy, the couple did not belong there; they had long since been officially "resettled." They had lived in their own home for thirty years, though their command of English was shaky. They were denied admission, and pronounced "no worse off than any other elderly couple living in a small village."[39]

For elderly Poles, insisting on admission to Ilford Park was yet another way to resist the state's vision of resettlement. Jane St. Keverne, a social worker, urged Ilford Park to admit Stanislaw and Halina and consider more lenient admissions policies for "the most culturally dependent people."[40] After this entreaty, Stanislaw and Halina were finally (re)admitted to Ilford Park, rejoining the place from which they had been "resettled" some thirty years before. The case forced the acknowledgment that "integration" was not a singular act, to be achieved in a moment, but an ongoing process that could unravel in old age. Resettlement could be undone, or reversed over the course of a lifetime.[41]

In the 1980s, relief organizations in London desperately tried to use Ilford Park to billet refugees from Poland's new political upheavals. As the ranks of wartime refugees thinned through old age, the DHSS had hoped to close the camp soon; if another generation of refugees arrived from Poland, Ilford Park could easily be open another fifty years. The DHSS claimed that they were only responsible for the welfare of Polish ex-servicemen and their dependents from the Second World War; they had no authority to take in new Polish refugees.[42] The arrival of refugees from Vietnam sparked new debates about the parameters of Polish resettlement. In 1982, twenty-three Catholic Vietnamese families (more than 100 people) applied to live at Ilford Park. The request was denied on the grounds that Ilford Park was still in use for the Poles.[43] In this sense, the immediate "emergency" in Vietnam was trumped by the long history of Polish unsettling and resettling.

Here, the state was compelled to rethink the ethics of its wartime commitments, and how these promises played out in the postwar world. How long could resettlement possibly take? At stake were the precise moral obligations of the Polish Resettlement Act, and whether these were still in force forty years after the war's end. The parameters of the act became more controversial over time, as its demographic became increasingly vulnerable. Some argued that, "if the Polish Resettlement Act 1947 had any meaning it is now [in the 1980s] when it should be most fully implemented."[44] New social-scientific studies suggested that refugees became especially vulnerable in old age. Even those who had assimilated into British life had lost spouses and jobs, and they might find themselves "flooded" with nostalgia (or dementia). The refugee who had been in Britain for thirty or forty years remained "as complex a person as ever."[45]

In 1987, the Department of Social Security undertook a review of Ilford Park. The department sold some of the land and demolished old buildings, but also built a new home for pensioners who wished to live in an exclusively Polish community.[46] Ilford Park was full of "highly individualistic people... Residents are free to plan their own lives and their privacy is respected."[47] In 1990, 128 Poles were still in residence, with an average age of 82. Several of these residents had lived at Ilford Park since 1948. Much had changed since the early days of camp life, though the residents—many of whom continued to hoard bread in their beds—were largely living in the past. Wondering how much to try to rouse the residents to engage with the outside world, the camp leader, Peter Dukes, mused, "Has it really been a success or a failure? I cannot decide."[48]

Camp closures—as lengthy as they were—cannot be taken as the final chapter to the story of Polish resettlement in Britain. The Polish Resettlement Act was never rescinded. Indeed, the act was revived in Parliament in the 1990s, after the fall of the communist regime in Poland. Barry Field, Conservative MP for the Isle of Wight, noted in 1990 that the Russians had finally admitted to the massacre of 15,000 Polish officers in Katyn Wood during the Second World War. This event galvanized a new debate about whether the act could be used to help Poles in Britain go back to the "new," post-communist Poland. Field proposed that the best tribute to those murdered officers would be aid for Poles in Britain who might wish to return—at last—to their homeland.[49]

The long life of Polish encampment was exceptional. The camps for other refugees in Britain closed far more hastily, with their residents shuttled away with alarming speed. Like the Basques and the Jews, the Hungarians in Britain were rapidly moved out of camps. In January of 1957, there were more than 10,000 Hungarians in hostels; by December, only 1,426 remained.[50] But they were not necessarily peacefully "settled." After the hostel closures, reports continued for months about "Central European teddy boys" invading nearby neighborhoods.[51] In 1958, hostels for Anglo-Egyptians were rapidly shut down. The "hard core" of uncooperative residents were handed over to local authorities, and their services were promptly withdrawn.[52]

The Ugandan Asian and Vietnamese camp closures also took place in great haste. By the end of 1973, the Ugandan Asian camps had been emptied (sometimes forcibly) of most of their 21,000 residents. Rukshana Smith described refugees' relatives coming to claim their family members "like people collecting packages from a Lost Property Office."⁵³ One resident explained, "the camps were 'closed down over our heads...because there was a general election coming and the government wanted everything cleared away.'"⁵⁴ Cooks were withdrawn, readmission was forbidden, and the work of maintaining the camp fell entirely to the residents.⁵⁵ At one point, Ugandan Asians were leaving the camps at a rate of 1,000 people per week.⁵⁶

From the URB's perspective, this phase of rapid camp closures was wholly positive. The URB's bulletins printed letters from happily resettled Ugandan Asians to inspire other residents to decamp. Zulfikar Somani wrote from his new home in Slade Green, Kent, to thank the West Malling staff:

> We are leaving the camp with heavy hearts but still we are pleased, we have got a house and a job by your kind help. When we left Uganda we were on the verge of a nervous breakdown, on our arrival here we were received by kindhearted people who were doing all they could to make us happy and forget our bad yesterdays...our bad dreams were forgotten wherever we used to see your smiling faces.⁵⁷

The final days of encampment saw a flurry of gifts exchanged between refugees and camp workers. Ugandan Asians at Greenham Common offered framed pictures of Ugandan wildlife to the station commander and the county council.⁵⁸ As the Ugandan Asian residents of Tonfanau left for Gaydon, they were presented with pieces of locally made pottery and Welsh slate.⁵⁹ Some staff were wistful as their camp days came to an end. Praising the "polite manners and gentleness" of the Ugandan Asians, Nurse Amos added, "I think they are charming. I love them."⁶⁰

But these cheerful exchanges masked an uglier reality. Any person who ever registered in camp and then left it, even if they had only stayed in camp for one day, was considered to be "resettled." What looked like success—that is, the speedy closure of camps—actually led to renewed (and often compulsory) mobility for refugees who were left behind. Some Ugandan Asians at Kensington Barracks had already moved camps four times in two months by the time they arrived in London. Faced with further moves, some simply left—and the URB counted them as resettled. But, according to Mamdani, the board had not "resettled" them as much as just "got rid of them."⁶¹

The rules about who could enter camps also became more haphazard in the final months. New arrivals were only allowed into camps if they were dependents of camp residents. If they were not related by blood to a camp resident, then they were not allowed to enter at all. Instead, they might be given housing by local authorities ahead of Ugandan Asians who had arrived in Britain much earlier.⁶² Furthermore, the URB's haste to close the camps led to people being "pushed out" into half-finished houses. After being discharged from one camp, the Trivedi family immediately sent a desperate telegram to the URB: "House not completed. No Carpets No bath no heaters we have no money arrange immediately or send van to collect us."⁶³ Having just been officially "resettled," the Trivedis immediately sought to return to camp. Stories of these unfinished homes circulated in the camps, making residents reluctant to leave. One confidential memo described Ugandan Asians being "conned" by resettlement officers into inferior housing, and moving multiple times after leaving camp.[64] If this was "resettlement," many thought little of it.[65]

Some "resettled" individuals expressed their longing to return to camp life. Champak Ganatra, for example, wrote plaintively from her new home in Leicester to a refugee worker, Molly, to thank her for a birthday gift and to ask, "How is it all at the camp? I hope it is all right. I remember there very much and I want to come there for a visit but I can't because of transport. I am looking forward to meet you again." Champak lamented that it would take another six months at least to get a place at school: "if I had stayed there [in camp] I could go to school but here I cry because I don't go to school. I sit home all day and I am lonely. I remember very much the school that I used to go to when I was in the camp." Champak implored Molly to put a notice in the camp newspaper that she thought about the camp fondly.[66]

The disruption of social networks after rehousing (perhaps a more accurate term than "resettlement") could be profoundly dislocating. One pensioner recalled that "the days passed very joyfully" when he was in a camp of 1,000 people. When he moved to a private house, the isolation of being in England suddenly became much more painful. It had been good living in the camp, he remembered. Since it was "a big open airfield we stayed in people would roam about in groups and enjoy the sunshine…we never realized the difference whether it was India, East Africa, or England."[67] For him, the move out of camp involved its own traumas and a new recognition of loss.

The last of the Ugandan Asian camps in Britain, West Malling, closed in 1974. The residents were sent to stress boroughs in London: a clear sign that dispersal had been abandoned. In London, the LCSS hired one welfare worker, Jan Romijn, to offer support to Ugandan Asians who were "experiencing particular difficulty."[68] The Greater London Council and London Boroughs Association set up a Uganda Asian Unit, which stayed active until 1977. At this point, the myth of Ugandan Asians as the model minority ran up against new socioeconomic realities. There were high rates of poverty among Ugandan Asians who had left the camps. After twelve to sixteen months in Britain, 22 percent of Ugandan Asians had tried to find work and failed.[69] One study of Ugandan Asians in Wandsworth estimated that 75 percent were living in substandard housing.[70] Another survey showed that of the last 300 families to be resettled, 45 percent of their heads of family were unemployed, 69 percent did not speak English, and 80 percent felt "completely at a loss." Many were elderly, widowed, or disabled, and all were "terrified" to face their new life in Britain outside the camp. From military insecurity in Uganda, one social worker noted, these individuals had fallen into financial, social, and moral insecurity in Britain.[71]

So, had the Ugandan Asians been "resettled"? Even the URB's final report acknowledged that the answer was no. The camps had provided for the basic material needs of thousands of people who had suddenly been rendered homeless. But true resettlement involved more than simply being rehoused outside a camp. According to the aid organizations that worked with Ugandan Asians, resettlement required "the creation of conditions in which human beings can live in dignity in a new country—perhaps with a new job, new responsibilities, new hopes."[72] One camp resident, Manu Lakhani, recalled how family members were "settled" at different times by camp authorities, and then had to reunite (and find larger houses) elsewhere. According to the URB's own statistics, it had only a 30-percent success rate in tracing relatives and friends of those who were encamped.[73] Other reunions would have to take place at a later date, beyond the eye of officialdom. In 1973, as one Community Relations Councilor wrote, "the Ugandan Asians are no less refugees today than they were when they arrived."[74]

The closure of Vietnamese camps was equally chaotic. In 1981, one Sopley staff member wrote, "Sopley has been a unique, unpredictable but strangely invigorating experience, and I cannot really believe it will ever come to an end!"[75] But when the end came, the camp collapsed quickly. In 1982, the Home Office announced without warning that Sopley was needed as a training facility for the British Army. The furniture was hauled away even as 300 refugees stayed behind, still unhoused. The final edition of Sopley's newsletter featured a mournful quote from Kahlil Gibran's poem "This Day Has Ended": "what was given us here, we shall keep . . . our dream is over." Sopley's families were in a state of "acute depression and near panic. 'Some of them believe the Government is trying to wash its hands of them . . . They feel like refugees again.'"[76] In order to accommodate Sopley's residents, the Home Office proposed to reopen camps that had already been closed. But it refused to fund educational programs for the transfers, on the pretext that these individuals had already received their allotted three months of education. Thus, Sopley's refugees who moved to new centers were left without language instruction.[77] In this sense, "resettlement" terminated one of the most important forms of aid.

Refugee workers acknowledged that for the Vietnamese to leave the "insulating" environment of the camps was "a traumatic event."[78] Yet they had little sense of who should take responsibility for refugees after they left the camps: "any care during resettlement is likely to be arbitrary and therefore, unsystematic."[79] Many of Sopley's residents decided to try to resettle themselves. Those who had come to regard Sopley as their home felt strongly that they should stay close to the camp, but only a few were able to realize this hope. A Sopley worker reported that one family had "taken matters into their own hands and have independently settled themselves with Pakistani landlords in Birmingham!"[80] In fact, two large, extended families—the Dangs (80 people) and the Le (175 people) moved themselves into substandard housing in Birmingham. The Le family, devout Catholics and fishermen from North Vietnam, had first occupied a disused convent in Lanark, Scotland, but the renovations would have taken more than a year, and the Home Office's reversal of support left them with few options. Sopley's staff considered this move "disastrous." A major influx of refugees into an urban area without any official aid was the opposite of what camp leaders had sought to achieve.

In 1988, the British government began to treat arrivals from Vietnam in Hong Kong as illegal immigrants. In 1989, the Home Office created a voluntary repatriation scheme to try to control the ever-growing camp population in Hong Kong. Britain's Foreign Secretary, Sir Geoffrey Howe, also threatened to introduce mandatory repatriation. In December 1989, the British government forcibly returned fifty-one "illegal immigrants" from Hong Kong to Vietnam, offering to pay $620 for each returned person in order to ensure that the returnees would not be persecuted. New arrivals were reclassified as economic migrants, rather than refugees.[81] Officially, there *was* no such thing as a Vietnamese refugee in Britain after 1989.

Whether after days or years (and whether happily resettled or forcibly evicted), most refugees did eventually leave the camps behind. What happened to the sites of encampment? The movement of refugees in and out of camps was part of the larger recrafting of the British landscape that took place over the twentieth century. The sites of refugeedom were put to many uses. They were not truly "emptied," but repopulated. In some cases, spaces that were created for refugees became part of the apparatus of welfare for all Britons, revealing the complexity of who enjoyed welfare's protections and suffered its intrusions. Just as many refugee camps had grown out of militarized spaces, some of them morphed back into military usage in the aftermath of refugee crises. Many camps never "closed" at all, but were redeployed to serve new schemes in the history of welfare and warfare.

THE FATES OF THE CAMPS: WARFARE, AID, AND DETENTION

Refugee camps in Britain met uneven fates, from the menacing to the banal. Many camps simply receded into invisibility, leaving no physical or documentary trace. Some, such as Greenham Common, had famous (or infamous) afterlives in the protest politics of the late twentieth century. Northwick Park Hostel for Poles was neglected for many years, and then converted to a business park; the Nissen huts were updated as offices, and luxury flats replaced the walled garden and orchards. Raleigh Hall, which housed both Ugandan Asians and Vietnamese, became an upscale industrial estate. Other camps reverted back to the uses they had served before, though never in quite the same way.

The Polish hostel at Daglingworth was scheduled to close in 1961. Before the Poles had even vacated the premises, Prison Commissioners began planning a detention center on this site for convicted boys, aged 14 to 17, whom the courts felt "would benefit from the short, sharp shock treatment."[82] Locals objected strongly to this plan, especially the proposed 12-foot fence. One councilor remarked that he had guarded just such a fence during the war, and "I can personally affirm that its appearance is more in keeping with Nazi Germany and the Iron Curtain than with our mellow Cotswold Hills." If this social experiment failed, then they would be left with "57 square feet of useless brick buildings surrounded by eight feet of concrete slabs performing no function other than the destruction of beauty in our countryside."[83] The county planning officer rejected the plan, claiming the site was too bleak even for juvenile detention. But he agreed that modern prison buildings would be vastly superior to the huts Poles had occupied.

Another proposal was to develop Daglingworth as a housing estate. But planners agreed that if the site was unsuitable for housing Polish families permanently, then placing British families there could only lead to isolation and sprawl. The Polish hostel had been conjured up by expediency, but "it was ironic having moved out the Poles on sociological considerations to suggest housing local English people on this bleak and windswept site."[84] Why should Britons be subjected to the plight of the Poles?[85] Ultimately, the Nissen huts at Daglingworth were pulled down, and the site returned to agriculture. Today, there is no trace on the open fields of the Polish families who lived there for fifteen years.

As refugees decamped, the spaces they had inhabited were reappraised. Some sites rose in public estimation, while others fell. Many of the Polish hostels and camps were abandoned or destroyed. Some were rented to British families, who had been looking for housing for years. Local authorities publicized the barracks to Britons as "Homes to let—at 'Little Poland.'"[86] The camps for Hungarians and Anglo-Egyptians were converted to sites of rehabilitation and detention. According to the National Assistance Board, the Hungarian hostels were much better built than the military camps that had been used for Poles, and were cheaper and more desirable to maintain. Styal Hostel, the Board claimed, was as solidly built as the best private houses in England. In 1959, the Hungarian hostels (and some of the Anglo-Egyptian ones) were taken over by the Prison Commission to be used as open prisons for women.[87] The British Red Cross Society adapted the Sheepcote Hostel in Harrow to use as a home for the aged. Anglo-Egyptians continued to live at Sheepcote, "until such time as this need has been met, when the home will presumably cater for local old folk."[88]

Once the camps were "empty," British officials offered competing visions of their future. In a 1962 debate about the Commonwealth Immigrants Act, which restricted the right of entry to Britain for individuals from South Asia, Africa, and the Caribbean, the Earl of Iddesleigh hearkened back to what he saw as happier days of resettlement. In setting up Polish refugee camps, he recalled, Labour had found an ideal method of "gradually and gently" integrating Poles into British life. Perhaps, he suggested, "something of the kind could be done for the immigrant communities we have today." This scheme—to place migrants in camps—collapsed the distinction between refugees and migrants. The camp became a model for the "integration" of migrants of color. Iddesleigh proposed that camps might alleviate the ill effects of migration and racial disharmony. After all, he suggested, many Britons knew that life in a Nissen hut was not "wholly intolerable," and perhaps West Indian and Pakistani workers might find camp life even more congenial.[89]

Other proposals to repurpose the camps proliferated. In November of 1972, while thousands of Ugandan Asians were still living in British camps, the Labour politician Arthur Lewis suggested that these camps might be used for housing the aged, the sick, and the poor of Britain.[90] Other groups lobbied to use the Ugandan Asian camps to provide holidays for children from deprived homes, or to house the homeless, "whether new immigrants, or people who have been here all their lives."[91] If such plans had been executed, they would have returned the camps to the days of the Poles, when poor or homeless Britons had often shared spaces with "foreign" refugees.

The Ministry of Defence rejected all of these proposals. Nine of the Ugandan Asian camps would be disposed of; the others would revert to active military bases.[92] Gaydon was envisioned as a long-term RAF base. The Home Office would take over West Malling as a young offenders' establishment.[93] The initial plan for Piddlehinton, the first Ugandan Asian camp to close, was that it should either revert to the agricultural use it had enjoyed before the Second World War, or be used for homeless British families. Neither proposal was enacted. In 1975, another scheme was to bulldoze all of Piddlehinton's Nissen huts off their concrete bases and replace them with mobile homes for young married couples. The derelict gymnasium, mess halls, and workshops would be revived "to serve the newly built village lived in by people who had themselves done a large part of the work."[94] The refugee camp could be resuscitated as a "truly British home."[95] In 1977, as the Home Office responded to rising rates of incarceration in Britain, Stradishall was turned into a prison built by its own prisoners. One official proposed that the Stradishall jail should house a memorial to its Ugandan Asian residents—an oak seat, surrounded by trees.[96] This memorial never took place, and Stradishall's life as a camp quickly became invisible.

The Ugandan Asian camp with the most famous afterlife was undoubtedly Greenham Common. After the departure of the Ugandan Asians, the camp reverted to the United States Air Force and became a visible marker of America's influence on British defense policy. Greenham was one of six sites in Europe to house Tomahawk ground-launched cruise missiles; it housed eighty-six missiles in 1986. Greenham became a focal point of the anti-bases movement that led to the discrediting of Cold War policies, sparking national debate about the unequal alliance between Britain and the United States in the nuclear age.[97] Women's peace camps were established at all seven of its gates. When the Americans left Greenham in 1992, the land was given not to the British military, but to the local people to again become common agricultural land; the barracks were converted to a business park.[98] Recently, the Common has reverted to an area of plateau heathland. The signs of its history as the epicenter of the Cold War in Britain are already fading away, just as its life as a refugee camp was erased earlier.[99]

Aid workers continued to urge the state to think outside the framework of emergency. In 1975, the Standing Conference of British Organizations for Aid to Refugees sought to create a permanent center for "newcomers"—both immigrants and refugees. This center would be capable of housing 200 people for stays of up to two months. It would be centrally located, within reach of Heathrow, and accessible to the main Channel ports. This center would not be a long-stay "camp," but a short-stay facility in pleasant surroundings for residents arriving from traumatic experiences.[100] The Home Office's response was strongly negative. From the Home Office's perspective, there was a real danger of this center acting as a "magnet" to attract other newcomers. Roy Jenkins, then the Home Secretary, also rejected a proposal that the Home Office should have a dispersal unit, since the government had no power to direct immigrants to different parts of the country. Aiding migrants and refugees together struck him as impossible. The constant stream of migrants would block refugees when they needed the center, and refugees were too "unpredictable and variable" to warrant anything other than an emergency response.[101]

As ever, the Home Office insisted on the specificity (and disconnectedness) of each refugee crisis—as well as a sharp distinction between migrants and refugees. The Home Office did acknowledge an ongoing need for refugee camps. In practice, the report concluded, there was "no real alternative to ex-military camps."[102] But the Home Office insisted that no money should be spent in maintaining such camps, and "a chance would have to be taken on camps falling out of use."[103] In other words, refugees did not warrant enduring structures of aid. They would continue to be treated as an emergency.

Even as the Home Office denied the scope and scale of displacement for Britons and others, displacement persisted. Some Britons were still living in Nissen huts as late as 1975.[104] But this landscape of dislocation disappeared rapidly, subject to excavation only through archives and personal memory. Betty Kellar, the young English girl who lived in a Nissen hut with her family outside of Torpoint, returned to Borough Gun site as an adult, but "could not find a single trace of the old gun site. It was as though it never existed."[105] Many people living on a new housing estate built over it did not even know of its existence. As these structures met multiple fates—from upcycling to abandonment—their lives as camps were often the least visible and most easily forgotten part of their history.

FORGETTING AND REMEMBERING ENCAMPMENT

Some refugee stories and spaces have suffered more erasures than others. The privileged place of the *Kinder* as a marker of British tolerance contrasts strikingly with the absence of memory around the rescue of the Basque children, which took place at almost precisely the same moment. The story of Hungarian refugees has been largely forgotten in the wider narrative of migrant settlement, and the Vietnamese "boat people" have never been incorporated into a wider British "island" story.[106] For Ugandan Asians, time in camps may disrupt the compelling narrative of the model minority and the Thatcherite trajectory toward wealth. All of which is to say: the state and refugees may have many different reasons for amnesia around camps, but the cumulative effect is the same. Rather than thinking in terms of total amnesia, we should think instead of a tension—and mutual dependence—between remembering and forgetting.

Not all refugee camps have been erased. Some former sites of encampment elsewhere—for example, the camp for Spanish Civil War refugees and Jewish internees at Gurs, and the refugee camp at Rivesaltes, or the camp for European refugees at Bonegilla in Victoria, Australia—are starting to be memorialized or enshrined. Why, then, has the erasure of such sites in Britain been so persistent? What is it about the project of encampment in Britain that lends itself to amnesia?

In part, this is an issue of vocabulary. Why should Britain memorialize its refugee camps when the camps are not camps, and the people in them are not refugees? Such categorizations make it possible to sustain the fiction—all the more urgent in the present-day political climate as Britain's refusal to admit refugees from Calais spurs the growth of camps elsewhere—that Britain is not a land of encampment.

The current global refugee crisis has activated interest in refugee memories (at least, of certain kinds), and brought back into view the recollections of "successful" refugees from earlier generations. The Labour peer Alf Dubs, for example, who came to Britain on a *Kindertransport* from Czechoslovakia in 1939, has campaigned to allow the entry of unaccompanied Syrian children to Britain.[107] In the context of wars in Afghanistan and Iraq, refugees of past wars have been recruited to testify to the gift of freedom.[108] Such testimonies leave little space for memories of camps in Britain.

Most memorials to refugees in Britain—the statue of the *Kinder* outside of Liverpool Street Station in London, for example—speak to the fetish of the moment of arrival, rather than the longer life of encampment.[109] The physical structures of Kitchener Camp no longer exist, but there is now a plaque to acknowledge it by the local toll bridge. Unveiled in 1971, it reads, "This plaque is to commemorate the Richborough Transit Camp 1939–1940 where 5,000 men found refuge from Nazi persecution on the Continent. During the Second World War most of them volunteered to fight for the Allied cause. Erected in gratitude to the citizens of Sandwich and East Kent who, as in the past, welcomed the refugees."[110] Others have focused on communal events of remembrance. In 2007, the Eastleigh Borough Council marked the seventieth anniversary of the Basque refugees' arrival with performances and an art installation; a park in Southampton restaged the famed bell tents of North Stoneham.[111]

Some refugees have returned to their former camps, mostly finding ruins. Zosia Hartman recorded a gathering at Northwick in 2007, as 300 former residents united to unveil a plaque commemorating the eight Polish camps in Gloucestershire, and sing the Polish and British national anthems. Many residents had not seen each other for forty years. The camp "resonated with Polish speech, laughter and joy, awakening many memories and ghosts that lingered in the barracks and nissen huts in the camp." Hartman voiced how

> children of the 50s, we still seem to have some sort of an affinity with the camp. Many of us still visit the camp when in the area although it has changed with some huts knocked down others altered to suit the small businesses. The park, lakes and fields where we once roamed freely are not accessible any more. I wonder if by going there we are chasing ghosts of our youth or searching for our roots buried somewhere in the grounds of Northwick Park.[112]

In 2011, Kaz Janowski returned to Kelvedon, where he had spent his childhood in the 1950s, revisiting the building that had been the camp church, as well as the space where his family's own "barrel" (Nissen hut) had stood.[113] Tracing where the kitchen and beds had been, Janowski recorded his brother talking about his memories, while his wife found an old medicine bottle at the ruins of the bathhouse.[114]

In the Ugandan Asian case, the major anniversaries of expulsion have been important markers for creating collective narratives of the flight to Britain.[115] In 1997, the twenty-fifth anniversary of the expulsion, commemorative events testified to the presence of Ugandan Asians in British culture; a special service was held at Westminster Abbey, where former volunteers read poems by Rabindranath

Fig. 7.1. The Kindertransport statue, Liverpool Street Station, London. Steve Vidler/ Alamy Stock Photo.

Tagore. But the camps were never mentioned. Following the fortieth anniversary in 2012, community activists have produced a slew of exhibitions and digital projects in order to preserve Ugandan Asian memories.[116]

For the Ugandan Asians, expulsion—and the subsequent experience of encampment—both broke down boundaries and created new ones.[117] In 1976, the Uganda Asian Relief Trust was created to begin the process of restitution for Ugandan Asian assets. After 1997, Ugandan Asians were invited back to Uganda, including those who had never lived there before. Uganda became subject to stipulations to return nationalized properties to their original Asian owners.[118] This effort to mobilize Ugandan Asian nostalgia and financial investment in Uganda is ongoing. In 2012, the "Let's Go Home" campaign invited expelled Asians in Europe, Canada, and the United States to reinvest in Uganda, exploiting the memory of expulsion for new generations. The aftermath of the (largely unsuccessful) campaign exposed the myth of a unified Ugandan Asian "community," even as many Ugandan Asians continued to emphasize their collective experience of expulsion.[119]

Fig. 7.2. Zosia Biegus returns to Northwick Park in 1980 to visit her Nissen hut. Photograph from http://www.polishresettlementcampsintheuk.co.uk, by kind permission of Zosia Biegus.

Refugees, then, have been celebrated and commemorated as camps have not. What is it about these sites that so fail to fit with existing narratives that they have been expurgated from collective memory? Camps were at odds with how Britons saw themselves: that is, not as people who had "camps" for their own citizens. But what was equally unsettling about this story was how it thwarted British expectations about where (and between whom) encounters across ethnicities, races, and classes took place. Camps are places where relationships were forged between groups who have been expected to stay separate, and who continue to be segregated in contemporary political discourse.

What is most easily remembered is British generosity to outsiders; what is most often obscured or forgotten is the fact that camps were not only for outsiders at all. The presence of citizens within the camps was perhaps one of the most volatile and troubling parts of the story. Their existence transforms the history of refuge from one of British aid to foreigners into a narrative of failed aid for citizens. Ironically, the refugee camp is where the unsettled nature of Britons themselves became visible.

This history—and its erasure—shows just how implicated citizens have been in the lives of refugee camps. It suggests that the refugee camp reveals a larger, ongoing segregation in Britain between the settled and the unsettled, and how their relationship is forged in a liberal democracy. The realignments of politics, feeling, and place that Britain's camps prompted are ongoing, and their histories are still unfinished.

THE FUTURE OF ENCAMPMENT

Why end this story in the 1980s? As we know all too well, refugee crises did not stop there. Many other refugee populations were still to enter Britain—Kurds, Bosnians, and Somalis, to name a few—and continue to do so today. As I write, there have been calls to establish new camps (or reopen old ones) in Britain for Syrian refugees. But the moral economy of asylum has shifted over the last thirty years.[120] Refugees did not stop trying to come to Britain in the 1980s, but the era of the refugee camp in Britain came to an end. Britain's shifting policies of refuge have had two key effects: first, they have pushed camps for those seeking refuge in Britain to other countries, and, second, they have spurred the growth of detention centers for "illegal immigrants" who would formerly have been considered refugees. Refugee camps in Britain provide a genealogy not only for the widely castigated spaces of the detention center, but for the ongoing existence of refugee camps in other parts of Europe and the world.

To return to the problem of names. Since the 1980s, which also inaugurated a harsh disavowal of multiculturalism by European leaders, "refugees" have been increasingly differentiated from (and, arguably, supplanted by) "asylum seekers."[121] Indeed, the terms "refugee" and "asylum seeker" are often confused or used interchangeably; United Nations High Commissioner for Refugees (UNHCR) defines an asylum seeker as someone who says they are a refugee, but whose claim has not yet been validated.[122] The proportion of asylum seekers to refugees is rapidly increasing.[123] Asylum claims in Western countries have risen sharply, from 13,000 in the 1970s to 690,000 in 1992. Between 1985 and 1996, more than 5 million claims for asylum were lodged in Western states.[124] Most asylum applicants are no longer considered to be political exiles, but economic migrants who are abusing protections designed for "true" asylum seekers.[125] Since the 1990s, as fears of the "fake refugee" have risen, states have required medical and psychiatric experts to verify accounts of persecution and abuse. Refugees can demand protection without prior evaluation, whereas asylum seekers are relentlessly assessed.

Paradoxically, even as Western states continue publicly to acknowledge their legal responsibilities to refugees, these same states have instituted more severe practices to deter asylum seekers: visa regimes, airport liaison officers, detention and dispersal, and restricted access to welfare and housing. The principle of asylum is still theoretically intact, but refugees are increasingly prevented from reaching the state where they could actually receive asylum.[126] In Britain, the merging of refugee policy and immigration controls has been heightened by the Immigration (Carriers' Liability) Act of 1987, which made it an offense for carriers to bring passengers without valid visas or asylum status to the UK; carriers who violate the act can be charged £1,000 per passenger.[127] This act significantly reduced asylum applications at British seaports and airports. It also prompted public criticism about the privatization of immigration control, as it placed decisions about refugee status in the hands of airline companies.[128]

For a time, the combination of this law and Britain's geography ensured that many asylum seekers were simply physically unable to reach the United Kingdom.

The opening of the Chunnel in 1994, along with increased smuggling and organized trafficking, galvanized anti-asylum policies. Britain imposed new visa requirements on countries sending asylum seekers, and strengthened its powers of executive discretion to remove unsuccessful asylum seekers. In 1999, Labour abolished welfare payments for all asylum applicants. In 2002, Tony Blair considered radical new options to reduce the number of asylum seekers, from mobilizing Royal Navy warships to intercept traffickers in the Mediterranean to pursuing aggressive deportation policies.[129] For these reasons, Britain has been called a "master" of asylum degradation.[130]

Strikingly, Britain's policies around refuge have not eradicated the refugee camp, but relocated it. For example, in the recently dismantled "jungle" of Calais, where most residents were trying to get to the UK, the camp was spurred by Britain's refusal to accept these residents. The end of the era of encampment in Britain has only accelerated the production of camps elsewhere. The refugee camp has been pushed out of Britain and across the Channel—or, in some cases, back to the global South.

Within Britain, the detention center has replaced the refugee camp.[131] Some of the very structures that were once used in Britain to house refugees have been redeployed as detention centers for "illegals" (who are often also asylum seekers). The industry that has sprung up around the detention of migrants offers important continuities and discontinuities with earlier forms of refugee aid.[132] Such projects reflect an ongoing—and rapidly increasing—intermeshing of refugee care and the security state. Detention was always an element of refugee work. But new sites for asylum seekers are more explicitly penal, shading into something that looks very much like criminal detention. The ties between aid and detention continue to shift, though the origins of their interconnection are largely forgotten. Given the increased use of forced detention in Britain, we can only expect these pathways between refuge and detention to multiply in the future.

The expanded use of forced detention has coincided with the revival of dispersal. The Immigration and Asylum Act, introduced by New Labour in 1999 and implemented in 2000, treated dispersal as a normal feature of asylum policy.[133] The National Asylum Support Service now disperses asylum seekers around the UK: typically, in deprived urban areas. In 2014, 26,350 asylum seekers were sent to dispersal housing on a no-choice basis. Anyone who refused to be dispersed forfeited their entitlement to housing altogether.[134] In 2002, the Home Office announced that fifteen new British "asylum accommodation centres" (housing up to 750 people each) would be built on former military sites in rural areas.[135] The Refugee Council urged the Home Office to focus instead on urban middle England as the ideal site for refugee housing. The Home Office's plan suggests that dispersal is still part of the shifting geography of encampment. Once again, policies of refuge are reshaping the landscape, generating new sites that recalibrate the ratio of aid and detention.

The scandalous conditions of detention elsewhere—for example, the human rights crisis that has developed at the Australian immigration detention center in Nauru—should not blind us to the crisis of detention within Britain. At the time of my writing, Britain has one of the largest networks of immigration detention facilities in Europe. When Tony Blair came to power in 1997, there were around 700 people in detention centers in Britain at any given time. By 2005, that number was up to 1,800.[136] In 2016, the total number of immigration detainees in Britain was 32,526.[137] By far the most common category of detainee—around 45 percent—are asylum seekers.[138] The future of refuge in Britain is not in a camp, but in a cell.

Michel Agier has suggested that the twentieth century was the "century of camps." What, then, is the future of the camp in the twenty-first? Despite their failures and tragedies, refugee camps have remained an intractable part of the political and physical landscape. Agier predicts the extension and multiplication of forms of encampment, all of which will continue to entrench aid as a new form of policing. He envisages that "camps will no longer be used just to keep vulnerable refugees alive, but rather to park and guard all kinds of undesirable populations."[139] As Hannah Arendt foresaw after the Second World War, policing refugees promotes the growth of the police state. The unrestricted, arbitrary domination of those seeking refuge tends to chip away at resistance to this state. The greater the ratio of stateless and potentially stateless to the population at large, the greater the danger of a transformation to a police state for everyone.[140] As Britain and Europe (and indeed, the rest of the world) are now encountering new prospects for mass detention, remembering the complexities of refugee camps, and the relationship they continue to bear to multiple forms of detention, is all the more important.

The politics of this project oppose encampment. But most of all, it is committed to seeing people who are encamped as "us" rather than "them." This was indeed the historical reality of encampment in Britain, and it is one of the most crucial lessons that British camps have to offer. In Britain, it proved impossible to segregate citizens and refugees. The categories kept falling apart—the Irish poor bunked with Belgians in flight, English women moved into camps to join their Polish husbands, while homeless Britons squatted in camps designed for foreigners. At the same time, refugees often did not represent the ethnically "pure" populations the British imagined. This was no rosy tale of multicultural harmony. But the contact between refugees and citizens within these camps—unsettling though it may have been—made it impossible for Britons to think of refugees only in terms of difference.

In Britain, the fate of refugees and citizens was always intertwined. But they were more closely allied at the beginning of the century than at the end. At specific moments, citizens were able to see refugees as being like themselves—at least, in terms of temporary and extreme conditions of need. It was, perhaps, easier for Britons to empathize with "foreign" refugees when many of them were themselves living in huts, experiencing mass feeding, and so on. We might say that the twentieth century witnessed not so much a decline in comparative thinking about citizens and refugees as a shift in the nature of the comparison. Over the course of the century, refugees went from being compared to the poor (though largely also deemed superior to them) to being grouped with "normal" migrants. The shift was largely to their detriment. Refugees were incorporated into the increasingly punitive regimes of immigration law instead of the uneven regimes of welfare.

Britain's response to the "unsettled"—whoever they were—suggests that a society's response to refugees has much to do with how it perceives categories of freedom and mobility for its own citizens. Refugee camps illuminate not only how democracies think about people in flight from persecution abroad, but also how they conceive of populations in need at home—and perhaps more strikingly, how they understand the fluidity with which people move in and out of states of aid. Camps were supposed to transform people—whether citizens or refugees—from unsettled to settled. The prospect of settling refugees was, in general, treated with more optimism, and the mobility of refugees was imagined as easier to change. The problem of unsettled citizens seemed far more intractable.

Throughout this book, we have seen how the realities of refugee aid and encampment meshed with fantasy. We might say that fantasy always played a crucial role in the process of encampment, though it was more visible in some moments than others. In particular, we have seen how the governmental fantasy of refugee aid as a series of discontinuous, unanticipated emergencies clashed with the realities of the constancy of refugee needs. This gap of perception shaped the physical structures of aid and the conditions of encampment. Here, I wish to focus on an episode of pure fantasy within the history of humanitarian intervention and encampment: the planning for aid to refugees from Rhodesia. It is a story of racialized invention, pointing to discomfiting gulfs between "real" and "ideal" refugees that continue to shape the politics of local and global aid. Above all, it is a story of the refugees who never arrived and the camps that were never inhabited.

THE REFUGEE CAMP THAT NEVER WAS: RHODESIA AND BRITISH FANTASIES OF EMERGENCY

In 1976, the British government began contingency planning for the emergency in Rhodesia. Clearly, this was a special case of refugee aid. All 6.5 million Rhodesian citizens were British subjects, but the administration there had been in rebellion against the Crown since 1965. By this point, a civil war was in progress, in which many more blacks were being killed than whites. Most of the whites were either UK citizens or had, as one document cagily put it, "other ties with the UK": that is, the intimate bonds of "kith and kin." As the civil war escalated, multiple state departments in Britain began drawing up plans for the evacuation, reception, and resettlement of those who might flee Rhodesia.[141]

Who might decide to flee? There was much uncertainty on this point. British officials estimated that anywhere from 75,000 to 100,000 whites would leave the country; some thought as many as 180,000. Many British officials were aware that this single crisis could generate diverse (and politically opposed) groups of refugees. Black Africans who feared retribution for their part in the war were another population at risk, along with leaders of the African nationalist parties.[142] C.W. Fogarty from the Ministry of Overseas Development warned the Home Office not to focus their rescue plans on white Rhodesians alone. Rather, this conflict would produce "profoundly mingled blocks of refugees of widely different national status and racial origin."[143] The British government would prompt great hostility "if we cannot at the same time show that we are assisting black Rhodesians as well as white."[144]

Were the Rhodesians refugees at all? Not everyone was convinced. The Foreign and Commonwealth Office thought that many Rhodesians would "irrationally" object to the term "refugee," and proposed "former residents in Rhodesia" instead.[145] For a person to be deemed a refugee depended on satisfying particular conditions of persecution; individual Rhodesians would have to prove that this definition pertained to them. Also, "refugees" were typically assumed to be outside the country of their nationality. But Rhodesians were British subjects under the British Nationality Act 1948, and therefore were—when in Britain—not outside the country of their nationality at all.[146] As the 1951 Convention had understood the term "refugee," Rhodesians clearly fell outside it.[147] Both black and white Rhodesians might be motivated to flee to Britain by genuine fear, but that did not make them refugees.

The question of race played a crucial role in this imagined refugee crisis. The English press typically depicted white settlers in Rhodesia as closer to conservative "middle England" than to Kenya's degenerate Happy Valley set or the unreconstructed racists of South Africa.[148] Even the *Guardian*, generally progressive, reported of Rhodesia's white suburbanites that "there are no beatniks."[149] One official argued that "anyone with a white face" (that is, not just UK passport holders and patrials) would have to receive the same humanitarian assistance as British citizens in a military rescue operation, though "we would argue that this was not just because they were white but because their race put them in special danger" in the context of an African emergency.[150] The prospect of racial mixing and hostility *within* a refugee population—as opposed to projected tensions between "ethnic" refugees and "white" Britons—was a new problem in refugee aid.

Despite the British government's efforts, it proved impossible to obtain detailed information about the origins and nationalities of white Rhodesians, let alone the black Africans who might flee with them.[151] From the social-scientific standpoint, the group—such as it was—was a blank. The Rhodesian census offered no equivalent to the UK's sophisticated grouping of social classes, and such statistics would have been skewed anyway by the significantly higher standard of living of white Europeans in Rhodesia, where taxes were lower and most families had at least one servant.[152] Ultimately, there was very little that could be known about the tens, or hundreds, of thousands of people who might arrive.

With great reluctance, British officials faced yet another situation in which they would have to deploy military camps for a civilian refugee population. They began assessing (in secret) the number of camp spaces that could be made available immediately. Camp spaces numbered only around 17,000; up to 28,000 could be ready within three weeks. If the Rhodesian crisis took on the proportions imagined by many Britons, the existing camp provisions were wholly inadequate. Airport staff would have to be very restrictive about offering places in camps, reserving them for refugees who could not make up their mind about where to go, or for areas where local authorities were becoming overburdened.[153]

One striking element of the Rhodesian crisis was the radical rebirth of dispersal. British authorities were absolutely clear: Rhodesian refugees (or whatever they were) must be "maximally dispersed." Stays in camp should be very short, even more so than for the Ugandan Asians. Interestingly, the Home Office warned that local authorities would not necessarily be more forthcoming with housing just because most of the Rhodesian refugees were likely to be white. For this reason, camps were, unfortunately, still necessary. But if maximum dispersal worked correctly, then camps could be minimized. The assumption was that white Rhodesians with the right of abode would likely have family connections in Britain. Yet the Home Office warned that many refugees' family ties in Britain might actually be quite "tenuous" and could not be depended upon as a resettlement strategy.[154]

The Rhodesian crisis offered a way to revisit the troubled past of refugee camps in Britain, and to imagine the future of the white, post-imperial refugee. The prospect of Rhodesian encampment in Britain represented the culmination of comparative thinking about refuge and refugees. West Malling, one of the key sites of Ugandan Asian encampment, was revisited for Rhodesians, and officials frequently reminded each other that they must not appear to be more generous to white refugees than they had been to Ugandan Asians.[155] One key element of the Rhodesian plan was to avoid what many now saw as a pattern of "compulsory" internment that had plagued the Ugandan Asian crisis.

In this sense, the Rhodesian situation created an opportunity to rethink past (and present) experiences of encampment.[156] Looking through the National Archives files on the Rhodesian crisis reveals official memories of *all* the refugee crises of the twentieth century, and lessons learned or ignored. The Immigrants Advisory Service sought assurance that UK passport holders of Asian origin would be included in any emergency evacuations, while others lobbied for the interests of Poles in Rhodesia. British officials hoped that the projected influx of Rhodesians would not coincide with the very real influx of refugees from Vietnam, already underway.[157] One discussion about housing refugees in New Towns revealed that whereas the Vietnamese were supposed to be relocated in groups of no fewer than five families in order to prevent their cultural and social isolation, the Rhodesians were to be dispersed as widely as possible.[158] Indeed, Thatcher's attitude toward "boat people" from Vietnam was shaped in part by her concerns about potential refugees from Rhodesia, underscoring how real and imagined refugees figured together in her calculations.

The Foreign and Commonwealth Office commissioned elaborate plans for evacuations, airlifts, parachute drops, and combat supplies. Detailed rules of engagement were forged. Contracts with the Civil Service Catering Organization for unspecified resettlement camps were drawn up as well. The idea of setting up a central authority like the Uganda Resettlement Board (itself modeled on the Anglo-Egyptian Resettlement Board) was discussed, though no one wanted to leak information to the local authorities too early. Given how contentious the provision of food had been in British camps, perhaps it is unsurprising that the caterers lobbied for more demographic information. They were told that any influx from Rhodesia would probably be mostly European, with only a small minority of

Asians and Africans (by which was meant black Africans). The caterers replied, "If all these people eat the same food, the exercise will, of course, be quite simple." But if different ethnic or religious groups required their own foods, it might be necessary to segregate them and feed them separately.[159]

Because these plans were made in great secrecy, there was little public response. But some Britons did make their views on the imagined Rhodesian refugees known to the government. Mrs. Winifred E. Curtis wrote an angry missive to the Conservative politician Michael Heseltine to denounce "special treatment" for the Rhodesians. Her pleas combined wartime memories with the new demands of Thatcherite politics.[160] She herself had spent three years as a POW in Shanghai during the Second World War and had experienced "tremendous loss," but "Never mind, we were coming home." The Rhodesians had never been in camps, and would not "come home" penniless. Yes, they would leave their lovely homes, but so had she. After detailing her brutal treatment at the hands of the Japanese, when she had lived in a converted stable with 2,000 people, Mrs. Curtis noted that she was a true Thatcherite. But, she warned, if Thatcher's government insisted on "mollycoddling" the Rhodesians, "you will be making for one heck of a row." When every budget was being cut, no one could condone housing and funding a single population on this scale.[161]

Unlike the other cases of "emergency" we have seen in this book, this was the one time where little was left to chance. Had the Rhodesians actually fled to Britain, this would have been the largest exodus in this book. And, had the Rhodesians arrived in Britain by the tens or hundreds of thousands, they would have found a resettlement plan far more assiduously crafted than any other group. No other resettlement was more lovingly detailed; no other plans were as carefully considered. But, they did not arrive. The Rhodesian refugee crisis was the crisis that never took place, outside the imagination. It was the one case in which emergency was foretold, but not staged. We might say that the best-planned refugee crisis in British history was the one that never happened.

Endnotes

NOTES TO INTRODUCTION

1. Caroline Shaw, *Britannia's Embrace: Modern Humanitarianism and the Imperial Origins of Refugee Relief* (Oxford, 2015), p. 99.
2. Shaw, *Britannia's Embrace*, p. 55.
3. Shaw, *Britannia's Embrace*, p. 99.
4. Bruno Cabanes, *The Great War and the Origins of Humanitarianism, 1918–1924* (Cambridge, 2014), p. 302.
5. Dan Stone, *Concentration Camps: A Short History* (Oxford, 2017), p. 28.
6. Although there were scattered references to "refugee studies" as early as the 1920s, the term began to appear more frequently in geography and anthropology journals in the 1970s and 1980s. Panikos Panayi and Pippa Virdee, eds., *Refugees and the End of Empire: Imperial Collapse and Forced Migration in the Twentieth Century* (Basingstoke, 2011).
7. Matthew J. Gibney, *The Ethics and Politics of Asylum: Liberal Democracy and the Response to Refugees* (Cambridge, 2004), p. 6.
8. On the inadequacy of law in describing refugee experiences, see Laura Madokoro, *Elusive Refuge: Chinese Migrants in the Cold War* (Cambridge, MA, 2016); Patricia Tuitt, *False Images: The Law's Construction of the Refugee* (London, 1996).
9. Tony Kushner notes that the Jewish Refugee Committee changed its title to the German Jewish Aid Committee in 1938 because the word "refugee" aroused so much hostility. Tony Kushner, *Remembering Refugees: Then and Now* (Manchester, 2006), p. 6.
10. "Clause I.—(Power to apply Royal Warrant as to pensions, etc. to certain Polish forces)," *Hansard's Parliamentary Debates*, HC 433, February 10, 1947.
11. Shiva Naipaul, "Passports to Dependence," in *Beyond the Dragon's Mouth: Stories and Pieces* (London, 1984), pp. 221–9.
12. Some English writers believed that different terms—such as "homeless Ugandan Asians" or "newcomers"—might evoke more public sympathy than "refugee." "260 Asians Arrive at Doniford," *West Somerset Free Press*, October 27, 1972.
13. http://webarchive.nationalarchives.gov.uk/±/http://www.movinghere.org.uk/stories/story_EMMHUganda29/story_EMMHUganda29.htm?identifier=stories/story_EMMHUganda29/story_EMMHUganda29.htm.
14. Mahmood Mamdani, *From Citizen to Refugee: Uganda Asians Come to Britain* (Cape Town, 2011), p. 9.
15. Mamdani, *From Citizen to Refugee*, p. 81.
16. Madokoro, *Elusive Refuge*, p. 6.
17. Ilana Feldman, "The Challenge of Categories: UNRWA and the Definition of a 'Palestine Refugee,'" *Journal of Refugee Studies* 25.3 (2012): 387–406.
18. Pamela Ballinger, "Entangled or 'Extruded' Histories? Displacement, National Refugees, and Repatriation after the Second World War," *Journal of Refugee Studies* 25.3 (2012): 366–86; see also Didier Fassin, "The Precarious Truth of Asylum," *Public Culture* 25.1 (2013): 39–63; Md. Mahbubar Rahman and Willem Van Schendel, "'I Am Not a Refugee': Rethinking Partition Migration," *Modern Asian Studies* 37.3 (July 2003):

551–84, and Roger Zetter, "More Labels, Fewer Refugees: Remaking the Refugee Label in an Era of Globalization," *Journal of Refugee Studies* 20.2 (2007): 172–92.

19. Robert Humphreys, *No Fixed Abode: A History of Responses to the Roofless and the Rootless in Britain* (Basingstoke, 1999).

20. Humphreys, *No Fixed Abode*; M.D.R. Melles, "Vagrancy in Hampshire and the Unsuccessful Response of the Authorities," *Southern History* 35 (2013): 77–97.

21. David Feldman, "Migrants, Immigrants and Welfare from the Old Poor Law to the Welfare State," *Transactions of the Royal Historical Society* 13 (2003): 79–104.

22. David Arnold, "European Orphans and Vagrants in India in the 19th Century," *Journal of Imperial and Commonwealth History* 7.2 (1979): 104–27; Harold Fischer-Tiné, "Britain's Other Civilizing Mission: Class Prejudice, European 'Loaferism' and the Workhouse System in Colonial India," *Indian Economic and Social History Review* 42.3 (2005): 295–338.

23. Tehila Sasson, "The Problem of Homelessness in Postwar Britain," in Beate Althammer, Lutz Raphael, and Tamara Stazic-Wendt, eds., *Rescuing the Vulnerable: Poverty, Welfare and Social Ties in Nineteenth- and Twentieth-Century Europe* (New York, 2014), pp. 212–34.

24. Slum clearance began in the 1930s, and 321,444 houses were closed or destroyed by 1945. Harold Macmillan renewed the slum clearance campaign in 1954; it peaked in the 1970s and fell dramatically thereafter. Jim Yelling, "The Incidence of Slum Clearance in England and Wales, 1955–1985," *Urban History* 27.2 (2000): 234–53.

25. Tara Zahra, *The Great Departure: Mass Migration from Eastern Europe and the Making of the Free World* (New York, 2016), p. 7.

26. Hagar Kotef, *Movement and the Ordering of Freedom: On Liberal Governances of Mobility* (Durham, NC, 2015).

27. Maja Janmyr, *Protecting Civilians in Refugee Camps: Unable and Unwilling States, UNHCR and International Responsibility* (Leiden, 2014), p. 99.

28. Aidan Forth, *Barbed-Wire Imperialism: Britain's Empire of Camps, 1876–1903* (Berkeley, 2017). For a more detailed discussion of the influence of the South African War on refugee camps, see Chapter 1.

29. Stone, *Concentration Camps*, p. 17.

30. Elizabeth van Heyningen, *The Concentration Camps of the Anglo-Boer War: A Social History* (Johannesburg, 2013); Tehila Sasson and James Vernon, "Practising the British Way of Famine: Technologies of Relief, 1770–1985," *European Review of History* 22.6 (2015): 860–72.

31. Forth, *Barbed-Wire Imperialism*.

32. Rebecca Gill, *Calculating Compassion: Humanity and Relief in War, Britain 1870–1914* (Manchester, 2013).

33. Richard Bessel and Claudia B. Haake, "Introduction: Forced Removal in the Modern World," in Richard Bessel and Claudia B. Haake, eds., *Removing Peoples: Forced Removal in the Modern World* (London, 2009), pp. 3–11; Anna C. Bramwell, ed., *Refugees in the Age of Total War* (London, 1988).

34. Michael Marrus, "Introduction," in Anna Bramwell, ed., *Refugees in the Age of Total War* (London, 1988), pp. 1–6.

35. Gerard Daniel Cohen, *In War's Wake: Europe's Displaced Persons in the Postwar Order* (Oxford, 2012).

36. Liisa Malkki, "Refugees and Exile: From 'Refugee Studies' to the National Order of Things," *Annual Review of Anthropology* 24 (1995): 495–523; Ilana Feldman, "What Is

a Camp? Legitimate Refugee Lives in Spaces of Long-Term Displacement," *Geoforum* 66 (2015): 244–52.

37. Peter Gatrell, *A Whole Empire Walking: Refugees in Russia During World War One* (Bloomington, IN, 2005); Peter Gatrell, "Refugees—What's Wrong with History?" *Journal of Refugee Studies* 30.2 (2017): 170–89.

38. Michael R. Marrus, *The Unwanted: European Refugees in the Twentieth Century* (New York, 1985), pp. 299–300.

39. Cohen, *In War's Wake*, pp. 66–7.

40. Cohen, *In War's Wake*, p. 68.

41. Arendt, who had fled Nazi Germany for Paris and then the United States, objected to the term "refugee." As she said, "We don't like to be called 'refugees' . . . We ourselves call each other 'newcomers' or 'immigrants.'" Quoted in Daniel Snowman, *The Hitler Émigrés: The Cultural Impact on Britain of Refugees from Nazism* (London, 2002), p. xviii.

42. Hannah Arendt, *The Origins of Totalitarianism* (New York, 1968), p. 445.

43. Czeslaw Maryszczak, "Foreword," in Zosia Biegus and Jurek Biegus, *Polish Resettlement Camps in England and Wales* (Essex, 2013).

44. Francesca M. Wilson, *In the Margins of Chaos: Recollections of Relief Work in and between Three Wars* (New York, 1945).

45. I am indebted to James Vernon for this insight.

46. "The Government's Camp Policy," *Hansard's Parliamentary Debates*, HL 111, February 22, 1939.

47. Emergency Accommodation Committee, "Polish Dependents' Hostels and Family Group Camps" (AST 18/74, TNA), March 15, 1948.

48. Jan Nowak, "Wheaton Aston" (AST 18/80, TNA), February 11, 1951.

49. http://www.northwickparkpolishdpcamp.co.uk/northwick06.htm.

50. "Confidential. UK Passport Holders" (BD 65/46, TNA), September 27, 1972.

51. Lewis Donnelly, "Emergency Arrangements for the British Asians from Uganda" (ACC/1888/203, LMA), August 17, 1972.

52. Quoted in Valerie Marett, *Immigrants Settling in the City* (London, 1989), p. 72.

53. Daphne M.F. Byrne, "Thorney Island," Vietnamese Centre Records (ACC 15240, WSRO, Chichester), 1995. Another refugee worker in a Vietnamese center argued, "we are trying to run a community not a camp." Georgina Ashworth, "Who Cares for the Boat People?" *Voluntary Action* (December 1979): 15–16.

54. Sir Charles Cunningham, "The Work of the Uganda Resettlement Board," *Contemporary Review* 222 (May 1973): 225–30.

55. The term "relocation center" was popular in the United States. Jana K. Lipman, "A Refugee Camp in America: Fort Chaffee and Vietnamese and Cuban Refugees, 1975–1982," *Journal of American Ethnic History* 33.2 (Winter 2014): 57–87.

56. On the proliferation of terms around refugees and asylum seekers in France, as well as the spaces they inhabit, see Didier Fassin, *Humanitarian Reason: A Moral History of the Present* (Berkeley, 2012), p. 152.

57. Jana Lipman, "'The Fish Trusts the Water and It Is In the Water That It Is Cooked': The Caribbean Origins of the Krome Detention Center," *Radical History Review* 115 (Winter 2013): 115–41; and see also Mamphela Ramphele's powerful *A Bed Called Home: Life in the Migrant Labour Hostels of Cape Town* (Cape Town, 1993).

58. Giorgio Agamben, "The Camp as the 'Nomos' of the Modern," in *Homo Sacer: Sovereign Power and Bare Life* (Stanford, 1998), pp. 166–80.

59. Lipman, "A Refugee Camp in America."

60. Robert Kee, *Refugee World* (London, 1961), p. 4.

61. Peter Gatrell, *The Making of the Modern Refugee* (Oxford, 2013), p. 296.
62. Bülent Diken and Carsten Bagge Laustsen, *The Culture of Exception: Sociology Facing the Camp* (London, 2005).
63. Diken and Laustsen, *The Culture of Exception*, p. 192.
64. Vivek Bald, *Bengali Harlem and the Lost Histories of South Asian America* (Cambridge, MA, 2013), pp. 225–6.
65. Refugees in Britain were usually not placed in purpose-built camps, but sites created for other functions. Some sites, such as Damfield Lane, Maghull, were built to house displaced Britons in anticipation of bombing during the Second World War. But the Blitz ended before the camp was completed, and it became a home for Poles in 1947. http://www.polishresettlementcampsintheuk.co.uk/maghull.htm.
66. Unlike in the United States, the British military was not typically involved in large-scale refugee operations, and participated in the project of refugee aid mostly through housing refugees on its bases. Lipman, "A Refugee Camp in America."
67. David Edgerton, *Britain's War Machine: Weapons, Resources, and Experts in the Second World War* (Oxford, 2011); Edgerton, *Warfare State: Britain, 1920–1970* (Cambridge, 2006).
68. Shaw, *Britannia's Embrace*.
69. Panayi and Virdee, eds., *Refugees and the End of Empire*.
70. Stephen Howe, "Decolonisation and Imperial Aftershocks: The Thatcher Years," in Ben Jackson and Robert Saunders, eds., *Making Thatcher's Britain* (Cambridge, 2012), pp. 234–51.
71. Larissa MacFarquhar, *Strangers Drowning: Grappling with Impossible Idealism, Drastic Choices, and the Overpowering Urge to Help* (New York, 2015).
72. For brilliant examples of scholarship that explore the history of empathy in British contexts, see Deborah Cohen, *Family Secrets: Shame and Privacy in Modern Britain* (Oxford, 2013); Seth Koven, *Slumming: Sexual and Social Politics in Victorian London* (Princeton, 2004); Koven, *The Match Girl and the Heiress* (Princeton, 2014).
73. Leslie Jamison, *The Empathy Exams* (Minneapolis, 2014), p. 5.
74. Michael Barnett, *Empire of Humanity: A History of Humanitarianism* (Ithaca and London, 2011); Julia F. Irwin, *Making the World Safe: The American Red Cross and a Nation's Humanitarian Awakening* (Oxford, 2013); Keith David Watenpaugh, "The League of Nations' Rescue of Armenian Genocide Survivors and the Making of Modern Humanitarianism, 1920–1927," *American Historical Review* 115.5 (December 2010): 1315–39; Watenpaugh, *Bread from Stones: The Middle East and the Making of Modern Humanitarianism* (Berkeley, 2015).
75. Geoff Eley, "End of the Post-War? The 1970s as a Key Watershed in European History," *Journal of Modern European History* 9.1 (2011): 12–17.
76. Cabeiri Debergh Robinson, "Too Much Nationality: Kashmiri Refugees, the South Asian Refugee Regime, and a Refugee State, 1947–74," *Journal of Refugee Studies* 25.3 (2012): 344–65.
77. Sana Aiyar, "Anticolonial Homelands Across the Indian Ocean: The Politics of the Indian Diaspora in Kenya, ca. 1930–1950," *American Historical Review* 116.4 (2011): 987–1013.
78. Gatrell, "Refugees."
79. Geoff Eley, "A Disorder of Peoples: The Uncertain Ground of Reconstruction in 1945," in Jessica Reinisch and Elizabeth White, eds., *The Disentanglement of Populations: Migration, Expulsion and Displacement in Post-War Europe, 1944–9* (Basingstoke, 2011), pp. 291–314.

80. "Evacuation of British Subjects from Overseas in Circumstances Short of Global War" (HO 297/29, TNA), n.d.
81. In the United States, this work was handled by the Office of Refugee Resettlement, which has no British counterpart.
82. Gatrell, *Making of the Modern Refugee*, p. 172.
83. Kushner, *Remembering Refugees*, p. 9. See also Maya Parmar, "Memorialising 40 Years since Idi Amin's Expulsion: Digital 'Memory Mania' to the 'Right to be Forgotten,'" *South Asian Popular Culture* 12.1 (2014): 1–14; Glenda Sluga, "Bonegilla and Migrant Dreaming," in Kate Darian-Smith and Paula Hamilton, eds., *Memory and History in Twentieth-Century Australia* (Oxford, 1994), pp. 195–209.
84. Tony Kushner, "Finding Refugee Voices," in Anthony Grenville and Andrea Reiter, eds., *Political Exile and Exile Politics in Britain after 1933* (Amsterdam, 2011), pp. 121–37.
85. I am grateful to Sarah Stein for this point.
86. Watenpaugh, *Bread from Stones*, pp. 25 and 33. Similarly, see Ballinger, "Entangled or 'Extruded' Histories?"
87. Michel Agier, *Managing the Undesirables: Refugee Camps and Humanitarian Government* (Cambridge, 2011), p. 65; Emma Haddad, *The Refugee in International Society: Between Sovereigns* (Cambridge, 2008), p. 3.
88. This is especially true for refugees from Vietnam, as many of the National Archives files on these individuals are still classified or heavily redacted.
89. Tony Kushner and Katharine Knox, *Refugees in an Age of Genocide: Global, National, and Local Perspectives during the Twentieth Century* (London, 1999), p. 5.
90. Didier Fassin, "Introduction: Governing Precarity," in Didier Fassin et al., eds., *At the Heart of the State: The Moral World of Institutions* (London, 2015), p. 5.
91. Gatrell, *Making of the Modern Refugee*, p. 219.
92. See, e.g., http://media.nationalarchives.gov.uk/index.php/karim-hussain-ugandan-asian-talk/.

NOTES TO INTERLUDE

1. G.A. Powell, *Four Years in a Refugee Camp: Being an Account of the British Government War Refugees Camp, Earl's Court, London, 1914–1919* (London, 1919).
2. Kushner and Knox, *Refugees in an Age of Genocide.*
3. Peter Cahalan, *Belgian Refugee Relief in England During the Great War* (New York, 1982), p. 1.
4. *The Times* (London), October 14, 1914.
5. Katherine Storr, *Excluded from the Record: Women, Refugees and Relief, 1914–1929* (Oxford, 2009), p. 40.
6. Lady Flora Lugard, "The Work of the War Refugees' Committee," *Journal of the Royal Society of Arts* 63 (March 26, 1915): 429–40.
7. This account draws heavily on Kushner and Knox, *Refugees in an Age of Genocide*, ch. 4.
8. Leah Manning, *A Life for Education: An Autobiography* (London, 1960), p. 131.
9. Alicia Pozo-Gutiérrez and Padmini Broomfield, *"Here, look after him": Voices of Basque Evacuee Children of the Spanish Civil War* (Southampton, 2012).
10. Manning, *A Life for Education*, p. 131.
11. Pozo-Gutiérrez and Broomfield, *"Here, look after him."*
12. Barry Turner, *. . . And the Policeman Smiled* (London, 1990).
13. Vera Gissing, *Pearls of Childhood* (New York, 1989).

14. Mark Jonathan Harris and Deborah Oppenheimer, *Into the Arms of Strangers: Stories of the Kindertransport* (London, 2005), p. 101.
15. Britain eventually gave (mostly temporary) refuge to 80,000 Jews. Kushner, *Remembering Refugees*, p. 6; Gerhard Hirschfield, "Introduction," in Gerhard Hirschfield, ed., *Exile in Great Britain: Refugees from Hitler's Germany* (Warwickshire, 1984), pp. 1–9.
16. Anita J. Prazmowska, "Polish Refugees as Military Potential: Policy Objectives of the Polish Government in Exile," in Anna Bramwell, ed., *Refugees in the Age of Total War* (London, 1988), pp. 219–32.
17. Halik Kochanski, *The Eagle Unbowed: Poland and the Poles in the Second World War* (London, 2012), p. 531.
18. Kochanski, *The Eagle Unbowed*, pp. 553 and 557–8.
19. Sheila Patterson, "The Polish Exile Community in Britain," *Polish Review* 6.3 (Summer 1961): 69–97.
20. Quoted in Wendy Webster, "Transnational Communities of Allies," in Wendy Ugolini and Juliette Pattinson, eds., *Fighting for Britain: Negotiating Identities in Britain During the Second World War* (Oxford, 2015), pp. 209–33.
21. "Assistance for Former Members of the Polish Regular Armed Forces" (LAB 8/2633, TNA), n.d.
22. The Act came into force on April 1, 1947.
23. Marrus, *The Unwanted*.
24. Many of these Hungarians (5,822 of them) re-emigrated, leaving 14,312 in Britain. Kushner and Knox, *Refugees in an Age of Genocide*, p. 248.
25. David Sanders, *Losing an Empire, Finding a Role: An Introduction to British Foreign Policy since 1945* (New York, 1989), pp. 102–3.
26. Camilla Schofield, *Enoch Powell and the Making of Postcolonial Britain* (Cambridge, 2013), p. 114.
27. Siberry to Dibney (WORK 22/376, TNA), November 27, 1956.
28. On the vexed history of the Maltese in British and French territory, see Julia A. Clancy-Smith, *Mediterraneans: North Africa and Europe in an Age of Migration, c. 1800–1900* (Berkeley, 2011); Clancy-Smith, "Mediterranean Historical Migrations," in Immanuel Ness, ed., *The Encyclopedia of Global Human Migration* (Hoboken, NJ, 2013), pp. 1–19; and Mary Dewhurst Lewis, *Divided Rule: Sovereignty and Empire in French Tunisia, 1881–1938* (Berkeley, 2014).
29. *Manchester Guardian*, August 2, 1957.
30. *The Times* (London), February 6, 1957.
31. "Hungarian Refugees" (T 220/553, TNA), November 7, 1956; J.W.M. Siberry to K. Whalley (WORK 22/376, TNA), November 26, 1956.
32. "Hungarian Refugees. Conference of Local Authorities, Leeds Civic Hall" (HLG 107/5, TNA), December 10, 1956.
33. "UK Citizens. Position at Independence of Persons Registered or Nationalised as Citizens of the UK and Colonies in Territories Concerned. Why They Have Remained Citizens of the UK and Colonies" (HO 213/1709, TNA), 1964.
34. "Problems Which Will Arise When the Gold Coast Achieves Independence" (CO 554/803, TNA), 1954–7; "Asian Immigration into Tanganyika" (CO 822/868, TNA), 1954; "Immigration of Asians from East Africa" (DO 175/92, TNA), 1963.
35. http://media.nationalarchives.gov.uk/index.php/ugandan-asians-in-britain-journeys-across-three-continents-to-find-a-home/.
36. Peter Busch, *All the Way with JFK? Britain, the United States, and the Vietnam War* (Oxford, 2003).

37. Rhiannon Vickers, "Harold Wilson, the British Labour Party, and the War in Vietnam," *Journal of Cold War Studies* 1.2 (Spring 2008): 41–70. See also Kevin Boyle, "The Price of Peace: Vietnam, the Pound, and the Crisis of the American Empire," *Diplomatic History* 27.1 (2003): 37–72; Busch, *All the Way with JFK?*; John Dumbrell and Sylvia Ellis, "British Involvement in Vietnam Peace Initiatives, 1966–67: Marigolds, Sunflowers, and 'Kosygin Week,'" *Diplomatic History* 27.1 (2003): 113–49; Geraint Hughes, "A 'Missed Opportunity' for Peace? Harold Wilson, British Diplomacy, and the *Sunflower* Initiative to End the Vietnam War, February 1967," *Diplomacy and Statecraft* 14.3 (September 2003): 106–30; John W. Young, "Britain and 'LBJ's War,' 1964–68," *Cold War History* 2.3 (April 2002): 63–92.

38. Nick Thomas, "Protests Against the Vietnam War in 1960s Britain: The Relationship Between Protestors and the Press," *Contemporary British History* 22.2 (2008): 335–54.

39. "Vietnamese Refugees," *Hansard's Parliamentary Debates*, HC 891, May 8, 1975.

40. Kushner and Knox, *Refugees in an Age of Genocide*, p. 309.

41. *The Times* (London), October 19 and 21, 1978.

42. The previous Labour government had already accepted 1,500 refugees from the Southeast Asian camps.

43. Kushner and Knox, *Refugees in an Age of Genocide*, p. 330.

44. Kushner, *Remembering Refugees*, p. 77.

45. Vijay Mishra, *The Literature of the Indian Diaspora: Theorizing the Diasporic Imaginary* (London, 2007), p. 1.

46. Craig Calhoun, "The Idea of Emergency: Humanitarian Action and Global (Dis)-Order," in Didier Fassin and Mariella Pandolfi, eds., *Contemporary States of Emergency: The Politics of Military and Humanitarian Interventions* (New York, 2010), pp. 29–58. See also Peter Nyers, *Rethinking Refugees: Beyond States of Emergency* (London, 2006); Watenpaugh, *Bread from Stones*.

47. Matthew Frank and Jessica Reinisch, "Refugees and the Nation-State in Europe, 1919–59," *Journal of Contemporary History* 49.3 (July 2014): 477–90.

48. Michal Levin, *What Welcome? Reception and Resettlement of Refugees in Britain* (London, 1982), p. 103.

49. Quoted in Vaughan Robinson, "The Vietnamese Reception and Resettlement Programme in the UK: Rhetoric and Reality," *Ethnic Groups* 6 (1985): 305–30.

50. Aid workers and refugees have typically been more critical of the emergency paradigm, forging alliances between refugee experiences instead of insisting on disconnection. Gatrell, "Refugees."

NOTES TO CHAPTER 1

1. On the politics of space in twentieth-century Britain, see Stephen Brooke, "Space, Emotions, and the Everyday: Affective Ecologies in 1980s London," *Twentieth-Century British History* 28.1 (2017): 110–42; Paul Farley and Michael Symmons Roberts, *Edgelands: Journeys into England's True Wilderness* (London, 2012); David Gilbert, David Matless, and Brian Short, eds., *Geographies of British Modernity* (Malden, MA, 2003); Kitty Hauser, *Shadow Sites: Photography, Archaeology, and the British Landscape, 1927–1955* (Oxford, 2007); David Matless, *Landscape and Englishness* (London, 1998); Laura McAtackney, *An Archaeology of the Troubles: The Dark Heritage of Long Kesh/Maze Prison* (Oxford, 2014).

2. Aidan Forth, "Britain's Archipelago of Camps: Labor and Detention in a Liberal Empire, 1871–1903," *Kritika* 16.3 (2015): 651–80.

3. John Schofield, *Aftermath: Readings in the Archaeology of Recent Conflict* (Swindon, 2008).
4. Romola Sanyal, "Squatting in Camps: Building and Insurgency in Places of Refuge," *Urban Studies* 48 (2011): 877–90.
5. Clancy-Smith, *Mediterraneans*, pp. 9–10.
6. *Daily Mail*, February 6, 1917.
7. Adam Momement, "Gimme Shelter," *RIBA Journal* 114.8 (2007): 48–52.
8. *Daily Mail*, February 6, 1917.
9. Fred McCosh, *Nissen of the Huts: A Biography of Lt. Col. Peter Nissen* (Bourne End, 1997). See also Stephen Van Dulken, *Inventing the Twentieth Century: 100 Inventions that Shaped the World* (New York, 2000), p. 44.
10. Quoted in McCosh, *Nissen of the Huts*, pp. 112–14.
11. "Building Costs," *Hansard's Parliamentary Debates*, HC 391, July 23, 1943.
12. John A. Richards to Aneurin Bevan (HLG 101/488, TNA), August 18, 1945.
13. *Observer*, November 12, 1944.
14. S.W. Sherry to Housing and Local Government (HLG 101/488, TNA), August 13, 1945.
15. Greta Clench to Aneurin Bevan (HLG 101/488, TNA), March 22, 1946.
16. G.J.M. Gray to G. Clench (HLG 101/488, TNA), April 4, 1946.
17. L. Wright to Ministry of Health (HLG 101/488, TNA), n.d.; see also "Petition from Hereford Branch of Standing Conference of Women's Organizations" (HLG 101/488, TNA), n.d. 1945?
18. A.K. Green to Aneurin Bevan (HLG 101/488, TNA), October 22, 1945.
19. "Housing (Service Huts)," *Hansard's Parliamentary Debates*, HC 445, December 9, 1947.
20. Personal correspondence with Betty Kellar, January 2014.
21. "Building Materials," *Hansard's Parliamentary Debates*, HC 421, March 25, 1946.
22. "Housing (Temporary Accommodation) Bill," *Hansard's Parliamentary Debates*, HC 411, June 5, 1945.
23. E.J.R. Edwards to I.F. Armer (HLG 101/488, TNA), July 17, 1945.
24. I.F. Armer to E.J.R. Edwards (HLG 101/488, TNA), August 11, 1945.
25. "Huts (Heating)," *Hansard's Parliamentary Debates*, HC 445, December 9, 1947.
26. "Housing (Service Huts)," *Hansard's Parliamentary Debates*, HC 445, December 9, 1947.
27. "Housing, Ashford (Army Hutments)," *Hansard's Parliamentary Debates*, HC 511, February 16, 1953.
28. "Nissen Huts," *Hansard's Parliamentary Debates*, HC 485, March 20, 1951.
29. Sherman Stonor to Duncan Sandys (HLG 101/867, TNA), November 16, 1954; Sandys to Stonor (HLG 101/867, TNA), November 27, 1954.
30. "Nissen Hut," *Hansard's Parliamentary Debates*, HC 485, March 20, 1951.
31. "Housing (Service Huts)," *Hansard's Parliamentary Debates*, HC 445, December 9, 1947.
32. W.G. Hoskins, *The Making of the English Landscape* (London, 1955).
33. Richard Vinen, *National Service: Conscription in Britain, 1945–1963* (London, 2014).
34. http://www.dailymail.co.uk/news/article-2257101/Three-bedroom-WWII-Nissen-hut-home-wartime-land-girls-56-years-emerges-sale.html; http://www.keele.ac.uk/alumni/thekeeleoralhistoryproject/hutlife/.
35. https://www.keele.ac.uk/thekeeleoralhistoryproject/hutlife/.
36. "Vandalism," *Hansard's Parliamentary Debates*, HC 902, December 19, 1975.
37. *Guardian*, December 2, 1993, p. 26.
38. David Kynaston, *Modernity Britain: Opening the Box, 1957–59* (London, 2013), p. 128.

39. Forth, *Barbed-Wire Imperialism*.
40. Forth, "Britain's Archipelago of Camps."
41. Forth, "Britain's Archipelago of Camps."
42. John Field, *Working Men's Bodies: Work Camps in Britain, 1880–1940* (Manchester, 2013).
43. Forth, "Britain's Archipelago of Camps."
44. Marouf Hasian, Jr., *Restorative Justice, Humanitarian Rhetorics, and Public Memories of Colonial Camp Cultures* (Basingstoke, 2014), p. 70; Jonathan Hyslop, "The Invention of the Concentration Camp: Cuba, Southern Africa, and the Philippines, 1896–1907," *South African Historical Journal* 63.2 (2011): 251–76.
45. Forth, "Britain's Archipelago of Camps," p. 663.
46. Forth, "Britain's Archipelago of Camps," p. 662.
47. Aidan Forth, "The Birth of the Concentration Camp? British Imperialists and the Origins of Modern Detention," *Perspectives on Europe* 43.2 (2013): 54–8.
48. Forth, "Britain's Archipelago of Camps."
49. Weyler did not actually encamp these civilians. Forth, *Barbed-Wire Imperialism*.
50. Stone, *Concentration Camps*, p. 17.
51. Forth, *Barbed-Wire Imperialism*.
52. Gill, *Calculating Compassion*.
53. Hasian, *Restorative Justice*, p. 70.
54. Forth, "Britain's Archipelago of Camps," pp. 670 and 675.
55. Hasian, *Restorative Justice*, p. 70; see also Forth, "Birth of the Concentration Camp?"
56. Van Heyningen, *The Concentration Camps of the Anglo-Boer War*; Sasson and Vernon, "Practising the British Way of Famine."
57. Bronwen Everill, "Freetown, Frere Town, and the Kat River Settlement: Nineteenth-Century Humanitarian Intervention and Precursors to Modern Refugee Camps," in Bronwen Everill and Josiah Kaplan, eds., *The History and Practice of Humanitarian Intervention and Aid in Africa* (Basingstoke, 2013), pp. 23–42; Eyal Weizman, *The Least of All Possible Evils: Humanitarian Violence from Arendt to Gaza* (London, 2011).
58. Olivier Razac, *Barbed Wire: A Political History* (New York, 2002).
59. Adrian Myers and Gabriel Moshenska, eds., *Archaeologies of Internment* (New York, 2011), p. 4.
60. "Ula Szwabiak's Recollections of Life in the Camp," http://www.northwickparkpolish-dpcamp.co.uk/springhill04.htm.
61. One interned woman illustrated this confusion when she wrote to the *News Chronicle* in 1940 from the Isle of Man to express her gratitude that, "We have been sent to the safest, most beautiful part of Britain. We will never forget what Britain has done for us refugees." Quoted in Ronald Stent, *A Bespattered Page? The Internment of His Majesty's "most loyal enemy aliens"* (London, 1980), p. 198.
62. Alon Rachamimov, *POWs and the Great War: Captivity on the Eastern Front* (Oxford, 2002), p. 123.
63. Tammy Proctor, *Civilians in a World at War, 1914–1918* (New York, 2010); Proctor, "Feeding Internees: Food Politics in the Isle of Man," Paper delivered at the Pacific Coast Conference on British Studies (2015).
64. Proctor, *Civilians*, p. 205.
65. Around 10,000 more were deported. Richard Dove, ed., *"Totally Un-English"? Britain's Internment of "Enemy Aliens" in Two World Wars* (New York, 2005).
66. Reviel Netz, *Barbed Wire: An Ecology of Modernity* (Middletown, CT, 2004).
67. Interview with Rudolph Munster (IWM 3899), September 27, 1979.

68. Zoe Denness, "A Question Which Affects Our Prestige as a Nation: The History of British Civilian Internment, 1899–1945," Ph.D. Thesis, University of Birmingham, 2012.

69. Jennifer Kewley Draskau, "*Kulturkrieg* and *Frontgeist* from Behind the Wire: World War I Newspapers from Douglas Internment Camp," in Gilly Carr and Harold Mytum, eds., *Cultural Heritage and Prisoners of War: Creativity Behind Barbed Wire* (New York, 2012), pp. 208–26.

70. Panikos Panayi, *The Enemy in Our Midst: Germans in Britain during the First World War* (New York, 1991).

71. Panikos Panayi, "An Intolerant Act by an Intolerant Society: The Internment of Germans in Britain During the First World War," in David Cesarani and Tony Kushner, eds., *The Internment of Aliens in Twentieth-Century Britain* (London, 1993), pp. 53–78.

72. Dove, ed., *"Totally Un-English?"*

73. Suzanne Snizek, "'Spiritual Vitamins': Music in Huyton and Central Internment Camps May 1940 to January 1941," in Gilly Carr and Harold Mytum, eds., *Cultural Heritage and Prisoners of War: Creativity Behind Barbed Wire* (New York, 2012), pp. 34–50.

74. Connery Chappell, *Island of Barbed Wire: Internment on the Isle of Man in World War Two* (London, 1984), p. 110.

75. Snizek, "Spiritual Vitamins."

76. Rachel Dickson, Sarah MacDougall, and Ulrike Smalley, "'Astounding and Encouraging': High and Low Art Produced in Internment on the Isle of Man during the Second World War," in Carr and Mytum, eds., *Cultural Heritage and Prisoners of War*, pp. 186–204.

77. Interview with Hellmuth Weissenborn (IWM 3771), June 16 1978.

78. Interview with Klaus Ernst Hinrichsen (IWM 3789), June 1978.

79. Interview with Rudolph Munster (IWM 3899), September 27, 1979.

80. Interview with Peter Midgley (IWM 3941), October 18, 1978.

81. Wendy Ugolini and Gavin Schaffer, "Victims or Enemies? Italians, Refugee Jews and the Reworking of Internment Narratives in Post-War Britain," in Monica Riera and Gavin Schaffer, eds., *The Lasting War: Society and Identity in Britain, France and Germany after 1945* (Houndmills, 2008), pp. 207–25.

82. Quoted in Miriam Kochan, *Britain's Internees in the Second World War* (London, 1983), p. 77.

83. Stent, *A Bespattered Page?*, p. 89.

84. Uhlman had escaped from Germany to Paris in 1936, and began painting professionally when he was forbidden to practice as a lawyer. He married an Englishwoman, Diana Croft, and settled in London. During Uhlman's internment, he produced 150 drawings. Fred Uhlman, *The Making of an Englishman* (London, 1960), p. 226.

85. Interview with Rudolph Munster (IWM 3899), September 27, 1979.

86. Uhlman, *Making of an Englishman*, p. 230.

87. Charmian Brinson, "Exile, Internment—and a Camp 'Full of Once and Future Very Important Persons,'" in Charmian Brinson, Anna Müller-Härlin, and Julia Winckler, *His Majesty's Loyal Internee: Fred Uhlman in Captivity* (London, 2009), pp. 13–33.

88. In Leo Kahn's novel about internment during the Second World War, *Obliging Fellow* (1946), one internee described the tin bowls in his British camp as "incredibly filthy. You can say what you like, but that sort of thing couldn't have happened in Germany. Not even in a concentration camp. Beat you to death, yes—but no dirty bowls." Leo Kahn, *Obliging Fellow* (London, 1946), p. 23.

89. Uhlman, *Making of an Englishman*, p. 229.

90. Steve Cohen, *From the Jews to the Tamils: Britain's Mistreatment of Refugees* (Manchester, 1988).

91. Alfred Lomnitz, *"Never Mind, Mr. Lom!" or The Uses of Adversity* (London, 1941), p. 39.

92. Walter Igersheimer, *Blatant Injustice: The Story of a Jewish Refugee from Nazi Germany Imprisoned in Britain and Canada during World War Two* (Montreal, 2005).

93. Peter Gillman and Leni Gillman, *"Collar the Lot!" How Britain Interned and Expelled its Wartime Refugees* (London, 1980), p. 33.

94. Eugen Spier, *The Protecting Power* (London, 1951), pp. 29–31.

95. This shift echoed the euphemistic vocabulary of "reception centers" for refugees; see the Introduction. Sasson, "The Problem of Homelessness in Postwar Britain."

96. Dominic Sandbook, *Never Had It So Good: A History of Britain from Suez to the Beatles* (London, 2005), pp. 98 and 102. Brian Harrison, *Finding a Role? The United Kingdom, 1970—1990* (Oxford, 2010), pp. 364–5.

97. Pat Thane, "Family Life and 'Normality' in Postwar British Culture," in Richard Bessel and Dirk Schuman, eds., *Life After Death: Approaches to a Cultural and Social History of Europe During the 1940s and 1950s* (Washington, D.C., 2003), pp. 193–210.

98. Dominic Sandbrook, *Seasons in the Sun: The Battle for Britain, 1974–1979* (London, 2012), pp. 15 and 29.

99. Don Watson, *Squatting in Britain: Housing, Politics, and Direct Action, 1945–1955* (London, 2016).

100. Stone, *Concentration Camps*, p. 26.

101. Lugard, "Work of the War Refugees' Committee."

102. *The Times* (London), September 22, 1914.

103. *The Times History of the War*, vol. 4 (London, 1915).

104. Tony Kushner, "Local Heroes: Belgian Refugees in Britain During the First World War," *Immigrants and Minorities* 18.1 (1999): 1–28.

105. Powell, *Four Years in a Refugee Camp*, p. 16.

106. *The Times* (London), August 16, 1918.

107. Jim Fyrth, *The Signal Was Spain: The Spanish Aid Movement in Britain, 1936–39* (New York, 1986), p. 223.

108. Major Neil Hunter to Wilfred Roberts (MSS 308/3/CA/1, MRC), August 10, 1937.

109. Fyrth, *The Signal Was Spain*, p. 222.

110. Sir Wilfred Roberts to Sir John Simon (MH 57/322, TNA), April 27, 1937.

111. "Care of Basque Children," *The Times* (London), October 4, 1937.

112. Hywel Davies, *Fleeing Franco: How Wales Gave Shelter to Refugee Children from the Basque Country During the Spanish Civil War* (Cardiff, 2011), p. 47.

113. Yvonne Cloud, *The Basque Children in England: An Account of their Life at North Stoneham Camp* (London, 1937), p. 26.

114. "Home from Home," Basque Refugees on ITV Meridian (AV 1150/1/V1, HALS), November 2006.

115. Davies, *Fleeing Franco*, p. 47.

116. "Basque Children's Fear of Aeroplanes," *The Times* (London), May 25, 1937.

117. "The Basque Camp, Volume I" (173A12/A4/4/1/3, HALS), May 23, 1937.

118. "The Basque Camp, Volume I" (173A12/A4/4/1/3, HALS), May 24, 1937.

119. Davies, *Fleeing Franco*, p. 50.

120. Adrian Bell, *Only for Three Months: The Basque Children in Exile* (Norwich, 1996).

121. Natalia Benjamin, *Recuerdos: Basque Children Refugees in Great Britain* (Oxford, 2007), pp. 8–9.
122. Some of the specialists in child education who worked with the Basques were themselves Jewish refugees.
123. N. de Selincourt, "Report on a Visit to Dovercourt Refugee Camp" (MH 55/689, TNA), January 12, 1939.
124. Turner, ... *And the Policeman Smiled*, p. 55.
125. Lore Segal, *Other People's Houses* (New York, 1964), p. 36.
126. Karen Gershon, *We Came as Children: A Collective Autobiography* (London, 1966), pp. 31–2.
127. C.F. Roundell, "Jewish Refugees Camp" (MH 55/689, TNA), December 21, 1938.
128. C.F. Roundell and Miss Montagnon, "Jewish Refugees Camp. Dovercourt, Essex" (MH 55/689, TNA), n.d.
129. Bill Williams, *"Jews and other foreigners": Manchester and the Rescue of the Victims of European Fascism, 1933–1940* (Manchester, 2011) p. 117.
130. Clare Ungerson, *Four Thousand Lives: The Rescue of German Jewish Men to Britain, 1939* (Stroud, 2014).
131. Transcription of Phineas May, "Kitchener Camp Diary" (644/1, Institute of Contemporary History and Wiener Library, London), January 29–August 30, 1939.
132. Memoirs of Peter Mansbacher (644/8, Institute of Contemporary History and Wiener Library, London), 1988.
133. *Kitchener Camp Review*, May 1939.
134. *Kitchener Camp Review*, July 1939.
135. Emergency Accommodation Committee. Polish Dependents Hostels and Family Group Camps. Memorandum by Parliamentary Secretary to Minister of Health (AST 18/48, TNA), March 15, 1948.
136. "The Rights of Members of the Polish Resettlement Corps Based on Government Promises" (AST 18/84, TNA), n.d.
137. In 1946, there were 160,000 men who were eligible to join the PRC; 114,000 enrolled by the end of the year.
138. Kochanski, *The Eagle Unbowed*, p. 560.
139. Poles moving from military to civilian camps often experienced a gap of several weeks, in which no one was officially in charge of their care. *Dziennik Polski*, September 15, 1948, p. 3.
140. Jerzy Zubrzycki, *Polish Immigrants in Britain: A Study of Adjustment* (The Hague, 1956), p. 95.
141. "Resettlement of British Subjects from Egypt" (T 221/651, TNA), n.d.
142. National Assistance Board, "Polish Camps and Hostels Circular" (AST 18/85, TNA), 1947.
143. *The Times* (London), January 12, 1956.
144. "The Homeless in London," *Economist*, September 22, 1956, pp. 941–3.
145. "Britain's Free Hotels," *Manchester Guardian*, December 22, 1954.
146. *Evening Standard*, February 14, 1957.
147. *Evening News*, December 13, 1956.
148. H. Fieldhouse to Sir Henry Hancock (AST 7/1031, TNA), April 6, 1951.
149. *Daily Express*, July 4, 1961.
150. *Daily Express*, July 4, 1961.
151. "Notes for Guidance of Reception Centre Staffs" (AST 7/1728, TNA), n.d.

152. "Vagrancy in the Welfare State," *County Councils Association Official Gazette* (May 1955): 109–10; Memorandum to Rt. Hon. Osbert Peake (AST 7/1295, TNA), n.d.
153. Geoffrey Hutchinson to Rev. P.B. Clatyon (AST 7/1735, TNA), February 1960.
154. *Hospital and Social Service Journal*, July 25, 1958.
155. "Suggested Sites for Polish Dependents Hostels. London and Southeastern Region" (AST 18/71, TNA), July 5, 1947.
156. National Assistance Board, "Polish Camps and Hostels Circular" (AST 18/85, TNA), 1947.
157. D.M. Rees to H.W. Hart (AST 7/1254, TNA), May 31, 1960.
158. R.K. Jago, "Hostels for Polish Dependents and Family Group Camps" (AST 18/74, TNA), n.d.
159. O.J.R. Whetmath to R. Jago (AST 18/63, TNA), April 2, 1949.
160. "Accommodation for Polish Soldiers and Dependents Sojourning in England—Standards for Domestic Sanitation" (AST 18/75, TNA), n.d. (1947?).
161. "Polish Resettlement: Accommodation and Administration of Polish Dependents' Hostels" (AST 18/48, TNA), 1948.
162. Cabinet, Home Affairs Committee "Polish Resettlement—Long Term Housing Problem" (AST 18/61, TNA), n.d.
163. J.R. Lambie, "General Inspection at Keevil Polish Hostel" (AST 18/67, TNA), December 10, 1949.
164. *Exeter Express and Echo*, February 14, 1951; Mrs. Lawinski Maddicott to Brig. Rayner (AST 18/46, TNA), n.d. (1951?).
165. "Progress Report, Fairford Hostel" (AST 18/77, TNA), December 3, 1951.
166. *Dziennik Polski*, October 15, 1946, p. 3.
167. *Dziennik Polski*, October 20, 1948, p. 3.
168. *Dziennik Polski*, December 2, 1948, p. 1.
169. "Remarks in Connection with the Schedule of Charges for Maintenance and Lodging in the Dependents' Camps" (AST 18/11, TNA), February 4, 1947; Stanislaw Sobanski to War Office (AST 18/74, TNA), July 14, 1948.
170. *Dziennik Polski*, October 23, 1948, p. 3.
171. http://www.leicestershirevillages.com/meltonmowbray/thedifferentsites.html [website discontinued].
172. *Dziennik Polski*, September 15, 1948, p. 3.
173. *Dziennik Polski*, October 3, 1950, p. 4.
174. Refugee Council, *Credit to the Nation: A Study of Refugees in the United Kingdom* (London, 1997), p. 15.
175. Urszula Szulakowska, "Life at Melton Mowbray Polish Resettlement Camp, 1957–58," https://www.academia.edu/8329878/LIFE_AT_MELTON_MOWBRAY_POLISH_RESETTLEMENT_CAMP_1957-58.
176. http://www.northwickparkpolishdpcamp.co.uk/northwick01.htm.
177. The fence and watchtowers were taken down shortly thereafter. http://www.northwickparkpolishdpcamp.co.uk/northwick02.htm.
178. "Quarterly Progress Report: Northwick" (AST 18/68, TNA), July 31, 1958.
179. Bogusia J. Wojciechowska, ed., *Waiting to Be Heard: The Polish Christian Experience under Nazi and Stalinist Oppression, 1939–1955* (Bloomington, IN, 2009), p. 310.
180. Wojciechowska, ed., *Waiting to Be Heard*, p. 312.
181. Wojciechowska, ed., *Waiting to Be Heard*, pp. 304–5.
182. "Report on Fairford Hostel" (AST 18/100, TNA), December 5, 1951.

183. Biegus and Biegus, *Polish Resettlement Camps*, p. 101.
184. Kaz Janowski, "Memories of a Happy Childhood in Kelvedon Camp," http://www.polishresettlementcampsintheuk.co.uk/kelvedon01.htm.
185. http://www.polishresettlementcampsintheuk.co.uk/burtononthewolds.htm.
186. Barbara Fisher, "Memories of My Life at Doddington Park," http://www.polishresettlementcampsintheuk.co.uk/doddingtoncamp6.htm.
187. http://www.polishresettlementcampsintheuk.co.uk/tweedsmuir.htm.
188. Henry Pavlovich, *Worlds Apart: Surviving Identity and Memory* (UK, 2006), p. 29.
189. Kushner and Knox, *Refugees in an Age of Genocide*, p. 245.
190. Political and Economic Planning, "Refugees in Britain: Hungarians and Anglo-Egyptians," February 17, 1958.
191. Men identified as miners were collected into special hostels run by the National Coal Board.
192. *Report on 25 Years Work* (London, 1963).
193. J. Shields Smith to N. Digney (HO 352/143, TNA), March 28, 1957.
194. Quoted in Tony Kushner, *The Battle of Britishness: Migrant Journeys, 1685 to the Present* (Manchester, 2012), p. 77.
195. "Report and Covering Letter pertaining to Chiseldon, Hungarian Refugees" (SCF A53, Heslop 1175, Special Collections, Cadbury Research Library, Birmingham), 1956.
196. "Hungarian Refugee Camp, Chiseldon, Wilts. Report" (SCF A53, Heslop 1175, Special Collections, Cadbury Research Library, Birmingham), December 29, 1956.
197. Vera Sheridan, "The Inadvertent Cosmopolitan: A Refugee Tale from Hungarian to English," in Patrick O'Donovan and Laura Rascaroli, eds., *The Cause of Cosmopolitanism: Dispositions, Models, Transformations* (Oxford, 2011), pp. 357–74.
198. W. Owen Cole, *Cole Sahib: The Story of a Multifaith Journey* (Eastbourne, 2009), p. 27.
199. "Notes of an Interview between Mr. Morley and Mr. Knowles, Deputy Chief Welfare Officer, Sheffield C.B. and of visit to Hungarian Refugee Hostel at Crimicar Lane Sanitorium, Sheffield" (HLG 107/5, TNA), February 8, 1957.
200. "Hungarian Refugees. Thorney Pits Hostel Corsham Wiltshire. Adaptations Required to Accommodate Refugees" (WORK 22/375, TNA), n.d.
201. "Plight of Hungarians in Britain" (FO 371/127700, TNA), n.d.
202. Magda Czigány, *"Just Like Other Students": Reception of the 1956 Hungarian Refugee Students in Britain* (Newcastle upon Tyne, 2009), p. 23.
203. "Elderly and Infirm Refugees—Statistics and General Information" (HO 240/47, TNA), 1957–9.
204. "Egyptian Evacuees. Eastwood Hostel near Nottingham" (HO 240/94, TNA), February 14, 1957.
205. For more on the British state's expectations about norms of behavior for Anglo-Egyptian men and women, see Chapter 4.
206. H. Trevelyan to Lord Colyton (HO 240/94, TNA), February 28, 1957.
207. As Chapter 3 suggests, the Eastwood residents took a different view.
208. *Daily Telegraph*, November 4, 1972.
209. Marett, *Immigrants*, pp. 76–7.
210. Sasson, "The Problem of Homelessness in Postwar Britain."
211. Richard Bourne, "The Last Asians," *New Society* (May 31, 1973): 484–5.
212. Marett, *Immigrants*, p. 76.
213. John Schofield, "Monuments and the Memories of War: Motivations for Preserving Military Sites in England," in John Schofield, William Gray Johnson, and Colleen

M. Beck, eds., *Matériel Culture: The Archaeology of Twentieth-Century Conflict* (London, 2002), pp. 143–58; Michael Anderton, "Social Space and Social Control: Analysing Movement and Management on Modern Military Sites," in Schofield et al., eds., *Matériel Culture*, pp. 189–97.

214. Jo Guldi, "World Neoliberalism as Rebellion from Below? British Squatters and the Global Interpretation of Poverty, 1946–1974," *Humanity* (forthcoming, 2018). On British squatters' occupation of military bases, see Chapter 5.

215. *The Times* (London), December 29, 1958.

216. See, e.g., *The Times* (London), April 29, 1948.

217. Whitney to Secretary of State (RG 59 741.56311/9-360, NARA), November 8, 1960.

218. "U.S. Bases and Operating Facilities (United Kingdom)" (RG 59 711.56341/3-457, NARA), March 4, 1957.

219. Loyd V. Steere, Agricultural Attaché, to Secretary of State, "Article on Evacuation of Large Agricultural Area for Use of U.S. Forces" (RG 59 811.24541, NARA), December 11, 1943.

220. Veronica Fiorato, "Greenham Common: The Conservation and Management of a Cold War Archetype," in John Schofield and Wayne Cocroft, eds., *A Fearsome Heritage: Diverse Legacies of the Cold War* (Walnut Creek, CA, 2007), pp. 129–54.

221. "Greenham Common U.S. Air Force Base, near Newbury, Berks." (RG 59 741.56311/9-360, NARA), 1960.

222. On the 1980s protests at Greenham Common, see the Epilogue.

223. "U.S. Bases and Operating Facilities (United Kingdom)" (RG 59 711.56341/3-457, NARA), March 4, 1957.

224. James F. Grady to Department of State (RG 59 741.56311/9-360, NARA), September 7, 1960.

225. John Schofield and Mike Anderton, "The Queer Archaeology of Green Gate: Interpreting Contested Space at Greenham Common Airbase," *World Archaeology* 32 (2000): 236–51.

226. "Greenham Common Resettlement Centre" (RVS), October 8, 1972.

227. "From Grief and Fear to Over Here," *Independent*, July 31, 1992.

228. http://www.piddlevalley.info/history/piddlehinton/sop/piddlehinton_chap10.php.

229. "Ugandan Immigrants," *Hansard's Parliamentary Debates*, HC 849, February 1, 1973.

230. "Report on Visit to the Centre on 23 October 1972" (RVS), 1972.

231. David Reynolds, *Rich Relations: The American Occupation of Britain, 1942–1945* (Glasgow, 1995), p. 297.

232. Elizabeth J. Hawkins to National Parks Commission (COU 6/74, TNA), March 26, 1967; Elizabeth J. Hawkins to Parliamentary Under-Secretary of State (COU 6/74, TNA), February 5, 1967.

233. Reynolds, *Rich Relations*, p. 123.

234. *The Times* (London), September 30, 1972.

235. *The Times* (London), March 22, 1973.

236. "Tea and Biscuits for Apprehensive Exiles," *Telegraph*, September 19, 1972.

237. "Big Log-Jam Builds Up in Asian Transit Camps," *The Times*, October 1, 1972.

238. *Evening Echo*, November 8, 1972.

239. *The Times* (London), September 30, 1972.

240. Brian Jackson, *Starting School* (London, 1979), p. 61.

241. According to Tailor, "nobody regrets being here [in Britain] ... there isn't anybody." Interview with Vinod Tailor, December 10, 2014.

242. "260 Asians Arrive at Doniford," *West Somerset Free Press*, October 27, 1972.

243. *Tommies Holiday Camp Bugle* 1–12 (incomplete), DD/X/NAS 1, Somerset Heritage Centre, Somerset, 1972–3.

244. Naipaul, "Passports to Dependence."

245. http://www.movinghere.org.uk/stories/story_EMMHUganda22/story_EMMHU ganda22.htm?identifier=stories/story_EMMHUganda22/story_EMMHUganda22. htm&ProjectNo=38.

246. Atul Patel, www.exilesproject.org [website discontinued; documents now housed at the London Metropolitan Archives].

247. Interview with Atul Patel, July 14, 2014.

248. James Hamilton-Paterson, "Camp on John Bull's Island," *Nova* (April 1973): 68–75.

249. *The Times* (London), November 12, 1972.

250. *The Times* (London), October 10, 1972.

251. Interview with Chandrika Joshi, July 24, 2017.

252. Personal communication with James Hamilton-Paterson, July 1, 2017.

253. Emma Robertson, " 'Green for Come': Moving to York as a Ugandan Asian Refugee," in Panayi and Virdee, eds., *Refugees and the End of Empire*, pp. 245–67.

254. *The Times* (London), November 12, 1972.

255. Hamilton-Paterson, "Camp on John Bull's Island."

256. Derek Humphrey and Michael Ward, *Passports and Politics* (London, 1974), p. 64.

257. Hamilton-Paterson, "Camp on John Bull's Island."

258. See, e.g., the study of the Tai Ah Chau center in Joe Thomas, *Ethnocide: A Cultural Narrative of Refugee Detention in Hong Kong* (Aldershot, 2000).

259. See, e.g., Adeline Hartcup, "Hong Kong's Closed and Open Centres," *Contemporary Review* 247 (1985): 298–303.

260. Kwok B. Chan and David Loveridge, "Refugees in Transit: Vietnamese in a Refugee Camp in Hong Kong," *International Migration Review* 21.3 (1987): 745–59.

261. Peter R. Jones, *Vietnamese Refugees: A Study of their Reception and Resettlement in the United Kingdom*. Research and Planning Unit Paper 13 (London, 1982).

262. Felicity Edholm et al., *Vietnamese Refugees in Britain* (London, 1983); Becky Taylor, "Refugees, Ghost Ships, and Thatcher," *History Workshop Online* 26 (January 2015); http://www.historyworkshop.org.uk/ghostships/.

263. Edholm et al., *Vietnamese Refugees in Britain*, p. 30.

264. Rachel Whitham (née Pearson), "A Health Visitor's View of Reception and Resettlement of Indo-Chinese Refugees into the United Kingdom," in Ron Baker, ed., *The Psychosocial Problems of Refugees* (London, 1983), pp. 50–6.

265. Jones, *Vietnamese Refugees*.

266. Interview with Tam Ly (C1055/82, Vietnamese Oral History Project, BLSA), 2002.

267. Interview with Cuu Luc (C1055/83, Vietnamese Oral History Project, BLSA), 2002.

268. Levin, *What Welcome?*

269. Joyce Pearce to Barrie Denton (7155/7/3/2, Ockenden Files, Surrey History Centre), October 10, 1979.

270. *Times Educational Supplement*, April 18, 1975.

271. A.M. Agathangelous, "Evaluation of Vietnamese Refugee Reception and Resettlement Programme, 1979–1989" (1989), EV/QU40.5 RCA, Box 1, Refugee Council Archives, University of East London.

272. Interview with Colin Hodgetts, June 12, 2017; interview with Julia Meiklejohn, June 12, 2017.

273. E.G. Bennett, *In Search of Freedom: The Story of Some Refugees and Exiles who Found a Haven in Bournemouth and District* (Bournemouth, 1985).

274. Ockenden Files 7155/4/6/17, Surrey History Centre, n.d.
275. Vu Khanh Thanh with Christina Puryear, *Catholic with Confucian Tendencies: The True Story of the Extreme Adventures of a Vietnamese Boat Person* (2016), p. 131.
276. Colin Hodgetts, *Action! A Cleric Off the Leash: An Autobiography* (CreateSpace, 2016).
277. *Guardian*, September 3, 1979.
278. J. Legg to Sturgess (H/ED1/4B/5, File 1, HALS), December 3, 1979; "Report on Plan for Full-Day Adult Education at Sopley Reception Centre" (H/ED1/4B/5, File 1, HALS), January 6, 1980.
279. Wendy Orr, "Adult Education Sopley Reception Centre" (H/ED1/4B/5, File 1, HALS), n.d.
280. Thanh, *Catholic with Confucian Tendencies*, p. 133.
281. Jones, *Vietnamese Refugees*.
282. "Education at Thorney Island," *New Homeland* (Par/196/7/8, WSRO), 1980.
283. Daphne M.F. Byrne, "Thorney Island," Vietnamese Centre Records (Acc 15240, WSRO), 1995.
284. Daphne Byrne and Heather Lewis, "Emsworth Memories" (AV 637/63/51, HALS), 2007.
285. Daphne Byrne, "The Fair Island," *Acorn* (Acc 15420, WSRO), n.d.
286. "Minutes of the Heads of Sections Committee Meeting (Acc 15240, WSRO), September 16, 1981.

NOTES TO CHAPTER 2

1. Proctor, "Feeding Internees."
2. "Notes for Guidance in the Preparation of Various Hungarian Dishes" (HLG 107/5, TNA), December 17, 1956.
3. James Vernon, *Hunger: A Modern History* (Cambridge, MA, 2007), p. 159; see also Tom Scott-Smith, "Control and Biopower in Contemporary Humanitarian Aid: The Case of Supplementary Feeding," *Journal of Refugee Studies* 28.1 (March 2015): 21–37.
4. Proctor, "Feeding Internees."
5. Eric Koch, *Deemed Suspect: A Wartime Blunder* (Toronto, 1980), p. 19.
6. F. Lafitte, *The Internment of Aliens* (Harmondsworth, 1940), p. 114.
7. British Patriotic Fun to Algernon Maudsley (MH 8/2, TNA), October 15, 1915.
8. Powell, *Four Years in a Refugee Camp*.
9. *Manchester Guardian*, April 28, 1915, p. 8.
10. *The Times* (London), February 8, 1915.
11. Vernon, *Hunger*, p. 125.
12. Vernon, *Hunger*, ch. 5.
13. *Guardian*, May 22, 2002.
14. Cloud, *Basque Children in England*, pp. 28–9.
15. Pozo-Gutiérrez and Broomfield, *"Here, look after him."*
16. Cloud, *Basque Children in England*, pp. 30–1.
17. Cloud, *Basque Children in England*, p. 30.
18. E.G. Colles, "Arrangements for Basque Children. Nazareth House, Southampton" (MH 57/323, TNA), June 8, 1937.
19. M.A. Quinlan, "Basque Children at Wattermillock" (MH 57/323, TNA), June 17, 1937.
20. Benjamin, *Recuerdos*.
21. Bell, *Only for Three Months*.

22. Gershon, *We Came as Children*, p. 36.
23. C.F. Roundell, "Jewish Refugees Camp" (MH 55/689, TNA), December 21, 1938.
24. *Kitchener Camp Review*, June 1939.
25. Elaine May, "Reception in the United Kingdom of Jewish Refugees with Special Emphasis on the Role of the Kitchener Camp, 1938–1939," MA in History, Polytechnic of Central London, 1989.
26. May, "Reception."
27. Szulakowska, "Life at Melton Mowbray."
28. Janowski, "Memories."
29. Pavlovich, *Worlds Apart*.
30. "Quarterly Progress Report: Northwick" (AST 18/68, TNA), July 31, 1958.
31. "Polish Resettlement Act 1947. Rules for the Separate Hostels" (AST 12/129, TNA), 1947.
32. http://www.polishresettlementcampsintheuk.co.uk/northwick07.htm.
33. J.H. Johnson, "Stover" (AST 18/22, TNA), July 1948.
34. Warden, "Progress Report" (AST 18/22, TNA), October 1952.
35. Warden, Stover Hostel to H.W. Hart (AST 18/100, TNA), May 31, 1960.
36. H.W. Hart, "Polish Hostel, Stover—Catering" to F.W. Goodchild (AST 18/86, TNA), October 23, 1961.
37. H.W. Hart to W. Gardiner (AST 18/22, TNA), February 24, 1960.
38. In contrast to the United States, where federal programs to feed the hungry ballooned during the 1960s and 1970s, the state's assumption in Britain was that income supports combined with rationing long after the war were sufficient for most Britons. The Food Welfare Scheme served around 50,000 mothers and young children, but hungry Britons did not play a major role in postwar public debates about hunger until Thatcher's cuts to the school-meal program in 1980. Personal communication with Caitlin Rathe, March 21, 2017.
39. *Evening Echo*, November 8, 1972.
40. Brigadier G.H.B. Beyts, *The Path of Duty: The Life and Times of Bill Beyts*, pp. 50–1; quoted in http://www.asiansfromuganda.org.uk/uganda_asian_interlude.php; "The Uganda Asians. West Sussex," RVS, 1972. On white youth cultures and South Asian food in Britain, see Elizabeth Buettner, "Going for an Indian: South Asian Restaurants and the Limits of Multiculturalism in Britain," *Journal of Modern History* 80.4 (2008): 865–901.
41. Interview with Shirin Abdul Hussein, Millennium Memory Bank Project (C900/00048, BLSA), 2000.
42. Humphrey and Ward, *Passports and Politics*, p. 63.
43. Quoted in Humphrey and Ward, *Passports and Politics*, p. 63.
44. "260 Asians Arrive at Doniford," *West Somerset Free Press*, October 27, 1972.
45. Humphrey and Ward, *Passports and Politics*, p. 64.
46. Marett, *Immigrants*.
47. Interview with Chandrika Joshi, July 24, 2017.
48. http://www.itv.com/news/wales/story/2012-07-27/40-years-since-ugandan-asians-made-wales-their-home/.
49. Interview with Atul Patel, July 14, 2014.
50. Sandra Penelope Hunt, "Adaptation and Nutritional Implications of Food Habits among Uganda Asians Settling in Britain," Ph.D. Thesis in Nutrition, University of London, 1977.

51. "A Traditional English Christmas for Asians in Camps," *The Times* (London), December 19, 1972.
52. http://webarchive.nationalarchives.gov.uk/20091002212758/http://test.movinghere.org.uk/stories/story_EMMHUganda08/story_EMMHUganda08.htm?identifier=stories/story_EMMHUganda08/story_EMMHUganda08.htm.
53. Bourne, "The Last Asians."
54. Jane Kramer, "The Uganda Asians," *New Yorker* 50.7 (April 8, 1974): 47–93.
55. Jackson, *Starting School.*
56. On the longer history of hunger strikes in British and imperial settings, see Kevin Grant, "The Transcolonial World of Hunger Strikes and Political Fasts, c. 1909–1935," in Durba Ghosh and Dane Kennedy, eds., *Decentering Empire: Britain, India, and the Transcolonial World* (Hyderabad, 2006), pp. 243–69; Tim Pratt and James Vernon, "Appeal from this Fiery Bed: The Colonial Politics of Gandhi's Fasts and Their Metropolitan Reception," *Journal of British Studies* 44.1 (2005): 92–114; Vernon, *Hunger.*
57. At the Warth Mills internment camp, hunger strikes prompted a visit from R.A. Haccius, the delegate to Britain of the Red Cross; Haccius condemned the entire camp shortly thereafter. Cohen, *From the Jews to the Tamils.*
58. Proctor, "Feeding Internees."
59. "Northern Command Coordinating Committee Meeting for Polish Welfare" (AST 18/99, TNA), September 4, 1947.
60. Leonard Leybourne to W. Walton (AST 18/19, TNA), July 30, 1947; "Petition to National Assistance Board" (AST 18/19, TNA), September 26, 1947.
61. Marian Czuchnowski, "Polish Camps Near Liverpool: A Report by Our Special Correspondent," *Dziennik Polski*, December 27, 1946.
62. "Remarks in Connection with the Schedule of Charges for Maintenance and Lodging in the Dependents' Camps" (AST 18/11, TNA), February 4, 1947.
63. "Petition from Petworth Camp" (AST 18/19, TNA), January 2, 1948.
64. Monica Janowski, "Food in Traumatic Times: Women, Foodways and 'Polishness' During a Wartime 'Odyssey,'" *Food and Foodways* 20.3–4 (2012): 236–349.
65. Vernon, *Hunger*, p. 167.
66. R.K. Jago, "Hostels for Polish Dependents and Family Group Camps" (AST 18/74, TNA), n.d.
67. H.W. Ward, "Catering Residents Taking Meals from Dining Room" (AST 18/22, TNA), December 16, 1958.
68. *Dziennik Polski*, July 11, 1949, p. 3; August 6, 1949, p. 3.
69. http://www.northwickparkpolishdpcamp.co.uk/northwick02.htm.
70. *Dziennik Polski*, November 3, 1949, pp. 1 and 4.
71. "Tea Bars in Housing Hostels. Daglingworth" (AST 18/82), n.d.
72. *Dziennik Polski*, August 10, 1949, p. 3.
73. *Melton Times*, December 2, 1949; http://www.leicestershirevillages.com/meltonmowbray/newspaperclippings,254415.html [website discontinued].
74. *Dziennik Polski*, November 8, 1949, p. 3.
75. Wojciechowska, ed., *Waiting to Be Heard*, p. 310.
76. *Melton Times*, December 2, 1949; http://www.leicestershirevillages.com/meltonmowbray/newspaperclippings,254415.html [website discontinued].
77. Nadja Durbach, "Nations Out of Nurseries, Empires into Bottles: The Colonial Politics of Welfare Orange Juice," Paper presented at North American Conference on British Studies (Little Rock, 2015).

78. "Report on Visit to Eastwood Hostel" (HO 240/94, TNA), n.d.
79. "Residents' Committee Meeting" (HO 240/95, TNA), April 26, 1957.
80. S.J. Dibble, "Anglo-Egyptian Resettlement Board Standing Instructions to Hostels" (WORK 22/376, TNA), September 1957.
81. "Report re Complaint of Catering at Summerfield Hostel" (HO 240/95, TNA), n.d.
82. "Summerfield Hostel. Minutes of the Working Committee" (HO 240/100, TNA), August 13, 1957.
83. Clynes to Stebbing (HO 240/95, TNA), September 12, 1957.
84. *Daily Telegraph*, February 17, 1958.
85. Mamdani, *From Citizen to Refugee*, p. 76.
86. "Statement by Representatives of the Asian Community at Stradishall following a meeting on Thursday, December 28 1972" (HO 289/93, TNA), 1972.
87. *Telegraph*, November 11, 1972.
88. "Resettlement Centres—Control of, and Accounting for Expenditure" (HO 289/64, TNA), December 1972.
89. Bourne, "The Last Asians."
90. Jones, *Vietnamese Refugees*, p. 39.
91. Eleanor Carlson, M. Kipps, and J. Thomson, "Feeding the Vietnamese in the UK and the Rationale behind their Food Habits," *Proceedings of the Nutrition Society* 41 (1982): 229–37.
92. Interview with Julia Meiklejohn, June 12, 2017.
93. Interview with Colin Hodgetts, June 12, 2017.
94. Eleanor Carlson et al., "Feeding the Vietnamese in the UK," *Nutrition and Food Science* 80.4 (1980): 2–5.
95. Interview with Cuu Luc (C1055/83, Vietnamese Oral History Project, BLSA), 2002.
96. Interview with Tam Ly (C1055/82, Vietnamese Oral History Project, BLSA), 2002.
97. Levin, *What Welcome?*
98. Daphne M.F. Byrne, Vietnamese Centre Records, Thorney Island (Acc 15240, WSRO), 1995.
99. Vietnamese Centre Records, Thorney Island (Acc 15240, WSRO), May 28, 1980.
100. "Minutes of the Vietnamese Committee" (Acc 15240, WSRO), December 31, 1979.
101. "Minutes of the Vietnamese Committee" (Acc 15240, WSRO), December 3, 1980.
102. Thanh, *Catholic with Confucian Tendencies*, p. 135.
103. "Minutes of a Special Meeting of the Vietnamese Sub-Committee" (Acc 15420, WSRO), February 12, 1981.

NOTES TO CHAPTER 3

1. Julie Peteet, "Cartographic Violence, Displacement and Refugee Camps: Palestine and Iraq," in Are Knudsen and Sari Hanafi, eds., *Palestinian Refugees: Identity, Space and Place in the Levant* (London, 2011), pp. 13–28. See also Bassem Sirhan, "Palestinian Camp Life in Lebanon," *Journal of Palestine Studies* 4.2 (Winter 1975): 91–107; Julie Peteet, *Landscape of Hope and Despair: Palestinian Refugee Camps* (Philadelphia, 2005); and Margaret Myers Feinstein, *Holocaust Survivors in Postwar Germany, 1945–1957* (Cambridge, 2010).
2. Michel Agier, Richard Nice, and Loïc Wacquant, "Between War and City: Towards an Urban Anthropology of Refugee Camps," *Ethnography* 3.3 (2002): 317–41.
3. Liisa Malkki, *Purity and Exile: Violence, Memory and National Cosmology Among Hutu Refugees in Tanzania* (Chicago, 1995), p. 237.

4. Liisa Malkki, "Speechless Emissaries: Refugees, Humanitarianism, and Dehistoricization," *Cultural Anthropology* 11.3 (August 1996): 377–404.

5. Gatrell, *Making of the Modern Refugee*, pp. 220–1; similarly, see Meryn McLaren, "'Out of the Huts Emerged a Settled People': Community-Building in West German Refugee Camps," *German History* 28.1 (2010): 21–43.

6. Monique Scheer, "Captive Voices: Phonographic Records in the German and Austrian Prisoner-of-War Camps of World War One," in Reinhard Johler et al., eds., *Doing Anthropology in Wartime and War Zones: World War One and the Cultural Sciences in Europe* (New Brunswick, 2010), pp. 279–309. See also Alon Rachamimov, "The Disruptive Comforts of Drag: (Trans)Gender Performances among Prisoners of War in Russia, 1914–1920," *American Historical Review* 111.2 (April 2006): 362–82.

7. Powell, *Four Years in a Refugee Camp*, p. 54.

8. *The Times* (London), August 16, 1918.

9. Powell, *Four Years in a Refugee Camp*, p. 12.

10. *Kitchener Camp Review*, April 1939.

11. Lafitte, *The Internment of Aliens*, p. 36.

12. Ungerson, *Four Thousand Lives*.

13. Marion Berghahn, "German Jews in England: Aspects of the Assimilation and Integration Process," in Gerhard Hirschfield, ed., *Exile in Great Britain: Refugees from Hitler's Germany* (Warwickshire, 1984), pp. 285–306.

14. "Director's Message," *Kitchener Camp Review*, August 1939.

15. A.W.W., "Song for the Campmen," *Kitchener Camp Review*, July 1939.

16. *Kitchener Camp Review*, June 1939.

17. *Kitchener Camp Review*, May 1939.

18. May, "Kitchener Camp Diary," February 25, 1939.

19. *Kitchener Camp Review*, June 1939.

20. *Kitchener Camp Review*, June 1939.

21. *Kitchener Camp Review*, September 1939.

22. May, "Kitchener Camp Diary," February 25, 1939.

23. May, "Kitchener Camp Diary," March 16, 1939.

24. Judith Tydor Baumel, "The Kitchener Transmigration Camp at Richborough," *Yad Vashem Studies* 14 (1981): 233–46.

25. Margaret Goldsmith, "The Refugee Transit Camp at Richborough," *Nineteenth Century and After* 126 (September 1939): 315–21.

26. Alfred Perles, *Alien Corn* (London, 1944), pp. 21–2.

27. For a woman's perspective on the Isle of Man camps, see Livia Laurent, *A Tale of Internment* (London, 1942).

28. Koch, *Deemed Suspect*.

29. Quoted in Cohen, *From the Jews to the Tamils*, p. 29.

30. Spier, *The Protecting Power*, p. 105.

31. George W. Brandt, "Thespis Behind the Wire, Or Entertainment in Internment—A Personal Recollection," in Michael Balfour, ed., *Theatre and War 1933–1945: Performance in Extremis* (New York, 2001), pp. 117–23.

32. Stent, *A Bespattered Page?*, p. 193.

33. "Detentions," *Hansard's Parliamentary Debates*, HC 368, January 30, 1941; "Refugees," *Hansard's Parliamentary Debates*, HC 362, July 10, 1940.

34. "Internment Camps," *Hansard's Parliamentary Debates*, HL 123, July 2, 1942.

35. Stent, *A Bespattered Page?*, p. 34.

36. Igersheimer, *Blatant Injustice*, p. 23.

37. Quoted in Kochan, *Britain's Internees*, p. 76.
38. Uhlman, *Making of an Englishman*, p. 226.
39. Interview with Rudolph Munster (IWM 3899), September 27, 1979.
40. Interview with Klaus Ernst Hinrichsen (IWM 3789), June 1978.
41. Interview with Hellmuth Weissenborn (IWM 3771), June 16, 1978.
42. Interview with Klaus Ernst Hinrichsen (IWM 3789), June 1978.
43. Judith Tydor Baumel-Schwartz, *Never Look Back: The Jewish Refugee Children in Great Britain* (West Lafayette, IN, 2012), p. 113.
44. Quoted in Gershon, *We Came as Children*, pp. 171–3.
45. C.F. Roundell, "Jewish Refugees Camp" (MH 55/689, TNA), December 21, 1938.
46. *Manchester Guardian*, December 25, 1938, p. 11.
47. Segal, *Other People's Houses*.
48. Cloud, *Basque Children in England*, p. 38.
49. Pozo-Gutiérrez and Broomfield, "*Here, look after him,*" p. 180.
50. "Refugees Other than German—Spanish" (HO 213/287, TNA), 1937.
51. Sir Wilfred Roberts to Sir Samuel Hoare (HO 213/288, TNA), June 8, 1937.
52. G.T. Garratt to E.N. Cooper (HO 213/289, TNA), March 18, 1938.
53. "Notes of a Conference held in the Home Secretary's Room" (HO 213/288, TNA), May 13, 1937.
54. Interview with Herminio, Basque Children's Recording Project (AV1273/1/S2, HALS), 2008?
55. Patterson, "The Polish Exile Community in Britain."
56. Wojciechowska, ed., *Waiting to Be Heard*, p. 315.
57. Wojciechowska, ed., *Waiting to Be Heard*, p. 310.
58. Biegus and Biegus, *Polish Resettlement Camps*.
59. Personal communication with Henry Pavlovich, June 3, 2017.
60. http://www.northwickparkpolishdpcamp.co.uk/northwick04.htm.
61. Zubrzycki, *Polish Immigrants in Britain*, p. 124.
62. *Dziennik Polski*, December 9, 1948, p. 3.
63. M. Jakubik, A. Nahajski, and B.W. Studzinki to Warden, Polish Hostel, Wheaton Aston (AST 18/66, TNA), July 29, 1953.
64. Stafford Rural District Council to M. Jakubik, A. Nahajski, and B.W. Studzinki (AST 18/66, TNA), August 27, 1953.
65. http://www.polishresettlementcampsintheuk.co.uk/northwick09.htm.
66. http://www.northwickparkpolishdpcamp.co.uk/northwick05.htm.
67. Biegus and Biegus, *Polish Resettlement Camps*, p. 110.
68. Biegus and Biegus, *Polish Resettlement Camps*, p. 35.
69. Szulakowska, "Life at Melton Mowbray."
70. Aihwa Ong, *Buddha is Hiding: Refugees, Citizenship, the New America* (Berkeley, 2003).
71. Annette Saville, *Only A Kindertransportee* (London, 2002), p. 32.
72. "Evacuation of British Subjects from Overseas" (HO 297/29, TNA), n.d.
73. Interview with Colin Hodgetts, June 12, 2017.
74. Interview with Sue Millman, June 19, 2017.
75. Cahalan, *Belgian Refugee Relief*, p. 81.
76. Powell, *Four Years in a Refugee Camp*, p. 17.
77. *The Times* (London), September 7, 1914.
78. Storr, *Excluded from the Record*, p. 76.
79. *New York Times*, February 28, 1915, p. 3.

80. Edith Sellers, "On the Entertaining of Refugees," *Nineteenth Century* 360 (June 1915): 1371–83.
81. *The Times History of the War*, vol. 4 (London, 1915).
82. Francesca M. Wilson, *They Came as Strangers: The Story of Refugees to Great Britain* (London, 1959), p. 215.
83. Government Belgian Refugees Committee, *First Report of the Departmental Committee Appointed by the President of the Local Government Board to Consider and Report on Questions Arising in Connection with the Reception and Employment of the Belgian Refugees in this Country* (London, 1914).
84. Cahalan, *Belgian Refugee Relief*, pp. 76–7.
85. "Belgian Refugees in the United Kingdom" (CAB 37/121/115, TNA), 1914.
86. William Buck, "'Come and Find Sanctuary in Eire': The Experiences of Ireland's Belgian Refugees During the First World War," *Immigrants and Minorities* 34.2 (2016): 192–209.
87. Sir Ernest Hatch, "The Belgian Refugees in the United Kingdom," *Quarterly Review* 225 (January 1916): 188–214.
88. *The Times* (London), September 22, 1914.
89. Storr, *Excluded from the Record*, p. 76.
90. Powell, *Four Years in a Refugee Camp*, p. 52.
91. *The Condition of the Belgian Workmen Now Refugees in England* (London, 1917).
92. *The Times* (London), August 16, 1918.
93. Paul Cohen-Portheim, *Time Stood Still: My Internment in England, 1914–1918* (New York, 1932), p. 20.
94. Cohen-Portheim, *Time Stood Still*, p. 41.
95. Interview with Klaus Ernst Hinrichsen (IWM 3789), June 1978.
96. Interview with Leo Kahn (IWM 4300), February 8, 1979.
97. Tydor Baumel, "Kitchener."
98. May, "Reception."
99. Warden, Stover Hostel to National Assistance Board (AST 18/11, TNA), July 31, 1963.
100. Residents Committee Submission Regarding Krysiak Family (AST 18/81, TNA), November 29, 1951.
101. "Polish Resettlement Bill," *Hansard's Parliamentary Debates*, HC 433, February 12, 1947.
102. "Poles (Assistance)," *Hansard's Parliamentary Debates*, HC 458, November 30, 1948.
103. *Citizen*, December 11, 1956. See also "Egypt: British Subjects' Losses," *Hansard's Parliamentary Debates*, HL 202, February 28, 1957.
104. On special provisions for Anglo-Egyptian Jews, see Addison, "The Case for the 1951 Victims of Suez" (HO 240/7, TNA), n.d.; "Special Food for Orthodox Jews" (HO 240/26, TNA), 1957–8; "Anglo-Egyptian Resettlement: Particulars of Aged Jewish Evacuees who are being maintained by the Board" (HO 240/45, TNA), 1959; and Dario Miccoli, *Histories of the Jews of Egypt: An Imagined Bourgeoisie, 1880s–1950s* (New York, 2015).
105. Marion E. Massey to S.J. Dibble (HO 240/54, TNA), August 25, 1959; S.J. Dibble to R. Davies (HO 240/54, TNA), August 26, 1959.
106. "Proposed Anglo-Egyptian Charity" (CHAR 7/67, TNA), February 7, 1957.
107. "Anglo-Egyptian Resettlement Board," *Hansard's Parliamentary Debates*, HC 573, July 15, 1957.
108. "Egypt (Expelled British Subjects)," *Hansard's Parliamentary Debates*, HC 592, August 1, 1958.

109. "Egypt: Distress of Expelled British Nationals," *Hansard's Parliamentary Debates*, HL 212, November 12, 1958.
110. "Refugees from Hungary and Egypt," *Hansard's Parliamentary Debates*, HC 563, January 29, 1957.
111. *Manchester Guardian*, February 11, 1957, p. 11.
112. *Sunday Times*, December 15, 1956.
113. *Manchester Guardian*, December 13, 1956.
114. "Refugees," *Hansard's Parliamentary Debates*, HC 566, March 8, 1957.
115. B. Tollinton to T.E. Evans (HO 240/68, TNA), December 10, 1958.
116. O.M. Fillery, "Anglo-Egyptian Resettlement Board" (FO 371/142039, TNA), August 18, 1959.
117. "Egypt: Distress of Expelled British Nationals."
118. G.M. Wilcox, "The Anglo-Egyptian Hostels. A Brief Survey and Summing Up, Resultant from Visits Paid to Summerfield, Bridgend, and Frobisher Hall" (HO 240/101, TNA), May 21, 1958.
119. "Evacuation of British Subjects from Overseas" (HO 297/29, TNA), n.d.
120. "Evacuation of British Subjects from Overseas in Circumstances Short of Global War" (HO 297/29, TNA), n.d.
121. Lord Colyton, "Anglo-Egyptian Aid Society" (HO 240/43, TNA), October 14, 1957.
122. R. Clare Martin and R.R. Brewis to Sir Frank Newsam (HO 297/8, TNA), January 25, 1957.
123. "British Subjects from Egypt in Receipt of National Assistance" (HO 240/81, TNA), February 20, 1957.
124. "Anglo-Egyptian Resettlement Board" (CAB 128/32, TNA), July 1958.
125. "Resettlement Grants" (HO 240/37, TNA), October 17, 1957.
126. "Egypt: Hardships of Expelled Britons," *Hansard's Parliamentary Debates*, HL 211, July 23, 1958.
127. "Egypt: British Subjects' Losses," *Hansard's Parliamentary Debates*, HL 202, February 28, 1957.
128. Anglo-Egyptian Resettlement Board, "Minutes of a Meeting held on Thursday, 17th October, 1957" (HO 240/16, TNA), 1957.
129. R.R. Brewis to D.A. Peach (HO 240/16, TNA), August 7, 1957.
130. Anglo-Egyptian Aid Society, "Memorandum re Resettlement of Elderly People" (HO 240/43, TNA), September 17, 1957.
131. Victor Lagnardo to Lord Coylton (HO 240/95, TNA), March 15, 1957.
132. "Complaints on Eastwood Hostel" (HO 240/95, TNA), 1957.
133. *Daily Telegraph*, October 31, 1958.
134. "Duration of Relief and Resettlement Scheme" (HO 297/19, TNA), 1959.
135. Anglo-Egyptian Resettlement Board, "Minutes of a Meeting Held on Friday, 20th June, 1958" (HO 240/37, TNA), 1958.
136. David L.M. Renton to Patricia Hornsby-Smith (PIN 70/7, TNA), December 4, 1957; "Cases of Post-Resettlement Difficulties" (HO 240/34, TNA), n.d.
137. Herbert Addison, Association of (Former) British Officials of the Egyptian Government to Lord Colyton (HO 240/7, TNA), October 4, 1957.
138. "Manpower Planning Unit Background Brief. The Manpower Characteristics and Importance to Uganda of (a) Asian Residents, (b) British Supplemented Personnel" (BD 65/46, TNA), n.d.
139. Christie Davis, "Interviews with East African Asians" (C1067, BLSA), 1969.

140. "Preparing for the Ugandan Asians," *Observer*, August 20, 1972.
141. Vaughan Robinson, *Transients, Settlers and Refugees: Asians in Britain* (Oxford, 1986).
142. Yumiko Hamai, "'Imperial Burden' or 'Jews of Africa'? An Analysis of Political and Media Discourse in the Uganda Asian Crisis," *Twentieth-Century British History* 22.3 (2011): 415–36.
143. "Preparing for the Ugandan Asians," *Observer*, August 20, 1972.
144. http://media.nationalarchives.gov.uk/index.php/ugandan-asians-in-britain-journeys-across-three-continents-to-find-a-home/.
145. British politicians feared that rumor and paranoia would take hold if they did not provide the news in Hungarian. The Ministry of Labour employed 342 interpreters for Hungarian refugees, all of whom were screened extensively. "Hungarian and British Refugees," *Hansard's Parliamentary Debates*, HC 563, January 31, 1957; "Hungarian Refugees," *Hansard's Parliamentary Debates*, HC 568, April 11, 1957; J.D. Morley to P.G. Knowles (HLG 107/5, TNA), February 18, 1957.
146. D.W. Tanner, "Further Education Provision at Ugandan Asian Resettlement Centres" (CC26/1, Surrey History Centre), December 8, 1972.
147. *Daily Telegraph*, October 25, 1972.
148. D.O. Mcl. Thorne, "Points Stressed at Briefing of Staff Officers" (HO 289/60, TNA), November 8, 1972.
149. Interview with Chotalal Vadhia Mohan (C900/00003, BLSA), 1998.
150. Kramer, "The Uganda Asians."
151. Marett, *Immigrants*, p. 79.
152. http://media.nationalarchives.gov.uk/index.php/ugandan-asians-in-britain-journeys-across-three-continents-to-find-a-home/.
153. Naipaul, "Passports to Dependence."
154. *The Times* called for Asian "experts" to provide a more accurate picture. See, e.g., the reliance on Praful Patel in "Big Log-Jam Builds Up in Asian Transit Camps," *The Times* (London), October 1, 1972.
155. "Case No. 4, West Malling" (HO 289/50, TNA), February 2, 1973.
156. Camilla Schofield, "'A Nation or No Nation?' Enoch Powell and Thatcherism," in Jackson and Saunders, eds., *Making Thatcher's Britain*, pp. 95–110.
157. Mihir Bose, "The Ugandan Asian Success Magic," *New Community* (September 16, 1982): 456–8.
158. Quoted in Rina Valeny, "From Pariah to Paragon: The Social Mobility of Ugandan Asian Refugees in Britain," Ph.D. Thesis, University of Wales, 1998, p. 220.
159. P. Lashmar and A. Harris, "Who Wants to be a Millionaire?" *Independent*, March 1, 1997, pp. 12–20.
160. Quoted in Valeny, "From Pariah to Paragon," p. 236.
161. On the persistence of the Ugandan Asian success story, see "Ugandan Asians," *Hansard's Parliamentary Debates*, HC, December 6, 2012.
162. Vaughan Robinson, "Marching into the Middle Classes? The Long-term Resettlement of East African Asians in the United Kingdom," *Journal of Refugee Studies* 6.3 (1993): 230–47.
163. Dominic Sandbrook, *State of Emergency: The Way We Were: Britain, 1970–1974* (London, 2010), pp. 295–6. See also Shaila Srinivasan, *The South Asian Petty Bourgeoisie in Britain: An Oxford Case Study* (Aldershot, 1995).
164. D.W. Tanner, "Further Education Provision at Ugandan Asian Resettlement Centres" (CC26/1, Surrey History Centre), December 8, 1972.

165. Janie Thomas and Diane Mak, "Social Work and the Boat People," *Social Work Today* 10 (August 10, 1979): 11–14. On the tensions between North Vietnamese and South Vietnamese at Thorney Island, see Thanh, *Catholic with Confucian Tendencies*, p. 149.

166. Daphne M.F. Byrne, Vietnamese Centre Records, Thorney Island (Acc 15240, WSRO), 1995.

167. Thanh, *Catholic with Confucian Tendencies*, p. 136.

168. "Minutes of Heads of Section Committees" (Acc 15240, WSRO), July 23, 1980.

169. "Minutes of the Vietnamese Committee" (Acc 15240, WSRO), November 5, 1980.

170. "Minutes of Heads of Section Committees" (Acc 15240, WSRO), November 14, 1979.

NOTES TO CHAPTER 4

1. Susan Pedersen, *Family, Dependence, and the Origins of the Welfare State* (Cambridge, 1993); see also Lynne Haney, *Inventing the Needy: Gender and the Politics of Welfare in Hungary* (Berkeley, 2002), and Jane Lewis, "Gender, the Family and Women's Agency in the Building of 'Welfare States': The British Case," *Social History* 19.1 (1994): 37–56.

2. Claire Langhamer, *The English in Love: The Intimate Story of an Emotional Revolution* (Oxford, 2013); Langhamer, "Feelings, Women and Work in the Long 1950s," *Women's History Review* 26.1 (2017): 77–92; Laura King, *Family Men: Fatherhood and Masculinity in Britain, c. 1914–1960* (Oxford, 2015); Frank Mort, "Social and Symbolic Fathers and Sons in Postwar Britain," *Journal of British Studies* 38.3 (1999): 353–84.

3. Stephen Brooke, *Sexual Politics: Sexuality, Family Planning and the British Left from the 1880s to the Present Day* (Oxford, 2011); Thane, "Family Life and 'Normality' in Postwar British Culture." See also Teri Chettiar, "'More than a Contract: The Emergence of a State-Supported Marriage Welfare Service and the Politics of Emotional Life in Post-1945 Britain," *Journal of British Studies* 55.3 (2016): 566–91; Cohen, *Family Secrets*; Selina Todd, "Family Welfare and Social Work in Post-War England, c. 1948–c.1970," *English Historical Review* 129 (2014): 362–87.

4. Tara Zahra, *The Lost Children: Reconstructing Europe's Families after World War Two* (Cambridge, MA, 2011); see also Ruth Balint, "Children Left Behind: Family, Refugees and Immigration in Postwar Europe," *History Workshop Journal* 82 (2016): 151–72.

5. Seth Koven and Sonya Michel, eds., *Mothers of a New World: Maternalist Politics and the Origins of Welfare States* (London: Routledge, 1993); Sarah Gregson, "Women and Children First? The Administration of Titanic Relief in Southampton, 1912–1959," *English Historical Review* 128 (February 2012): 83–109; Marjorie Levine-Clark, *Unemployment, Welfare, and Masculine Citizenship: So Much Honest Poverty in Britain, 1870–930* (Basingstoke, 2015); Susan Pedersen, "The Maternalist Moment in British Colonial Policy: The Controversy Over 'Child Slavery' in Hong Kong, 1917–1941," *Past and Present* 171.1 (2001): 161–202.

6. G. Ivor Thomas to Sir Godfrey Ince (AST 18/60, TNA), January 12, 1948.

7. G. Ivor Thomas to Sir Godfrey Ince (AST 18/60, TNA), January 12, 1948.

8. Interestingly, the British state's understanding of dependents was not confined to family relationships. Anyone who had worked with Polish education, medical, or welfare organizations during the Second World War was a "dependent" as well. "Welfare of Dependents in the Polish Resettlement Corps" (AST 18/199, TNA), n.d.

9. "Report on a Visit to Haydon Park: The Settling Down of the Lebanese Intake" (AST 18/97, TNA), August 17 and 18, 1950; "Intake of Poles from East Africa" (AST 18/97, TNA), September 11, 1950.

10. One Pole at Tengeru claimed allegiance to the Masai and threatened to massacre the whites in his camp with his African friends. The Kenyans were "horrified," and insisted that the British leave no Poles behind. T.W.E. Roche to Mr. Howard (AST 18/96, TNA), June 4, 1950.

11. T.W.E. Roche, "Report of the British Mission to East Africa on Polish Refugees" (AST 18/96, TNA), July 6, 1950.

12. "Accommodation—Families and Dependents" (AST 18/75, TNA), November 3, 1947.

13. G. Ivor Thomas to Sir Godfrey Ince (AST 18/60, TNA), January 12, 1948.

14. Emergency Accommodation Committee, "Draft Memorandum. Accommodation of Polish Dependents" (AST 18/61, TNA), n.d.

15. *Dziennik Polski*, August 10, 1949, p. 3.

16. *Dziennik Polski*, November 15, 1949, p. 3.

17. Emergency Accommodation Committee, "Draft Memorandum. Accommodation of Polish Dependents" (AST 18/61, TNA), n.d.

18. Manning protested that many Polish men did not know whether their Polish wives were dead or alive, and therefore could not legalize their relationships with English women. "Polish Resettlement Bill."

19. Webster, "Transnational Communities of Allies."

20. Kushner and Knox, *Refugees in an Age of Genocide*.

21. "Polish Resettlement. Civilians in Dependents Hostels" (AST 18/85, TNA), 1947.

22. G.A. Isaacs to James Chuter Ede (AST 18/60, TNA), July 4, 1947.

23. E. Whyte to D.J. Hope-Wallace (AST 18/60, TNA), March 15, 1947.

24. "Accommodation of Families and Dependents of Poles in Military Camps" (AST 18/60, TNA), January 9, 1948.

25. Sir Harry Methven, "National Service Hostels Corporation" (AST 18/60, TNA), January 27, 1948.

26. *Dziennik Polski*, April 26, 1948.

27. Peter Somerville, "The Making and Unmaking of Homelessness Legislation," in Susan Hutson and David Clapham, eds., *Homelessness: Public Policies and Private Troubles* (London, 1999), pp. 29–57.

28. Maud Bülbring, "Post-War Refugees in Great Britain," *Population Studies* 8.2 (November 1954): 99–112.

29. R. Perun to Manager, Kelvedon Hostel (AST 18/81, TNA), February 2, 1951.

30. Mrs. L. Kiczorowska to Kelvedon Hostel (AST 18/81, TNA), June 29, 1950.

31. Estate Manager, Kelvedon Hostel to Mrs. L. Kiczorowska (AST 18/81, TNA), July 20, 1950.

32. F. Hajduczek to Ministry of Pensions (AST 18/114, TNA), October 19, 1959; National Assistance Board to F.A. Cullum (AST 18/114, TNA), November 3, 1959.

33. Stefan Kuchta to Queen of England (AST 18/114, TNA), November 8, 1959.

34. S. Kuchta and E. Holownia to National Assistance Board (AST 18/114, TNA), n.d.

35. The Board viewed both men as "troublesome," and doubted their ability to be "clean and tidy householders." Edward Holownia to Queen of England (AST 18/114, TNA), November 9, 1959.

36. Northwick Park Hostel Residents Single Persons Group to National Assistance Board (AST 18/114, TNA), October 21, 1959.

37. Northwick Park Hostel Residents Single Persons Group to National Assistance Board (AST 18/114, TNA), October 21, 1959.
38. *Melton Times*, February 25, 1955. http://www.leicestershirevillages.com/meltonmowbray/newspaperclippings,279277.html [website discontinued].
39. "Evictions from Hostels" (AST 18/53, TNA), February 14, 1949.
40. Warden, Northwick Hostel to National Assistance Board (AST 7/1255, TNA), June 27, 1956.
41. C.W. Berry to Mrs. J. Stopa (AST 7/1255, TNA), October 23, 1956.
42. Warden of Northwick Hostel to Jan Ozga (AST 18/69, TNA), May 20, 1955.
43. "British Refugees. British Subjects from Egypt" (HO 297/3, TNA), January 18, 1957.
44. "Policy Governing the Future of Elderly and Infirm Refugees" (HO 240/46, TNA), 1957–60.
45. Prof. S.E. Finer, "Rec. 4 of Employment Sub-Committee, adopted by Consultative Committee at its meeting on the 28th May 1957" (HO 240/90, TNA), 1957.
46. O.G. Ommanney to A.W. Peterson (HO 297/4, TNA), April 4, 1957.
47. O.G. Ommanney to A. Peach (HO 297/4, TNA), March 20, 1957.
48. *Daily Nation* (Nairobi), December 21, 1972.
49. "WVS Anglo-Egyptian Dossier" (HO 240/23, TNA), n.d.
50. "Greenbanks Hostel" (HO 240/89, TNA), 1957.
51. H.L. Evans, "Resettlement Grants on Marriage" (HO 240/33, TNA), July 29, 1958.
52. S.J. Dibble to H.B. Wilson (HO 240/42, TNA), August 22, 1957.
53. "Refugees from Uganda" (DD/X/NAS 1, Somerset Heritage Centre, Somerset), n.d.
54. Nicholas Winterton in "Ugandan Asians," *Hansard's Parliamentary Debates*, HC 847, December 6, 1972.
55. *Daily Nation* (Nairobi), December 12, 1972.
56. Canon L. John Collins to Prime Minister (ACC 1888/203, LMA), December 15, 1972.
57. *The Times* (London), September 26, 1973.
58. "Absent Asian," *The Times* (London), January 1973.
59. "Stranded in India" (ACC/1888/200, LMA), 1973.
60. *Sunday Telegraph*, February 18, 1973.
61. *Guardian*, January 27, 1973, p. 12.
62. "Ugandan Asians," *Hansard's Parliamentary Debates*, HL 337, December 6, 1972.
63. "British Citizens from Uganda" (ACC 1888/203, LMA), August 30, 1972.
64. Mary Dines, "Ugandan Asians—One Year On," *New Community* 12 (1973): 380–3.
65. Yasmin Alibhai-Brown, *No Place Like Home: An Autobiography* (London, 1995), p. 186.
66. Bourne, "The Last Asians."
67. M.G. Fowler, "'Split Family' Interviews at West Malling Centre" (HO 289/76, TNA), May 17, 1973.
68. Marett, *Immigrants*, p. 76.
69. ACC/1888/203, LMA, August 30, 1972.
70. *The Times*, March 22, 1973.
71. M.G. Fowler to A.J. Rutherford, "Employment—'Single' Persons in Resettlement Centres, West Malling" (HO 289/76, TNA), July 12, 1973.
72. "Interviews at West Malling Centre" (HO 289/76, TNA), July 10 and 11, 1973.
73. Town Clerk, Andover to W.L. Mees (HO 289/76, TNA), June 27, 1973.
74. A.J. Rutherford to Uganda Resettlement Board (HO 289/76, TNA), May 1973.
75. S.A. Dharamshi to Uganda Resettlement Board (HO 289/51, TNA), March 11, 1973.

76. Jan Romijn, *Tabu: Uganda Asians—the Old, the Weak, the Vulnerable. A Report on his Work with the Elderly and Handicapped among the Uganda Asian Evacuees in London* (London, 1976), p. 32.

77. Brian Jackson and Barrie Knight, "As the Camps Close: Prospects for a Continuing Commitment to the Needs of Refugees in Britain" (July 1973), ACC/1888/200, LMA.

78. Janie Thomas, "Where Have All the Refugees Gone?" *Community Care* (October 29, 1981): 19–21.

79. "British Committee for Vietnamese Refugees" (BS 18/18, TNA), June 16, 1981.

80. "Home Office/UNHCR Procedure and Guidelines for Family Reunions" (Acc 15240, WSRO), n.d.

81. Thomas and Mak, "Social Work and the Boat People."

82. "Minutes of the Vietnamese Sub-Committee" (Acc 15240, WSRO), April 3, 1980.

83. "Minutes of Heads of Section Committees" (Acc 15240, WSRO), November 28, 1979.

84. Simon Philips and Jane Pearson, "Dealing with Vietnamese Refugees: Our Plans," *British Medical Journal* 282 (February 14, 1981): 525–7.

85. Whitham, "A Health Visitor's View."

86. Daphne M.F. Byrne, Vietnamese Centre Records, Thorney Island (Acc 15240, WSRO), 1995.

87. Daphne M.F. Byrne, Vietnamese Centre Records, Thorney Island (Acc 15240, WSRO), 1995.

88. "Minutes of Heads of Section Committee" (Acc 15240, WSRO), December 10, 1980.

89. *Daily Telegraph*, June 12, 1980.

90. *Observer*, September 12, 1982.

91. "Minutes of the Heads of Sections Committee Meeting" (Acc 15240, WSRO), May 13, 1981.

92. "Vietnamese Committee Meeting" (Acc 15240, WSRO), April 13, 1981.

93. Suzanne Bang, *We Come as a Friend: Towards a Vietnamese Model of Social Work* (Derby, 1983).

94. "Minutes of the Vietnamese Committee" (Acc 15240, WSRO), November 27, 1979.

95. Laura King, "Future Citizens: Cultural and Political Conceptions of Children in Britain, 1930s–1950s," *Twentieth-Century British History* 27.3 (2016): 389–411.

96. Sir Wilfred Roberts to Sir John Simon (MH 57/322, TNA), April 27, 1937.

97. Manning, *A Life for Education*, p. 130.

98. "Note of Conference held in the Home Secretary's Room" (HO 213/288, TNA), May 18, 1937.

99. Benjamin, *Recuerdos*, p. 3.

100. W.S. Craig, "Basque Children" (MH 57/322, TNA), May 20, 1937.

101. Of course, as Chapter 1 suggests, the Basque children at North Stoneham camp had little choice but to use the latrines together.

102. W.S. Craig, "Spanish Refugee Children" (MH 57/322, TNA), May 25, 1937.

103. "Basque Children at Oakley Park, Oakley" (MH 57/323, TNA), August 16, 1937.

104. Miss Montagnon, "Basque Refugee Children, North Stoneham Camp" (MH 57/322, TNA), May 28, 1937.

105. "The Basque Camp, Volume I" (173A12/A4/4/1/3, HALS), May 23, 1937.

106. "Rusthall Beacon, Tunbridge Wells" (MH 57/323, TNA), n.d.; Mr. Hobbs, "Basque Children at Woodberry Piercing Hall" (MH 57/323, TNA), June 30, 1937.

107. Interview with Klaus Ernst Hinrichsen (IWM 3789), June 1978.

108. Interview with Leo Kahn (IWM 4300), February 8, 1979.

109. "Eighty Girls in Polish Camp" (AST 18/9, TNA), December 1946.
110. "Northern Command Meeting for Polish Welfare" (AST 18/99, TNA), April 21, 1947.
111. *Dziennik Polski*, October 12, 1946, p. 3.
112. Warden, Stowell Park, to Mrs. M.A. Patterson (AST 18/107, TNA), November 18, 1948.
113. Warden, Northwick to National Assistance Board (AST 7/1255, TNA), September 19, 1956.
114. Dingle to Walton (AST 18/14, TNA), August 17, 1948.
115. Letter to Miss Dingle (AST 18/14, TNA), December 17, 1948.
116. "Assessment and Maintenance Charges in Cases of Co-habitation" (AST 18/14, TNA), August 19, 1948.
117. Walton to Dixon (AST 18/14, TNA), December 7, 1948.
118. J.S. Balderstone, "Training Courses for Polish Women" (AST 18/8, TNA), May 1949.
119. "Conference on WVS Work for Anglo-Egyptian Repatriates" (HO 240/23, TNA), April 12, 1957.
120. "WVS Anglo-Egyptian Dossier" (HO 240/23, TNA), n.d.
121. "Conference on WVS Work for Anglo-Egyptian Repatriates" (HO 240/23, TNA), April 12, 1957.
122. Helen McCarthy, "Women, Marriage and Paid Work in Post-War Britain," *Women's History Review* 26.1 (2017): 46–61.
123. Helen McCarthy, "Social Science and Married Women's Employment in Post-War Britain," *Past and Present* 233 (2016): 269–305.
124. *Kidderminster Shuttle*, August 30, 1957.
125. Anglo-Egyptian Resettlement Board, "Minutes of Inaugural Meeting of Consultative Committee of the Summerfield Hostel" (HO 240/95, TNA), June 24, 1957.
126. *Telegraph*, September 25, 1972.
127. BCAR, "Reception of Vietnamese Boat Refugees (rescued by *S.S. Sibonga*) at the RAF Camp Sopley, Hants." (H/ED1/4B/5, File 1, HALS), June 18, 1979.
128. Interview with Lee Allane, July 18, 2014.
129. Interview with Peter Rimmer, June 2, 2017; interview with Sue Millman, June 19, 2017.
130. Interview with Atul Patel, July 14, 2014.
131. Interview with Atul Patel, The Exiles Project.
132. Interview with Atul Patel, July 14, 2014.

NOTES TO CHAPTER 5

1. Maria Pfister-Ammende, "Mental Hygiene in Refugee Camps," in Charles Zwingmann and Maria Pfister-Ammende, eds., *Uprooting and After...* (New York: Springer Verlag, 1973), p. 248.
2. Cohen, *From the Jews to the Tamils*, p. 55; David Glover, *Literature, Immigration, and Diaspora in Fin-de-Siècle England: A Cultural History of the 1905 Aliens Act* (Cambridge, 2012); Williams, *"Jews and other foreigners,"* pp. 99–100.
3. Agier et al., "Between War and City"; Sanyal, "Squatting in Camps"; Romola Sanyal, "Urbanizing Refuge: Interrogating Spaces of Displacement," *International Journal of Urban and Regional Research* 38.2 (2014): 558–72.
4. Simon Turner, "What Is a Refugee Camp? Exploration of the Limits and Effects of the Camp," *Journal of Refugee Studies* 29.2 (2015): 139–48.
5. Kushner, "Local Heroes"; M. Radford, *Our Friends the Belgians: Sketches of Belgian Life in England* (London, 1921), p. 20.

6. Kushner, "Local Heroes."
7. Government Belgian Refugees Committee, *First Report*, p. 43.
8. Sellers, "On the Entertaining of Refugees."
9. Refugee Council, *Credit to the Nation.*
10. "The Basque Camp, Volume I" (173A12/A4/4/1/3, HALS), May 22, 1937.
11. Theo Montagnon, "Basque Refugee Children. The Grange, Somerset" (MH 57/323, TNA), June 18, 1937.
12. E.P. Harries, W.M.C., "Basque Camp, Eastleigh, Report" (292/946/39/111i, MRC), May 27, 1937.
13. "The Basque Camp, Volume I" (173A12/A4/4/1/3, HALS), May 26, 1937.
14. "The Basque Camp, Volume I" (173A12/A4/4/1/3, HALS), May 27, 1937; May 28, 1937; May 31, 1937.
15. "The Basque Camp, Volume I" (173A12/A4/4/1/3, HALS), May 25, 1937.
16. Celia Lee (née Cilly Horwitz), "Our Life in Dovercourt-Bay Camp" (Typescript from C526/44, BLSA), June 19, 1941.
17. May, "Kitchener Camp Diary," March 12, 1939.
18. May, "Reception."
19. "This Lovely England," *Kitchener Camp Review*, July 1939.
20. A.W.W., "Sandwich," *Kitchener Camp Review*, August 1939.
21. Ungerson, *Four Thousand Lives.*
22. Kushner and Knox, *Refugees in an Age of Genocide*, p. 151.
23. Memoirs of Peter Mansbacher (644/8, Institute of Contemporary History and Wiener Library, London), 1988.
24. *Kitchener Camp Review*, June 1939.
25. *Kitchener Camp Review*, July 1939.
26. Lomnitz, *"Never Mind, Mr. Lom!,"* p. 94.
27. Gatrell, *Making of the Modern Refugee*, p. 114.
28. *Evening Argus*, May 3, 1960.
29. Peter Gatrell, *Free World? The Campaign to Save the World's Refugees, 1956–1963* (Cambridge, 2011).
30. Webster, "Transnational Communities of Allies."
31. *Listener*, January 16, 1941. Quoted in Webster, "Transnational Communities of Allies."
32. Quoted in Kochanski, *The Eagle Unbowed*, p. 478.
33. Webster, "Transnational Communities of Allies," p. 231.
34. Quoted in Kochanski, *The Eagle Unbowed*, p. 562.
35. "Ex-Service Men (Resettlement)," *Hansard's Parliamentary Debates*, HC 448, March 10, 1948. On interethnic and interracial tensions at the Ministry of Labour hostels, which were disrupted by violence between Polish, Irish, and Jamaican workers, see Kevin Searle, "'Mixing of the Unmixables': The 1949 Causeway Green 'Riots' in Birmingham," *Race and Class* 54.3 (2013): 44–64; *Dziennik Polski*, August 23, 1949, p. 3.
36. "Report on Ashby Hostel" (AST 18/100, TNA), December 4, 1951.
37. "Report on Marsworth Hostel" (AST 18/100, TNA), December 6, 1951.
38. J.R. Lambie, "General Inspection at Keevil Polish Hostel" (AST 18/67, TNA), December 10, 1949.
39. *Loughborough Monitor*, January 27, 1949.
40. http://www.tweedsmuirmilitarycamp.co.uk/ch4.html.
41. http://www.northwickparkpolishdpcamp.co.uk/northwick03.htm.
42. Biegus and Biegus, *Polish Resettlement Camps.*
43. Szulakowska, "Life at Melton Mowbray."

44. Watson, *Squatting in Britain*.
45. Guldi, "World Neoliberalism as Rebellion from Below?"
46. "Requisition Camps in Use for Housing" (HLG 101/867, TNA), n.d. (1954?).
47. Watson, *Squatting in Britain*, p. 69.
48. "Squatters in Army Camps" (PREM 8/227, TNA), August 13, 1946.
49. Janine Hansen, "Sympathy, Antipathy, Hostility: British Attitudes to Non-Repatriable Poles and Ukrainians after the Second World War and to the Hungarian Refugees of 1956," Ph.D. Thesis, University of Sheffield, 1995.
50. Cabinet, "Squatters in Army Camps" (PREM 8/227, TNA), August 13, 1946.
51. At the Auchenraith Camp for Poles in Scotland, nineteen Britons were fined for squatting in the camp's Nissen huts. Watson, *Squatting in Britain*, p. 83.
52. "Tilstock Anglo-Polish Housing Units" (AST 18/66, TNA), February 3, 1951.
53. The vacant huts at a Polish hostel in Amersham were also used in this way. Bülbring, "Post-War Refugees in Great Britain."
54. F.F. Jones to C.H. Simmons (AST 18/66, TNA), August 8, 1952; C.H. Simmonds to National Assistance Board (AST 18/66, TNA), August 26, 1952.
55. *Birmingham Gazette*, September 12, 1949.
56. Biegus and Biegus, *Polish Resettlement Camps*.
57. http://www.bbc.co.uk/stoke/content/articles/2009/04/15/poles_lost_found_feature.shtml.
58. *Manchester Guardian*, August 4, 1951.
59. *Staffordshire Advertiser*, August 3, 1951.
60. Jan Nowak, "Wheaton Aston" (AST 18/80, TNA), February 11, 1951.
61. *Daily Telegraph*, September 17, 1951.
62. http://www.polishresettlementcampsintheuk.co.uk/wheatonaston1.htm.
63. *Staffordshire Advertiser*, November 25, 1950.
64. Janowski, "Memories."
65. http://foxley.org/Camp-barracks.
66. Pavlovich, *Worlds Apart*, pp. 84 and 91.
67. L.W. Moore to National Assistance Board (AST 7/1298, TNA), May 30, 1950; L.W. Moore, "Hours of Duty" (AST 9/143, TNA), June 12, 1950.
68. G.C. Seager, "Visit by Chairman to Reception Centre and Polish Hostel at Kelvedon on 2nd May 1952" (AST 7/1299, TNA), May 16, 1952.
69. L.W. Moore to National Assistance Board (AST 7/1298, TNA), November 16, 1950.
70. J.W.M. Siberry to K. Whalley (AST 9/142, TNA), July 26, 1956.
71. "Notes on Vagrancy and the Future Provision of Reception Centres" (AST 9/142, TNA), n.d.
72. Humphrey and Ward, *Passports and Politics*, p. 61.
73. On the "mutually dependent, unequal, and often antagonistic" relationship between camp and town in a German context, see Adam R. Seipp, *Strangers in the Wild Place: Refugees, Americans, and a German Town, 1945–1952* (Bloomington, 2013), p. 72.
74. Lawrence Black, Hugh Pemberton, and Pat Thane, eds., *Reassessing 1970s Britain* (Manchester, 2013).
75. Robert Saunders, "Crisis? What Crisis? Thatcherism and the Seventies," in Ben Jackson and Robert Saunders, eds., *Making Thatcher's Britain* (Cambridge, 2012), pp. 25–42.
76. Sandbrook, *State of Emergency*. See also Richard Clutterbuck, *Britain in Agony: The Growth of Political Violence* (London, 1978); Francis Wheen, *Strange Days Indeed—the 1970s: The Golden Age of Paranoia* (New York, 2009).
77. Andy Beckett, *When the Lights Went Out: Britain in the Seventies* (London, 2009); Lawrence Black and Hugh Pemberton, "Introduction: The Benighted Decade?

Reassessing the 1970s," in Lawrence Black, Hugh Pemberton, and Pat Thane, eds., *Reassessing 1970s Britain* (Manchester, 2013), pp. 1–24; Thomas Borstelmann, *The 1970s: A New Global History from Civil Rights to Economic Inequality* (Princeton, 2012).

78. Tehila Sasson, "Milking the Third World? Humanitarianism, Capitalism, and the Moral Economy of the Nestlé Boycott," *American Historical Review* 121.4 (2016): 1196–224.

79. Eve Colpus, "'The Screen Is Two-Way': That's Life! Television and Social Activism in Britain, 1973–1994," Paper delivered at Burdens Conference: Writing History after 1945, University of California at Berkeley, 2012; Vanessa Pupavac, "Between Compassion and Conservatism: A Genealogy of Humanitarian Sensibilities," in Didier Fassin and Mariella Pandolfi, eds., *Contemporary States of Emergency: The Politics of Military and Humanitarian Interventions* (New York, 2010), pp. 129–49.

80. Matthew Hilton, "Politics is Ordinary: Non-Governmental Organizations and Political Participation in Contemporary Britain," *Twentieth-Century British History* 22.2 (2011): 230–68; Matthew Hilton, James McKay, Nicholas Crowson, and Jean-Francis Mouhot, *The Politics of Expertise: How NGOs Shaped Modern Britain* (Oxford, 2013).

81. Sandbrook, *State of Emergency*, p. 29; Sandbrook, *Seasons in the Sun*, p. 22.

82. Andy McSmith, *No Such Thing as Society* (London, 2010). On Thatcherite social policy, see Florence Sutcliffe-Braithwaite, "Neo-Liberalism and Morality in the Making of Thatcherite Social Policy," *Historical Journal* 55.2 (2012): 497–520.

83. Jodi Burkett, *Constructing Post-Imperial Britain: Britishness, "Race" and the Radical Left in the 1960s* (Basingstoke, 2013).

84. J.N.M. Parry to Dr. R.T. Bevan, "Visit to Tonfannau, October 29–30 1972" (BD 103/82, TNA), October 31, 1972.

85. Sir Charles Cunningham, "The Uganda Resettlement Board and Hiving-Off: Some Possibilities for Future Research," *Public Administration* 51.3 (1973): 251–60.

86. *The Times* (London), November 8, 1972.

87. P.J. Fox to Henderson (HO 289/82, TNA), July 17, 1973.

88. Jenny Bourne, "Resettlement Blues," *Race Today* 4.11 (November 1972): 357.

89. http://www.bbc.co.uk/devon/community_life/features/uganda_story.shtml.

90. "Faldingworth Resettlement Camp" (RVS), November 17, 1972.

91. "Report on Plasterdown Camp" (RVS), November 19–26, 1972.

92. Nadine Peppard, "End of a Chapter," *Uganda Resettlement News Bulletin* 3 (5380/1/8, SHC), 1972?

93. http://www.itv.com/news/wales/story/2012-07-27/40-years-since-ugandan-asians-made-wales-their-home/.

94. Brenda Kidman, *A Handful of Tears* (London, 1975), pp. 75 and 79.

95. "Uganda Asian Reception and Resettlement" (HO 289/95, TNA), n.d.

96. "Military Camp, Tonfanau (Closure)," *Hansard's Parliamentary Debates*, HC 715, July 6, 1965; Humphrey and Ward, *Passports and Politics*.

97. http://www.bbc.co.uk/legacies/immig_emig/england/suffolk/article_5.shtml.

98. "Note of Meeting, Uganda Asians, Welsh Office, Cathays Park" (BD 103/82, TNA), October 25, 1972.

99. Jackson, *Starting School*, p. 63.

100. Jackson, *Starting School*.

101. Interview with Atul Patel, July 14, 2014.

102. On the racial antipathies of Tower Hamlets, see Brooke, "Space, Emotions and the Everyday."

103. "Ugandan Asians," *Hansard's Parliamentary Debates*, HC 847, December 6, 1972.

104. In the United States, refugee resettlement programs relied on labor exploitation, grouping refugees with Mexican migrant workers or "Negro" sharecroppers. Latvian refugees in the United States complained about being compelled to live in "Negro" huts and work as sharecroppers. Stephen R. Porter, *Benevolent Empire: U.S. Power, Humanitarianism, and the World's Dispossessed* (Philadelphia, 2017).

105. Linda McDowell, *Migrant Women's Voices: Talking about Life and Work in the UK since 1945* (London, 2016), p. 22; see also Katy Long, "When Refugees Stopped Being Migrants: Movement, Labour, and Humanitarian Protection," *Migration Studies* 1.1 (2013): 4–26; Kushner, *Battle of Britishness*; http://www.newsweek.com/refugee-vs-migrants-whats-right-term-use-371222; https://www.washingtonpost.com/news/worldviews/wp/2015/07/30/why-the-language-we-use-to-talk-about-refugees-matters-so-much/?utm_term=.a9b3efd2894e; and https://www.washingtonpost.com/news/worldviews/wp/2015/08/24/is-it-time-to-ditch-the-word-migrant/.

106. The refugee might be read as a version of what Sara Ahmed has called the "melancholic migrant," who clings to the racist tragedies of the past—but, distinctively, is also supposed to view Britain with gratitude as the source of salvation from persecution. Migrants, she suggests, are bound to tell certain (highly positive) stories about their arrival. For refugees, the narrative of arrival is linked to the assertion that the prejudice the refugee has endured elsewhere will not be echoed in Britain. Sara Ahmed, *The Promise of Happiness* (Durham, NC, 2010).

107. Gatrell, "Refugees."

108. Ronald Kaye, "Defining the Agenda: British Refugee Policy and the Role of Parties," *Journal of Refugee Studies* 7.2 (1994): 144–59.

109. Kushner, *Battle of Britishness*, p. 44.

110. *The Times* (London), September 20, 1972.

111. "Preparing for the Ugandan Asians," *Observer*, August 20, 1972.

112. *Refuge or Home? A Policy Statement on the Resettlement of Refugees* (London, 1976), p. 52.

113. Interview with Shirin Abdul Hussein, Millennium Memory Bank Project (C900/00048, BLSA), 2000.

114. Interview with Lee Allane, July 18, 2014.

115. "Resettlement Centre Gaydon Warwickshire" (RVS), n.d.

116. Interview with Praful Thakrar, "Preserving Asian Heritage: An Oral History Project in Leicester" (BLSA), 2005.

117. Interview with Chandrika Joshi, July 24, 2017.

118. Alibhai-Brown, *No Place Like Home*, p. 186.

119. Alibhai-Brown, *No Place Like Home*, p. 187.

120. Alibhai-Brown, *No Place Like Home*, pp. 190–1.

121. Mahmood Mamdani, "The Ugandan Asian Expulsion: Twenty Years After," *Journal of Refugee Studies* 6.3 (1993): 265–73.

122. Mamdani, *From Citizen to Refugee*, p. 79.

123. Mamdani, *From Citizen to Refugee*, p. 71.

124. P.D. Bird, "In Confidence. Anti-Asian Demonstrations. Instructions for the Staff" (5380/1/8, Surrey History Centre), November 27, 1972; "Right-Wing Political Demonstrators" (5380/1/8, Surrey History Centre), n.d.

125. "Ugandan Asians," *Hansard's Parliamentary Debates*, HL 337, December 6, 1972.

126. Naipaul, "Passports to Dependence."

127. Bourne, "Resettlement Blues."

128. "Hobbs Barracks" (53801/1/8, SHC), n.d.

129. Humphrey and Ward, *Passports and Politics*, p. 65.
130. Humphrey and Ward, *Passports and Politics*, p. 65.
131. On Afro-Asian solidarity and frictions, see Antoinette Burton, *Brown Over Black: Race and the Politics of Postcolonial Citation* (Gurgaon, 2012), p. 5.
132. E.A. Markham and Arnold Kingston, *Merely a Matter of Colour: The Uganda Asian Anthology* (Edgware: "Q" Books, 1973), pp. 91–4.
133. Quoted in Harrison, *Finding a Role?*, p. 203.
134. Harrison, *Finding a Role?*, pp. 262–3.
135. Kushner and Knox, *Refugees in an Age of Genocide*, p. 313.
136. McSmith, *No Such Thing as Society*, p. 80.
137. Simon Field, *Resettling Refugees: The Lessons of Research* (London: HMSO, 1985); Jones, *Vietnamese Refugees*.
138. "In Confidence. Notes on Visit to Nelson Hall" (Ockenden Files, 7155/7/3/17, Surrey History Centre), December 1980.
139. Le Con (translated by Le Chan Vinh and Ian Stone), "Untitled," Surrey History Centre, 1979.
140. Pham Thanh, "The Memories Have Never Been Forgotten," *New Homeland* (Par 196/7/8, WSRO), 1980.
141. *Sopley Newsletter* (EV/QU 50, RCA, Box 1, Refugee Council Archives, University of East London), July 1981.
142. Interview with Julia Meiklejohn, June 12, 2017.
143. "What a Volunteer Can Do" (H/ED1/4B/5, File 1, HALS), n.d.
144. Interview with Thanh Cherry, June 26, 2017.
145. Daphne M.F. Byrne, Vietnamese Centre Records, Thorney Island (Acc 15240, WSRO), 1995.
146. BBC Solent, "The Sounds of '79" (AV74/SOSN/S1, HALS), 1979.
147. "Vietnamese Committee Meeting" (Acc 15240, WSRO), July 1, 1981.
148. "Vietnamese Committee Meeting" (Acc 15240, WSRO), March 25, 1981.

NOTES TO CHAPTER 6

1. On refugee politics, see Agier, *Managing the Undesirables*, p. 215.
2. On the history of depoliticizing the refugee, see Emily Baughan and Juliano Floriani, "Save the Children, the Humanitarian Project, and the Politics of Solidarity: Reviving Dorothy Buxton's Vision," *Disasters* Special Issue: *Aid in the Archives: Academic Histories for a Practitioner Audience* 39.2 (2015): 129–45.
3. Weizman, *The Least of All Possible Evils*, p. 60.
4. When a deputation of Jewish refugees at Kitchener approached Phineas May to protest the long work hours, he delivered a "very good" speech about how thousands of German Jews were still waiting to come to Britain, and it would be very selfish of them to wish for a free day. After this rebuke, he claimed, "they are all willing to work like good boys on Sunday mornings." May, "Kitchener Camp Diary," March 24, 1939.
5. Gatrell, *Making of the Modern Refugee*, p. 9.
6. Interview with Rudolph Munster (IWM 3899), September 27, 1979.
7. Interview with Klaus Ernst Hinrichsen (IWM 3789), June 1978.
8. Stent, *A Bespattered Page?*, p. 162.
9. Interview with Klaus Ernst Hinrichsen (IWM 3789), June 1978.
10. "On Self-Government in Civilian Dependents' Camps in Great Britain" (AST 18/99, TNA), n.d.

11. Balderstone to Walton (AST 18/25, TNA), June 27, 1947.
12. "Polish Hostels: Rules for Conduct" (AST 18/25, TNA), June 26, 1947.
13. "New Clause.—Provisions as to Discipline and Internal Administration of Certain Polish Forces," *Hansard's Parliamentary Debates*, HC 434, March 4, 1947.
14. "Polish Hostels. Rules for Conduct" (AST 18/25, TNA), June 26, 1947.
15. "Polish Resettlement Act 1947. Rules for the Separate Hostels" (AST 12/129, TNA), 1947.
16. "Notes for the Guidance of Residents at Polish Hostels" (AST 18/25, TNA), n.d.
17. Balderstone to Walton (AST 18/25, TNA), June 27, 1947.
18. "Resettlement Grants" (HO 240/37, TNA), February 20, 1958 and May 8, 1958.
19. On the politics of self-rationing, see Chapter 2.
20. "State of Hostel Grounds, etc.—Complaint by Ministry of Works" (AST 18/75, TNA), April 14, 1950.
21. "Welfare of Residents" (AST 18/100, TNA), June 4, 1951.
22. *Dziennik Polski*, August 3, 1949, p. 3.
23. See, e.g., "Quarterly Progress Report: Northwick" (AST 18/68, TNA), January 31, 1956.
24. "Quarterly Progress Report: Northwick" (AST 18/68, TNA), July 31, 1954.
25. "Quarterly Progress Report: Northwick" (AST 18/68, TNA), October 31, 1955.
26. Warden, Stover Hostel to National Assistance Board (AST 18/39, TNA), July 31, 1963.
27. Warden, Stover to Chief Officer, Polish Hostels (AST 18/39, TNA), August 5, 1949.
28. Celezewski Franciszek to National Assistance Board (AST 18/39, TNA), November 19, 1950.
29. Warden, Mepal Polish Hostel to National Assistance Board (AST 18/39, TNA), November 28, 1950.
30. "Clothing Needs in Hostels" (AST 18/39, TNA), February 22, 1950.
31. W.H. Hart to Ottley (AST 18/39, TNA), February 24, 1950.
32. Warden of Northwick Polish Hostel to J.H.C. Ottley (AST 18/39, TNA), February 24, 1950.
33. Jozef Skrzypiniak to National Assistance Board (AST 18/39, TNA), August 27, 1951.
34. F.A. Cullum to Hostel Warden, Northwick (AST 18/39, TNA), August 15, 1955.
35. W.S. Smethurst to K.R. Stoew (AST 18/121, TNA), May 20, 1964.
36. "Duties of Liaison Assistants" (AST 18/87, TNA), October 1947.
37. "Constitution and Duties of the Residents' Committee" (AST 18/100, TNA), n.d.
38. "Polish Dependents' Hotels—Conduct of Staff, Complaints Regarding" (AST 7/1254, TNA), n.d.
39. Residents' Committee, Mepal Hostel to National Assistance Board (AST 7/1254, TNA), February 26, 1954.
40. George B. Kidd to National Assistance Board (AST 7/1254, TNA), March 12, 1954.
41. Warden, Stover to National Assistance Board, "Mrs. Jozefa Wierszycka, Letter of Complaint" (AST 7/1254, TNA), March 14, 1961.
42. J. Reich to Stover Hostel (AST 7/1254, TNA), February 15, 1961; Petition to Stover Hostel (AST 7/1254, TNA), February 20, 1961.
43. Mrs. Jozefa Wierszycka to National Assistance Board (AST 7/1254, TNA), n.d.
44. N.E. Clarke to W.S. Smethurst (AST 18/121, TNA), May 2, 1966.
45. J.R. Lambie, "General Inspection at Fairford Polish Hostel" (AST 18/67, TNA), November 25, 1949.
46. J.R. Lambie, "General Inspection at the East Moor Polish Hostel" (AST 18/67, TNA), April 17, 1950.

47. "Memorandum to Hostel Wardens and BCAR Representatives" (HO 352/149, TNA), n.d.; "Hungarian Refugees—Discipline" (HO 352/149, TNA), 1957.
48. "Hungarian Refugees—Draft H Code Amendments" (AST 7/1622, TNA), n.d.
49. J. Blake to W.B. Lyon (HO 352/149, TNA), May 6, 1957.
50. Becky Taylor, "Their Only Words of English Were 'Thank You': Rights, Gratitude, and 'Deserving' Hungarian Refugees to Britain in 1956," *Journal of British Studies* 55.1 (January 2016): 120–44.
51. "Hostels for Hungarian Refugees. National Assistance Board Memorandum 994" (AST 7/1621, TNA), n.d.
52. "Crimicar Lane Sanitorium" (HLG 107/5, TNA), December 31, 1956.
53. S.J. Partridge to A.G. Merritt (HLG 107/5, TNA), April 8, 1957.
54. "Hungarian Refugees. Discipline" (HO 352/149, TNA), January 10, 1957.
55. Dorothy Richard, "Reports on Visits to Hostels by WVS" (HO 352/143, TNA), n.d.
56. "Work with the Hampshire Police on Aliens' Registration" (HO 352/145, TNA), 1957.
57. W.B. Lyon to Major Sir John Ferguson (HO 352/145, TNA), February 22, 1957.
58. "Grange Farm Camp" (HO 352/143, TNA), November 21, 1956.
59. "Report on a Visit to Eastwood Hostel" (HO 240/94, TNA), 1957–8.
60. Michael Micaleff to Anglo-Egyptian Resettlement Board (HO 240/95, TNA), n.d.
61. Interview with Lee Allane, July 18, 2014.
62. The official report on these incidents concluded that misunderstandings were inevitable when people of different cultures were brought together in stressful conditions to work out "roles which were not clearly defined and to establish relationships for which it would be hard to find a precedent." S. Barraclough, "Report of Enquiry into the Role of Volunteers at Greenham Common" (HO 289/82, TNA), March 30, 1973.
63. http://www.telegraph.co.uk/news/obituaries/1327382/Brigadier-Geoffrey-Billy-Beyts.html.
64. At Faldingworth, all staff were forbidden to communicate with the press without an administrator's permission. "Faldingworth Resettlement Centre Information Bulletin" (RVS), November 9, 1972.
65. "Report on Greenham and Piddlehinton Centres" (RVS), n.d. (1972?).
66. Interview with Peter Rimmer, June 2, 2017.
67. Thanh, *Catholic with Confucian Tendencies*, p. 142.
68. "Dr. Schenk" (HO 352/145, TNA), January 14, 1957.
69. Roger Hammett, "The BCAR Camp for Vietnamese Refugees, Sopley" (H/ED1/2/210, HALS), November 1979.
70. Colin Hodgetts and Jane Shackman, *First Impressions: Project Leaders with Save the Children Fund Talk about the Reception Programme for Refugees from Vietnam between 1979 and 1983* (London, 1983), p. 11.
71. "Minutes of the Vietnamese Sub-Committee" (Acc 15240, WSRO), April 3, 1980.
72. Edholm et al., *Vietnamese Refugees in Britain*, p. 21.
73. Ashworth, "Who Cares for the Boat People?"
74. *The Times* (London), August 14, 1980.
75. "Minutes of Heads of Section Committees" (Acc 15240, WSRO), June 26, 1980.
76. Suzanne Bang and Rosalind Finlay, *Working to Support Refugees: A Report of a Training Project to Prepare Vietnamese and Chinese Field Staff to Work Amongst their own People Resettled in the United Kingdom* (London, 1982).
77. Bang, *We Come as a Friend*, p. 17.

78. Peter Gatrell, "Trajectories of Population Displacement in the Aftermaths of Two World Wars," in Jessica Reinisch and Elizabeth White, eds., *The Disentanglement of Populations: Migration, Expulsion and Displacement in Post-War Europe, 1944–9* (Basingstoke, 2011), pp. 3–26.
79. Malkki, "Speechless Emissaries."
80. Malkki, "Refugees and Exile," p. 518.
81. On the political protests of Vietnamese refugees at an American refugee camp, see Jana Lipman, "'Give Us a Ship': The Vietnamese Repatriate Movement on Guam, 1975," *American Quarterly* 64 (2012): 1–31.
82. Dorothy Legarreta, *The Guernica Generation: Basque Refugee Children of the Spanish Civil War* (Reno, 1984), p. 125.
83. Williams, *"Jews and other foreigners,"* p. 125.
84. W.S. Craig, "Spanish Children—Eastleigh Camp" (MH 57/322, TNA), May 24, 1937.
85. Cloud, *Basque Children in England*, pp. 26–7.
86. "Spanish Refugee Children," *Hansard's Parliamentary Debates*, HC 335, May 5, 1938.
87. "Suggestions for Press" (HO 213/288, TNA), n.d.
88. Cloud, *Basque Children in England*, p. 36.
89. Cloud, *Basque Children in England*, p. 54.
90. Cloud, *Basque Children in England*, p. 61.
91. "The Fall of Bilbao: Sorrow of Refugee Children," *The Times* (London), June 21, 1937; *New York Times*, June 20, 1937, p. 28.
92. "The Basque Camp, Volume I" (173A12/A4/4/1/3, HALS), July 14, 1937.
93. One colony in West Derby described the Basque boys as "big in build." They did not attend lessons and "just amuse themselves all day." They smoked cigarettes in their beds, and had unexplained amounts of money. They did not try to run away, but only asked for large quantities of olive oil. "West Derby Certified School for Boys" (MH 57/323, TNA), 1937?
94. Williams, *"Jews and other foreigners,"* p. 119.
95. Kevin Myers, "The Ambiguities of Aid and Agency: Representing Refugee Children in England, 1937–8," *Cultural and Social History* 6.1 (2009): 29–46.
96. M.A. Quinlan, "Basque Children at Wattermillock" (MH 57/323, TNA), June 17, 1937.
97. "The Basque Camp, Volume I" ((173A12/A4/4/1/3, HALS), June 25, 1937.
98. "The Basque Camp, Volume I" (173A12/A4/4/1/3, HALS), July 13, 1937.
99. "Basque Children at Hexham" (MH 57/323, TNA), 1937?
100. Cloud, *Basque Children in England*, p. 32.
101. "Basque Children at Burmaston House, Etwall, Derby" (MH 57/323, TNA), August 16, 1937.
102. "Basque Girls Rebel," *South London Press*, October 14, 1937; "Basque Children at Manningham Lane, Bradford, Yorks." (MH 57/323, TNA), October 11, 1937.
103. E.G. Colles, "Arrangements for Basque Children" (MH 57/323, TNA), June 8, 1937.
104. *Western Mail and South Wales News*, July 24, 1937.
105. "Basque Children in Britain," *The Times* (London), August 13, 1937.
106. Davies, *Fleeing Franco*, pp. 71–2.
107. Davies, *Fleeing Franco*, p. 79.
108. "Spanish Refugees (Basque Children)," *Hansard's Parliamentary Debates*, HC 326, July 28, 1937.
109. Interview with Erich Duschinsky (C526/21/01, BLSA), 1988.

110. Pozo-Gutiérrez and Broomfield, "*Here, look after him*," p. 65.
111. "Polish Resettlement Bill. General Note by the Treasury" (AST 18/9, TNA), n.d.
112. Cohen, *In War's Wake*, p. 158.
113. F.F. Turnbill, "Hungarian Refugees" (T 225/875, TNA), December 10, 1956.
114. "Crookham Camp" (HO 352/145, TNA), n.d.
115. See, e.g., G.P. Pratt to Critchley (HO 289/50, TNA), December 5, 1972.
116. Bussy, "Maresfield" (HO 289/50, TNA), n.d. 1972.
117. "Uncooperative Residents" (HO 289/50, TNA), December 1972.
118. Sir Richard Turnbull, "Trouble-Makers" (HO 289/50, TNA), November 16, 1972.
119. Mamdani, *From Citizen to Refugee*, p. 103.
120. Thomas and Mak, "Social Work and the Boat People."
121. Daphne M.F. Byrne, Vietnamese Centre Records, Thorney Island (Acc 15240, WSRO), 1995.
122. "Minutes of Heads of Section Committees" (Acc 15240, WSRO), June 26, 1980 and May 28, 1981.
123. "Minutes of Heads of Section Committees" (Acc 15240, WSRO), November 14, 1979.
124. "Penalty for Not Taking Part in the communal Life of Thorney Island. Minutes of the Vietnamese Sub-Committee" (Acc 15240, WSRO), June 24, 1981.
125. "Minutes of the Vietnamese Committee" (Acc 15240, WSRO), January 2, 1981.
126. "Minutes of the Vietnamese Committee" (Acc 15240, WSRO), April 1, 1980.
127. Ashworth, "Who Cares for the Boat People?"
128. "Minutes of the Vietnamese Committee" (Acc 15240, WSRO), February 5, 1980 and March 6, 1980.
129. "A Code of Thorney Island Centre" (Acc 15240, WSRO), n.d.
130. Vu Khanh Thanh to Arrowsmith (Acc 15240, WSRO), April 3, 1980.
131. Vu Khanh Thanh to Major Arrowsmith (Acc 15240, WSRO), June 5, 1980.
132. Joya Chatterji, "'Dispersal' and the Failure of Rehabilitation: Refugee Camp-dwellers and Squatters in West Bengal," *Modern Asian Studies* 41.5 (2007): 995–1032.
133. Greg Robinson, *After Camp: Portraits in Midcentury Japanese American Life and Politics* (Berkeley, 2012); Ellen Wu, *The Color of Success: Asian Americans and the Origins of the Model Minority* (Princeton, 2014).
134. Wu, *The Color of Success*.
135. Robinson, *After Camp*.
136. Brett Bebber, "'We Were Just Unwanted': Bussing, Migrant Dispersal, and South Asians in London," *Journal of Social History* 48.3 (Spring 2015): 635–51.
137. Jacqueline Jenkinson, "Soon Gone, Long Forgotten: Uncovering British Responses to Belgian Refugees During the First World War," *Immigrants and Minorities* 34.2 (2016): 101–12.
138. Sir H.C. Monro, "Belgian Refugees on East Coast" (HO 45/10737/261921, TNA), October 21, 1914.
139. Tydor Baumel-Schwartz, *Never Look Back*, p. 119.
140. Bell, *Only for Three Months*.
141. Vaughan Robinson, Roger Andersson, and Sako Musterd, *Spreading the "Burden"? A Review of Policies to Disperse Asylum Seekers and Refugees* (Bristol: Policy Press, 2003), p. 109.
142. *Manchester Guardian*, November 26, 1946, p. 8.
143. "Polish Resettlement Bill," *Hansard's Parliamentary Debates*, HC 433, February 12, 1947.

144. Johannes-Dieter Steinart, "British Post-War Migration Policy and Displaced Persons in Europe," in Jessica Reinisch and Elizabeth White, eds., *The Disentanglement of Populations: Migration, Expulsion and Displacement in Post-War Europe, 1944–9* (Basingstoke, 2011), pp. 229–47.
145. The Ministry of Labour planned to disperse Hungarian refugees as widely as possible, and advocated the use of smaller camps and hostels to ease the transition to dispersed resettlement. "Accommodation and Staffing in Hostels" (HO 352/143, TNA), n.d.
146. Alice Bloch and Liza Schuster, "At the Extremes of Exclusion: Deportation, Detention, and Dispersal," *Ethnic and Racial Studies* 28.3 (2005): 491–512.
147. "Draft. Voluntary Dispersal of Commonwealth Immigrants" (HO 376/41, TNA), April 22, 1969.
148. "Dispersal of Commonwealth Immigrants" (HO 376/41, TNA), 1968.
149. "Draft. Information Relevant to Dispersal" (HO 376/41, TNA), 1969.
150. J.T.A. Howard-Drake to Morrison (HO 376/41, TNA), April 24, 1969.
151. "Dispersal of Immigrants" (HO 376/41, TNA), n.d.
152. "Voluntary Dispersal of Commonwealth Immigrants. Headings for a Paper by the Working Party" (HO 376/41, TNA), May 9, 1969.
153. Patrick Cosgrave to Lord Windlesham (HO 376/41, TNA), July 7, 1970.
154. "Dispersal of Immigrants" (HO 376/41, TNA), n.d.; John Barr, "New Towns as Anti-Ghettoes?" *New Society* 5 (April 1, 1965): 5–6; Nicholas Deakin and Clare Ungerson, *Leaving London: Planned Mobility and the Inner City* (London, 1977).
155. "Movement of Coloured Immigrants to New Towns, Analysis of Chairman's Replies to Minister's Letter of 31st July 1970" (HLG 116/492, TNA), 1970. Many thanks to Milla Schofield for bringing this file to my attention, and sharing her digital copies of the file.
156. Cunningham, "The Work of the Uganda Resettlement Board."
157. *Refuge or Home?*, p. 51.
158. "Preparing for the Ugandan Asians," *Observer*, August 20, 1972.
159. Mike Bristow, "Britain's Response to the Ugandan Asian Crisis: Government Myths versus Political and Resettlement Realities," *Journal of Ethnic and Migration Studies* 5.3 (1976): 265–79.
160. "Ugandan Asians," *Hansard's Parliamentary Debates*, HL 337, December 6, 1972.
161. *The Times* (London), September 2, 1972.
162. *The Times* (London), October 2, 1972.
163. *The Times* (London), September 15, 1972.
164. Mike Bristow and Bert N. Adams, "Ugandan Asians and the Housing Market in Britain," *New Community* 6 (1977): 65–77.
165. "UK Passport Holders in Uganda. Confidential" (BD 65/46, TNA), n.d.
166. S.T. Charles to O.H. Morris (BD 65/46, TNA), August 15, 1972.
167. J.H. Waddell, "Confidential. UK Passport Holders: Contingency Planning" (BD 65/46, TNA), August 10, 1972.
168. S.T. Charles to O.H. Morris (BD 65/46, TNA), August 15, 1972.
169. "Ugandan Asians," *Hansard's Parliamentary Debates*, HC 847, December 6, 1972.
170. *The Times* (London), October 20, 1972.
171. Interview with Chandrika Joshi, July 24, 2017.
172. Kushner and Knox, *Refugees in an Age of Genocide*.
173. Robinson, *Transients*, p. 45.
174. D.W. Plampling to J.N. Pearson (HLG 118/2138/2, TNA), February 2, 1977.

175. "Contingency Planning for the Reception and Resettlement of Refugees and Other Emergency Influxes in the UK" (HLG 118/2138/2, TNA), n.d.
176. Thomas, "Where Have All the Refugees Gone?"
177. Paul Rushton, "Request to the City of Southampton" and "The Present Situation in Great Britain" (H/ED1/4B/5, File 2, HALS), n.d.
178. Felicity Somerset, "Vietnamese Refugees in Britain: Resettlement Experiences," *Journal of Ethnic and Migration Studies* 10.3 (1983): 454–63. By this point, refugee workers in the United States—who had witnessed the failures of Indo-Chinese dispersal—had begun to recommend larger clusters of several hundred people. Julia Vadala Taft, David S. North, and David A. Ford, *Refugee Resettlement in the U.S.: Time for a New Focus* (Washington, DC, 1979), pp. 23 and 89.
179. Thanh, *Catholic with Confucian Tendencies*, p. 146.
180. A.M. Agathangelous, "Vietnamese Refugee Reception and Resettlement, 1979–1988" (EV/QU40.5 RCA, Box 1, Refugee Council Archives, University of East London, London), 1989.
181. "Anchored in London: The Long Journey of Lambeth's Vietnamese Refugees," https://www.youtube.com/watch?v=v16zmFZWT-Y.
182. Interview with Sue Millman, June 17, 2017.
183. Interview with Colin Hodgetts, June 12, 2017.
184. BBC TV South, "The Boat People" (AV18/157/V1, HALS), 1990.
185. Diken and Laustsen, *The Culture of Exception*, p. 87.
186. *Independent*, February 13, 2017.
187. *The Times* (London), August 16, 1918.
188. R. Reynolds Garrett to C.F. Roundell (MH 57/323, TNA), June 24 and 26, 1937.
189. W.S., "Confidential. Spanish Refugee Children—Eastleigh Camp" (MSS 308/3/N5/4i, MRC), n.d.
190. Ernest R. Cockburn to Johnson (MH 57/322, TNA), May 31, 1937.
191. Lilian Smith, "An Unofficial Report on the Camp" (MSS 308/3/N5/44i, MRC), n.d.
192. May, "Reception," p. 66.
193. "Basque Children's Camps," *The Times* (London), August 11, 1937.
194. Robert Bernays to Eustace Percy (MH 57/323, TNA), June 23, 1937.
195. On the long life of the Polish camps, see the Epilogue.
196. "Notes of a Meeting on 25th February 1957 to discuss action to be taken against uncooperative residents" (HO 352/149, TNA), 1957.
197. "Polish Housing Estate. Great Bower Wood" (TS 51/3, TNA), 1955–6.
198. W.W. Alison, "Minute" (AST 18/53, TNA), January 12, 1949.
199. "Polish Camps and Hostels Circular (No. 4. Evictions from Hostels. General" (PIN 31/7, TNA), 1949.
200. "Northwick Park" (AST 18/68, TNA), February 3, 1955.
201. H.W. Hart, "Audit Report" (AST 18/68, TNA), November 1958.
202. "Polish Dependents Hostels: Admission and Re-admission Policy" (AST 18/50, TNA), August 1947.
203. "Polish Dependents Hostels: Eviction" (AST 18/53, TNA), n.d.
204. National Assistance Board, "Memorandum No. 600. Polish Hostels: Applications for Admission and Unauthorized Entrants" (AST 18/50, TNA), February 3, 1950.
205. "Quarterly Progress Report: Northwick" (AST 18/68, TNA), July 9 and 16, 1964 and October 7, 1964.
206. "Conversion of Northwick Polish Hostel" (AST 18/114, TNA), October 26, 1959.

207. "Closure of Northwick. Report on a Visit 21/23 March 1968" (AST 8/124, TNA), 1968.
208. W. Hartman to National Assistance Board (AST 7/1255, TNA), April 22, 1955.
209. C.W. Berry to Warden, Northwick Hostel (AST 7/1255, TNA), May 21, 1955. Similarly, see J. Kupferblum to National Assistance Board (AST 18/114, TNA), October 20, 1959.
210. "Resettlement Grants" (HO 240/37, TNA), May 22, 1958.
211. Robert Gautier, "Anglo-Egyptian Resettlement Board" (HO 240/36, TNA), June 11, 1958.
212. "Re: John Abela and His Family" (HO 240/36, TNA), n.d.
213. "Functions of the Board. Residual Cases in Which Resettlement Cannot be Effected by the Board" (HO 240/6, TNA), 1959–60.
214. "Hungarian Refugees" (HO 352/143, TNA), November 28, 1956.
215. BCAR, "Hungarian Refugees" (HLG 107/5, TNA), n.d.
216. Albert Vajda, *Remade in England: From Her Majesty's Alien to Her Majesty's Loyal Subject* (Edinburgh, 1981), p. 14.
217. Vajda, *Remade in England*, pp. 16–17 and 20.
218. "Hungarian Refugees" (HLG 107/5, TNA), n.d.
219. "Refugees," *Hansard's Parliamentary Debates*, HC 566, March 8, 1957.
220. "Uganda Asian Reception and Resettlement" (HO 289/95, TNA), 1974.
221. A.J. Rutherford, "Resettlement" (HO 289/64, TNA), November 13, 1972.
222. Interview with Chotalal Mohan Vadhia (C900/00003, BLSA), 1998.
223. Securicor was also contracted to run a smaller facility at Manchester Airport. Christine Bacon, "The Evolution of Immigration Detention in the United Kingdom: The Involvement of Private Prison Companies," RSC Working Paper No. 27, 2005.
224. J.H. Waddell, "Confidential. UK Passport Holders: Contingency Planning" (BD 65/46, TNA), August 10, 1972.
225. ACC/1888/205, LMA, October 16, 1972.
226. "Immigration Control: E.E.C. and Commonwealth Citizens," *Hansard's Parliamentary Debates*, HL 337, December 6, 1972.
227. Mrs. Turner to Brigadier Beyts (HO 289/41, TNA), December 5, 1972.
228. *Observer*, October 29, 1972, p. 2.
229. Bristow and Adams, "Ugandan Asians."
230. "Asian Refugees Reach First Base," *Guardian*, September 19, 1972.
231. Interview with Chotalal Vadhia Mohan (C900/00003, BLSA), 1998.
232. *The Times*, November 8, 1972.
233. *Daily Telegraph*, November 4, 1972.
234. Markham and Kingston, *Merely a Matter of Colour*, p. 34.
235. Mamdani, *From Citizen to Refugee*, p. 96.
236. The press coverage was largely negative, accusing the Ugandan Asians of ingratitude. See, e.g., "Angry Asians Refuse to Move Camp," *Guardian*, December 22, 1972.
237. Peter Hellyer, "Hobbs Barracks" (CC26/1, Surrey History Centre), n.d.
238. Hellyer, "Hobbs Barracks."
239. "Hobbs Barracks Report" (CC26/1, Surrey History Centre), December 12, 1972.
240. "Asian Resettlement Camp—Hobbs Barracks, Lingfield" (RVS), n.d.
241. Ockenden Files, 7155/7/3/18, Surrey History Centre, n.d.
242. *Guardian*, October 12, 1979.
243. Nora Morley Fletcher to Mike Laloe (BS 18/28, TNA), March 12, 1981.
244. "Minutes of the Heads of Section Committees" (Acc 15240, WSRO), June 11, 1980.

245. Daphne M.F. Byrne, Vietnamese Centre Records, Thorney Island (Acc 15240, WSRO), 1995. Daphne Byrne and Heather Lewis, "Emsworth Memories" (AV 637/63/51, HALS), 2007.
246. Edholm et al., *Vietnamese Refugees in Britain*, p. 34.
247. Janmyr, *Protecting Civilians in Refugee Camps*, p. 113.

NOTES TO EPILOGUE

1. Jenkinson, "Soon Gone, Long Forgotten."
2. Kushner, "Local Heroes."
3. *Report on the Work Undertaken by the British Government in the Reception and Care of the Belgian Refugees* (London, 1920).
4. Wilson, *They Came as Strangers*, p. 215; Cahalan, *Belgian Refugee Relief*, p. 3.
5. Oliver Marshall, *Ship of Hope* (London, 1991).
6. Bell, *Only for Three Months*.
7. *Daily Herald*, January 8, 1938.
8. *Manchester Guardian*, January 8, 1938.
9. Pozo-Gutiérrez and Broomfield, *"Here, look after him,"* p. 98.
10. Pozo-Gutiérrez and Broomfield, *"Here, look after him,"* p. 102.
11. Susana Sabín-Fernández, "The Basque Refugee Children of the Spanish Civil War in the UK: Memory and Memorialisation," Ph.D. Thesis, University of Southampton, 2010.
12. Turner, ... *And the Policeman Smiled*, p. 68.
13. Turner, ... *And the Policeman Smiled*, p. 264.
14. Saville, *Only a Kindertransportee*, p. 43.
15. Interview with Klaus Ernst Hinrichsen (IWM 3789), June 1978.
16. Ungerson, *Four Thousand Lives*.
17. At the peak of the Board's involvement with Polish hostels in 1948, they cost £1,450,000; in 1958, only £64,000. "Memorandum 1051. Polish Hostels" (AST 18/114, TNA), February 20, 1959.
18. "Memorandum 1051. Polish Hostels" (AST 18/114, TNA), February 20, 1959.
19. http://www.tweedsmuirmilitarycamp.co.uk/ch5.html.
20. Biegus and Biegus, *Polish Resettlement Camps*, p. 96.
21. Szulakowska, "Life at Melton Mowbray."
22. *Dziennik Polski*, April 27, 1953.
23. "Report on a Visit to Ilford Park, Stover" (AST 18/125, TNA), 1965.
24. *Dziennik Polski*, October 12, 1964.
25. https://www.gov.uk/government/publications/ilford-park-polish-home/ilford-park-polish-home.
26. Robert Sparke, "Still Happy After 20 Years in Huts," *Independent*, June 3, 1966.
27. "Polish Dependents Hostel—Ilford Park—Stover" (AST 18/126, TNA), 1966.
28. Charlotte Greenhalgh, "An Age of Emotion: Expertise and Subjectivity in Old Age in Britain, 1937–1970," Ph.D. Thesis, Oxford University, 2012.
29. The Supplementary Benefits Commission replaced the National Assistance Board in 1966.
30. "Ilford Park" (AST 18/127, TNA), August 5, 1968.
31. Peter Townsend, *The Last Refuge: A Survey of Residential Institutions and Homes for the Aged in England and Wales* (London, 1962), p. 148.

32. R.J. Raymont, "Ilford Park Polish Home—Visit on 21 Sept 81" (AST 18/117, TNA), November 6, 1981.
33. Ursula Brennan, "The Future of Ilford Park Polish Home" (AST 18/117, TNA), n.d.
34. "SDG Visit to Ilford Park Polish Home" (AST 18/131, TNA), March 15, 1982.
35. "Ilford Park Polish Home" (AST 18/133, TNA), n.d.
36. "Refugee Camp's Future 'Safe,'" *Herald Express*, September 13, 1985.
37. Hilary Kingsley, "Up the Poles," *Daily Mirror*, June 18, 1986.
38. M.T. Benford to T.G. Roberts (AST 18/138, TNA), October 5, 1987.
39. F.W. Kearns, "Admission to Ilford Park Polish Home: Mr. and Mrs. SG Zosz-Zuchowski" (AST 18/138, TNA), May 15, 1985.
40. Jane St. Keverne to Mr. Kearns (AST 18/138, TNA), June 25, 1985.
41. "Report on a Visit to Ilford Park, Stover on 10 February 1965" (AST 18/125, TNA), 1965.
42. "Polish Problem," *Herald Express*, January 29, 1982.
43. Jim G. Lee to R.M. Orton (AST 18/130, TNA), January 23, 1981.
44. Marie Denham, "The Future of Ilford Park Polish Home" (AST 18/130, TNA), February 24, 1982.
45. Walter Jagucki, "The Polish Experience: Forty Years On," in Ron Baker, ed., *The Psychosocial Problems of Refugees* (London, 1983), pp. 32–8.
46. Hansen, "Sympathy."
47. "SDG Visit to Ilford Park Polish Home" (AST 18/131, TNA), March 15, 1982.
48. *Guardian*, November 12, 1990, p. 6.
49. "Business of the House," *Hansard's Parliamentary Debates*, HC 170, April 19, 1990.
50. Levin, *What Welcome?*
51. Taylor, "Their Only Words of English Were 'Thank You.'"
52. S.J. Dibble to S.E. Finer (HO 240/86, TNA), August 13, 1958.
53. Rukshana Smith, *Sumitra's Story* (New York, 1982), p. 26.
54. Marett, *Immigrants*, p. 79.
55. "Ugandan Asians," *Hansard's Parliamentary Debates*, HC 855, May 4, 1973.
56. *Uganda Resettlement Board News Bulletin* 5 (ACC/1888/200, LMA, London).
57. *Uganda Resettlement Board News Bulletin* 5 (5380/1/8, Surrey History Centre).
58. Quoted in http://www.asiansfromuganda.org.uk/uganda_asian_interlude.php.
59. *Uganda Resettlement Board News Bulletin* 8 (5380/1/8, Surrey History Centre).
60. *Uganda Resettlement Board News Bulletin* 5 (5380/1/8, Surrey History Centre).
61. Mamdani, *From Citizen to Refugee*, p. 102.
62. J. Romijn to Sir Charles Cunningham (ACC 1888/201, LMA), December 16, 1973.
63. Mr. Trivedi to Uganda Resettlement Board (HO 289/76, TNA), May 7, 1973.
64. Nicholas Brown, "A Survey of Ugandan Asian Families Resettled in Scotland" (ACC 1888/204, LMA), July–August 1973.
65. CCWEU (Father Romijn, Liaison Officer), "Situation in the Camp" (ACC 1888/201, LMA), December 13, 1973.
66. Champak Ganatra to Molly (ACC 1888/204, LMA), November 23, 1972.
67. Pam Schweitzer, ed., *A Place to Stay: Memories of Pensioners from Many Lands* (London, 1984), p. 46.
68. London Council of Social Service, *London's Response to Uganda Asians: Implications for Social Services Arising Out of LCSS's Work with Disadvantaged Uganda Asians in London* (London, 1978).
69. Bert N. Adams and Victor Jesudason, "The Employment of Ugandan Asian Refugees in Britain, India, and Canada," *Ethnic and Racial Studies* 7 (1984): 462–77.

70. Brian Jackson and Barrie Knight, "As the Camps Close: Prospects for a Continuing Commitment to the Needs of Refugees in Britain" (ACC 1888/200, LMA), July 1973.

71. Romijn, *Tabu*.

72. "The Uganda Asians: The Reality of Resettlement" (ACC 1888/205, LMA), n.d.

73. *Uganda Resettlement Board News Bulletin* 4 (ACC 1888/200, LMA).

74. Mike McCart, "Wandsworth: Unsettled Ugandan Refugees," *Journal of Ethnic and Migration Studies* 2 (1973): 383–6.

75. Pamela Clifford to J.H. Aldam (H/ED1/2/210, HALS), March 21, 1981.

76. *Observer*, September 12, 1982.

77. Pamela Clifford to J.H. Aldam (H/ED1/2/210, HALS), August 4, 1982.

78. Gordon Griffiths, "General and Educational Notes in the Background of Vietnamese Refugees" (H/ED1/4B/5, File 1, HALS), n.d.

79. "Proposed Project on ESL for Vietnamese Refugees" (H/ED1/4B/5, File 2, HALS), n.d.

80. Pamela Clifford to J.H. Aldam (H/ED1/2/210, HALS), September 20, 1982.

81. Andrew Cunliffe, "The Refugee Crisis: A Study of the United Nations High Commission for Refugees," *Political Studies* 43.2 (June 1995): 278–90.

82. "Ex-Polish Hostel—Cirencester Gloucester Road—Proposed Detention Centre" (DA 4/140/87, Gloucestershire Archives, Gloucester), January 31, 1962.

83. "Daglingworth" (DA 4/140/87, Gloucestershire Archives, Gloucester), n.d.

84. Eric Lewis Higgins, "Proposed Detention Centre, Daglingworth" (DA 4/140/87, Gloucestershire Archives, Gloucester), n.d.

85. Eric L. Higgins to W.E. Lloyd (DA 4/140/87, Gloucestershire Archives, Gloucester), January 16, 1961.

86. *Dziennik Polski*, January 26, 1949, p. 3.

87. "Final Report on Hungarian Hostels. National Assistance Board Memorandum 1078" (AST 7/1621, TNA), October 23, 1959; "Resettlement Grants" (HO 240/37, TNA), May 8, 1958.

88. H.L. Evans to Mrs. D. Balsom (HO 240/51, TNA), March 17, 1959; *Observer*, March 12, 1959.

89. "Commonwealth Immigrants Bill," *Hansard's Parliamentary Debates*, HL 238, March 12, 1962.

90. "Ugandan Asian Resettlement Camps," *Hansard's Parliamentary Debates*, HC 846, November 23, 1972.

91. Bristol Quaker Co-ordinating Committee for Evacuees, "Resettlement."

92. "Ugandan Asians' Accommodation," *Hansard's Parliamentary Debates*, HL 352, June 10, 1974.

93. "Ugandan Asian Resettlement Camps," *Hansard's Parliamentary Debates*, HC 855, April 30, 1973.

94. "Housing," *Hansard's Parliamentary Debates*, HC 893, June 16, 1975.

95. Piddlehinton was ultimately converted to an industrial estate; it is no longer open to the public. Over massive local objections, the site has also become a temporary home for travelers; http://www.bournemouthecho.co.uk/news/11211235.Travellers__site_proposed_for_village__like_a_concentration_camp__says_Gypsy_Council/.

96. "Resettlement Centres" (HO 289/93, TNA), March 19, 1973.

97. Cynthia Enloe, *Bananas, Beaches, and Bases: Making Feminist Sense of International Politics* (Berkeley, 2014), p. 170.

98. Enloe, *Bananas, Beaches, and Bases*, p. 172.

99. John Kippin, *Cold War Pastoral: Greenham Common* (London, 2001).

100. "Standing Conference of British Organizations for Aid to Refugees" (HO 376/209, TNA), October 1975.
101. R.A. Birch to G.P. Renton (HO 376/204, TNA), December 2, 1975.
102. "Confidential. Refugee Contingency Planning" (HLG 118/2138/2, TNA), November 21, 1975.
103. "Refugee Contingency Planning" (HO 376/207, TNA), November 21, 1975.
104. "Amendment of the Law," *Hansard's Parliamentary Debates*, HC 890, April 15, 1975.
105. Betty Kellar, "Nissen Hut Was Home for Two Years," *Western Morning News*, June 10, 2008, p. 10.
106. Kushner, *Battle of Britishness*; Williams, *"Jews and other foreigners."*
107. *New York Times*, May 4, 2016. On applying the lessons of the Ugandan Asians to the "jungle" at Calais, see http://www.ibtimes.co.uk/calais-crisis-what-david-cameron-can-learn-edward-heath-britains-ugandan-asians-1514044.
108. Mimi Thi Nguyen, *The Gift of Freedom: War, Debt, and Other Refugee Passages* (Durham, NC, and London, 2012), p. 29.
109. See also the plaque at Stansted Airport that commemorates the arrival of the Ugandan Asians.
110. May, "Reception."
111. Sabín-Fernández, "The Basque Refugee Children of the Spanish Civil War in the UK"; Pozo-Gutiérrez and Broomfield, *"Here, look after him."*
112. http://www.northwickparkpolishdpcamp.co.uk/northwick14.htm.
113. For one example of this nostalgic "camp tourism," see http://www.polishresettle-mentcampsintheuk.co.uk/springhill05.htm.
114. Janowski, "Memories."
115. Parmar, "Memorialising 40 Years."
116. See, e.g., http://www.newburytoday.co.uk/news/news/3670/Former-refugee-marks-40th-anniversary-of.html; http://www.bbc.com/news/uk-england-berkshire-20641636; http://www.soas.ac.uk/news/newsitem91636.html. The Exiles Project, organized in London by Sunil Shah, traced the lives of Ugandan Asians before and after their arrival in Britain.
117. Edgar Taylor, "The Asian Expulsion and Cultural Intimacy in Contemporary Uganda," Paper delivered at the American Historical Association, Washington, DC, January 2014.
118. Margaret Frenz, "Migration, Identity and Post-Colonial Change in Uganda: A Goan Perspective," *Immigrants and Minorities* 31.1 (2013): 48–73.
119. Frenz, "Migration, Identity, and Post-Colonial Change in Uganda."
120. Fassin, "Introduction: Governing Precarity," in Fassin et al., *At the Heart of the State*, p. 9.
121. Rita Chin, *The Crisis of Multiculturalism in Europe: A History* (Princeton, 2017); see also Buettner, "Going for an Indian"; David Feldman, "Why the English Like Turbans: Multicultural Politics in British History," in David Feldman and Jon Lawrence, eds., *Structures and Transformations in Modern British History* (Cambridge, 2011), pp. 281–302.
122. http://www.unhcr.org/pages/49c3646c137.html.
123. Gibney, *The Ethics and Politics of Asylum*, p. 10.
124. Gibney, *The Ethics and Politics of Asylum*, p. 3.
125. Carolina Kobelinsky, "In Search of Truth: How Asylum Applications are Adjudicated," in Didier Fassin et al., *At the Heart of the State: The Moral World of Institutions* (London, 2015), pp. 67–89.

126. Gibney, *Ethics and Politics of Asylum*, p. 3.

127. Didier Fassin and Richard Rechtman, *The Empire of Trauma: An Inquiry into the Condition of Victimhood* (Princeton, 2009), p. 273.

128. Gibney, *Ethics and Politics of Asylum*, p. 123.

129. Gibney, *Ethics and Politics of Asylum*, p. 107.

130. Jeremy Harding, "The Uninvited," *London Review of Books* 22.3 (February 3, 2000): 3–25.

131. A. Naomi Paik, "Carceral Quarantine at Guantánamo: Legacies of U.S. Imprisonment of Haitian Refugees, 1991–1994," *Radical History Review* 115 (Winter 2013): 142–68.

132. Ruben Andersson, *Illegality, Inc.: Clandestine Migration and the Business of Bordering Europe* (Berkeley, 2014).

133. Bloch and Schuster, "At the Extremes of Exclusion."

134. Andrew Burridge and Nick Gill, "Conveyor-Belt Justice: Precarity, Access to Justice, and Uneven Geographies of Legal Aid in UK Asylum Appeals," *Antipode* 49.1 (2017): 23–42.

135. Tony Kushner, "Meaning Nothing But Good: Ethics, History, and Asylum-Seeker Phobia in Britain," *Patterns of Prejudice* 37.3 (2003): 257–76.

136. Diken and Laustsen, *The Culture of Exception*, p. 90.

137. As a point of comparison, the total prison population of England in 2015 was 94,889. https://www.globaldetentionproject.org/countries/europe/united-kingdom.

138. http://www.migrationobservatory.ox.ac.uk/resources/briefings/immigration-detention-in-the-uk/.

139. Agier, *Managing the Undesirables*, p. 3. Similarly, see A. Naomi Paik, *Rightlessness: Testimony and Redress in U.S. Prison Camps since World War Two* (Chapel Hill, 2016).

140. Arendt, *The Origins of Totalitarianism*, pp. 288–9.

141. "Rhodesia: Evacuation Planning for British Citizens" (FCO 36/2280, TNA), n.d.

142. "Refugees from Rhodesia: Contingency Planning" (FCO 36/2282, TNA), 1978.

143. C.W. Fogarty to P.J. Woodfield (FCO 36/2283, TNA), August 24, 1978.

144. Mrs. Hart, "Rhodesia: Plans for Possible Evacuation" (FCO 36/2283, TNA), September 28, 1978.

145. P.J. Barlow to P.R. Burleigh (FCO 36/2284, TNA), October 19, 1978.

146. A.D. Watts, "Rhodesian 'Refugees' in the UK" (FCO 36/2590, TNA), May 9, 1979.

147. R.J. Spencer, "Confidential. Considerations: Refugee Status" (FCO 36/2590, TNA), March 8, 1979.

148. John Darwin, "Orphans of Empire," in Robert Bickers, ed., *Settlers and Expatriates: Britons Over the Seas* (Oxford, 2010), pp. 329–45; see also Luise White, *Unpopular Sovereignty: Rhodesian Independence and African Decolonization* (Chicago, 2015).

149. Martin Thomas, *Fight or Flight: Britain, France, and their Roads from Empire* (Oxford, 2014), p. 343.

150. P.J. Barlow to Mr. Jones (FCO 36/2284, TNA), November 9, 1978.

151. "Rhodesia: Composition of the European Population" (FCO 36/2284, TNA), October 16, 1978.

152. P.J. Barlow to G.P. Renton (HGL 118/2136, TNA), May 20, 1976.

153. "Refugees from Rhodesia. Practicality of Maximum Dispersal" (HLG 118/2136, TNA), June 6, 1976.

154. "Refugees from Rhodesia: Social and Occupational Status" (HO 376/218, TNA), June 8, 1976.

155. Roy Jenkins, "Refugees from Rhodesia" (OD 66/50, TNA), April 2, 1976.

156. T.L. Holmes, "Refugees from Rhodesia" (HLG 118/3314, TNA), August 25, 1978.
157. T.L. Jones to Geoffrey de Deney (FCO 36/2285, TNA), December 22, 1978.
158. Geoffrey de Deney to J.C. O'Neill (FJ 2/374, TNA), July 31, 1979.
159. B.O. Bassett to G.P. Renton (HO 376/216, TNA), December 9, 1976.
160. On the role of wartime memories in the charged racial politics of the 1970s and 1980s, see Schofield, *Enoch Powell*.
161. Mrs. Winifred E. Curtis to M. Heseltine (HLG 118/3314, TNA), March 5, 1980.

Bibliography

ARCHIVES CONSULTED

British Library Sound Archive, London (BLSA)
Cadbury Research Library, Birmingham
Gloucestershire Archives
Hampshire Archives and Local Studies (HALS)
Imperial War Museum, London (IWM)
Institute of Contemporary History and Wiener Library, London
London Metropolitan Archives (LMA)
Modern Records Centre, University of Warwick (MRC)
National Archives, Kew (TNA)
National Archives and Records Administration, College Park, Maryland (NARA)
Refugee Council Archives, University of East London
Royal Voluntary Service Archive and Heritage Collection (RVS)
Somerset Heritage Centre
Surrey History Centre
West Sussex Record Office (WSRO)

WORKS CITED

Adams, Bert N. and Victor Jesudason. "The Employment of Ugandan Asian Refugees in Britain, India, and Canada," *Ethnic and Racial Studies* 7 (1984): 462–77.
Agamben, Giorgio. "The Camp as the 'Nomos' of the Modern." In *Homo Sacer: Sovereign Power and Bare Life* (Stanford: Stanford University Press, 1998), 166–80.
Agier, Michel. *Managing the Undesirables: Refugee Camps and Humanitarian Government* (Cambridge: Polity, 2011).
Agier. Michel. "Afterword: What Contemporary Camps Tell Us About the World To Come." *Humanity* 7.3 (2016): 459–68.
Agier, Michel, Richard Nice, and Loïc Wacquant. "Between War and City: Towards an Urban Anthropology of Refugee Camps." *Ethnography* 3.3 (2002): 317–41.
Ahmed, Sara. *The Promise of Happiness* (Durham, NC: Duke University Press, 2010).
Aiyar, Sana. "Anticolonial Homelands Across the Indian Ocean: The Politics of the Indian Diaspora in Kenya, ca. 1930–1950," *American Historical Review* 116.4 (2011): 987–1013.
Alibhai-Brown, Yasmin. *No Place Like Home: An Autobiography* (London: Virago, 1995).
Andersson, Ruben. *Illegality, Inc.: Clandestine Migration and the Business of Bordering Europe* (Berkeley: University of California Press, 2014).
Anderton, Michael. "Social Space and Social Control: Analysing Movement and Management on Modern Military Sites." In *Matériel Culture: The Archaeology of Twentieth-Century Conflict*, edited by John Schofield et al. (London: Routledge, 2002), 189–97.
Arendt, Hannah. *The Origins of Totalitarianism* (New York: Harvest, 1968).
Arnold, David. "European Orphans and Vagrants in India in the 19th Century," *Journal of Imperial and Commonwealth History* 7.2 (1979): 104–27.
Ashworth, Georgina. "Who Cares for the Boat People?" *Voluntary Action* (December 1979): 15–16.

Bacon, Christine. "The Evolution of Immigration Detention in the United Kingdom: The Involvement of Private Prison Companies," RSC Working Paper No. 27, 2005.

Bailkin, Jordanna. *The Afterlife of Empire* (Berkeley: University of California Press, 2012).

Bald, Vivek. *Bengali Harlem and the Lost Histories of South Asian America* (Cambridge, MA: Harvard University Press, 2013).

Balint, Ruth. "Children Left Behind: Family, Refugees and Immigration in Postwar Europe," *History Workshop Journal* 82 (2016): 151–72.

Ballinger, Pamela. "Entangled or 'Extruded' Histories? Displacement, National Refugees, and Repatriation after the Second World War," *Journal of Refugee Studies* 25.3 (2012): 366–86.

Bang, Suzanne. *We Come as a Friend: Towards a Vietnamese Model of Social Work* (Derby: Refugee Action, 1983).

Bang, Suzanne and Rosalind Finlay. *Working to Support Refugees: A Report of a Training Project to Prepare Vietnamese and Chinese Field Staff to Work Amongst their own People Resettled in the United Kingdom* (London: Save the Children Fund and Refugee Action, 1982).

Barnett, Michael. *Empire of Humanity: A History of Humanitarianism* (Ithaca and London: Cornell University Press, 2011).

Barr, John. "New Towns as Anti-Ghettoes?" *New Society* 5 (April 1, 1965): 5–6.

Baughan, Emily and Juliano Floriani. "Save the Children, the Humanitarian Project, and the Politics of Solidarity: Reviving Dorothy Buxton's Vision," *Disasters* Special Issue: *Aid in the Archives: Academic Histories for a Practitioner Audience* 39.2 (2015): 129–45.

Bebber, Brett. "'We Were Just Unwanted': Bussing, Migrant Dispersal, and South Asians in London," *Journal of Social History* 48.3 (Spring 2015): 635–51.

Beckett, Andy. *When the Lights Went Out: Britain in the Seventies* (London: Faber and Faber, 2009).

Bell, Adrian. *Only for Three Months: The Basque Children in Exile* (Norwich: Mousehold Press, 1996).

Benjamin, Natalia. *Recuerdos: Basque Children Refugees in Great Britain* (Oxford: Mousehold Press, 2007).

Bennett, E.G. *In Search of Freedom: The Story of Some Refugees and Exiles who Found a Haven in Bournemouth and District* (Bournemouth: Bournemouth Local Studies Publications, 1985).

Berghahn, Marion. "German Jews in England: Aspects of the Assimilation and Integration Process." In *Exile in Great Britain: Refugees from Hitler's Germany*, edited by Gerhard Hirschfield (Warwickshire: Berg, 1984), 285–306.

Bessel, Richard and Claudia B. Haake, eds., *Removing Peoples: Forced Removal in the Modern World* (London: German Historical Institute for Oxford University Press, 2009).

Biegus, Zosia and Jurek Biegus. *Polish Resettlement Camps in England and Wales* (Essex: PB Software, 2013).

Black, Lawrence and Hugh Pemberton. "Introduction: The Benighted Decade? Reassessing the 1970s." In *Reassessing 1970s Britain*, edited by Lawrence Black, Hugh Pemberton, and Pat Thane (Manchester: Manchester University Press, 2013), 1–24.

Bloch, Alice and Liza Schuster. "At the Extremes of Exclusion: Deportation, Detention and Dispersal," *Ethnic and Racial Studies* 28.3 (2005): 491–512.

Borstelmann, Thomas. *The 1970s: A New Global History from Civil Rights to Economic Inequality* (Princeton: Princeton University Press, 2012).

Bose, Mihir. "The Ugandan Asian Success Magic," *New Community* (September 16, 1982): 456–8.

Bourne, Jenny. "Resettlement Blues," *Race Today* 4.11 (November 1972): 357.

Bourne, Richard. "The Last Asians," *New Society* (May 31, 1973): 484–5.

Boyle, Kevin. "The Price of Peace: Vietnam, the Pound, and the Crisis of the American Empire," *Diplomatic History* 27.1 (2003): 37–72.

Bramwell, Anna C., ed. *Refugees in the Age of Total War* (London: Unwin Hyman, 1988).

Brandt, George W. "Thespis Behind the Wire, Or Entertainment in Internment—A Personal Recollection." In *Theatre and War 1933–1945: Performance in Extremis*, edited by Michael Balfour (New York: Berghahn, 2001), 117–23.

Brinson, Charmian. "Exile, Internment—and a Camp 'Full of Once and Future Very Important Persons.'" In *His Majesty's Loyal Internee: Fred Uhlman in Captivity*, edited by Charmian Brinson, Anna Müller-Härlin, and Julia Winckler (London: Valentine Mitchell, 2009), 13–33.

Bristow, Mike. "Britain's Response to the Ugandan Asian Crisis: Government Myths versus Political and Resettlement Realities," *Journal of Ethnic and Migration Studies* 5.3 (1976): 265–79.

Bristow, Mike and Bert N. Adams. "Ugandan Asians and the Housing Market in Britain," *New Community* 6 (1977): 65–77.

Brooke, Stephen. *Sexual Politics: Sexuality, Family Planning and the British Left from the 1880s to the Present Day* (Oxford: Oxford University Press, 2011).

Brooke, Stephen. "Living in 'New Times': Historicizing 1980s Britain," *History Compass* 12.1 (January 2014): 20–32.

Brooke, Stephen. "Space, Emotions, and the Everyday: Affective Ecologies in 1980s London," *Twentieth-Century British History* 28.1 (2017): 110–42.

Buck, William. "'Come and Find Sanctuary in Eire': The Experiences of Ireland's Belgian Refugees During the First World War," *Immigrants and Minorities* 34.2 (2016): 192–209.

Buettner, Elizabeth. "Going for an Indian: South Asian Restaurants and the Limits of Multiculturalism in Britain," *Journal of Modern History* 80.4 (2008): 865–901.

Bülbring, Maud. "Post-War Refugees in Great Britain," *Population Studies* 8.2 (November 1954): 99–112.

Burkett, Jodi. *Constructing Post-Imperial Britain: Britishness, "Race" and the Radical Left in the 1960s* (Basingstoke: Palgrave Macmillan, 2013).

Burridge, Andrew and Nick Gill. "Conveyor-Belt Justice: Precarity, Access to Justice, and Uneven Geographies of Legal Aid in UK Asylum Appeals," *Antipode* 49.1 (2017): 23–42.

Burton, Antoinette. *Brown Over Black: Race and the Politics of Postcolonial Citation* (Gurgaon: Three Essays Collective, 2012).

Busch, Peter. *All the Way with JFK? Britain, the United States, and the Vietnam War* (Oxford: Oxford University Press, 2003).

Cabanes, Bruno. *The Great War and the Origins of Humanitarianism, 1918–1924* (Cambridge: Cambridge University Press, 2014).

Cahalan, Peter. *Belgian Refugee Relief in England During the Great War* (New York: Garland Press, 1982).

Calhoun, Craig. "The Idea of Emergency: Humanitarian Action and Global (Dis)Order." In *Contemporary States of Emergency: The Politics of Military and Humanitarian Interventions*, edited by Didier Fassin and Mariella Pandolfi (New York: Zone Books, 2010), 29–58.

Carlson, Eleanor et al. "Feeding the Vietnamese in the UK," *Nutrition and Food Science* 80.4 (1980): 2–5.

Carlson, Eleanor, M. Kipps, and J. Thomson. "Feeding the Vietnamese in the UK and the Rationale Behind their Food Habits," *Proceedings of the Nutrition Society* 41 (1982): 229–37.

Carr, Gilly and Harold Mytum, eds. *Cultural Heritage and Prisoners of War: Creativity Behind Barbed Wire* (New York: Routledge, 2012).

Cesarani, David and Tony Kushner, eds. *The Internment of Aliens in Twentieth-Century Britain* (London: Frank Cass, 1993).

Chan, Kwok B. and David Loveridge. "Refugees in Transit: Vietnamese in a Refugee Camp in Hong Kong," *International Migration Review* 21.3 (1987): 745–59.

Chappell, Connery. *Island of Barbed Wire: Internment on the Isle of Man in World War Two* (London: Robert Hale, 1984).

Chatterji, Joya. "'Dispersal' and the Failure of Rehabilitation: Refugee Camp-dwellers and Squatters in West Bengal," *Modern Asian Studies* 41.5 (2007): 995–1032.

Chettiar, Teri. "'More than a Contract': The Emergence of a State-Supported Marriage Welfare Service and the Politics of Emotional Life in Post-1945 Britain," *Journal of British Studies* 55.3 (2016): 566–91.

Chin, Rita. *The Crisis of Multiculturalism in Europe: A History* (Princeton: Princeton University Press, 2017).

Clancy-Smith, Julia A. *Mediterraneans: North Africa and Europe in an Age of Migration, c. 1800–1900* (Berkeley: University of California Press, 2011).

Clancy-Smith, Julia A. "Mediterranean Historical Migrations." In *The Encyclopedia of Global Human Migration*, edited by Immanuel Ness (Hoboken, NJ: Wiley-Blackwell, 2013), 1–19.

Cloud (Kapp), Yvonne. *The Basque Children in England: An Account of their Life at North Stoneham Camp* (London: Victor Gollancz, 1937).

Clutterbuck, Richard. *Britain in Agony: The Growth of Political Violence* (London: Faber and Faber, 1978).

Cohen, Deborah. *Family Secrets: Shame and Privacy in Modern Britain* (Oxford: Oxford University Press, 2013).

Cohen, Gerard Daniel. *In War's Wake: Europe's Displaced Persons in the Postwar Order* (Oxford: Oxford University Press, 2012).

Cohen, Steve. *From the Jews to the Tamils: Britain's Mistreatment of Refugees* (Manchester: Manchester Law Centre, 1988).

Cohen-Portheim, Paul. *Time Stood Still: My Internment in England, 1914–1918* (New York: E.P. Dutton, 1932).

Cole, W. Owen. *Cole Sahib: The Story of a Multifaith Journey* (Eastbourne: Sussex Academic Press, 2009).

Colpus, Eve. "'The Screen Is Two-Way': That's Life! Television and Social Activism in Britain, 1973–1994," Paper delivered at Burdens Conference: Writing History after 1945, University of California at Berkeley, 2012.

The Condition of the Belgian Workmen Now Refugees in England (London: J.J. Keliher, 1917).

Cunliffe, Andrew. "The Refugee Crisis: A Study of the United Nations High Commission for Refugees," *Political Studies* 43.2 (June 1995): 278–90.

Cunningham, Sir Charles. "The Uganda Resettlement Board and Hiving-Off: Some Possibilities for Future Research," *Public Administration* 51.3 (1973): 251–60.

Cunningham, Sir Charles. "The Work of the Uganda Resettlement Board," *Contemporary Review* 222 (May 1973): 225–30.

Czigány, Magda. *"Just Like Other Students": Reception of the 1956 Hungarian Refugee Students in Britain* (Newcastle upon Tyne: Cambridge Scholars, 2009).

Darwin, John. "Orphans of Empire." In *Settlers and Expatriates: Britons Over the Seas*, edited by Robert Bickers (Oxford: Oxford University Press, 2010), 329–45.

Davies, Hywel. *Fleeing Franco: How Wales Gave Shelter to Refugee Children from the Basque Country During the Spanish Civil War* (Cardiff: University of Wales Press, 2011).

Deakin, Nicholas and Clare Ungerson. *Leaving London: Planned Mobility and the Inner City* (London: Heinemann, 1977).

Denness, Zoe. "A Question Which Affects Our Prestige as a Nation: The History of British Civilian Internment, 1899–1945," Ph.D. Thesis, University of Birmingham, 2012.

Dickson, Rachel, Sarah MacDougall, and Ulrike Smalley. "'Astounding and Encouraging': High and Low Art Produced in Internment on the Isle of Man during the Second World War." In *Cultural Heritage and Prisoners of War*, edited by Carr and Mytum, 186–204.

Diken, Bülent and Carsten Bagge Laustsen. *The Culture of Exception: Sociology Facing the Camp* (London: Routledge, 2005).

Dines, Mary. "Ugandan Asians—One Year On. Cool Reception," *New Community* 12 (1973): 380–3.

Dove, Richard, ed. *"Totally Un-English"? Britain's Internment of "Enemy Aliens" in Two World Wars* (New York: Rodopi, 2005).

Dow, Mark. *American Gulag: Inside U.S. Immigration Prisons* (Berkeley: University of California Press, 2004).

Draskau, Jennifer Kewley. "*Kulturkrieg* and *Frontgeist* from Behind the Wire: World War I Newspapers from Douglas Internment Camp." In *Cultural Heritage and Prisoners of War*, edited by Carr and Mytum (New York: Routledge, 2012), 208–26.

Dumbrell, John and Sylvia Ellis. "British Involvement in Vietnam Peace Initiatives, 1966–67: Marigolds, Sunflowers, and 'Kosygin Week,'" *Diplomatic History* 27.1 (2003): 113–49.

Durbach, Nadja. "Nations Out of Nurseries, Empires into Bottles: The Colonial Politics of Welfare Orange Juice," Paper presented at North American Conference on British Studies (Little Rock, 2015).

Edgerton, David. *Warfare State: Britain, 1920–1970* (Cambridge: Cambridge University Press, 2006).

Edgerton, David. *Britain's War Machine: Weapons, Resources, and Experts in the Second World War* (Oxford: Oxford University Press, 2011).

Edholm, Felicity et al. *Vietnamese Refugees in Britain* (London: Commission for Racial Equality, 1983).

Eley, Geoff. "A Disorder of Peoples: The Uncertain Ground of Reconstruction in 1945." In *The Disentanglement of Populations: Migration, Expulsion and Displacement in Post-War Europe, 1944–9*, edited by Jessica Reinisch and Elizabeth White (Basingstoke: Palgrave Macmillan, 2011), 291–314.

Eley, Geoff. "End of the Post-War? The 1970s as a Key Watershed in European History," *Journal of Modern European History* 9.1 (2011): 12–17.

Enloe, Cynthia. *Bananas, Beaches, and Bases: Making Feminist Sense of International Politics* (Berkeley: University of California Press, 2014). 2nd ed.

Everill, Bronwen. "Freetown, Frere Town, and the Kat River Settlement: Nineteenth-Century Humanitarian Intervention and Precursors to Modern Refugee Camps." In *The History and Practice of Humanitarian Intervention and Aid in Africa*, edited by Bronwen Everill and Josiah Kaplan (Basingstoke: Palgrave Macmillan, 2013), 23–42.

Farley, Paul and Michael Symmons Roberts. *Edgelands: Journeys into England's True Wilderness* (London: Vintage, 2012).

Fassin, Didier. *Humanitarian Reason: A Moral History of the Present* (Berkeley: University of California Press, 2012).

Fassin, Didier. "The Precarious Truth of Asylum," *Public Culture* 25.1 (2013): 39–63.

Fassin, Didier, "Introduction: Governing Precarity." In *At the Heart of the State: The Moral World of Institutions*, edited by Didier Fassin et al. (London: Pluto, 2015), pp. 1–11.

Fassin, Didier and Richard Rechtman. *The Empire of Trauma: An Inquiry into the Condition of Victimhood* (Princeton: Princeton University Press, 2009).

Feinstein, Margaret Myers. *Holocaust Survivors in Postwar Germany, 1945–1957* (Cambridge: Cambridge University Press, 2010).

Feldman, David. "Migrants, Immigrants and Welfare from the Old Poor Law to the Welfare State," *Transactions of the Royal Historical Society* 13 (2003): 79–104.

Feldman, David. "Why the English Like Turbans: Multicultural Politics in British History." In *Structures and Transformations in Modern British History*, edited by David Feldman and Jon Lawrence (Cambridge: Cambridge University Press, 2011), 281–302.

Feldman, Ilana. "The Challenge of Categories: UNRWA and the Definition of a 'Palestine Refugee,'" *Journal of Refugee Studies* 25.3 (2012): 387–406.

Feldman, Ilana. "What Is a Camp? Legitimate Refugee Lives in Spaces of Long-Term Displacement," *Geoforum* 66 (2015): 244–52.

Field, John. *Working Men's Bodies: Work Camps in Britain, 1880–1940* (Manchester: Manchester University Press, 2013).

Field, Simon. *Resettling Refugees: The Lessons of Research* (London: HMSO, 1985).

Fiorato, Veronica. "Greenham Common: The Conservation and Management of a Cold War Archetype." In *A Fearsome Heritage: Diverse Legacies of the Cold War*, edited by John Schofield and Wayne Cocroft (Walnut Creek, CA: Left Coast Press, 2007), 129–54.

Fischer-Tiné, Harold. "Britain's Other Civilizing Mission: Class Prejudice, European 'Loaferism' and the Workhouse System in Colonial India," *Indian Economic and Social History Review* 42.3 (2005): 295–338.

Forth, Aidan. "The Birth of the Concentration Camp? British Imperialists and the Origins of Modern Detention," *Perspectives on Europe* 43.2 (2013): 54–8.

Forth, Aidan. "Britain's Archipelago of Camps: Labor and Detention in a Liberal Empire, 1871–1903," *Kritika* 16.3 (2015): 651–80.

Forth, Aidan. *Barbed-Wire Imperialism: Britain's Empire of Camps, 1876–1903* (Berkeley: University of California Press, 2017).

Frank, Matthew and Jessica Reinisch. "Refugees and the Nation-State in Europe, 1919–59," *Journal of Contemporary History* 49.3 (July 2014): 477–90.

Frenz, Margaret. "Migration, Identity and Post-Colonial Change in Uganda: A Goan Perspective," *Immigrants and Minorities* 31.1 (2013): 48–73.

Fyrth, Jim. *The Signal Was Spain: The Spanish Aid Movement in Britain, 1936–39* (New York: St. Martin's Press, 1986).

Gatrell, Peter. *A Whole Empire Walking: Refugees in Russia During World War One* (Bloomington, IN: Indiana University Press, 2005).

Gatrell, Peter. *Free World? The Campaign to Save the World's Refugees, 1956–1963* (Cambridge: Cambridge University Press, 2011).

Gatrell, Peter. "Trajectories of Population Displacement in the Aftermaths of Two World Wars." In *The Disentanglement of Populations*, edited by Reinisch and White (Basingstoke: Palgrave Macmillan, 2011), 3–26.

Gatrell, Peter. *The Making of the Modern Refugee* (Oxford: Oxford University Press, 2013).

Gatrell, Peter. "Refugees—What's Wrong with History?" *Journal of Refugee Studies* 30.2 (2017): 170–89.

Gershon, Karen. *We Came as Children: A Collective Autobiography* (London: Victor Gollancz, 1966).

Gibney, Matthew J. *The Ethics and Politics of Asylum: Liberal Democracy and the Response to Refugees* (Cambridge: Cambridge University Press, 2004).

Gilbert, David, David Matless, and Brian Short, eds. *Geographies of British Modernity* (Malden, MA: Blackwell, 2003).

Gill, Rebecca. *Calculating Compassion: Humanity and Relief in War, Britain 1870–1914* (Manchester: Manchester University Press, 2013).

Gillman, Peter and Leni Gillman. *"Collar the Lot!" How Britain Interned and Expelled its Wartime Refugees* (London: Quartet Books, 1980).

Gissing, Vera. *Pearls of Childhood* (New York: St. Martin's, 1989).

Glover, David. *Literature, Immigration, and Diaspora in Fin-de-Siècle England: A Cultural History of the 1905 Aliens Act* (Cambridge: Cambridge University Press, 2012).

Goldsmith, Margaret. "The Refugee Transit Camp at Richborough," *Nineteenth Century and After* 126 (September 1939): 315–21.

Government Belgian Refugees Committee, *First Report of the Departmental Committee Appointed by the President of the Local Government Board to Consider and Report on Questions Arising in Connection with the Reception and Employment of the Belgian Refugees in this Country* (London: HMSO, 1914).

Grant, Kevin. "The Transcolonial World of Hunger Strikes and Political Fasts, c. 1909–1935." In *Decentering Empire: Britain, India, and the Transcolonial World*, edited by Durba Ghosh and Dane Kennedy (Hyderabad: Orient Longman, 2006), 243–69.

Greenhalgh, Charlotte. "An Age of Emotion: Expertise and Subjectivity in Old Age in Britain, 1937–1970," Ph.D. Thesis, Oxford University, 2012.

Gregson, Sarah. "Women and Children First? The Administration of Titanic Relief in Southampton, 1912–1959," *English Historical Review* 128 (February 2012): 83–109.

Guldi, Jo. "World Neoliberalism as Rebellion from Below? British Squatters and the Global Interpretation of Poverty, 1946–1974," *Humanity* (forthcoming, 2017).

Haddad, Emma. *The Refugee in International Society: Between Sovereigns* (Cambridge: Cambridge University Press, 2008).

Hamai, Yumiko. " 'Imperial Burden' or 'Jews of Africa'? An Analysis of Political and Media Discourse in the Uganda Asian Crisis," *Twentieth-Century British History* 22.3 (2011): 415–36.

Hamilton-Paterson, James. "Camp on John Bull's Island," *Nova* (April 1973): 68–75.

Haney, Lynne. *Inventing the Needy: Gender and the Politics of Welfare in Hungary* (Berkeley: University of California Press, 2002).

Hansen, Janine. "Sympathy, Antipathy, Hostility: British Attitudes to Non-Repatriable Poles and Ukranians after the Second World War and to the Hungarian Refugees of 1956," Ph.D. Thesis, University of Sheffield, 1995.

Harding, Jeremy. "The Uninvited," *London Review of Books* 22.3 (February 3, 2000): 3–25.

Harris, Mark Jonathan and Deborah Oppenheimer. *Into the Arms of Strangers: Stories of the Kindertransport* (London: Bloomsbury, 2005).

Harrison, Brian. *Finding a Role? The United Kingdom, 1970–1990* (Oxford: Clarendon Press, 2010).

Hartcup, Adeline. "Hong Kong's Closed and Open Centres," *Contemporary Review* 247 (1985): 298–303.

Hasian, Jr., Marouf. *Restorative Justice, Humanitarian Rhetorics, and Public Memories of Colonial Camp Cultures* (Basingstoke: Palgrave Macmillan, 2014).

Hatch, Sir Ernest. "The Belgian Refugees in the United Kingdom," *Quarterly Review* 225 (January 1916): 188–214.

Hauser, Kitty. *Shadow Sites: Photography, Archaeology, and the British Landscape, 1927–1955* (Oxford: Oxford University Press, 2007).

Hilton, Matthew. "Politics is Ordinary: Non-Governmental Organizations and Political Participation in Contemporary Britain," *Twentieth-Century British History* 22.2 (2011): 230–68.

Hilton, Matthew, James McKay, Nicholas Crowson, and Jean-Francis Mouhot. *The Politics of Expertise: How NGOs Shaped Modern Britain* (Oxford: Oxford University Press, 2013).

Hirschfeld, Gerhard. "Introduction." In *Exile in Great Britain: Refugees from Hitler's Germany*, edited by Gerhard Hirschfeld (Warwickshire: Berg, 1984), 1–9.

Hodgetts, Colin. *Action! A Cleric Off the Leash: An Autobiography* (CreateSpace, 2016).

Hodgetts, Colin and Jane Shackman. *First Impressions: Project Leaders with Save the Children Fund Talk about the Reception Programme for Refugees from Vietnam between 1979 and 1983* (London: Refugee Action, 1983).

"The Homeless in London," *Economist* (September 22, 1956): 941–3.

Hoskins, W.G. *The Making of the English Landscape* (London: Hodder and Stoughton, 1955).

Howe, Stephen. "Decolonisation and Imperial Aftershocks: The Thatcher Years." In *Making Thatcher's Britain*, edited by Jackson and Saunders, 234–51.

Hughes, Geraint. "A 'Missed Opportunity' for Peace? Harold Wilson, British Diplomacy, and the *Sunflower* Initiative to End the Vietnam War, February 1967," *Diplomacy and Statecraft* 14.3 (September 2003): 106–30.

Humphrey, Derek and Michael Ward. *Passports and Politics* (London: Penguin, 1974).

Humphreys, Robert. *No Fixed Abode: A History of Responses to the Roofless and the Rootless in Britain* (Basingstoke: Macmillan, 1999).

Hunt, Sandra Penelope. "Adaptation and Nutritional Implications of Food Habits among Uganda Asians Settling in Britain," Ph.D. Thesis in Nutrition, University of London, 1977.

Hyslop, Jonathan. "The Invention of the Concentration Camp: Cuba, Southern Africa, and the Philippines, 1896–1907," *South African Historical Journal* 63.2 (2011): 251–76.

Igersheimer, Walter. *Blatant Injustice: The Story of a Jewish Refugee from Nazi Germany Imprisoned in Britain and Canada during World War Two* (Montreal: McGill-Queen's University Press, 2005).

Irwin, Julia F. *Making the World Safe: The American Red Cross and a Nation's Humanitarian Awakening* (Oxford: Oxford University Press, 2013).

Jackson, Ben and Robert Saunders, eds. *Making Thatcher's Britain* (Cambridge: Cambridge University Press, 2012).

Jackson, Brian. *Starting School* (London: Croom Helm, 1979).

Jagucki, Walter. "The Polish Experience: Forty Years On." In *The Psychosocial Problems of Refugees*, edited by Ron Baker (London: British Refugee Council, 1983), 32–8.

Jamison, Leslie. *The Empathy Exams* (Minneapolis: Graywolf, 2014).

Janmyr, Maja. *Protecting Civilians in Refugee Camps: Unable and Unwilling States, UNHCR and International Responsibility* (Leiden: Martinus Nijhoff, 2014).

Janmyr, Maya and Are J. Knudsen. "Hybrid Spaces," *Humanity* 7.3 (Winter 2016): 391–4.

Janowski, Monica. "Food in Traumatic Times: Women, Foodways and 'Polishness' During a Wartime 'Odyssey,'" *Food and Foodways* 20.3–4 (2012): 236–349.

Jenkinson, Jacqueline. "Soon Gone, Long Forgotten: Uncovering British Responses to Belgian Refugees During the First World War," *Immigrants and Minorities* 34.2 (2016): 101–12.

Jones, Peter R. *Vietnamese Refugees: A Study of their Reception and Resettlement in the United Kingdom*. Research and Planning Unit Paper 13 (London: Home Office, 1982).

Kahn, Leo. *Obliging Fellow* (London: Nicholson and Watson, 1946).

Kaye, Ronald. "Defining the Agenda: British Refugee Policy and the Role of Parties," *Journal of Refugee Studies* 7.2 (1994): 144–59.

Kee, Robert. *Refugee World* (London: Oxford University Press, 1961).

Kidman, Brenda. *A Handful of Tears* (London: BBC, 1975).

King, Laura. *Family Men: Fatherhood and Masculinity in Britain, c. 1914–1960* (Oxford: Oxford University Press, 2015).

King, Laura. "Future Citizens: Cultural and Political Conceptions of Children in Britain, 1930s–1950s," *Twentieth-Century British History* 27.3 (2016): 389–411.

Kippin, John. *Cold War Pastoral: Greenham Common* (London: Black Dog, 2001).

Kobelinsky, Carolina. "In Search of Truth: How Asylum Applications are Adjudicated." In *At the Heart of the State: The Moral World of Institutions*, edited by Didier Fassin et al. (London: Pluto, 2015), 67–89.

Koch, Eric. *Deemed Suspect: A Wartime Blunder* (Toronto: Methuen, 1980).

Kochan, Miriam. *Britain's Internees in the Second World War* (London: Macmillan, 1983).

Kochanski, Halik. *The Eagle Unbowed: Poland and the Poles in the Second World War* (London: Allen Lane, 2012).

Kotef, Hagar. *Movement and the Ordering of Freedom: On Liberal Governances of Mobility* (Durham, NC: Duke University Press, 2015).

Koven, Seth. *Slumming: Sexual and Social Politics in Victorian London* (Princeton: Princeton University Press, 2004).

Koven, Seth. *The Match Girl and the Heiress* (Princeton: Princeton University Press, 2014).

Koven, Seth and Sonya Michel, eds. *Mothers of a New World: Maternalist Politics and the Origins of Welfare States* (London: Routledge, 1993).

Kramer, Jane. "The Uganda Asians," *New Yorker* 50.7 (April 8, 1974): 47–93.

Kushner, Tony. "Local Heroes: Belgian Refugees in Britain During the First World War," *Immigrants and Minorities* 18.1 (1999): 1–28.

Kushner, Tony. "Meaning Nothing But Good: Ethics, History, and Asylum-Seeker Phobia in Britain," *Patterns of Prejudice* 37.3 (2003): 257–76.

Kushner, Tony. *Remembering Refugees: Then and Now* (Manchester: Manchester University Press, 2006).

Kushner, Tony. "Finding Refugee Voices." In *Political Exile and Exile Politics in Britain after 1933*, edited by Anthony Grenville and Andrea Reiter (Amsterdam: Rodopi, 2011), 121–37.

Kushner, Tony. *The Battle of Britishness: Migrant Journeys, 1685 to the Present* (Manchester: Manchester University Press, 2012).

Kushner, Tony and Katharine Knox. *Refugees in an Age of Genocide: Global, National, and Local Perspectives during the Twentieth Century* (London: Frank Cass, 1999).

Kynaston, David. *Modernity Britain: Opening the Box, 1957–59* (London: Bloomsbury, 2013).

Lafitte, F. *The Internment of Aliens* (Harmondsworth: Penguin, 1940).

Langhamer, Claire. *The English in Love: The Intimate Story of an Emotional Revolution* (Oxford: Oxford University Press, 2013).

Langhamer, Claire. "Feelings, Women and Work in the Long 1950s," *Women's History Review* 26.1 (2017): 77–92.

Laurent, Livia. *A Tale of Internment* (London: George Allen and Unwin, 1942).

Legarreta, Dorothy. *The Guernica Generation: Basque Refugee Children of the Spanish Civil War* (Reno: University of Nevada Press, 1984).

Levin, Michal. *What Welcome? Reception and Resettlement of Refugees in Britain* (London: Acton Society Trust, 1982).

Levine-Clark, Marjorie. *Unemployment, Welfare, and Masculine Citizenship: So Much Honest Poverty in Britain, 1870–1930* (Basingstoke: Palgrave Macmillan, 2015).

Lewis, Jane. "Gender, the Family and Women's Agency in the Building of 'Welfare States': The British Case," *Social History* 19.1 (1994): 37–56.

Lewis, Mary Dewhurst. *Divided Rule: Sovereignty and Empire in French Tunisia, 1881–1938* (Berkeley: University of California Press, 2013).

Lipman, Jana. "'Give Us a Ship': The Vietnamese Repatriate Movement on Guam, 1975," *American Quarterly* 64 (2012): 1–31.

Lipman, Jana. "'The Fish Trusts the Water and It Is In the Water That It Is Cooked': The Caribbean Origins of the Krome Detention Center," *Radical History Review* 115 (Winter 2013): 115–41.

Lipman, Jana. "A Refugee Camp in America: Fort Chaffee and Vietnamese and Cuban Refugees, 1975–1982," *Journal of American Ethnic History* 33.2 (Winter 2014): 57–87.

Lomnitz, Alfred. *"Never Mind, Mr. Lom!" or The Uses of Adversity* (London: Macmillan, 1941).

Long, Katy. "When Refugees Stopped Being Migrants: Movement, Labour, and Humanitarian Protection," *Migration Studies* 1.1 (2013): 4–26.

Lugard, Lady Flora. "The Work of the War Refugees' Committee," *Journal of the Royal Society of Arts* 63 (March 26, 1915): 429–40.

McAtackney, Laura. *An Archaeology of the Troubles: The Dark Heritage of Long Kesh/Maze Prison* (Oxford: Oxford University Press, 2014).

McCart, Mike. "Wandsworth: Unsettled Ugandan Refugees," *Journal of Ethnic and Migration Studies* 2 (1973): 383–6.

McCarthy, Helen. "Social Science and Married Women's Employment in Post-War Britain," *Past and Present* 233 (2016): 269–305.

McCarthy, Helen. "Women, Marriage and Paid Work in Post-War Britain," *Women's History Review* 26.1 (2017): 46–61.

McCosh, Fred. *Nissen of the Huts: A Biography of Lt. Col. Peter Nissen* (Bourne End: BD Publishing, 1997).

McDowell, Linda. *Migrant Women's Voices: Talking about Life and Work in the UK since 1945* (London: Bloomsbury, 2016).

MacFarquhar, Larissa. *Strangers Drowning: Grappling with Impossible Idealism, Drastic Choices, and the Overpowering Urge to Help* (New York: Penguin, 2015).

McLaren, Meryn. "'Out of the Huts Emerged a Settled People': Community-Building in West German Refugee Camps," *German History* 28.1 (2010): 21–43.

McSmith, Andy. *No Such Thing as Society* (London: Constable, 2010).

Madokoro, Laura. *Elusive Refuge: Chinese Migrants in the Cold War* (Cambridge, MA: Harvard University Press, 2016).

Malkki, Liisa. *Purity and Exile: Violence, Memory, and National Cosmology Among Hutu Refugees in Tanzania* (Chicago: University of Chicago Press, 1995).

Malkki, Liisa. "Refugees and Exile: From 'Refugee Studies' to the National Order of Things," *Annual Review of Anthropology* 24 (1995): 495–523.

Malkki, Liisa. "Speechless Emissaries: Refugees, Humanitarianism, and Dehistoricization," *Cultural Anthropology* 11.3 (August 1996): 377–404.

Mamdani, Mahmood. "The Ugandan Asian Expulsion: Twenty Years After," *Journal of Refugee Studies* 6.3 (1993): 265–73.

Mamdani, Mahmood. *From Citizen to Refugee: Uganda Asians Come to Britain* (Cape Town: Pambazuka Press, 2011).

Manning, Leah. *A Life for Education: An Autobiography* (London: Victor Gollancz, 1960).

Marett, Valerie. *Immigrants Settling in the City* (London: Leicester University Press, 1989).

Markham, E.A. and Arnold Kingston. *Merely a Matter of Colour: The Uganda Asian Anthology* (Edgware: "Q" Books, 1973).

Marrus, Michael. "Introduction." In *Refugees in the Age of Total War*, edited by Anna C. Bramwell (London: Unwin Hyman, 1988), 1–6.

Marrus, Michael R. *The Unwanted: European Refugees in the Twentieth Century* (New York: Oxford University Press, 1985).

Marshall, Oliver. *Ship of Hope* (London: Notting Dale Urban Studies Centre, 1991).

Marx, Emanuel. "The Social World of Refugees: A Conceptual Framework," *Journal of Refugee Studies* 3.3 (1990): 189–203.

Matless, David. *Landscape and Englishness* (London: Reaktion, 1998).

May, Elaine. "Reception in the United Kingdom of Jewish Refugees with Special Emphasis on the Role of the Kitchener Camp, 1938–1939," MA in History, Polytechnic of Central London, 1989.

Miccoli, Dario. *Histories of the Jews of Egypt: An Imagined Bourgeoisie, 1880s–1950s* (New York: Routledge, 2015).

Mishra, Vijay. *The Literature of the Indian Diaspora: Theorizing the Diasporic Imaginary* (London: Routledge, 2007).

Momement, Adam. "Gimme Shelter," *RIBA Journal* 114.8 (2007): 48–52.

Mort, Frank. "Social and Symbolic Fathers and Sons in Postwar Britain," *Journal of British Studies* 38.3 (1999): 353–84.

Myers, Adrian and Gabriel Moshenska, eds. *Archaeologies of Internment* (New York: Springer, 2011).

Myers, Kevin. "The Ambiguities of Aid and Agency: Representing Refugee Children in England, 1937–8," *Cultural and Social History* 6.1 (2009): 29–46.

Naipaul, Shiva. "Passports to Dependence." In *Beyond the Dragon's Mouth: Stories and Pieces* (London: Viking, 1984), 221–9.

Netz, Reviel. *Barbed Wire: An Ecology of Modernity* (Middletown, CT: Wesleyan University Press, 2004).

Nguyen, Mimi Thi. *The Gift of Freedom: War, Debt, and Other Refugee Passages* (Durham, NC and London: Duke University Press, 2012).

Nyers, Peter. *Rethinking Refugees: Beyond States of Emergency* (London: Routledge, 2006).

Ong, Aihwa. *Buddha is Hiding: Refugees, Citizenship, the New America* (Berkeley: University of California Press, 2003).

Paik, A. Naomi. "Carceral Quarantine at Guantánamo: Legacies of U.S. Imprisonment of Haitian Refugees, 1991–1994," *Radical History Review* 115 (Winter 2013): 142–68.

Paik, A. Naomi. *Rightlessness* (Chapel Hill: University of North Carolina Press, 2016).

Panayi, Panikos. *The Enemy in Our Midst: Germans in Britain during the First World War* (New York: Berg, 1991).

Panayi, Panikos. "An Intolerant Act by an Intolerant Society: The Internment of Germans in Britain During the First World War." In *The Internment of Aliens in Twentieth-Century Britain*, edited by David Cesarani and Tony Kushner (London: F. Cass, 1993), 53–78.

Panayi, Panikos and Pippa Virdee, eds. *Refugees and the End of Empire: Imperial Collapse and Forced Migration in the Twentieth Century* (Basingstoke: Palgrave Macmillan, 2011).

Parmar, Maya. "Memorialising 40 Years since Idi Amin's Expulsion: Digital 'Memory Mania' to the 'Right to be Forgotten,'" *South Asian Popular Culture* 12.1 (2014): 1–14.

Patterson, Sheila. "The Polish Exile Community in Britain," *Polish Review* 6.3 (Summer 1961): 69–97.

Pavlovich, Henry. *Worlds Apart: Surviving Identity and Memory* (UK: Lulu, 2006).

Pedersen, Susan. *Family, Dependence, and the Origins of the Welfare State* (Cambridge: Cambridge University Press, 1993).

Pedersen, Susan. "The Maternalist Moment in British Colonial Policy: The Controversy Over 'Child Slavery' in Hong Kong, 1917–1941," *Past and Present* 171.1 (2001): 161–202.

Perles, Alfred. *Alien Corn* (London: George Allen and Unwin, 1944).

Peteet, Julie. *Landscape of Hope and Despair: Palestinian Refugee Camps* (Philadelphia: University of Pennsylvania Press, 2005).

Peteet, Julie. "Cartographic Violence, Displacement and Refugee Camps: Palestine and Iraq." In *Palestinian Refugees: Identity, Space and Place in the Levant*, edited by Are Knudsen and Sari Hanafi (London: Routledge, 2011), 13–28.

Pfister-Ammende, Maria. "Mental Hygiene in Refugee Camps." In *Uprooting and After ...*, edited by Charles Zwingmann and Maria Pfister-Ammende (New York: Springer-Verlag, 1973), 241–51.

Philips, Simon and Jane Pearson. "Dealing with Vietnamese Refugees: Our Plans," *British Medical Journal* 282 (February 14, 1981): 525–7.

Political and Economic Planning. "Refugees in Britain: Hungarians and Anglo-Egyptians," (London: Weekend Publications, February 17, 1958).

Porter, Stephen R. *Benevolent Empire: U.S. Power, Humanitarianism, and the World's Dispossessed* (Philadelphia: University of Pennsylvania Press, 2017).

Powell, G.A. *Four Years in a Refugee Camp Being an Account of the British Government War Refugees Camp Earl's Court London 1914–1919* (London: Baynard Press, 1919).

Pozo-Gutiérrez, Alicia and Padmini Broomfield. *"Here, look after him": Voices of Basque Evacuee Children of the Spanish Civil War* (Southampton: University of Southampton, 2012).

Pratt, Tim and James Vernon. "Appeal from this Fiery Bed: The Colonial Politics of Gandhi's Fasts and Their Metropolitan Reception," *Journal of British Studies* 44.1 (2005): 92–114.

Prazmowska, Anita J. "Polish Refugees as Military Potential: Policy Objectives of the Polish Government in Exile." In *Refugees in the Age of Total War*, edited by Anna Bramwell (London: Unwin Hyman, 1988), 219–32.

Proctor, Tammy. *Civilians in a World at War, 1914–1918* (New York: New York University Press, 2010).

Proctor, Tammy. "Feeding Internees: Food Politics in the Isle of Man," Paper delivered at the Pacific Coast Conference on British Studies, 2015.

Pupavac, Vanessa. "Between Compassion and Conservatism: A Genealogy of Humanitarian Sensibilities." In *Contemporary States of Emergency: The Politics of Military and Humanitarian Interventions*, edited by Didier Fassin and Mariella Pandolfi (New York: Zone, 2010), 129–49.

Rachamimov, Alon. *POWs and the Great War: Captivity on the Eastern Front* (Oxford: Berg, 2002).

Rachamimov, Alon. "The Disruptive Comforts of Drag: (Trans)Gender Performances among Prisoners of War in Russia, 1914–1920," *American Historical Review* 111.2 (April 2006): 362–82.

Radford, M. *Our Friends the Belgians: Sketches of Belgian Life in England* (London: Arthur H. Stockwell, 1921).

Rahman, Md. Mahbubar and Willem Van Schendel. "'I Am Not a Refugee': Rethinking Partition Migration," *Modern Asian Studies* 37.3 (July 2003): 551–84.

Ramphele, Mamphela. *A Bed Called Home: Life in the Migrant Labour Hostels of Cape Town* (Cape Town: David Philip, 1993).

Razac, Olivier. *Barbed Wire: A Political History* (New York: New Press, 2002).

Refugee Council. *Credit to the Nation: A Study of Refugees in the United Kingdom* (London: Refugee Council, 1997).

Refuge or Home? A Policy Statement on the Resettlement of Refugees (London: Community Relations Commission, 1976).

Reinisch, Jessica and Elizabeth White, eds. *The Disentanglement of Populations: Migration, Expulsion and Displacement in Post-War Europe, 1944–9* (Basingstoke: Palgrave Macmillan, 2011).

Report on 25 Years Work (London: HMSO, 1963).

Reynolds, David. *Rich Relations: The American Occupation of Britain, 1942–1945* (Glasgow: HarperCollins, 1995).

Robertson, Emma. "'Green for Come': Moving to York as a Ugandan Asian Refugee." In *Refugees and the End of Empire*, edited by Panayi and Virdee, 245–67.

Robinson, Cabeiri Debergh. "Too Much Nationality: Kashmiri Refugees, the South Asian Refugee Regime, and a Refugee State, 1947–74," *Journal of Refugee Studies* 25.3 (2012): 344–65.

Robinson, Greg. *After Camp: Portraits in Midcentury Japanese American Life and Politics* (Berkeley: University of California Press, 2012).

Robinson, Vaughan. "The Vietnamese Reception and Resettlement Programme in the UK: Rhetoric and Reality," *Ethnic Groups* 6 (1985): 305–30.

Robinson, Vaughan. *Transients, Settlers, and Refugees: Asians in Britain* (Oxford: Clarendon Press, 1986).

Robinson, Vaughan. "Marching into the Middle Classes? The Long-term Resettlement of East African Asians in the United Kingdom," *Journal of Refugee Studies* 6.3 (1993): 230–47.

Romijn, Jan. *Tabu: Uganda Asians—the Old, the Weak, the Vulnerable. A Report on his Work with the Elderly and Handicapped among the Uganda Asian Evacuees in London* (London: London Council of Social Service, 1976).

Sabín-Fernández, Susana. "The Basque Refugee Children of the Spanish Civil War in the UK: Memory and Memorialisation," Ph.D. Thesis, University of Southampton, 2010.

Sandbrook, Dominic. *Never Had It So Good: A History of Britain from Suez to the Beatles* (London: Little, Brown, 2005).

Sandbrook, Dominic. *State of Emergency: The Way We Were: Britain, 1970–1974* (London: Allen Lane, 2010).

Sandbrook, Dominic. *Seasons in the Sun: The Battle for Britain, 1974–1979* (London: Allen Lane, 2012).

Sanders, David. *Losing an Empire, Finding a Role: An Introduction to British Foreign Policy since 1945* (New York: St. Martin's Press, 1989).

Sanyal, Romola. "Squatting in Camps: Building and Insurgency in Places of Refuge," *Urban Studies* 48 (2011): 877–90.

Sanyal, Romola. "Urbanizing Refuge: Interrogating Spaces of Displacement," *International Journal of Urban and Regional Research* 38.2 (2014): 558–72.

Sasson, Tehila. "The Problem of Homelessness in Postwar Britain." In *Rescuing the Vulnerable: Poverty, Welfare and Social Ties in Nineteenth- and Twentieth-Century Europe*, edited by Beate Althammer, Lutz Raphael, and Tamara Stazic-Wendt (New York: Berghahn, 2014), 212–34.

Sasson, Tehila. "Milking the Third World? Humanitarianism, Capitalism, and the Moral Economy of the Nestlé Boycott," *American Historical* Review 121.4 (2016): 1196–224.

Sasson, Tehila and James Vernon. "Practicing the British Way of Famine: Technologies of Relief, 1770–1985," *European Review of History* 22.6 (2015): 860–72.

Saunders, Robert. "Crisis? What Crisis? Thatcherism and the Seventies." In *Making Thatcher's Britain*, edited by Jackson and Saunders, 25–42.

Saville, Annette. *Only a Kindertransportee* (London: New Millennium, 2002).

Scheer, Monique. "Captive Voices: Phonographic Records in the German and Austrian Prisoner-of-War Camps of World War One." In *Doing Anthropology in Wartime and War Zones: World War One and the Cultural Sciences in Europe*, edited by Reinhard Johler et al. (New Brunswick: Transaction, 2010), 279–309.

Schofield, Camilla. "'A Nation or No Nation?' Enoch Powell and Thatcherism." In *Making Thatcher's Britain*, edited by Jackson and Saunders (Cambridge: Cambridge University Press, 2012), pp. 95–110.

Schofield, Camilla. *Enoch Powell and the Making of Postcolonial Britain* (Cambridge: Cambridge University Press, 2013).

Schofield, John. "Monuments and the Memories of War: Motivations for Preserving Military Sites in England." In *Matériel Culture: The Archaeology of Twentieth-Century Conflict*, edited by John Schofield, William Gray Johnson, and Colleen M. Beck (London: Routledge, 2002), 143–58.

Schofield, John. *Aftermath: Readings in the Archaeology of Recent Conflict* (Swindon: Springer, 2008).

Schofield, John and Mike Anderton. "The Queer Archaeology of Green Gate: Interpreting Contested Space at Greenham Common Airbase," *World Archaeology* 32 (2000): 236–51.

Schweitzer, Pam, ed. *A Place to Stay: Memories of Pensioners from Many Lands* (London: Age Exchange Theatre Company, 1984).

Scott-Smith, Tom. "Control and Biopower in Contemporary Humanitarian Aid: The Case of Supplementary Feeding," *Journal of Refugee Studies* 28.1 (March 2015): 21–37.

Searle, Kevin. "'Mixing of the Unmixables': The 1949 Causeway Green 'Riots' in Birmingham," *Race and Class* 54.3 (2013): 44–64.

Segal, Lore. *Other People's Houses* (New York: Harcourt, Brace, and World, 1964).

Seipp, Adam R. *Strangers in the Wild Place: Refugees, Americans, and a German Town, 1945–1952* (Bloomington: Indiana University Press, 2013).

Sellers, Edith. "On the Entertaining of Refugees," *Nineteenth Century* 360 (June 1915): 1371–83.

Shaw, Caroline. *Britannia's Embrace: Modern Humanitarianism and the Imperial Origins of Refugee Relief* (Oxford: Oxford University Press, 2015).

Sheridan, Vera. "The Inadvertent Cosmopolitan: A Refugee Tale from Hungarian to English." In *The Cause of Cosmopolitanism: Dispositions, Models, Transformations*, edited by Patrick O'Donovan and Laura Rascaroli (Oxford: Peter Lang, 2011).

Sirhan, Bassem. "Palestinian Camp Life in Lebanon," *Journal of Palestine Studies* 4.2 (Winter 1975): 91–107.

Sluga, Glenda. "Bonegilla and Migrant Dreaming." In *Memory and History in Twentieth-Century Australia*, edited by Kate Darian-Smith and Paula Hamilton (Oxford: Oxford University Press, 1994), 195–209.

Smith, Rukhsana. *Sumitra's Story* (New York: Coward McCann, 1982).

Snizek, Suzanne. "'Spiritual Vitamins': Music in Huyton and Central Internment Camps May 1940 to January 1941." In *Cultural Heritage and Prisoners of War*, edited by Carr and Mytum (New York: Routledge, 2012), 34–50.

Snowman, Daniel. *The Hitler Émigrés: The Cultural Impact on Britain of Refugees from Nazism* (London: Chatto and Windus, 2002).

Somerset, Felicity. "Vietnamese Refugees in Britain: Resettlement Experiences," *Journal of Ethnic and Migration Studies* 10.3 (1983): 454–63.

Somerville, Peter. "The Making and Unmaking of Homelessness Legislation." In *Homelessness: Public Policies and Private Troubles*, edited by Susan Hutson and David Clapham (London: Cassell, 1999), 29–57.

Spier, Eugen. *The Protecting Power* (London: Skeffington, 1951).

Srinivasan, Shaila. *The South Asian Petty Bourgeoisie in Britain: An Oxford Case Study* (Aldershot: Avebury, 1995).

Steedman, Carolyn. *Landscape for a Good Woman* (New Brunswick, NJ: Rutgers University Press, 1987).

Steinart, Johannes-Dieter. "British Post-War Migration Policy and Displaced Persons in Europe." In *The Disentanglement of Populations*, edited by Reinisch and White, 229–47.

Stent, Ronald. *A Bespattered Page? The Internment of His Majesty's "most loyal enemy aliens"* (London: Andre Deutsch, 1980).

Stone, Dan. *Concentration Camps: A Short History* (Oxford: Oxford University Press, 2017).

Storr, Katherine. *Excluded from the Record: Women, Refugees and Relief, 1914–1929* (Oxford: Peter Lang, 2009).

Sutcliffe-Braithwaite, Florence. "Neo-Liberalism and Morality in the Making of Thatcherite Social Policy," *Historical Journal* 55.2 (2012): 497–520.

Sword, Keith. "The Absorption of Poles into Civilian Employment in Britain, 1945–1950." In *Refugees in the Age of Total War*, edited by Bramwell (London: Unwin Hyman, 1988), 233–52.

Taft, Julia Vadala, David S. North, and David A. Ford. *Refugee Resettlement in the U.S.: Time for a New Focus* (Washington, DC: New TransCentury Foundation, 1979).

Taylor, Becky. "Refugees, Ghost Ships, and Thatcher," *History Workshop Online* 26 (January 2015), http://www.historyworkshop.org.uk/ghostships/.

Taylor, Becky. "Their Only Words of English Were 'Thank You': Rights, Gratitude, and 'Deserving' Hungarian Refugees to Britain in 1956," *Journal of British Studies* 55.1 (January 2016): 120–44.

Taylor, Edgar. "The Asian Expulsion and Cultural Intimacy in Contemporary Uganda," Paper delivered at the American Historical Association, Washington, DC, January 2014.

Thane, Pat. "Family Life and 'Normality' in Postwar British Culture." In *Life After Death: Approaches to a Cultural and Social History of Europe During the 1940s and 1950s*, edited by Richard Bessel and Dirk Schuman (Washington, DC: German Historical Institute, 2003), 193–210.

Thanh, Vu Khanh with Christina Puryear. *Catholic with Confucian Tendencies: The True Story of the Extreme Adventures of a Vietnamese Boat Person* (United States: CreateSpace, 2016).

Thomas, Janie. "Where Have All the Refugees Gone?" *Community Care* (October 29, 1981): 19–21.

Thomas, Janie and Diane Mak. "Social Work and the Boat People," *Social Work Today* 10 (August 10, 1979): 11–14.

Thomas, Joe. *Ethnocide: A Cultural Narrative of Refugee Detention in Hong Kong* (Aldershot: Ashgate, 2000).

Thomas, Martin. *Fight or Flight: Britain, France, and their Roads from Empire* (Oxford: Oxford University Press, 2014).

Thomas, Nick. "Protests Against the Vietnam War in 1960s Britain: The Relationship Between Protestors and the Press," *Contemporary British History* 22.2 (2008): 335–54.

Thomson, Mathew. *Lost Freedom: The Landscape of the Child and the British Post-War Settlement* (Oxford: Oxford University Press, 2013).

The Times History of the War, vol. 4 (London: The Times, 1915).

Todd, Selina. "Family Welfare and Social Work in Post-War England, c. 1948–c. 1970," *English Historical Review* 129 (2014): 362–87.

Townsend, Peter. *The Last Refuge: A Survey of Residential Institutions and Homes for the Aged in England and Wales* (London: Routledge and Paul, 1962).

Tuitt, Patricia. *False Images: The Law's Construction of the Refugee* (London: Pluto, 1996).

Turner, Barry.... *And the Policeman Smiled* (London: Bloomsbury, 1990).

Turner, Simon. "What Is a Refugee Camp? Exploration of the Limits and Effects of the Camp," *Journal of Refugee Studies* 29.2 (2015): 139–48.

Tydor Baumel, Judith. "The Kitchener Transmigration Camp at Richborough," *Yad Vashem Studies* 14 (1981): 233–46.

Tydor Baumel-Schwartz, Judith. *Never Look Back: The Jewish Refugee Children in Great Britain* (West Lafayette, IN: Purdue University Press, 2012).

Ugolini, Wendy and Gavin Schaffer. "Victims or Enemies? Italians, Refugee Jews and the Reworking of Internment Narratives in Post-War Britain." In *The Lasting War: Society and Identity in Britain, France and Germany after 1945*, edited by Monica Riera and Gavin Schaffer (Basingstoke: Palgrave Macmillan, 2008), 207–25.

Uhlman, Fred. *The Making of an Englishman* (London: Jonathan Cape, 1960).

Ungerson, Clare. *Four Thousand Lives: The Rescue of German Jewish Men to Britain, 1939* (Stroud: History Press, 2014).

"Vagrancy in the Welfare State," *County Councils Association Official Gazette* (May 1955): 109–10.

Vajda, Albert. *Remade in England: From Her Majesty's Alien to Her Majesty's British Subject* (Edinburgh: Polygon, 1981).

Valeny, Rina. "From Pariah to Paragon: The Social Mobility of Ugandan Asian Refugees in Britain," Ph.D. Thesis, University of Wales, 1998.

Van Heyningen, Elizabeth. *The Concentration Camps of the Anglo-Boer War: A Social History* (Johannesburg: Jacana, 2013).

Vernon, James. *Hunger: A Modern History* (Cambridge, MA: Harvard University Press, 2007).

Vickers, Rhiannon. "Harold Wilson, the British Labour Party, and the War in Vietnam," *Journal of Cold War Studies* 1.2 (Spring 2008): 41–70.

Vinen, Richard. *National Service: Conscription in Britain, 1945–1963* (London: Allen Lane, 2014).

Watenpaugh, Keith David. "The League of Nations' Rescue of Armenian Genocide Survivors and the Making of Modern Humanitarianism, 1920–1927," *American Historical Review* 115.5 (December 2010): 1315–39.

Watenpaugh, Keith David. *Bread from Stones: The Middle East and the Making of Modern Humanitarianism* (Berkeley: University of California Press, 2015).

Watson, Don. *Squatting in Britain: Housing, Politics, and Direct Action, 1945–1955* (London: Merlin Press, 2016).

Webster, Wendy. "Transnational Communities of Allies." In *Fighting for Britain: Negotiating Identities in Britain During the Second World War*, edited by Wendy Ugolini and Juliette Pattinson (Oxford: Peter Lang, 2015), 209–33.

Weizman, Eyal. *The Least of All Possible Evils: Humanitarian Violence from Arendt to Gaza* (London: Verso, 2011).

Wheen, Francis. *Strange Days Indeed—the 1970s: The Golden Age of Paranoia* (New York: Public Affairs, 2009).

White, Luise. *Unpopular Sovereignty: Rhodesian Independence and African Decolonization* (Chicago: University of Chicago Press, 2015).

Whitham (née Pearson), Rachel. "A Health Visitor's View of Reception and Resettlement of Indo-Chinese Refugees into the United Kingdom." In *The Psychosocial Problems of Refugees*, edited by Ron Baker (London: British Refugee Council, 1983), 50–6.

Williams, Bill. *"Jews and other foreigners": Manchester and the Rescue of the Victims of European Fascism, 1933–1940* (Manchester: Manchester University Press, 2011).

Wilson, Francesca M. *In the Margins of Chaos: Recollections of Relief Work in and between Three Wars* (New York: Macmillan, 1945).

Wilson, Francesca M. *They Came as Strangers: The Story of Refugees to Great Britain* (London: Hamish Hamilton, 1959).

Wojciechowska, Bogusia J., ed. *Waiting to Be Heard: The Polish Christian Experience Under Nazi and Stalinist Oppression, 1939–1955* (Bloomington, IN: Authorhouse, 2009).

Wu, Ellen. *The Color of Success: Asian Americans and the Origins of the Model Minority* (Princeton: Princeton University Press, 2014).

Yelling, Jim. "The Incidence of Slum Clearance in England and Wales, 1955–1985," *Urban History* 27.2 (2000): 234–53.

Young, John W. "Britain and 'LBJ's War,' 1964–68," *Cold War History* 2.3 (April 2002): 63–92.

Zahra, Tara. *The Lost Children: Reconstructing Europe's Families after World War Two* (Cambridge, MA: Harvard University Press, 2011).

Zahra, Tara. *The Great Departure: Mass Migration from Eastern Europe and the Making of the Free World* (New York: W.W. Norton, 2016).

Zetter, Roger. "More Labels, Fewer Refugees: Remaking the Refugee Label in an Era of Globalization," *Journal of Refugee Studies* 20.2 (2007): 172–92.

Zubrzycki, Jerzy. *Polish Immigrants in Britain: A Study of Adjustment* (The Hague: Martinus Nijhoff, 1956).

Index

Abela, John 185
Abela sisters 185
African Caribbean 143, 149; *see also* immigration, Jamaican, West Indians
Agamben, Giorgio 9
Agier, Michel 210
Aldershot 13, 185
Alexandra Palace 16, 40–1, 72, 98, 191
Alibhai-Brown, Yasmin 121, 150
Allane, Lee 131, 149, 165
Amin, Idi 2, 7, 20, 78, 119, 120, 149, 150, 151, 152, 189
Amos, Nurse 198
Anders, General Władysław 18, 95
Anglo-Egyptian Aid Society 101, 103, 104
Anglo-Egyptian camps 1, 2, 3, 12, 55, 145
  arrival at 19
  class and 96, 97, 100–5, 108, 109
  closures of 184–5, 197, 202
  discipline in 186
  family and 118–19, 123, 129–30
  food in 81–2
  Hungarians and 22, 53, 186, 202
  language and 106
  property and 14, 107, 108
  resistance in 164
Anglo-Egyptian Resettlement Board (AERB) 55, 101, 103, 104, 145, 164, 185
  failures of 185
  family and 118
  Uganda Resettlement Board and 105, 213
  women and 129–30
anti-Semitism 138, 144, 175
Antolin, Carmen 42
Antolin, Josephina 42
Arendt, Hannah 7, 210, 217 n41
Armenian 6, 87
Arrowsmith, Major B.J.
  background 145
  class 110
  discipline 84, 172–3
  dispersal 189
  politics 165
  resistance to 155–6
Ashby Hostel 140
asylum seekers 180, 208–10
Aylesbury 35

Badeshia, Ranchhod 58
Bagge Laustsen, Carsten 9
Bailey, Mike 50
Banks, Mr. 45
Bartlett, Charles 146

Basque camps 1, 2, 12, 19, 21, 101
  arrival at 16, 17
  children, definition of 126–7
  closures of 193, 197
  discipline in 167–70, 181–3
  dispersal from 175
  ethnic identity in 92, 96
  food in 73–4, 75
  Jewish camps and 22, 43, 44, 170, 226 n122
  locals and 135–6
  memorialization of 204, 205
  physical environment of 41, 42
  politics in 172
  repatriation from 192
  violence in 172
Basque Children's Committee 135
Basque House 43
Battle of Britain 140
Beckett, Joe 135
Belgian camps 1, 2, 7, 8
  arrival at 16
  class and 97–8
  closure of 191, 193
  ethnic identity in 87, 210
  food in 72
  freedom of movement in 175, 181
  locals and 135
  physical environment of 40–1
Belgian Cookbook, The 72
Benford, Mrs. M.T. (Mysia Rembowski) 196
Bentley, Gregory 60
Bergen-Belsen 7, 162
Bertram Mills Circus 38
Bevan, Aneurin 28, 46
Bicester 141
Biegus, Jurek 140
Biegus, Zosia 94, 96, 140, 207
Bilbao 16, 73, 92, 126, 170, 192
  fall of 42, 168
Blackmore, Penny Jones 31
Blair, Tony 209, 210
Blitz 3
  compensation for 102
  housing, impact on 25, 28, 29, 58, 193, 218 n65
  see also Second World War
Blyton, Billy 30
Bomzer, Moishe 38
Bonegilla 204
Bosnians 208
Bourne, Jenny 152
Bowman, Isaiah 175
Brabazon, James 139
Brandt, George W. 90

Brechfa 169–70
Bridgend Hostel 145, 185
British Council for Aid to Refugees (BCAR)
    Hungarians and 53–4, 163, 186
    Vietnamese and 64, 65, 67, 154, 155, 190
British Nationality Act 212
Britons 1, 9, 207
    displaced 2, 3, 4–5, 10, 14, 57, 204, 207
    elderly 195
    family and 111, 123, 128, 130
    food and 71, 72, 73, 76, 79, 80–1, 82, 83,
        85, 232 n38
    homeless 4, 8, 24, 27–8, 30, 32, 40, 48, 50,
        56, 70, 86, 97, 114, 141, 143, 144, 148,
        151–2, 202, 203, 210, 215 n12, 218 n65
    housing and 24–33, 40, 49, 55, 56
    Hungarians and 163
    locals 13, 38, 44, 50, 56, 58, 62, 64, 70, 72,
        77, 78, 81, 83, 110, 124, 127, 131, 134,
        135, 136–40, 144, 147, 155, 170, 179,
        183, 201–2
    Poles and 139, 141–4, 158, 162, 202
    poor 4, 33, 47, 48–9, 80, 82, 86, 96,
        97–8, 100, 102–3, 105, 109–10, 113–14,
        143, 144, 148–9, 151–2, 158, 161, 163,
        202, 210
    relationships with refugees and 11, 12, 13,
        113, 119, 130, 131–2, 135, 136–7, 139,
        176, 183, 210
    Rhodesians and 212, 214
    Spanish Civil War and 16
    standard of living for 50, 53, 194, 201
    Ugandan Asians and 105
    volunteers 1, 8, 12, 41, 43, 54, 59, 64, 65,
        67, 69, 70, 76, 77, 83, 84, 98, 102, 124,
        127, 131, 135, 144–56, 158, 165, 167,
        173, 178, 205
    see also Poor Law, vagrancy, wayfarers' center
Brockway, Fenner 43
Buckett, Charles 77
Buhagiar, Mr. and Mrs. 118
Bülbring, Maud 141, 246 n53
Burmaston House 169
Burton-on-the-Wolds Hostel 140
Butlin's holiday camps 39, 43, 62
Byrne, Daphne 69, 70, 84, 155, 189

Cahn, Lory 17
Calais 5, 204, 209
Campaign for Nuclear Disarmament (CND) 57
Camp Clearance Programme 139
Canada 25, 52, 72, 89, 128, 206
Carpathian Rifles, Battalions of 52
Carr, Robert 58
Catholics 2
    Basque camps and 42, 168
    Belgian camps and 16
    Jewish camps and 92
    Polish camps and 93–5, 145, 193
    Vietnamese camps and 196, 200

Catterick 31
Cekalski, Eugeniusz 140
Central British Fund for German Jewry 18
Chandler's Ford 113
Charles, Bunty 146
Checkendon Hostel 159
Chelsea Barracks 39
Cherry, Thanh 155
"Children's Exodus, The" 91
Chinese 153, 154, 166, 173, 176, 189
Chiseldon 54
Chunnel 209
Churchill, Winston 4, 18, 51; *see also*
        Spencer-Churchill family
Clench, Greta 28
Cohen-Portheim, Paul 99
Cold War 2, 13, 56, 57, 203
    Hungarian refugees and 81, 171
    Polish refugees and 95, 183
Collins, Canon L. John 119–20
colonialism 12, 34, 66, 145, 150,
        151, 153
    dispersal and 177
    Indian camps and 32–3, 174
    Polish camps and 160
    see also decolonization, empire
Colville, Viscount 187
Colyton, Lord 103, 104, 145
Commonwealth Immigrants Act 202
communists
    Basque camps and 41, 135, 168, 170
    Hungarian camps and 171, 185
    internment and 99
    Poland and 94, 197
    Vietnamese and 65, 66, 165, 172, 173
Community Service Volunteers 64, 145
Con, Le 154
concentration camps
    British camps and 33, 38, 45, 51, 56, 63,
        104, 164, 170, 224 n88
    European 18, 88, 89, 117
    Hong Kong camps and 64
    South African 5, 33
Cong, Lam 180
Conservative Party
    Anglo-Egyptians and 102, 145
    housing 29, 30
    immigration 22, 149, 176, 177
    Rhodesia 214
    Soviet history and 197
    Suez Crisis 57
    Ugandan Asians and 108, 178, 187
Coordinating Committee for the Welfare of
        Evacuees from Uganda (CCWEU) 187
Corpus Christi 93, 94
Crimicar Lane 54, 163
Crookham 55, 164, 166, 171
Crystal Palace 40, 139
Cunningham, Sir Charles 122, 145
Cunningham's holiday camp 35

Curtis, Mrs. Winifred E. 214
Cynarth 169
Cyprus 66, 145
Czak, Mr. and Miss 128
Czigány, Magda 55, 62

Daglingworth 11, 51, 95, 114, 145, 201–2
Dangerous Moonlight 140
Dartmoor 45, 56, 58, 152, 194
Davies, Christie 105
decolonization 10, 19, 20, 145;
    see also empire
Deedes, Bill 30
Delamere 142
De Souza, Joseph 122
Deverill 196
Devizes 124
Devonshire, Duke of 90
Dharamshi, S.A. 123
Diary of a Polish Airman 140
Dibble, S.J. 119
Digby, Simon Wingfield 58
Diken, Bülent 9
Dines, Mary 120
dispersal 174–81
    asylum seekers and 203, 208, 209
    Basques and 175
    Belgians and 175
    Commonwealth immigrants and 176–7
    India and 174–5
    Jews and 175
    Poles and 176
    Rhodesia and 213
    Ugandan Asians and 188, 199
    United States and 175
    Vietnamese and 189
Divers, Anthony 33
Dobson, Terry 194
Doddington 52, 93
Domingo, Rosina 192
Doniford 59–60, 61, 77, 123
Dorney Common Camp 28
Dover 185, 186
Dovercourt
    arrival at 18
    closure of 192
    discipline in 170
    ethnic identity in 91–2
    food in 74
    Kitchener Camp and 87
    locals and 97, 136
    physical environment of 43–6
Drake Hall 185
Drweski, Anton 114
Dubs, Alf 205
Dukes, Peter 197
Dunkirk 89
Dunston, Fred 74, 89
Duschinsky, Eric 170
Dymond, Dr. 145

Earl's Court 16
    class and 98
    closure of 191
    ethnic identity in 87
    food in 72
    freedom of movement in 181
    physical environment of 40–1
East Moor Hostel 162–3
Eastwood Hostel 55, 82, 104, 164
Ede, James Chuter 100, 113, 159
Eden, Sir Anthony 54
Eisenhower, General Dwight D. 57
Emergency Accommodation Committee 49
Emigranto 91
empire 1, 10, 11
    Anglo-Egyptians and 96, 105, 109
    Ugandan Asians and 96, 105, 109, 153
    see also colonialism, decolonization,
        India, South African War
Essinger, Anna 44
European Voluntary Workers (EVWs) 166

Fahmy, Ahmed 104
Fairfield 80
Fairford 51, 81, 92, 162
Faldingworth 47
    ethnic identity in 148
    food in 77
    locals and 178
    physical environment of 62
    volunteers at 146, 251 n64
famine camps 14, 33, 174
Farringdon, Lord 90
Field, Barry 197
First World War 1, 2, 6, 7, 16, 18, 45, 87
    Britons and 40
    freedom of movement and 34–5, 175
    internment and 34–5, 38, 39, 72, 87, 99
    Nissen huts and 25, 26
Fisher, Barbara (née Białozorska) 52
Fogarty, C.W. 211
Folkestone 16
Fowlmere 158
Foxley Camp 53, 75, 93, 95
Franciszek, Celezewski 160
Franco, General Francisco 16, 73, 135, 168,
    169, 170, 192; *see also* Spanish Civil War
Free French 52, 140
Frobisher Hostel 184
From Citizen to Refugee 150–1
Fuller, Captain Freddy 63

Gál, Hans 36
Ganatra, Champak 199
Garrana, Angel 185
Gatrell, Peter 6
Gaydon 76, 123, 149, 198, 203
Gentles, Mrs. E. 100
George VI 17
Gershon, Karen 44

Goizeka Izarra 16
Grange Farm 185
Great Bowerwood 183
Greenbanks Hostel 119
Greenham Common
  class and 107
  closure of 109, 201, 203
  Cold War and 57
  discipline in 165, 188
  family reunions and 121–2
  food in 68, 83
  physical environment of 58
  protests at 201, 203
  stateless residents at 187
Guernica 16
Gurs 7, 204

Habaña 16
Hague Convention 34
Hailsham, Viscount (Quintin McGarel
    Hogg) 102
Hajduczek, F. 115
Hamilton-Paterson, James 63
Harbottle, Brigadier Michael 66, 165
Harmondsworth 187
Harries, E.P. 135
Harrington House 98
Harris, Sir Percy 29
Hartman, Zosia 8, 51, 62, 93, 95, 205
Hassan, Akbar 78–9, 106
Haverhill 130
Hawke, Lord 178
Heathfield Camp 30, 106
Heathrow Airport
  detention at 187
  refugees and 203
  Ugandan Asians and 3, 20, 58, 62, 151, 187
  Vietnamese and 21
Hednesford 54
Hemswell 56, 59, 78, 178
Hertz, Chief Rabbi Joseph 91
Hexham 169
Hidalgo, Helvecia 73
Hiltingbury 128
Hindus 62, 132, 146, 149, 150, 179
  food and 77
  in India 174
Hinrichsen, Klaus Ernst 37, 99, 127, 158
Hitler, Adolf 35, 90
Hobbs Barracks 151, 189
Hodgetts, Colin 97
Holownia, Edward 116
Hong Kong 10, 20, 21, 124, 153
  repatriation of Vietnamese from 200–1
  Vietnamese in 64, 66, 83, 172, 173
Honiton 30
  ethnic identity and 148
  family life in 131–3
  food in 77
  locals and 146

physical environment of 60, 62
  volunteers at 146
Hoskins, William 30–1
Hothfield 97
Howard-Drake, Jack Thomas 176
Howe, Sir Geoffrey 200
Huguenots 2
Hulme, Kathryn 6
Hungarian camps 1, 2, 62, 65
  Anglo-Egyptian camps and 20, 22, 53
  arrival at 19
  class and 96–7, 102
  closures of 197, 202
  discipline in 163–4
  dispersal from 254 n145
  food in 13, 71, 77, 81
  freedom of movement in 185–6
  language in 106, 165
  locals and 144
  memorialization of 204
  physical environment of 53–5
  Poles and 193
  politics in 171, 172
Hunt, Sandra 77–8
Huong, Dieu 154
Husen family 122–3
Hussein, Shirin Abdul 76, 149
Hutchinson 36–8, 91, 99, 127, 158
Huyton 36, 37, 39, 90, 139
Huyton Suite 36

Iddesleigh, Earl of 202
Igersheimer, Walter 38–9, 90
Ilford Park 194–7; *see also* Stover
Immigrants Advisory Service 213
immigration 16, 134, 153
  British history and 12, 204
  dispersal and 176–8, 181, 203
  illegal 187, 200–1, 208
  law and 123–4, 130
  opponents 152
  refugees and 4, 8, 71, 96–7, 120, 179, 201,
    202, 203–4, 217 n41, 248 n106
  Ugandan Asians and 105–6, 109, 149, 151
  United States and 248 n104
  Vietnamese and 200–1
  see also African Caribbean, Commonwealth
    Immigrants Act, Immigrants Advisory
    Service, immigration detention, Indians,
    Jamaican, Joint Council for the Welfare of
    Immigrants, Pakistani, race, South Asian,
    West Indians
Immigration and Asylum Act 209
Immigration (Carriers Liability) Act 208
immigration detention 208–10
India 7, 50
  camps in 14, 33, 174
  Poles and 112
  Ugandan Asians and 20, 105, 108, 121, 122,
    147, 159, 165, 199

Indians
  Ugandan Asians and 105, 106, 149, 152, 180
  see also immigration
Indochinese refugees 175, 255 n178
Institute of Race Relations 152
International Brigade 16
internment 7, 14, 90
  class and 99
  discipline and 158–9
  food and 72, 79–80
  Great War and 99
  Kitchener Camp and 89, 192
  physical environment of 34–9
  sexuality and 127
Irazola, Félix Amat 43
Irish 16, 143, 144, 245 n35
Isaji, Kurban 179
Isle of Man
  class and 99
  closure of 192
  discipline in 158
  ethnic identity in 90, 99
  food in 72, 79
  Kitchener Camp and 89
  physical environment of 35–6, 39

Jackson, Brian 59, 147
Jacobsthal, Paul 38
Jago, R.K. 49
Jamaican 245 n35; *see also*
  African Caribbean, immigration
Jamison, Leslie 10
Janowski, Kaz 51–2, 75, 143, 205
Japanese Americans 175
Jeffreys, Lord 103
Jenkins, Roy 21, 203
Jewish camps 1, 2, 57, 64, 101
  arrival at 17–18
  class and 97, 99
  closure of 192–3, 197
  discipline in 157, 170–1
  ethnic identity in 87–92, 96, 155, 175
  food in 74
  locals and 137–8
  physical environment of 43–6
  see also anti-Semitism, Dovercourt, internment, Kitchener Camp, Pakefield, Second World War
Joint Committee for Refugees from Vietnam (JCRV) 64, 189
Joint Council for the Welfare of Immigrants 120
Joshi, Chandrika 150, 179

Kahn, Leo 99, 127
Kai Tak 64
Kapp, Yvonne (pseud. Cloud) 73, 92, 167, 168, 169
Katyn Wood 197
Kee, Robert 9

Keele University 31
Keevil Polish Hostel 49, 113, 140
Kellar, Betty 29, 204
Kelvedon 205
  class and 100
  eviction from 184
  family and 115
  food in 75, 81
  locals and 143–4
  physical environment of 51–2
Kempton Park Racecourse 90
Kensington Barracks Camp
  Ugandan Asians 3, 7, 82, 85, 108, 151–2, 172, 188
  Vietnamese 21, 65, 84, 189
  see also Mamdani, Mahmood
Kenya 112, 165, 190, 212
Kidd, George B. 162
Kidman, Brenda 147
Kiersnowski, Ryszard 160
Killearn, Lord 103
Kinder 17
  arrival of 17, 43
  Basques and 19, 22, 44
  departure from Britain of 192
  memorialization of 204, 205, 206
Kindertransport 17, 45
Kitchener Camp
  arrival at 18
  class and 99
  closure of 192–3
  discipline in 157
  ethnic identity in 87–9
  food in 74, 75
  freedom of movement in 182
  locals and 136–9
  memorialization of 205
  physical environment of 44–6, 57
Kitchener Camp Review 45, 87, 88, 89, 137, 138
Kmita, Mr. 160
Knapp, Stefan 140
Knockaloe 35, 36, 72, 99
Koestler, Arthur 135
Kondratiew, Maria 128
Korean War 57
Kotecha, Mrs. Premkunvar 187
Kristallnacht 17
Kubinski, Mr. 184
Kuchta, Stefan 115–16
Kurds 208
Kushner, Tony 12

Labour Party
  asylum and 181, 205, 209
  Basques and 17, 43, 167
  housing and 28, 30, 40, 56
  Poles and 46, 100, 113, 202
  Vietnam War and 20
  see also New Labour

Lafitte, François 90
Lagnardo, Victor 104
Laing, R.D. 64
Lakhani, Manu 60, 62, 200
language training
    Anglo-Egyptian camps and 106
    Basque camps and 91
    Hungarian camps and 106, 165
    internment camps and 91
    Jewish camps and 44
    Ugandan Asian camps and 106
    Vietnamese camps and 66, 67, 124, 166,
        180, 200
Lansbury, George 167
Leadley, Joan 154
Lebanon 112
Lee, Celia 136
Legge-Bourke, Harry 29
Leggett, R.W. 56
"Let's Go Home" campaign 206
Lewis, Arthur 148–9, 202
Liberal Party 29
Lingfield Camp 37, 39
Lipowska, Mrs. Jozefa 117
Little Onn 143
Lloyd, Selwyn 170
Lofthouse Park 35, 99
Lomnitz, Alfred 37, 139
Long Marston 95, 115
Luc, Cuu 65, 84
Lugard, Lady Flora 41
Lusitania 35
Ly, Tam 65, 84
Ly, Thanh Chuong 68

Macaulay, Rose 139
Macmillan, Harold 140, 216 n24
McSmith, Andy 145
Mai, Hoang Thuy 124
Malaya 145
Malaysia 20, 60, 145
Malkki, Liisa 6, 167
Maltese 19, 55, 102, 104, 176
Mamdani, Mahmood 3, 7, 65, 150–2
    food and 82, 84, 85
    resistance and 172, 188
    see also Kensington Barracks Camp
Manning, Leah 17, 113, 126, 176
Mansbacher, Peter 45, 138
Maresfield 56, 122, 171, 179
Margate 43, 74
Marks & Spencer 44
Marsworth 140
Maryszczak, Czeslaw 7
Masefield, John 58
Mashru, Maz 78
May, Jonas 45
May, Phineas 45
    discipline and 249 n4
    ethnic identity and 87, 88, 89

freedom at Kitchener and 182
    friendship and 139
    locals and 136, 147
Meidner, Ludwig 36
Melton Mowbray
    closure of 193
    ethnic identity at 95
    food at 74, 81
    locals and 140
    physical environment of 50, 51
Mepal Hostel 160, 162
Micallef, Michael 164
Midgley, Peter 37, 38
Millet, Jean-François 98
Millman, Sue 97, 165
Mishra, Vijay 22
Modhwadia, Mrs. Sunibalu 120
Moghal, Manzoor 3
Mohan, Chotalal Vadhia 106, 186, 188
Moore, L.W. 143
Morrison, Herbert 90
Moyle Tower 155
Mughal, Mohamed 121–2
multicultural 11–12, 109, 146, 176, 181,
    208, 210
Munster, Rudolf 37, 90
Muraszko, Mr. 128
Muslims 60, 77, 121, 132, 146, 149, 179

Naipaul, Shiva 60, 152
Naipaul, V.S. 60
Nasser, Gamal Abdel 19, 102
National Archives 12, 13, 213, 219 n88
national assistance 103, 104, 128, 159,
    161, 163
National Assistance Act 40, 48, 114
National Assistance Board camps 47
    Britons and 48, 53, 102, 141, 142, 143,
        144, 246 n51
    class and 100
    closure of 193
    discipline in 158–63, 183–4
    family in 112–17, 128
    food in 76, 80, 81
    physical environment of 49–51, 52, 53,
        194–5, 202
    politics in 93
    see also welfare state
National Front 189
National Health Service 104
National Joint Committee for
    Spanish Relief 126, 135
National Service 31, 128, 163
Nauru 209
Nazareth House 73
Nelson Hall 154, 189
Nettlebed South Hostel 76
Newbury 35, 57, 83
New Homeland 154
New Labour 209; *see also* Labour Party

New Left 20
Newsam, Sir Frank 103
New Towns 4, 24, 177, 179, 213
Nissen, Peter 25, 26
Nissen hut 14, 25–32
  Anglo-Egyptians and 53, 55
  Basques and 170
  Britons and 202, 203, 204
  India and 174
  internment and 35
  Poles and 47, 49, 50, 51, 52, 116, 143, 183,
    184, 194, 201, 202, 205, 207
  Ugandan Asians and 70
North Stoneham 21, 136
  arrival at 17
  closure of 192
  discipline in 167–70
  Dovercourt versus 44
  ethnic identity in 82
  family in 127
  food in 73
  freedom of movement in 181–3
  locals and 135, 139
  memorialization of 205
  physical environment of 41–3
  Polish camps versus 46
  volunteers in 135
Northwick Park Hostel
  Catholicism at 93, 94
  closure of 201
  discipline in 115–16, 128, 160, 161,
    183, 184
  ethnic identity in 95
  family in 115–16, 117
  food in 75
  leisure at 96
  memorialization of 205, 206
  physical environment of 51
  resistance and 115–16
  Single Persons Group 116

Oakley Park 127
Ockenden Venture 64, 65, 109, 154
O'Garvaigh, Sean 147
Olympia 90
Onchan 36, 127
Operation Torch 57
Orbach, Maurice 102
Outward Bound 63
Ozga, Jan 117–18

Pajdzik, Maria 184
Pakefield 18
Pakistani 105–6, 149, 180, 200, 202
Palestine 1, 5, 17, 22, 50
Parkinson, Commander Reay 178
Partridge, S.J. 163
Patel, Atul 62, 77, 131–3, 148
Patel, C.B. 107
Patel, Chandrakant 108

Patel, Dawood 64
Patel, Hansa 188
Patel, Praful 56, 108
Pavlovich, Henry 75, 93, 143
People of Nowhere 139
Peppard, Nadine 146
Perles, Alfred 89
Petworth 80
Pfister-Ammende, Maria 134
Piddlehinton 58, 203
Pietrusiewicz, Piotr 52, 193
Pioneer Corps 89, 192
Pioneers (Keele University) 31
plague segregation camps 14, 33, 174
Plaisterdown 56, 60, 61, 123, 146
Platta, Mr. 184
Polish camps 1, 2, 7, 8, 12, 62, 64, 127
  arrival at 18–19
  class and 99–100, 101, 103
  closure of 193–7, 201–2
  discipline in 157, 158–63
  dispersal from 176
  ethnic identity in 92–6, 145
  family in 14, 112–18, 119, 122, 123, 124,
    127, 128–9, 133
  food in 74–6, 80–1, 83
  Hungarians and 54
  language and 166
  locals and 127–8, 129, 140–4, 202, 218 n65
  physical environment of 34, 46–53
  politics in 170–1, 172
  resistance and 167, 183–4
  Rhodesia and 213
  Second World War and 56
Polish Resettlement Act 18–19, 46–7, 197
  discipline and 159
  ethnic identity and 176
  family and 112
  National Assistance Board and 193
Polish Resettlement Corps (PRC) 46–7
Poor law 48, 98, 103, 114
Port Erin 36, 90
Portman, Lord 183
Port St. Mary 36, 90
Powell, Enoch 19, 153
Powell, G.A. 87
Powell, Tony 31
Price of Freedom, The 139
Probat, Prabha G. 120
Protestant 2, 6, 16, 92

Quach, Loi Binh 124

race 2, 4, 8, 83, 144–56, 207
  dispersal and 32, 174–81
  race relations 146, 245 n35
  racism 15, 24, 67, 104, 147, 148, 150,
    151–5, 177, 211–14, 248 n106
  see also immigration, Institute of Race
    Relations, multicultural

Raison, Timothy 22
Raleigh Hall 131, 149, 165, 201
Reading, Lady Stella 129, 176
Red Cross 53, 54, 146, 202
"red/green" policy 178–80
Reflex Alert Scheme 57
Refugee Council 209
Refugee World 9
Renton, David 28
repatriation 47, 175, 191, 192, 200
residents' committees 13
    Anglo-Egyptian camps and
        82, 104
    Polish camps and 100, 161–2
    Ugandan Asian camps and 77, 165
    Vietnamese camps and 84, 124, 125,
        172, 173–4
Rhodesia 211–14
Richard, Dorothy 163–4
Rimmer, Peter 165
Rivesaltes 204
Roberts, Sir Wilfred 126
Robeson, Paul 135
Robinson, Vaughan 108
Rogalski brothers 140, 193
Romijn, Jan 123, 199
Rommel, Erwin 103
Roosevelt, Eleanor 6
Roosevelt, Franklin D. 175
Rothwell, Captain Frederick 59
Royal Air Force (RAF) 31, 178, 203
    Britons and 142
    Hungarian camps and 54, 163
    Polish camps and 47, 52, 140, 142
    Ugandan Asian camps and 8, 57, 59,
        60, 146, 147
    Vietnamese camps and 66, 67, 69
Royal Navy 16, 69, 77, 145, 209
Rucker, Sir Arthur 53
Runnymede Trust 178
Rushton, Paul 180

St. Keverne, Jane 196
Sakaria, Arun 56
Salvation Army 32, 43, 98, 183
Samani, Mrs. S.B. 121
Sams, H.W.H. 41
Samy, Mrs. C.C. 104
Sandbrook, Dominic 108–9
Sandwich 45, 137–8, 192, 205
Sarton, Edgar 89–90
Save the Children (SCF)
    Basques and 92
    dispersal and 180, 190
    Vietnamese and 64, 66, 83–4, 97, 124,
        155, 166
Saville, Annette 192
Schwitters, Kurt 36
"Sea Fever" 58
Second World War 1, 2, 6, 8, 210

Britons and 3, 4, 27, 40, 49, 55, 101, 113,
    139, 141, 146, 214, 218 n65
Egypt and 103
European camps and 107, 134
internment and 34, 35, 38, 72, 99, 127,
    224 n88
Jews and 17, 175, 205
Ockenden Venture and 65
Poles and 18, 46, 52, 113, 115, 194, 196,
    197, 240 n8
Rhodesia and 214
Ugandan Asian camps and 56, 58, 203
Vietnamese camps and 67
Securicor 187
Segal, Lore 17, 43, 92
Shah, Nemchand 105
Sheepcote Hostel 202
Shell Oil 145
Sheridan, Vera 54
Sibonga 21
Sikhs 149, 179
Sikorski, Stanislaw 160
Singh, Jagit 153
Skrzypiniak, Jozef 161
Smith, Rukshana 197–8
Somalis 208
Somani, Zulfikar 198
Sopley 97
    closure of 200
    discipline in 172, 189
    family in 124–5, 130
    food in 83–4
    language and 166
    locals and 155
    physical environment of 65, 66, 67, 68
    politics in 165
Sorry for Them 139
South Africa 14, 33, 35, 54, 212; *see also*
    South African War
South African War 5–6, 33
Southall 78, 82, 106, 169, 188
South Asian 11, 105, 121, 153–4, 175, 202,
    232 n40; *see also* Indians, immigration,
    Pakistani
Soviet Union
    camps in 7
    Hungarians and 2, 19, 55, 102
    Poles and 2, 18, 115, 140, 193
Sower, The (Jean François Millet) 98
Spanish Civil War 2, 6, 16, 19, 126, 192, 204
Sparke, Robert 194
Spencer-Churchill family 51; *see also*
    Churchill, Winston
Spier, Eugen 37, 39, 90
Springhill Lodges 34, 95, 161
squatting 1, 4, 12, 24, 29
    Anglo-Egyptian 184
    British 1, 31–2, 56, 141–3, 210
    Hungarian 186
    Polish 112, 117, 141–3, 193

Standing Conference of British Organizations
  for Aid to Refugees 203
Stansted Airport 20, 59, 260 n109
stateless husbands 111, 118–22, 130, 187
Stonehouse 114
Stonor, Sherman 30
Stover 75–6, 81, 99, 160, 162, 194;
  see also Ilford Park
Stowell Park 128
Stradishall 8, 60, 147, 188
  family in 123, 130, 132
  food in 76, 82–3
  history of 56
  memorialization of 203
  physical environment of 59
Styal Hostel 202
Suez Crisis 2, 19–20, 57, 102, 104, 119
Summerfield Hostel 82, 129, 184
Sunshine House 154
Supplementary Benefits Commission 195
Swanwick Camp 38
Szulakowska, Urszula 50–1, 74, 95–6,
  140, 193
Szyszko, Mr. 161

Tagore, Rabindranath 205–6
Tai Ah Chau 64
Tailor, Vinod 59
Tanzania 112, 190
Taylorplan 77
Teviot, Lord 103
Thakrar, Praful 149–50
Thanh, Pham 154
Thanh, Vu Khanh 66, 67, 124, 173
Thatcher, Margaret 21, 149, 153, 213, 232 n38
Thatcherism, Thatcherite 14, 108, 145,
  204, 214
Thomas, Gwilym Ivor 112
Thorney Island 8, 145, 154
  class and 110
  discipline in 172–3
  dispersal from 189
  family in 124–5
  food in 84
  language and 166
  locals and 155
  physical environment of 67, 69
  politics and 165
  resettlement from 180, 189
Thorney Pits 54–5, 144, 163
Tilstock Anglo-Polish Housing Units 141
Tonfanau Camp
  closure of 198
  food in 7, 77, 79, 83, 85
  locals and 7, 64, 145, 146, 147, 150
  physical environment of 62–4
  politics in 153
  resettlement from 179
Torrano, Valentín Sagasti 74
Tower Hamlets 32, 148

Trades Union Congress 135
tribunals, Second World War 35, 89
Trivedi family 198
Tudor-Hart, Edith 21, 136
Tunbridge Wells 43, 127, 147
Tuncliffe, Martin 31
Tweedsmuir Camp 52, 140, 193

Ugandan Asian camps 1, 2, 3, 8, 11, 12
  Anglo-Egyptians and 14, 105–9
  arrival of 20
  class and 96, 97, 98, 105–9
  closures of 197–200, 201, 202–3
  discipline in 7, 157, 165, 167, 171–2
  dispersal from 177–80
  family in 118, 119–23, 125, 131, 132,
    133, 140
  food in 7, 76–8, 82–3, 84
  freedom of movement in 186–8
  locals and 144, 146–9, 149–53
  memorialization of 203, 204, 205–6
  physical environment of 46, 55–64
  politics in 171–2
  resistance and 157, 165, 167, 171–2
  Rhodesians and 213
  sources and archives and 13
  Vietnamese and 21, 65
Ugandan Asian Relief Trust 206
Uganda Resettlement Board (URB) 56, 62, 63,
  145, 147, 151
  Anglo-Egyptian Resettlement Board and 105,
    146, 213
  class and 106
  closures and 198, 199
  dispersal and 179, 188
  family reunions and 122, 123, 200
  food and 60
Uhlman, Fred 38, 90
Ukrainians 92
Umrania, Jayantila 188
Unemployment Assistance Act 33
United Nations 6, 21
United Nations Convention Relating to the
  Status of Refugees 2, 5
United Nations High Commissioner for
  Refugees (UNHCR) 208
United Nations Relief and Rehabilitation
  Administration (UNRRA) 6
United States
  Cold War and 203
  dispersal in 175
  Mahmood Mamdani in 150
  refugee care in 93, 217 n41, 217 n55, 218
    n66, 219 n81, 248 n104
  Suez Crisis and 19
  Ugandan Asians and 206
  Vietnam War and 20, 21
  Welfare in 232 n38
United States Air Force (USAF) 52, 57, 107
United States Army 52

vagrancy 4, 16, 48, 143–4, 190
Vajda, Albert 54, 186
Vale, Brian 31
Vernon, James 71
Vietnamese camps 1, 2, 7, 8, 10, 22
  arrival at 20–1
  class and 96, 97, 109, 149
  closures of 197, 200–1
  discipline in 157, 172–4, 189–90
  dispersal from 177, 180
  evictions from 189
  family in 14, 118, 123–5, 130–1
  food in 83–4
  freedom of movement in 187
  language and 166
  locals and 144, 145, 154–5
  memorialization of 204
  physical environment of 64–70
  Poles and 196
  politics in 165
  resistance at 172–4
  Rhodesians and 213
  sources and archives 13, 219 n88
  volunteers in 154–5
Vietnam War 20–1, 65, 165

Waddell, J.S. 187
Wakefield 35, 99
War Damage Acts 102
warfare state 10
War Office
  Basques and 41
  Hungarians and 53
  internment and 35, 39
  Poles and 8, 47, 49, 80, 112, 127, 141, 158
Warth Mills 38, 233 n57
Wattermillock 73, 169
Watton 127
wayfarers' center 48, 143–4
Wehner, Karl 39
Weissenborn, Hellmuth 36, 37, 91
Welcome Committee for British Asians 8
welfare state
  Anglo-Egyptians and 97, 100
  asylum seekers and 208, 209
  Belgians and 98
  colonial 32–3
  food and 81–2, 232 n38
  housing and 30
  Poles and 114, 161
  refugee care and 10, 12, 48, 98, 174, 194, 210
  Ugandan Asians and 107, 119, 148

Wellpark 21
West Indians 11, 106, 140, 144, 202;
  see also African Caribbean,
  immigration, Jamaican
West Malling
  class and 106
  closure of 198, 199, 203
  discipline in 186–7
  dispersal from 178
  family separations and 120, 121, 122
  food in 78
  freedom of movement in 186–7
  resettlement from 178, 188, 198
  Rhodesians and 213
Weston Green Camp 80
Weyler, General Valeriano 33
Wheaton Aston 94, 142–3
White, Baroness Eirene 120, 151–2
Whitham, Rachel 65
Wierszycka, Mrs. Jozefa 162
Wilcox, G.M. 102–3
Wild Place, The 6
Wojciechowska, Celina Kabala 51, 81, 92
Woolwich 183
Women's Royal Voluntary
  Service (WRVS)
  class and 106
  Faldingworth 146
  Greenham Common 58, 165
  Hemswell 59
  Honiton 146
  Piddlehinton 58
  Plaisterdown
  race and 152
  Southall 106
  Tonfanau 63, 64
  see also Women's Voluntary Service
Women's Voluntary Service (WVS)
  Anglo-Egyptians and 129, 185
  Hungarians and 54, 55, 163, 164, 165
  Poles and 176
  see also Women's Royal Voluntary Service
World Refugee Year 139

Young, Filson 25
Young-Jones, Edwin 77, 85, 147
Young-Jones, Margretta 77, 147

Zbyszewski, Karol 50
Zosz-Zuchowska, Halina 196
Zosz-Zuchoswki, Stanislaw 196
Zozial, Kazimierz 117